Essential Guide to Marketing Planning

Visit the *Essential Guide to Marketing Planning* second edition
Companion Website at **www.pearsoned.co.uk/wood-mp** to find
valuable **student** learning material including:

- Weblinks to relevant, specific Internet resources to facilitate
  in-depth independent research.
- An online glossary to explain key terms.

PEARSON
Education

We work with leading authors to develop the strongest
educational materials in marketing, bringing cutting-edge
thinking and best learning practice to a global market.

Under a range of well-known imprints, including
Financial Times Prentice Hall, we craft high quality
print and electronic publications which help readers
to understand and apply their content, whether
studying or at work.

To find out more about the complete range of our
publishing please visit us on the World Wide Web at:
www.pearsoned.co.uk

Marian Burk Wood

Essential Guide to
Marketing Planning

Second edition

**Financial Times
Prentice Hall
is an imprint of**

Harlow, England • London • New York • Boston • San Francisco • Toronto
Sydney • Tokyo • Singapore • Hong Kong • Seoul • Taipei • New Delhi
Cape Town • Madrid • Mexico City • Amsterdam • Munich • Paris • Milan

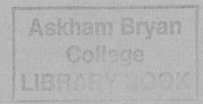

Pearson Education Limited
Edinburgh Gate
Harlow
Essex CM20 2JE
England

and Associated Companies throughout the world

Visit us on the World Wide Web at:
www.pearsoned.co.uk

First published 2007
Second edition published 2010

ISBN 978-0-273-72576-3

British Library Cataloguing-in-Publication Data
A catalogue record for this book is available from the British Library

Library of Congress Cataloging-in-Publication Data
Wood, Marian Burk.
    Essential guide to marketing planning / Marian Burk Wood. -- 2nd ed.
        p. cm.
    ISBN 978-0-273-72576-3 (pbk.)
 1. Marketing--Planning. I. Title.
    HF5415.13.W656 2010
    658.8'02--dc22

                                                        2010009679

10 9 8 7 6 5 4 3 2 1
14 13 12 11 10

Typeset in 10/12pt Palatino by 30
Printed and bound by Ashford Colour Press Ltd., Gosport

Brief contents

Full contents

Supporting resources
Visit **www.pearsoned.co.uk/wood-mp** to find valuable online resources:

Companion Website for students
- Weblinks to relevant, specific Internet resources to facilitate in-depth independent research.
- An online glossary to explain key terms.

For instructors
- PowerPoint slides that can be downloaded and used for presentations.
- Complete, downloadable Instructor's Manual.

For more information please contact your local Pearson Education sales representative or visit **www.pearsoned.co.uk/wood-mp**

Preface

A good marketing plan is essential to marketing success today. In a world where customers' needs and behaviours are always changing, economic circumstances are unpredictable, competitive pressure is a constant factor and every day brings new technological advances, you'll need careful planning to achieve your objectives.

This book is your essential guide to creating a practical, effective marketing plan. Through clear explanations, real-world examples and hands-on exercises, it will help you to:

- understand what marketing planning is, how it works and why it's important

- complete the seven stages of the marketing planning process

- formulate a marketing plan customised for your situation.

Chapter by chapter, you'll learn the language and basic concepts of planning, gain insights from the experiences of marketers worldwide and put your knowledge to work as you develop a marketing plan of your own. You'll find out how to research your market and marketing situation, set objectives, decide on marketing strategies and document your ideas in a marketing plan similar to the sample plan in the Appendix. Whether you go to work for a major corporation, start your own business or join a non-governmental organisation, your understanding of the marketing planning process will be a valuable asset.

NEW IN THIS EDITION

You'll find updated coverage of the latest developments in marketing, including definitions, descriptions and examples of:

- *social media* such as Twitter, YouTube and Bebo

- *crowdsourcing* product ideas and adverts

- *mobile marketing* to reach consumers on the go

- *greenwashing* and ecological concerns

- *marketing transparency* to build trust
- *scenario planning* to prepare for future possibilities
- *metrics* for evaluating marketing progress and performance
- *neuromarketing* for marketing research.

Every chapter has been thoroughly revised to reflect current marketing thought and practice. The new edition also contains dozens of new examples and cases showing how manufacturers, retailers, service firms and other organisations actually apply the principles of marketing planning to achieve their objectives. When you look up key terms in the glossary, you'll notice that every entry mentions the chapter number in which the definition appears. This change is intended to help you review the definition in context as you study or prepare for a class discussion or presentation.

YOUR STEP-BY-STEP GUIDE

Each chapter is packed with special features to assist you in understanding and completing the essential steps in formulating a marketing plan:

- *No-nonsense directions*. The 'how to' approach clearly explains the questions to be asked and the decisions to be made as you research and write your marketing plan.
- *Diagram of the planning process*. A diagram at the start of each chapter shows your progress through the seven stages of the marketing planning process.
- *Company examples*. Every chapter opens with an interesting example of marketing in action at a well-known organisation. Featured examples within each chapter demonstrate how marketers actually apply planning principles; several take a closer look at contemporary issues such as freemium pricing, sustainability, online prediction markets and price wars.
- *Practical exercises*. 'Apply your knowledge' exercises challenge you to translate principles into practice by analysing a specific organisation's marketing activities. 'Build your own marketing plan' exercises direct you through the main steps in preparing a strong, relevant marketing plan.
- *Case studies*. Every chapter closes with a case study of a company facing challenges and opportunities in consumer or business marketing. Answering the case questions will reinforce your understanding of the concepts and strengthen your planning skills.
- *Definitions*. Key terms defined in each chapter and in the glossary help you master the words and phrases every marketer must know.

SAMPLE MARKETING PLAN

The Appendix contains a detailed sample marketing plan showing how a fictional start-up company, Lost Legends Luxury Chocolatier, plans to launch its first products and compete with established confectionery companies. This sample plan includes background information about market trends and customer characteristics; analyses the company's strengths, weaknesses, opportunities and threats; sets specific objectives; and documents decisions about targeting, positioning, products and branding, pricing, distribution, marketing communications, customer service and internal marketing. It also summarises highlights of the company's marketing programmes, forecasts, metrics and control. As you learn about the planning process, refer to this sample plan to see how a company might present and explain its chosen marketing strategies and prepare for effective and efficient implementation.

ESSENTIAL MARKETING CHECKLISTS

This new edition includes 17 checklists to lead you through the essential aspects of the planning process. Checklist topics are keyed to the material in each chapter.

Chapter 1: Getting ready for situational analysis; the mission statement

Chapter 2: The internal environment; the external environment

Chapter 3: Analysing customers in consumer markets; analysing customers in business markets

Chapter 4: Evaluating market segments

Chapter 5: Evaluating objectives

Chapter 6: Planning for products; planning for brands

Chapter 7: Pricing through the product life cycle

Chapter 8: Planning for marketing channels; planning for logistics

Chapter 9: Planning for media

Chapter 10: Planning for customer service support

Chapter 11: Planning metrics

Chapter 12: Evaluating implementation

REAL-WORLD VIEW OF MARKETING PLANNING TODAY

Seeing how different organisations approach marketing can provoke new thinking, provide insights into marketing situations and lead to more creative marketing plans. How does Cadbury engage its customers and influence how they think, feel and act towards the brand (Chapter 1)? Why do marketers for McDonald's Europe see gourmet coffee as important for future growth in turnover and profits (Chapter 5)? How is Adidas using new products in its race for higher market share (Chapter 6)? What is Comic Relief doing to plan for marketing communications (Chapter 9)? How does Net-a-Porter use customer service to support its marketing (Chapter 10)? These and many other cases and chapter-opening examples reveal the contemporary realities of marketing planning around the world.

GUIDE TO THE BOOK

Essential Guide to Marketing Planning is divided into 12 chapters, each covering a key aspect of the planning process. Chapters 1–3 introduce marketing planning, explain how to analyse the current marketing situation and discuss how to research markets and customers. Chapter 4 examines the use of segmentation, targeting and positioning. Chapter 5 looks at planning direction, objectives and strategy. Chapters 6–9 focus on the marketing mix: product, price, place (channels and logistics) and promotion (marketing communications and customer influence). Chapter 10 discusses planning for customer service and internal marketing to support the marketing mix. Chapter 11 explores the use of metrics, forecasts, budgets and schedules in planning for measurement of marketing performance. Chapter 12 explains how to plan for implementation and control of your marketing plan.

ONLINE EXTRAS

Visit the companion blog at **http://essentialmarketingplanning.blogspot.com/** for updates to cases, concepts and companies and the latest news and views in the world of marketing.

Visit the companion website at **www.pearsoned.co.uk/wood-mp** for extras such as links to marketing-related websites and a key terms glossary. With a password, lecturers can access the Instructor's Manual with answers to case study questions plus additional resources.

About the author

Marian Burk Wood has held vice presidential-level positions in corporate and non-profit marketing with Citibank, JP Morgan Chase and the National Retail Federation. She has extensive practical experience in marketing planning, having developed and implemented many marketing plans over the years for a wide range of goods and services. Her US book, *The Marketing Plan Handbook,* now in its fourth edition, has introduced marketing planning to thousands of students worldwide.

Wood holds an MBA in marketing from Long Island University in New York and a BA from the City University of New York. She has worked with prominent academic experts to co-author college textbooks on principles of marketing, principles of advertising and principles of management. Her special interests in marketing include social media, ethics and social responsibility, segmentation, channels and metrics.

Visit her blog at: **http://essentialmarketingplanning.blogspot.com/**

Acknowledgements

I am sincerely grateful to the academic reviewers who so kindly provided detailed feedback on my ideas for this new edition, offered constructive insights on the previous edition and participated in reviewing my other European text, *Marketing Planning: Principles into Practice*. Thank you to Declan Bannon (University of Paisley Business School); Jill Brown (University of Portsmouth Business School); Noel Dennis (Teesside University); Niki Hynes (Napier University); Peter Lancaster (Sheffield Hallam University); Tony Lobo (Swinburne University of Technology); Paul Oakley (University of Brighton Business School); John Rudd (Aston Business School); Heather Skinner (Glamorgan Business School); Des Thwaites (University of Leeds); Peter Williams (Leeds Metropolitan University); Sarah Wren (North Hertfordshire College).

It was truly a pleasure to work with the talented professionals at Pearson Education, whose expertise and commitment I admire and appreciate. A special thank you to Rachel Gear, Publisher for Marketing, Leisure and Tourism, for all her knowledgeable suggestions and for lending her strong support from the very first day. Another special thank you to Emma Violet, Assistant Editor, who kept this project moving forward day after day with good cheer and incredible efficiency. For all they've done to transform my manuscript into a finished product to be proud of, I'm very grateful to Philippa Fiszzon, Desk Editor; Vivienne Church, Freelance Copy Editor; Jenny Kallin, Freelance Proofreader; Martin Hargreaves, Indexer; Kay Holman, Senior Production Controller and Kelly Miller, Senior Designer (for the cover design). Finally, I want to thank Stephen Jeffery, Executive Media Producer, and Emma De Oliveira, Media Producer, who did the eye-catching design and layout of the companion blog for this book.

This book is dedicated with much love to my husband Wally Wood, my sister Isabel Burk and the target market of the next generation: Amelia Biancolo, Ella Biancolo, Michael Werner, Gabriel Wood and Tobias Wood.

Marian Burk Wood

e-mail: MarianBWW@netscape.net
blog: http://essentialmarketingplanning.blogspot.com/

PUBLISHER'S ACKNOWLEDGEMENTS

We are grateful to the following for permission to reproduce copyright material:

Figures

Figure 1.2 after ANDREASEN, ALAN, KOTLER, PHILIP, *STRATEGIC MARKETING FOR NON-PROFIT ORGANIZATIONS*, 6th,©2003, Prentice Hall p.81. Reproduced by permission of Pearson Education, Inc., Upper Saddle River, New Jersey; Figure 2.3 adapted from BEST, ROGER J., *MARKET-BASED MANAGEMENT: STRATEGIES FOR GROWING CUSTOMER VALUE AND PROFITABILITY*, 2nd,©2000, Prentice Hall p.127. Reproduced by permission of Pearson Education, Inc., Upper Saddle River, New Jersey; Figure 6.1 from *Principles of Marketing*, 4th ed., Pearson Education Ltd (Kotler, P., Wang, V., Saunders, J. and Armstrong, G. 2005) p.604; Figure 6.2 after KELLER, KEVIN LANE, *STRATEGIC BRAND MANAGEMENT*, 2nd,©2003, Prentice Hall p.76. Reproduced by permission of Pearson Education, Inc., Upper Saddle River, New Jersey; Figure 7.1 adapted from NAGLE, THOMAS T.; HOGAN, JOHN, *THE STRATEGY AND TACTICS OF PRICING: GUIDE TO GROWING MORE PROFITABLY*, 4th,©2006, Prentice Hall p.4. Reproduced by permission of Pearson Education, Inc., Upper Saddle River, New Jersey; Figure 8.2 adapted from BEST, ROGER J., *MARKET-BASED MANAGEMENT: STRATEGIES FOR GROWING CUSTOMER VALUE AND PROFITABILITY*, 2nd,©2000, Prentice Hall p.199. Reproduced by permission of Pearson Education, Inc., Upper Saddle River, New Jersey; Figure 9.3 after SOLOMON, MICHAEL R., *CONSUMER BEHAVIOR: BUYING, HAVING, AND BEING*, 5th,©2002, Prentice Hall p.201. Reproduced by permission of Pearson Education, Inc., Upper Saddle River, New Jersey.

Tables

Table 3.4 adapted from *Principles of Marketing*, 4th European ed., Pearson Education Ltd (Kotler, P., Wang, V., Saunders, J. and Armstrong, G. 2005) p.309; Table 4.1 adapted from FLEISHER, CRAIG S.; BENSOUSSAN, BABETTE, *STRATEGIC AND COMPETITIVE ANALYSIS: METHODS AND TECHNIQUES FOR ANALYZING BUSINESS COMPETITION*, 1st,©2002, Prentice Hall p.173. Reproduced by permission of Pearson Education, Inc., Upper Saddle River, New Jersey; Table 4.2 adapted from FLEISHER, CRAIG S.; BENSOUSSAN, BABETTE, *STRATEGIC AND COMPETITIVE ANALYSIS: METHODS AND TECHNIQUES FOR ANALYZING BUSINESS COMPETITION*, 1st,©2002, Prentice Hall p.174. Reproduced by permission of Pearson Education, Inc., Upper Saddle River, New Jersey; Table 7.1 adapted from NAGLE, THOMAS T.; HOGAN, JOHN, *THE STRATEGY AND TACTICS OF PRICING: GUIDE TO GROWING MORE PROFITABLY*, 4th,©2006, Prentice Hall pp.275–77. Reproduced by permission of Pearson Education, Inc., Upper Saddle River, New Jersey; Table 11.2 adapted from BEST, ROGER J., *MARKET-BASED MANAGEMENT: STRATEGIES FOR GROWING CUSTOMER VALUE AND PROFITABILITY*, 2nd,©2000, Prentice Hall p.32. Reproduced by permission of Pearson Education, Inc., Upper Saddle River, New Jersey.

In some instances we have been unable to trace the owners of copyright material, and we would appreciate any information that would enable us to do so.

Introduction to marketing planning today

Comprehension outcomes

After studying this chapter, you will be able to:

- Outline the many benefits of marketing planning
- List the seven stages of the marketing planning process
- Describe the content of a marketing plan and explain why it must be dynamic
- Discuss how the mission statement guides marketing planning

Application outcomes

After studying this chapter, you will be able to:

- Begin the first stage of marketing planning
- Analyse and prepare or improve a mission statement
- Start documenting a marketing plan

CHAPTER PREVIEW: CADBURY'S MARKETING PLANS FOR GLOBAL GROWTH

Cadbury's vision is to be the 'biggest and best confectionery company in the world' by 'creating brands people love'. Despite worldwide economic woes, rising cocoa prices and aggressive competition, Cadbury's marketing plans have helped it make steady progress towards that vision. Already, Cadbury has achieved a global market share of 10.5 per cent, increased annual turnover beyond £5 billion and improved its profit margin to nearly 12 per cent.

The company's marketing plans put particular emphasis on such well-known brands as Dairy Milk and Green & Black's chocolates, Halls and Eclairs sweets and Trident and Dentyne chewing gums. New-product introductions as well as reintroductions (such as the Wispa bar) receive special marketing treatment. In addition, the plans make the most of timely opportunities, such as meeting higher demand for affordable treats during the recent economic downturn. They also reflect the company's commitment to sustainability, with more Fairtrade-certified cocoa and locally sourced ingredients used in each product year after year.

Finally, Cadbury's marketing plans rely on a variety of customer-engagement techniques to build buzz and sales. Cadbury brands have Facebook pages, channels on YouTube and tweets on Twitter. A few years ago, the famous 'drumming gorilla' advert for Cadbury Dairy Milk was viewed by tens of millions of consumers on television, Cadbury's website and YouTube – and it helped boost product purchases by 9 per cent. More recently, the 'eyebrow' advert became another word-of-mouth sensation. Cadbury's marketing director explains: 'If you can capture people's hearts and get them to like you as a brand, they will think better of you and purchase you.'[1]

Without marketing planning, Cadbury would have no clear course of action for reaching out to customers, improving market share and increasing profits. Yet the planning decisions that lead to growth for Cadbury will not necessarily work for Wrigley, Nestlé or any other competitor. Every marketing plan is therefore as unique as it is vital for the company's future. In this chapter, you'll learn about the vital role of marketing planning within today's ever-changing global marketplace, review the individual stages in the process and learn how to document a marketing plan. After you explore the three levels of planning, you'll see how a solid mission statement guides marketing planning. Take a quick look at the sample marketing plan in the Appendix for a preview of how to document your planning activities and decisions. And use this chapter's checklists to prepare for developing your own marketing plan.

THE ROLE OF MARKETING PLANNING

Marketing planning is the structured process that leads to a coordinated set of marketing decisions and actions, for a specific organisation and over a specific period, based on:

- an analysis of the current internal and external situation, including markets and customers

- clear marketing direction, objectives, strategies and programmes for targeted customer segments

- support through customer service and internal marketing programmes and

- management of marketing activities through implementation, evaluation and control.

The course of action that results from marketing planning is recorded in a **marketing plan**. This internal document outlines the marketplace situation and describes the marketing strategies and programmes that will support the achievement of business and organisational goals over a specified period, usually one year. Often firms create separate marketing plans for each brand and each market as well as for a new product launch or other special activities.

The benefits of marketing planning

In a world where brand reputations are won and lost with the click of a mouse and economic problems that originate far from home can disrupt local buying patterns, marketing planning is more important than ever before. You need a structured process to guide you through the examination of different opportunities for satisfying customers and achieving marketing goals, as well as for assessing the current and potential threats to overall performance. And you need it as a framework for systematically identifying and evaluating different marketing possibilities, priorities and outcomes.

Marketing planning keeps you focused on your customers, helps you determine what your organisation can do (and what it can't do) for customers, helps you examine offerings in the context of competition and the marketing environment, and sets up the rationale for allocating resources to achieve marketing efficiency and effectiveness. Marketing planning, in effect, deals with the *who, what, when, where, how* and *how much* of an organisation's marketing.

However, the marketing plan is not simply an account of what you as a marketer aspire to accomplish in the coming year. Your plan must allow for measuring progress towards objectives and making adjustments if actual results vary from projections. In other words, a marketing plan must be both specific and flexible to help you prepare for the new and the unexpected: an economic crisis, new competition, evolving technology, new laws, changing regulation and other shifts that can affect marketing performance.

The dynamic marketing plan

Today's marketing environment has become so volatile that successful companies like Cadbury continually update their marketing plans to maintain their competitive edge and provide goods or services that customers really value. A good marketing plan must be dynamic, not only anticipating changes but also providing guidelines for how to react with customer relationships in mind. No marketing plan lasts forever; even the most effective plan must be adjusted as the marketing situation is transformed. You may, in fact, want to have several alternative plans in mind that might be implemented if significant changes occur.

Consider the dramatic shifts that are bringing new urgency to the process of marketing planning. Both consumers and businesses have shown their willingness to stop buying or switch to cheaper brands at the first sign of economic trouble, forcing companies to fight harder for purchases. Some may, for instance, use discount vouchers as part of a marketing plan to attract first-time buyers, while others may use a loyalty scheme as part of a marketing plan to encourage customer loyalty. Marketing to maintain a good digital reputation is another key area for companies, now that consumers can quickly tell the world about their experiences with a good or service by e-mailing, blogging, tweeting, texting or posting YouTube videos.

Marketing planning also helps organisations stay ahead of competitors by anticipating and responding to what their customers want, need and require, as Ocado has done.

MARKETING IN PRACTICE: OCADO

Ocado.com was founded in 1999 with one basic purpose: 'to change the way people shop for their groceries every week'. The founders recognised that the UK grocery industry was a £120 billion business, they knew that many shoppers dislike pushing a trolley through store aisles week after week, and they believed that Internet technology was the key to faster, easier grocery shopping. For more than two years, they worked on the web-site while building a state-of-the-art distribution facility to hold food and household items for direct delivery to customers via satellite navigation-equipped vans.

Despite competition from supermarket giants such as Tesco, Ocado has been quite successful. Since the first day of business in 2002, in partnership with Waitrose, the firm has delivered more than one billion pounds (in weight) of groceries. Now serving 13.5 million loyal customers and growing by more than 10 per cent every year, Ocado is shaping the future of grocery shopping by using purchase data to predict when shoppers will need to reorder specific items they have ordered in the past. Ocado was also the first of the UK grocery retailers to add the convenience of shopping via iPhone. Knowing that shoppers keep their eyes on competitive pricing, Ocado matches Tesco's prices on certain items. Ocado's marketing has so impressed Procter & Gamble that the maker of Dash, Gillette, Pringles and other leading brands has bought a small stake in the retailer to learn more about its inner workings.[2]

Marketing planning is especially important for helping start-up businesses, such as London-based Two Chicks, establish themselves. One of the founders had noticed many liquid egg white products sold in US supermarkets, yet she had never seen something similar in UK shops. She and her business partner confirmed the growing trend of substituting egg whites for whole eggs in baked goods and other foods prepared by home cooks – and the lack of UK competition. They then created a plan to market preservative-free whites from eggs laid by free-range hens in an easy-pour container through major grocery chains such as Ocado, Waitrose and Sainsbury's. For a more personal connection with customers, the partners began blogging about recipes and special events on the company website. Demand has become so strong that Two Chicks recently expanded its distribution to grocery stores in Ireland.[3]

THE MARKETING PLANNING PROCESS

The marketing plan documents decisions and actions undertaken as a result of the seven-stage marketing planning process shown in Figure 1.1. Most organisations begin this process many months before a marketing plan is scheduled to take effect. Experts warn, however, that marketing planning should be ongoing, not a once-a-year exercise. Because the marketing environment is dynamic and can change at any time, managers should spread analysis and planning activities throughout the year and make strategic decisions after examining important issues at length.[4] This section will give you a brief overview of all seven stages and serve as a preview of the book.

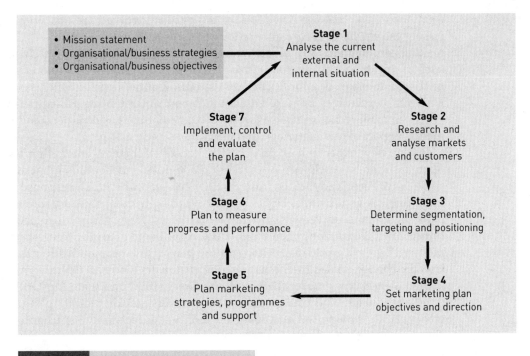

- Mission statement
- Organisational/business strategies
- Organisational/business objectives

Stage 1
Analyse the current external and internal situation

Stage 7
Implement, control and evaluate the plan

Stage 2
Research and analyse markets and customers

Stage 6
Plan to measure progress and performance

Stage 3
Determine segmentation, targeting and positioning

Stage 5
Plan marketing strategies, programmes and support

Stage 4
Set marketing plan objectives and direction

FIGURE 1.1   The marketing planning process

Stage 1: Analyse the current situation

The purpose of analysing your situation is to identify strengths, weaknesses, opportunities and threats (SWOT) for marketing purposes. You'll use an *internal audit* to examine the current situation within the organisation, including mission statement, resources, offerings, capabilities, important business relationships and – an important way of learning from the past – the results of earlier plans. As discussed later in this chapter, the mission statement is an overall guide to what the organisation wants to accomplish and where, in general terms, your marketing plan should take the organisation. Ocado's mission, which is 'to change the way people shop for their groceries every week', guides the firm's marketing decisions and activities.

Using an *external audit*, you'll study trends and changes in the broad political, economic, social–cultural, technological, legal and ecological environment (sometimes abbreviated as PESTLE) and analyse competitive factors. This audit should cover issues, threats and opportunities that might influence your ability to implement the marketing plan and achieve your objectives. The entrepreneurs who started Two Chicks identified an opportunity to be the first UK firm to market egg whites, thanks to the social–cultural trend of consumers becoming more conscious of healthy eating.

Due to external changes such as public pressure and internal changes such as forward-looking corporate leadership, a growing number of companies are adopting **sustainable marketing**, 'the establishment, maintenance and enhancement of customer relationships so that the objectives of the parties involved are met without compromising the ability of future generations to achieve their own objectives'.[5] This entails making commitments to a broader base of **publics** (also known as *stakeholders*), groups such as stockholders, reporters, citizen action groups and neighbourhood residents that have an interest in or an influence on the organisation's performance. As an example, Unilever's executives prepare an annual report documenting global performance on key sustainability factors such as water use, greenhouse gas emissions and the environmental impact of raw materials used in products and packaging.[6]

Publics now expect – and, on occasion, actually demand – **marketing transparency**, open and honest disclosure of marketing activities and decisions that affect them in some way. Perceived lack of transparency can lead to a harsh response from one or more publics. To illustrate, HSBC (among other high-street banks) traditionally offered bank accounts to university students with interest-free overdraft protection that continued after graduation. Then HSBC decided to begin charging interest on overdrafts incurred by new graduates. Although the bank provided notification as required by law, the change caused resentment among customers who had recently graduated. One started a Facebook group called 'Stop the Great HSBC Graduate Rip-Off!'. Thousands of new graduates joined the group and newspapers quickly picked up the story. Within weeks, HSBC apologised and reversed its pricing decision.[7] See Chapter 2 for more about assessing the current situation.

Stage 2: Research and analyse markets and customers

Next you should research your markets and customers (consumers, businesses, clients or constituents). Investigate trends in market share, product demand, customer needs and perceptions, demographics, buying patterns and customer satisfaction. Who is buying or would buy the product being marketed, and why? How are buying patterns changing, and why? What is in demand and when? Where is it in demand and how is demand expected to change over time? What experiences, services and benefits do customers need, want or expect before, during and after each purchase?

During this research and analysis stage, think about what your customers might need tomorrow as well as what they need today. This will help you formulate a plan for **relationship marketing**, building mutually satisfying ongoing connections with customers and other key publics.[8] Relationship marketing starts from the premise that when organisations look beyond the immediate transaction to build trust and meet customers' long-term needs, customers are more likely to remain loyal. Successful firms demonstrate a strong customer orientation through their marketing activities, recognising that satisfying customers will ultimately lead to satisfying shareholders and other stakeholders.[9] Increasingly, top executives are holding marketing personnel accountable for reinforcing customer loyalty and long-term relationships, purchase by purchase.[10] Marketing transparency contributes to relationship building, just as lack of transparency can undermine it. See Chapter 3 for more detail.

Before you continue, take a moment to review the first checklist in this book. The questions are designed to help you consider what you'll need as you begin the marketing planning process.

ESSENTIAL MARKETING PLAN CHECKLIST NO. 1:
GETTING READY FOR SITUATIONAL ANALYSIS

How much background information is available, and what sources should you be using? What trends and issues will influence your planning efforts? What should you be doing to prepare for the planning process? Answer the following as you get ready for analysing your current situation, putting a tick next to each question after you've written your answer.

☐ What sources of information will help you identify and understand important developments affecting your goods or services, customers and competition? How can you obtain this information?

_____

☐ What political changes, economic issues, social–cultural changes, technological trends, legal issues and ecological considerations are likely to influence your ability to attract and retain customers?

_____

☐ If you're marketing in more than one country, how will you uncover and monitor regional and international issues that can help or hurt your marketing efforts?

_____

☐ What insights into the marketing successes and failures of other organisations can help you anticipate or understand changes in the internal and external environment?

_____

☐ Who are your organisation's publics, and how is each important to the effective implementation of your marketing plan?

_____

Stage 3: Determine segmentation, targeting and positioning

No organisation has the resources (people, money or time) to serve every customer in every market. You will therefore use your research and customer knowledge to identify which specific subgroups can be effectively targeted through marketing. To do this, group customers into **segments** based on characteristics, behaviours, needs or wants that affect their demand for or usage of the product being marketed. A segment may be as small as one consumer or business customer or as large as millions of customers in multiple nations.

Next you will decide on your **targeting** approach. Will you focus on a single segment, on two or more segments or on one entire market? How will these segments be covered through marketing? Ford, for instance, creates new cars with specific targeted segments in mind. When Ford marketers redesigned the Fiesta, they targeted drivers under 30 years old who want small, affordable, fuel-efficient and stylish cars. They gave the diesel-equipped Fiesta a sporty, upmarket look to appeal especially to this targeted segment. 'The idea that large meant luxury, small meant cheap, is gone,' said Ford of Britain's marketing director.[11]

You also need to formulate a suitable **positioning**, which means using marketing to create a competitively distinctive place (position) for the product or brand in the mind of targeted customers. The purpose is to set your product apart from competing products in a way that is meaningful to customers. For example, in consumer markets, Prêt À Manger differentiates its sandwiches and other ready-to-eat foods using the positioning of 'made fresh daily'. Chapter 4 discusses segmentation, targeting and positioning in further detail.

Stage 4: Set marketing plan objectives and direction

The direction of a marketing plan is based on your organisation's mission statement and higher-level goals. Most use marketing plans to support a direction of growth in one of nine ways, as shown in Figure 1.2, including: penetrating existing markets, expanding within existing markets, adding new markets, offering existing products, modifying existing products and offering entirely new products.[12] A marketing plan for growth will define objectives in financial terms (such as higher turnover) and marketing terms (such as higher market share). High-performing firms such as Japan's Toyota may strive to retain or attain the role of **market leader**, hold the largest market share and lead other firms in new product introductions and other activities.[13]

Instead of driving for growth, companies trying to protect their current profit situation or their market share may use their marketing plans to sustain the current turnover level. During its two years of losses, Toyota created marketing plans to defend market share in mature markets while improving turnover in developing markets and aiming for future profitability. Firms under severe financial strain may develop plans to survive or to retrench; the US automaker General Motors did this during and after a period of insolvency in 2009.

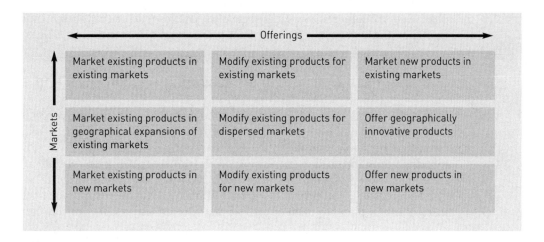

FIGURE 1.2   Growth grid

Source: After *ANDREASEN, ALAN; KOTLER, PHILIP, STRATEGIC MARKETING FOR NONPROFIT ORGANIZATIONS, 6th,©2003.* Prentice Hall, p.81. Reproduced by permission of Pearson Education, Inc., Upper Saddle River, New Jersey.

MARKETING IN PRACTICE: TOYOTA

During the worst of the recent global economic crisis, Toyota experienced two years of losses but retained its market leadership position despite declining sales of cars and trucks. However, after recalling millions of cars due to problems with acceleration and braking, Toyota now must rebuild its brand image, reassure customers about product quality and recapture growth momentum. The company is known for its commitment to marketing sustainability.

Since the introduction of the eco-friendly Toyota Prius in 1997, which runs on a fuel-efficient petrol-electric engine, more than 1 million units have been sold. Today Prius is the world's best-selling hybrid. By 2020, every Toyota model will be available with a hybrid motor or another 'green' power source. At design and development centres in the United Kingdom, Germany, France, the United States, Australia, Thailand and Japan, Toyota marketers research customers' life styles and preferences and apply the latest advances in vehicle technology, styling and production. Finally, Toyota is always exploring new ways to communicate with and influence car buyers through traditional media and YouTube videos, blogging, Twitter messages and event sponsorships.[14]

Note that goals and objectives are not the same, although the words are often used interchangeably. **Goals** are longer-term targets that help a business unit (or the entire organisation) achieve overall performance and fulfil its mission; **objectives** are shorter-term performance targets that lead to goal achievement. Marketing expert Tim Ambler notes that key corporate goals must be connected throughout the organisation, all the way down to the marketing plan and individual marketing programmes, if the company is to succeed. 'I would hope to see the marketing function become better integrated with the rest of the corporate machinery,' he says.[15] In addition to financial and marketing objectives, marketers may define societal objectives (such as for social responsibility and ecological protection). See Chapter 5 for more about direction and objectives.

Stage 5: Plan marketing strategies, programmes and support

In this stage, you will plan marketing strategies and tactics to achieve the objectives you set earlier. You will look not only at how to deliver value that meets customers' needs but also at the coordination of the basic marketing tools of product, price, place and promotion within individual marketing programmes. In addition, you should determine how to support the marketing effort with customer service and internal marketing. For practical reasons, you probably will not finalise all the details of your marketing activities until your plan has been approved and funded and is ready for implementation.

Product and branding

The product offering may be a tangible good such as a television or an intangible service such as expert tax-preparation assistance. Often, however, an offering combines the tangible and the intangible, as when a mobile phone company markets phones (tangible) along with phone service (intangible) or a manufacturer markets robotic assembly equipment (tangible) and provides repair services (intangible). Tangible elements of the product include: features, design, packaging, labelling and performance.

The brand is another intangible but extremely important aspect of the product offering. Every product must live up to the **brand promise,** which Philip Kotler and Kevin Keller define as 'the marketer's vision of what the brand must be and do for consumers'.[16] Other intangibles to consider in planning product strategy are: benefits, quality perceptions and related services. Process elements important to product planning are: the product mix/range, new product development, the product life cycle, ecological concerns and similar issues.

Changing a brand can be challenging but it can sometimes present new possibilities for satisfying customer needs. At the time of writing, Santander, a major Spanish bank, is in the process of putting its brand on the three UK high-street banks it owns. The banks, formerly known as Abbey, Alliance & Leicester and Bradford & Bingley, are being rebranded as Santander Bank branches. The switch means more convenience for customers, who can now make deposits and withdrawals at any of the 700 branches. To prepare for the rebranding, Santander began sponsoring Formula 1 motor racing so UK consumers would be more familiar with the brand.[17] Chapter 6 discusses how to plan product and brand strategy.

Price

What should you charge for your product offering? In planning price strategy, marketers must answer a number of key questions. Some are about external elements, such as: How do customers perceive the value of the good or service? What is the competition? How might market demand, channel requirements and legal or regulatory issues affect pricing? Internal elements raise questions such as: How can price be used to reflect the positioning of the product, brand or organisation? How do costs affect revenues and profitability? How does the price fit with other marketing decisions and planning for other products? And how can pricing capture value for the organisation and bring it closer to its objectives and goals?

Pricing is a vital ingredient in the marketing plan for Nestlé. This Swiss company, which specialises in food products, looks carefully at income levels, inflation and purchasing power to determine appropriate product prices (and potential profits) in its markets. For example, income in Russia has been rising and a large percentage of that income is disposable, which means consumers can afford foreign coffees and other extras. Nestlé's researchers learned that Russian consumers drink, on average, 250 cups of instant coffee each year – more than consumers anywhere else. Nestlé's marketers have therefore invested more than £600 million to market coffee, chocolates and other foods in Russia – and achieved annual turnover of £2 billion in that market alone. As the cost of ingredients increases due to Russia's high inflation rate, Nestlé's marketers also plan to increase product prices at least once a year.[18] See Chapter 7 for more about price and value.

Channel and logistics

Channel and logistics strategy – place strategy – is concerned with how customers gain access to the product offering, regardless of whether it is a tangible good or an intangible service. Will you market directly to your customers or make your products available through intermediaries such as wholesalers and retailers? If you market to businesses, will you go through wholesalers, distributors or agents that serve business buyers, or deal directly with some or all of your business customers?

Other channel decisions involve customer preferences, number of channel members, market coverage and ecological impact. Also consider logistics such as shipping, storage, inventory management, order fulfilment and related functions. Current channel and logistical arrangements should be evaluated as part of the internal audit. Whether you're marketing for a large corporation or a small business, the needs, expectations and preferences of customers should be deciding factors in planning your channels and logistics. Asda, the discount retail chain owned by Wal-Mart, has found a way to ask customers what they want.

These topics are covered in greater detail within Chapter 8.

MARKETING IN PRACTICE: ASDA

Asda's buyers frequently visit factories in the Far East to order products for resale in the firm's 363 UK stores. In the past, they had to make buying decisions without the benefit of customer input. Now Asda has teamed up with a research firm to create Pulse of the Nation, a panel of consumers willing to answer e-mail surveys about product preferences and other aspects of the shopping experience. The idea is to find out what panel members think before buyers place orders for certain non-food items. 'When our buyers in China are buying products nine months in advance, we will give them a phone, they will take a picture of the product and e-mail it to customers, and 1,000 customers will vote on whether we buy it,' explains Asda's chief merchandising officer.[19]

Marketing communications and influence

Marketing communications and influence strategy (also called promotion strategy) covers all the tools you use to reach customers in your targeted segments. The point is to encourage two-way communication and influence the way customers think, feel and act towards the goods, services or ideas you are marketing. Marketing in *social media* – online media such as blogs and YouTube that facilitate user interaction – has become increasingly popular because it can lead to *word of mouth*, which occurs when people tell other people about the brand or product.

Other tools include: public relations, sales promotion, special events and experiences, personal selling and direct marketing. Given the needs, interests, perceptions, expectations and buying patterns of customers in targeted segments, most organisations allow for a variety of messages and media in their marketing plans. However, you should be sure that the content and impact of the entire promotion strategy are consistent, unified and supportive of your positioning and objectives, which is what Fox's Biscuits has done (also see Table 1.1). See Chapter 9 for more on this topic.

MARKETING IN PRACTICE: FOX'S BISCUITS

Owned by Northern Foods, a top UK food manufacturer, Fox's Biscuits uses a variety of communications tactics (including TV advertising, radio, public relations and social media) to build demand for customer favourites such as Fox's Crunch Creams and Fox's Chocolatey. One campaign encouraged consumers to e-mail each other customised video and audio messages featuring the star of Fox's TV commercials, Vinnie the Panda. This campaign also increased brand involvement by inviting consumers to post questions for Vinnie on special Facebook and Twitter pages.

Fox's created an eBay auction page to sell Vinnie memorabilia, with proceeds donated to Crimestoppers, an independent charity that supports crime-fighting efforts. In addition, Fox's has been using communications to encourage convenience stores to devote more shelf space to Fox's biscuits and to expand the number of stores that carry the products. 'This is becoming increasingly important for us,' observes the brand category manager.[20]

Marketing support

You can plan to support your product, place, price and promotion strategies in two main ways. First, you should decide on an appropriate customer service level, in line with the chosen positioning, resource availability and customers' needs or expectations. Business customers often require service before, during and after a purchase, from tailoring product specifications to arranging installation to maintaining and repairing the product years later.

For example, Siemens, based in Munich, offers training and technical support for employees of hospitals and clinics that buy its sophisticated medical equipment.

Table 1.1　Vinnie the Panda and Fox's Biscuits

Communications tactic	Examples of use by Fox's Biscuits
Advertising	Vinnie the Panda television commercials, radio ads, billboards and posters
Social media	Vinnie the Panda Facebook page, Twitter messages and YouTube videos
Website	Vinnie the Panda pages on Fox's website
Public relations	Vinnie the Panda auctions items on eBay to raise money for Crimestoppers

Second, you will need the commitment and cooperation of others to implement and control your plan. This requires *internal marketing*, activities designed to build relationships with colleagues and staff members backed up by personnel policies that reinforce internal commitment to the marketing effort.[21] White Stuff, a fast-growing UK fashion retailer, uses internal marketing to help new employees understand their customer base and learn about the brand promise.[22] Chapter 10 describes customer service and internal marketing in more detail.

Stage 6: Plan to measure progress and performance

Before implementing the marketing plan, you must decide on measures to track marketing progress and performance towards achieving your objectives. This involves developing and documenting budgets, forecasts, schedules and responsibilities for all marketing programmes. You will also forecast the effect of the marketing programmes on future turnover, profitability, market share and other measures that signal progress towards objectives. The purpose is to see whether results are better than expected, lagging expectations or just meeting projections and objectives. For perspective, it is important to put recent marketing results into context through comparisons with competitors, the overall market and the organisation's previous results.

Often marketers establish quantifiable standards (*metrics*) to measure specific marketing outcomes and activities. In many cases, these metrics look at interim performance of specific brands, individual products or product lines, geographic results, financial results, customer relationship results and so on. Deciding exactly what to measure – and how – is critical to effective implementation and control of a marketing plan.

Siemens, which markets goods and services for industrial customers as well as consumers, applies metrics to track vital financial results. In particular, Siemens monitors growth in turnover and profit margins by SBU (strategic business unit), by product and by division in each geographic region.[23] Refer to Chapter 11 for more about planning to measure marketing progress and performance.

Stage 7: Implement, control and evaluate the plan

The real test of any marketing plan's effectiveness comes at implementation. For effective control, you will start with the objectives you have set, establish specific standards for measuring progress towards those targets, measure actual marketing performance, analyse the results and take corrective action if results are not as expected. Businesses generally apply several types of marketing control at different levels and intervals. The outcome of this stage feeds back to the beginning of the marketing planning process, paving the way for changes as needed.

Depending on your organisation and your plan, you may compare results with standards daily, weekly, monthly and quarterly; you may even compare results with standards on an hourly basis if you need to maintain extremely tight control over marketing. In addition, you and your managers should evaluate performance after all programmes are complete. See Chapter 12 for more about planning for effective implementation and control.

Documenting a marketing plan

As you move through each stage in the marketing planning process, take time to document your decisions and actions in a written marketing plan. Every marketing plan is unique, designed specifically for the individual organisation and its current marketing situation. Although some plans may be recorded in only a few pages, larger companies generally have a formal format for presenting detailed marketing plans by unit, brand and product.

Most marketing plans consist of the main sections shown in Table 1.2 (see the sample plan in the Appendix as another example). In practice, marketers cannot write the executive summary until all other sections have been completed, because its purpose is to offer a quick overview of the plan's highlights. With that exception, each section of the marketing plan is developed in order, building to the details documented in the financial plans and the implementation controls at the end of the plan. And when one section of the marketing plan is changed in response to competitive shifts or other environmental trends, other sections will need to be re-examined as well.

Table 1.2 Contents of a typical marketing plan

Section	Purpose
Executive summary	To describe, briefly, the plan's objectives and main points
Current marketing situation	In the context of the mission statement, to summarise the results of the PESTLE external audit and provide background about markets and customers, current marketing activities, previous results and competition
SWOT analysis	To discuss internal strengths and weaknesses, external opportunities and threats that can affect marketing performance
Segmentation, targeting and positioning	To identify the segments to be targeted and indicate how the product, brand or organisation will be positioned for the selected customer segment(s)
Objectives and issues	To show what the marketing plan is designed to achieve in terms of financial, marketing and societal objectives; to explain key issues that might affect the plan's implementation and success
Marketing strategy	To present the broad strategic approach that the plan will apply in providing value to achieve the objectives that have been set
Marketing programmes	To describe the set of coordinated actions that will be implemented to create, communicate and deliver value through product, pricing, place, promotion, customer service and internal marketing
Financial plans (budgets)	To back up the programmes with specifics about projected costs, revenue and sales forecasts, expected profit levels
Metrics and implementation controls	To indicate the organisation, responsibilities and schedule for implementation; explain metrics for monitoring and measuring progress towards objectives; and include contingency plans for dealing with unexpected results and future scenarios

Now you're ready to begin your own marketing plan. The final section of this chapter puts you into the first stage of the marketing planning process, analysing the current marketing situation. You'll continue your analysis in Chapter 2.

INTERNAL AUDIT: THE STARTING POINT FOR PLANNING

Plans and decisions made at the top levels of the organisation provide guidance for planning in each business unit and in the marketing function. To prepare for a thorough internal analysis, part of Stage 1 of the marketing planning process, you first need to understand the interaction among the plans at all three levels.

Three levels of planning for strategy

At the top level, planning for **organisational** (or **corporate**) **strategy** governs your organisation's overall purpose and its long-range direction and goals, establishes the range of businesses in which it will compete and shapes how it will create value for customers and other stakeholders (including shareholders). Corporate strategy includes extended plans for the long term, as far as five to ten years in the future. In turn, organisational strategy and goals provide a framework for the set of decisions made by business managers who must move their units forward towards the goals, given the organisation's resources and capabilities (see Figure 1.3).

Planning for organisational strategy ➡ Strategic plan (developed by top executives)

Planning for business strategy ➡ Business plan (developed by business unit managers)

Planning for marketing strategy ➡ Marketing plan (developed by marketing managers)

FIGURE 1.3   Planning on three organisational levels

Planning for **business strategy** covers the scope of each unit and how it will compete, what market(s) it will serve and how unit resources will be allocated and coordinated to create customer value. In establishing business strategy, senior managers must determine what portfolio of units is needed to support the organisation's overall goals and what functions should be emphasised or possibly outsourced. The business plan for one unit may span as long as three to five years.

Once the portfolio of business units is in place, planning for **marketing strategy** determines how each unit will use the *marketing-mix* tools of product, price, place and promotion – supported by customer service and internal marketing strategies – to compete effectively and meet business unit objectives. Typically, the marketing plan reflects the organisation's chosen marketing strategy for the coming year (but it may cover multiple years).

Because marketing is the organisational function closest to customers and markets, it is in the pivotal role of implementing higher-level strategies while informing the market and customer definitions of these strategies. In a customer-oriented organisation, marketing is a priority and concern of everyone at every level. Thus, marketing integrates floor-up, customer-facing knowledge of the market and the current environment with top-down development, direction and fine-tuning of organisational and business strategies. Table 1.3 illustrates decisions at the three levels of strategy, with examples showing how Cadbury might apply them.[24]

Be aware that the marketing plan (prepared on the level of the marketing function) is not the same as the business plan, although the two necessarily overlap to some extent. Sir George Bull, former chairman of J. Sainsbury, observed that the marketing plan, which results from the marketing planning process, is distinguished from the business plan by its focus. 'The business plan takes as both its starting point and its objective the business itself,' he said. In contrast, 'the marketing plan starts with the customer and works its way round to the business'.[25]

Marketing and the mission statement

Plans at all levels are made with the **mission statement** in mind. This statement explains the organisation's purpose, points the way towards a future vision of what the organisation aspires to become and drives planning at all levels. As you conduct an internal analysis of the current situation, take time to review your organisation's mission statement because it will be an important foundation for decisions about marketing activities and resources.

A mission statement should be more than mere words on a page. It should look to the future, be credible to the organisation's publics, contain or imply customer benefit and embrace the organisation's strengths.[26] A good mission statement will also clarify management's priorities and set the tone for all organisation members, including marketing staff, by touching on five areas:[27]

- *Customer focus*. Who does the organisation exist to serve? Businesses generally serve consumers, other businesses or government customers; non-profit organisations serve clients (such as patients, in the case of hospitals); government agencies serve constituents. For instance, the mission of Belgium's Médecins Sans Frontières (MSF), a non-profit international aid organisation, is to provide emergency medical assistance to populations in danger, to alleviate human suffering, to protect life and health, and to restore and ensure respect for human beings and fundamental human rights.[28]

Table 1.3 Levels of strategy

Strategy level	Decisions covered	Examples of application at Cadbury
Corporate	• Purpose	• Be the world's biggest, best confectionery by creating brands people love
	• Direction • Long-range goals	• Growth • 4–6% annual revenue growth; increase share of confectionery market; increase margin; increase shareowner returns
	• Focus • Value creation for customers	• Confectionery products • Brand-name, quality confectionery products that customers enjoy
	• Priorities	• Growth, efficiency, sustainability, quality
Business (implementing corporate strategy)	• Unit scope	• Chocolates, sweets and chewing gum
	• Competitive approach	• Exploit strength of market leadership
	• Markets served	• Americas, Britain, Ireland, Middle East, Europe, Asia Pacific
	• Allocation of resources	• Invest in high-potential business units, products and markets
Marketing (implementing business strategy, supporting corporate strategy)	• Product and brand strategy	• Offer world-class quality foods and make brands customer favourites
	• Pricing strategy • Channel/logistics [distribution] strategy	• Quality and value • Reach consumers through wide distribution via food wholesalers and retailers
	• Communications/influence strategy	• Use multimedia messages to encourage brand interaction and loyalty
	• Marketing support	• Fill channel orders completely and on time; share marketing news internally to reinforce cooperation

- *Value provided*. What value will the organisation provide for its customers and other stakeholders, and how will it do so in a competitively superior way? Companies profit only when offerings provide value that customers need or want. Siemens, for instance, makes energy-efficient lights, trains and gas turbine motors that are valued by industrial buyers and government agencies seeking to improve their energy efficiency and reduce their environmental impact. Siemens also creates value for employees (in the form of jobs) and shareholders (based on profits earned).[29]

- *Market scope.* Where and what will the organisation market? Defining the market scope helps management properly align structure, strategy and resources. Online retailer Zappos.com has chosen to market shoes, accessories and apparel in the United States and Canada. The size of the market opportunity in those two nations is one factor; another is the ability to provide speedy and cost-efficient service by limiting the geographic scope of the business.[30]

- *Guiding values.* What values will guide managers and employees in making decisions and dealing with stakeholders? What does the organisation want to stand for? Cadbury has five values: performance ('We compete in a tough but fair way'), quality ('We put quality and safety at the heart of all our activities'), respect ('We genuinely care for our business and our colleagues'), integrity ('We always strive to do the right thing') and responsibility ('We take accountability for our social, economic and environmental impact').[31]

- *Core competencies.* What employee, process and technological capabilities give your organisation its competitive edge? These are its **core competencies** (sometimes known as *distinctive competencies*) – capabilities that are not easily duplicated and that differentiate the organisation from its competitors.[32] The clothing retailer Zara, owned by Spain's Inditex, has expanded rapidly due to two core competencies: a short design-to-production-to-store cycle, based on customer buying patterns, and a constant stream of new products to freshen store inventories.[33] Competencies are 'core' when they are based on specific organisation capabilities *and* contribute to competitive differentiation.

Clearly, the challenge of a good mission statement is to convey all this information in as concise a manner as possible. Now continue with your marketing plan by completing the checklist below, then read Chapter 2 for more about analysing the current marketing situation.

ESSENTIAL MARKETING PLAN CHECKLIST NO. 2:
THE MISSION STATEMENT

Before you can develop a marketing plan, you need to know who the organisation exists to serve, what it expects to achieve in the long run and – in general terms – how it will compete, now and in the future. If you're preparing a plan for an existing organisation, obtain a copy of the mission statement and answer each of the questions below to evaluate both the content and the likely effect. Put a tick next to each question after you've written your answers in the space provided. If your organisation has no mission statement or if you're developing a marketing plan for a start-up or hypothetical company, use this checklist as you devise a suitable mission statement.

☐ Who will the organisation focus on as customers, clients or constituents?

☐ How will it provide value for customers and other stakeholders?

☐ What main markets (geographic, product) will the organisation serve?

☐ What guiding values will the organisation adopt?

☐ What core competencies will the organisation apply for competitive advantage?

☐ How can the mission statement be improved as a guide for marketing planning?

☐ Does the mission statement provide appropriate direction for organisational decisions, actions and resource allocation, including marketing planning?

☐ Is the mission statement credible to all publics?

☐ Is the statement capable of rallying employees and inspiring customers and other publics?

☐ Is the mission statement aspirational and enduring to guide the organisation into the future?

CHAPTER SUMMARY

Marketing planning is the structured process that leads to a coordinated set of marketing decisions and actions, for a specific organisation and period. This process consists of seven stages: (1) analyse the external and internal situation; (2) research and analyse markets and customers; (3) determine segmentation, targeting and positioning; (4) set marketing objectives and direction; (5) plan marketing strategies, programmes and support; (6) plan to measure progress; (7) implement, control and evaluate the plan. Marketing planning is used to examine opportunities and potential threats, identify and evaluate a variety of outcomes, focus on customers, assess offerings in a competitive and environmental context, and allocate resources for marketing.

The marketing plan outlines the marketplace situation and describes the marketing strategies and programmes that will support the achievement of business and organisational goals. Marketing plans must be both specific and flexible to help firms prepare for the new and the unexpected. Organisational (corporate) strategy sets the organisation's overall purpose, long-term direction, goals, businesses and approach to providing value. Business strategy sets the scope of individual units, how each will compete, the markets each will serve and how resources will be used. Marketing strategy shows how units will use the marketing mix plus service and internal marketing to achieve objectives. The mission statement outlines the organisation's fundamental purpose, the future vision of what it can become and its priorities, guiding the overall development of the marketing plan.

CASE STUDY: HOME RETAIL GROUP AIMS HIGHER

While retail rivals such as MFI and Woolworths were collapsing during the recent economic turmoil, Argos and Homebase – owned by Home Retail Group – were following marketing plans that aimed for higher turnover and market share. Argos sells a broad selection of general merchandise and consumer electronics, from sofas to snooker tables to sat-nav devices, through twice-yearly catalogues, 800 stores and its online retail site. Homebase is the UK's second-largest do-it-yourself home and garden retail chain, with more than 300 stores and a website offering 30,000 items.

Home Retail Group's marketers base their plans on in-depth analysis of customers' buying patterns and preferences. They know that the average customer purchase is £20–30 and that customers visit Argos or Homebase an average of five times per year. They also know that their shoppers are keen to choose the way they buy. Some prefer browsing in the stores; some like phoning in orders for home delivery; some buy online or click to reserve an item for immediate pickup at the local Argos or Homebase store. Whereas some catalogue retailers have been hurt by the rise of Internet shopping, Argos makes more than 25 per cent of its sales online. Now Home Retail Group views the ability to provide convenient multichannel shopping choices as a core competency.

During the economic downturn, when many shoppers were reluctant to spend, Home Retail Group's marketers created a marketing plan to introduce a Value range of merchandise with lower prices. A few Value products were actually priced lower than when the Argos catalogue debuted in 1973. Home Retail Group's marketers also planned many cost-cutting moves to try to preserve profit margins, yet higher raw-materials costs finally forced the decision to raise prices on many products. Looking ahead, competition and consolidation within the retail industry will be major factors in

Home Retail Group's ability to implement effective marketing plans for higher market share and turnover.[34]

Case questions

1. How does Home Retail Group's ability to provide multichannel shopping choices translate into value creation?

2. What marketing planning decisions are most affected by Argos's regular schedule of distributing catalogues every six months?

 **APPLY YOUR KNOWLEDGE**

Choose a particular industry (such as soft drinks or retailing) and research the mission statement and recent marketing activities of two competing businesses. Prepare a brief oral or written report summarising your comments.

• What do the mission statements say about the customer focus, value creation, market scope, guiding values and core competencies of these companies?

• For each company, how do specific marketing actions appear to relate to the stated mission? As an example, does the advertising reflect the customer focus in the mission statement?

• Now look more closely at the mission statement of one of these companies, keeping in mind the questions in Checklist No 2. What changes would you suggest to make the statement more effective as a guide for the marketing planning process or as an inspiration for managers and employees?

 **BUILD YOUR OWN MARKETING PLAN**

By the end of this course, you will know how to work through all the stages in the marketing planning process and how to document a marketing plan. Depending on your lecturer's instructions, you will base your marketing plan on an actual organisation (as if you were one of its marketing managers), a hypothetical company or a non-profit organisation. As you complete each of these cumulative exercises, record your findings and decisions in a marketing plan, following the order of topics shown in Table 1.2.

Define the mission statement of your hypothetical organisation or locate and analyse the mission statement of the organisation you have chosen. If necessary, amend an existing organisation's mission statement or create a new one according to Checklist #No 2. What does this mission statement suggest about the organisation's purpose? Include information about the mission statement when writing about the current marketing situation in your marketing plan.

In preparation for later stages of the marketing planning process, list your ideas about the markets and customers to be researched and analysed, the product offering(s) your plan will cover, the organisation's competitive stance and its guiding values. Also look at the general direction you expect the marketing plan to take: is it likely to drive a growth strategy, sustain current turnover or support retrenching? Finally, write a few lines about what a one-year marketing plan needs to accomplish in order to lead the organisation closer to its long-term goals. Save your notes for use in completing later assignments.

 ## ENDNOTES

1. 'Ferrero discusses Cadbury with Hershey, private equity', *Reuters*, 2 January 2010, www.reuters.com/article/idUSTRE6010G420100102. Mary-Louise Clews, 'Confectionery: speculation mounts over restructure at Cadbury', *Marketing Week*, 2 July 2009, www.marketingweek.com; Joe Leahy, 'Cadbury sees India as cocoa growth market', *Financial Times*, 31 May 2009, www.ft.com; Nick Hasell, 'Cadbury is not flavour of the month despite its sweet spot', *Times Online*, 1 May 2009, http://business.timesonline.co.uk; 'Cadbury feeling sweet', *Times Online*, 6 March 2009, http://business.timesonline.co.uk; Marcus Leroux, 'How Cadbury hope to beat their iconic drumming gorilla ad', *Times Online*, 2 February 2009, http://business.timesonline.co.uk; www.cadbury.com.

2. 'Ocado ordering comes to iPhone', *Daily Mirror*, 9 July 2009, www.mirror.co.uk/news; Marcus Leroux, 'Ocado will bring you things you didn't even know you needed', *The Times*, 19 June 2009, p. 58; Decca Aitkenhead, 'The G2 interview: 'I've got letters on my desk saying: 'Dear Jason, you have changed my life' – which is actually quite odd', *The Guardian*, 4 May 2009, p. 10; 'P&G venture into retail business, quite unusual', *The*

Economic Times, 22 January 2009, http://economictimes.indiatimes.com; www.ocado.com; Marcus Leroux, 'Snow fails to hamper Ocado's online sales', *Times Online*, 2 January 2010, http://business.timesonline.co.uk/tol/business/industry_sectors/retailing/article6973410.ece.

3. Andrew Stone, 'New firms discover upside to downturn', *Sunday Times*, 4 January 2009, www.timesonline.co.uk; Richard Tyler, 'Dreaming of an egg white Christmas', *Sunday Telegraph*, 28 September 2008, www.telegraph.co.uk; www.twochicks.co.uk.

4. Paul B. Brown, 'Don't plan too much. Decide', *New York Times*, 28 January 2006, p. C5.

5. Frances Brassington and Stephen Pettitt, *Principles of Marketing*, 3rd edn (Harlow, Essex: Financial Times Prentice Hall, 2003), p. 19.

6. 'The bigger picture', *Packaging Gateway.com*, 2 April 2009, www.packaging-gateway.com/features/feature52593/.

7. Clay Shirky, 'Transparency is the new marketing', *McKinsey: What Matters,* 26 February 2009, http://whatmatters.mckinseydigital.com; Patrick

Collinson and Tony Levene, 'Now it's Facebook vs. HSBC', *The Guardian*, 25 August 2007, www.guardian.co.uk; Sean Coughlan, 'Bank's U-turn on student charges', *BBC News*, 30 August 2007, http://news.bbc.co.uk/2/hi/uk_news/education/6970570.stm; Facebook page for 'Stop the Great HSBC Graduate Rip-Off!!!', www.facebook.com/group.php?gid=2371122959.

8. See Philip Kotler and Kevin Lane Keller, *Marketing Management*, 13th edn (Upper Saddle River, NJ: Pearson Prentice Hall, 2009), Chapter 1.

9. Tim Ambler, *Marketing and the Bottom Line* (London: Financial Times Prentice Hall, 2000), pp. 19–20.

10. See Roland T. Rust, Tim Ambler, Gregory S. Carpenter, V. Kumar and Rajendra K. Srivastava, 'Measuring marketing productivity: current knowledge and future directions', *Journal of Marketing*, October 2004, pp. 76–89.

11. Phil Patton, 'Before creating the car, Ford designs the driver', *New York Times*, 19 July 2009, www.nytimes.com; Jorn Madslien, 'New Ford targets fuel efficiency', *BBC News*, 22 July 2008, http://news.bbc.co.uk/2/hi/business/7519095.stm.

12. H. Igor Ansoff, 'Strategies for diversification', *Harvard Business Review*, September–October 1957, pp. 113–24; Ade S. Olusoga, 'Market concentration versus market diversification and internationalisation: implications for MNE performance', *International Marketing Review*, vol. 10, no. 2 (1993), pp. 40–59; Alan R. Andreasen and Philip Kotler, *Strategic Marketing for Non-profit Organisations*, 6th edn (Upper Saddle River, NJ: Prentice Hall, 2003), pp. 80–1.

13. See Philip Kotler, Veronica Wong, John Saunders and Gary Armstrong, *Principles of Marketing* (Harlow, Essex: Pearson Education, 2005), p. 33.

14. 'Toyota UK to make hybrids in 2010', *BBC News*, 17 July 2009, http://news.bbc.co.uk; John Arlidge, 'Toyota brings fun to its hybrid cars', *TimesOnline*, 26 April 2009, www.timesonline.co.uk; Justin McCurry, 'Toyota tailors cars to markets as it struggles to climb out of the red', *The Guardian*, 25 June 2009, www.guardian.co.uk/business. Justin McCurry, 'Toyota president Akio Toyoda "very sorry" for safety recalls', *The Guardian*, 5 February 2010, www.guardian.co.uk/business/2010/feb/05/toyota-president-very-sorry-recalls.

15. Tim Ambler, 'Set clear goals and see marketing hit its target', *Financial Times*, 29 August 2002, p. 8; 'Interregna in conversation with Tim Ambler', *Interregna*, February 2009, www.interregna.com/article_tim_ambler.php.

16. Philip Kotler and Kevin Lane Keller, *Marketing Management*, 13th edn (Upper Saddle River, NJ: Pearson Prentice Hall, 2009), p. 242.

17. Amy Wilson, 'Santander calls time on Abbey, Alliance & Leicester and Bradford & Bingley names', *Telegraph*, 27 May 2009, www.telegraph.co.uk/finance; Michael Kavanagh, 'When rebranding can come back to haunt you', *Financial Times*, 27 May 2009, www.ft.com.

18. Maria Kiselyova, 'Nestlé sees Russia as growth engine for Europe', *Reuters UK*, 27 March 2008, http://uk.reuters.com; Jason Bush, 'Shoppers gone wild', *BusinessWeek*, 20 February 2006, pp. 46–7.

19. Chloe Smith, 'Asda's Chinese democracy lets shoppers vote on new products', *The Grocer*, 7 July 2009, www.thegrocer.co.uk; Karen Talley, 'Wal-Mart's Asda to let customers help choose what stores sell', *Dow Jones Newswires*, 6 July 2009, www.wsj.com.

20. 'Fox's Biscuits creates eBay site for Vinnie the Panda merchandise', *The Drum*, 17 July 2009, www.thedrum.co.uk/news; Robert McLuhan, 'Field marketing report – FMCG brands and convenience stores', *Marketing*, 9 June 2009, www.marketing.co.uk; Danielle Long, 'Fox's Biscuits uses online to push Vinnie the Panda', *New Media Age*, 26 May 2009, www.nma.co.uk; 'Vinnie goes viral', *Talking Retail*, 29 May 2009, www.talking-retail.com.

21. See Ambler, *Marketing and the Bottom Line* (London: Financial Times Prentice Hall, 2000) Chapter 6.

22. 'Clothing retailer made of the white stuff', *Times Online*, 25 June 2009, http://business.timesonline. co.uk.

23. Mike Esterl, 'Siemens chief is setting a higher bar', *Wall Street Journal*, 24 January 2006, p. C3.

24. Based on information on Cadbury's website, www.cadbury.com.

25. Quoted in Sir George Bull, 'What does the term marketing really stand for?', *Marketing*, 30 November 2000, p. 30.

26. See 'Mission Statement', *The Chartered Institute of Marketing*, 2009, www.cim.co.uk/marketingresources.

27. Adapted from Stephen J. Porth, *Strategic Management* (Upper Saddle River, NJ: Prentice Hall, 2003), pp. 53–4; Forest R. David and Fred B. David, 'It's time to redraft your mission statement', *Journal of Business Strategy*, January–February 2003, pp. 11ff.

28. Médecins Sans Frontières website, www.msf.org.

29. Daniel Schäfer, 'Siemens expects boost to green sales', *Financial Times*, 23 March 2009, www. ft.com.

30. Carmine Gallo, 'Delivering happiness the Zappos way', *BusinessWeek*, 12 May 2009, www.business-week.com; www.zappos.com.

31. www.cadbury.com/ourcompany/ourculture/ Pages/OurValues.aspx.

32. Stephen J. Porth, *Strategic Management* (Upper Saddle River, NJ: Prentice Hall, 2003), pp. 85–6.

33. Graham Keeley and Andrew Clark, 'Retail: Zara bridges Gap to become world's biggest fashion retailer', *The Guardian,* 12 August 2008, www.guardian.co.uk/business/2008/aug/12/retail.spain.

34. Julia Finch, 'Price rises expected in new Argos catalogue to make up for weak pound', *The Guardian*, 19 July 2009, www.guardian.co.uk; Dominic Walsh, 'Sunshine brings out the punters and gives a healthy glow to Home Retail Group', *The Times*, 12 June 2009, p. 53; Jenny Davey, 'Sunshine revives Homebase', *Sunday Times*, 7 June 2009, p. 14; Marcus Leroux and Peter Stiff, 'Customers of Homebase and Argos told to brace for price rises of up to 10 per cent', *The Times*, 30 April 2009, p. 56; Zoe Wood, 'Argos Group sees weak pound raising prices', *The Guardian*, 30 April 2009, p. 30; www.homeretailgroup.com.

2 | Analysing the current situation

Comprehension outcomes

After studying this chapter, you will be able to:

- Explain the purpose of internal and external audits
- Discuss how the internal and external environments affect marketing planning
- Describe the use of SWOT analysis for marketing planning

Application outcomes

After studying this chapter, you will be able to:

- Conduct an internal audit
- Conduct an external audit
- Prepare a SWOT analysis for your marketing plan

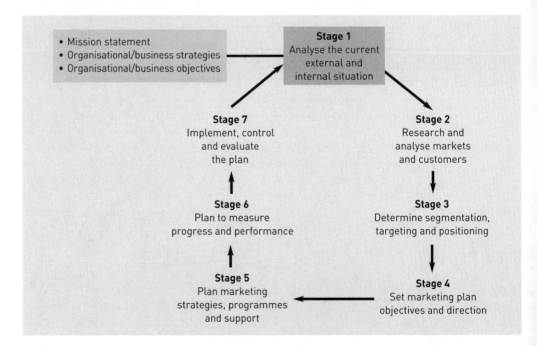

CHAPTER PREVIEW: MARKETING HELPS ROLLS-ROYCE MOTOR CARS ROLL TOWARDS PROFITABILITY

Marketing helps Rolls-Royce Motor Cars, owned by BMW since 2003, keep rolling along towards profitability. The recent global economic gyrations hurt sales of most car companies, yet purchases of Rolls-Royce's luxury vehicles dipped only slightly during that difficult period. In fact, Rolls-Royce's marketers continued driving towards their financial and marketing objectives, thanks to their knowledge of emerging trends in the marketing environment.

They noticed that public displays of wealth were being played down in certain regions and consumer confidence was not as strong as before the financial crisis. They also projected stronger economic growth and higher demand for upmarket vehicles in developing nations. They watched what competitors and new rivals were doing, taking particular notice when Geely, an auto manufacturer in China, announced a £30,000 car with a design very reminiscent of the Phantom, including a prominent radiator grill and luxurious styling.[1] Finally, they recognised that some competitors, such as Bentley, were increasingly appealing to affluent buyers who planned to drive themselves rather than ride in a chauffeur-driven luxury vehicle.

In response to these trends, Rolls-Royce's marketers prepared to introduce the new Ghost model, a smaller and less showy saloon than the well-known and more expensive Phantom, at a lower price (about £165,000). Knowing that even the smallest Rolls-Royce must deliver the smooth, silent and powerful driving experience for which the brand is known, they created marketing to communicate the benefits of the Ghost's unique engine and suspension technologies. The introductory campaign, which started more than a year before the Ghost's launch, included a direct-mail and e-mail programme, car show presentations, website preview photos and videos, and a worldwide tour to present the Ghost to selected customer and media audiences.[2]

This chapter continues with Stage 1 of the marketing planning process, in which you collect and interpret data about the internal and external environment. The first section is an overview of environmental scanning and analysis for the marketing plan. In the next two sections, you'll learn about performing internal and external audits. The final section looks at how to use the data collected to evaluate your organisation's strengths, weaknesses, opportunities and threats. Use the two checklists in this chapter as a guide to planning for environmental scanning. Also look at the sample marketing plan in the Appendix for ideas about how to present the outcome of your situation analysis when you document your planning.

ENVIRONMENTAL SCANNING AND ANALYSIS

Early in the marketing planning process, you have to look at the organisation's current situation, especially within the context of the mission, higher-level plans and higher-level goals. This is accomplished through **environmental scanning and analysis**, the systematic (and ongoing) collection and interpretation of data about both internal and external factors that may affect marketing and performance. When learning about the situation inside the organisation, you'll use an **internal audit**; when learning about the situation outside the organisation, you'll use an **external audit**.

Once you gather all the relevant information, you evaluate and distil it into a critique reflecting your firm's primary strengths, weaknesses, opportunities and threats, known as the **SWOT analysis**. In addition, many marketers conduct a SWOT analysis of current or potential rivals to clarify the competitive situation. The idea is to develop a marketing plan to leverage your internal strengths, bolster your internal weaknesses, take advantage of competitors' main weaknesses and defend against competitors' strengths, as shown in Figure 2.1.

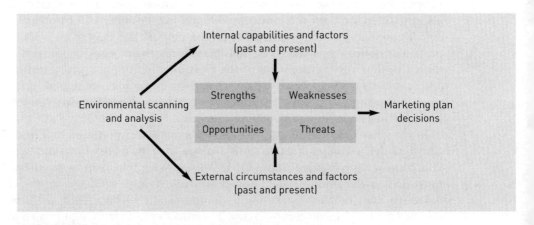

FIGURE 2.1   Environmental scanning and marketing planning

Details count in any environmental scan, but professional judgement plays a vital role as well. Use your best judgement (supported by other managers' insights, expert models and so on) to develop the most reasonable marketing plan under the circumstances. Over time, you'll develop a keener sense of how various environmental factors and trends interact and how they're likely to affect your organisation and marketing strategy. Also consider the resources and viewpoints of customers, partners, suppliers and other publics as you scan an uncertain marketing environment in search of creative opportunities and viable strategies. Having the flexibility to make changes during planning and implementation can give you an important competitive edge over organisations that do not or cannot react quickly and decisively under conditions of uncertainty.[3]

Internal audit: identifying strengths and weaknesses

The internal audit covers the mission statement (as discussed in Chapter 1) plus your organisation's resources and capabilities, current offerings, previous performance, business relationships and key issues. These internal factors, individually and in combination, are instrumental in the way your company fulfils its mission, serves customers and competes in the marketplace. And – just as important – these factors contribute to the firm's strengths and weaknesses in using marketing to deal with opportunities and threats.

A **strength** is an internal capability or factor that can help the organisation achieve its objectives, making the most of opportunities or deflecting threats. For example, three of Rolls-Royce's great strengths are the capability to engineer high-performance engines, the skill to hand-craft and finish every vehicle individually, and a long-standing worldwide reputation for quality and excellence.

A **weakness** is an internal capability or factor that may prevent the organisation from achieving its objectives or effectively handling opportunities and threats, especially within the competitive context. The high cost of hand-crafting every vehicle is one potential weakness for Rolls-Royce; another is limited production capacity, which could be a problem if the Ghost becomes unusually popular.

When auditing your internal strengths and weaknesses, search company records and databases for information such as current offerings, finances, personnel and skills, technological expertise, supplier relations, distributor connections, partnerships, previous marketing plans and results.

External audit: identifying opportunities and threats

The external audit covers political, economic, social–cultural, technological, legal and ecological factors in the environment (known as **PESTLE**) plus competitive factors that may present opportunities or pose threats. An **opportunity** is an external circumstance or factor that the organisation can attempt to exploit for higher performance. For example, Rolls-Royce identified the trend toward not showing off immense wealth as an opportunity to market the smaller, less expensive Ghost model. A **threat** is an external circumstance or factor that could inhibit organisational performance, if not addressed. The relatively low-priced luxury car recently introduced by the Chinese automaker Geely could be a threat to Rolls-Royce's ability to sell the Phantom at full price in Asia.

Sources for an external audit include internal information about customers, suppliers, partners, market share, technical standards; customer feedback through surveys, suggestions, complaints; government, academic or syndicated studies of the market, the industry, competition; industry groups; employees, suppliers and other partners; media and online reports; special interest groups. Later in this chapter you'll read more about the external audit.

SWOT analysis

Once you have data from internal and external audits, you'll prepare a SWOT analysis to make sense of what you have learned and interpret it in the context of the organisation's situation, mission and goals. The purpose of environmental scanning and SWOT analysis is to match key strengths with promising opportunities and use strengths to offset weaknesses and threats to marketing performance (see Table 2.1).

Table 2.1	The effects of strengths and weaknesses		
Strength or weakness (brief description)	**Internal source (resource, capability or factor)**	**Effect (on an opportunity or a threat and implications for marketing planning)**
Strength:		
Strength:		
Weakness:		
Weakness:		

How can you determine whether a particular internal capability, resource or factor is a strength or a weakness? Four criteria can be used:[4]

1. *Previous performance.* How has the factor affected earlier performance, as measured by trends in turnover and profitability, market share, employee productivity or other appropriate standards? Are prior trends and performance likely to continue?

2. *Outcomes.* How has the factor contributed to specific outcomes defined by objectives and goals? Will the factor be likely to influence short- and long-term outcomes in the future?

3. *Competitors.* How does the factor compare with that of competitors, and is significant change likely to occur in the future?

4. *Management judgement.* How do organisational managers view the factor and what changes, if any, do they foresee in the coming months or years?

The point is not to analyse every capability, resource or factor but to single out the most important as strengths (to be employed) and weaknesses (to be counteracted). When your environmental scans identify potentially profitable opportunities or challenging threats, you'll need the proper strengths to make the most of your marketing situation, as the fast-growing Irish airline Ryanair has done.

MARKETING IN PRACTICE: RYANAIR

Ryanair's marketers know that cost management is one of the budget airline's most critical competitive strengths. Selling tickets online keeps costs low and passengers pay for every extra. Ryanair is even trying to get government approval to remove some seats and sell cheap tickets to passengers willing to stand during flights. By continually lowering costs, the airline can offer ever-lower airfares and attract more passengers to achieve the objectives of filling each aircraft and increasing market share.

Costs that are out of Ryanair's control can therefore become real threats to marketing performance. Not long ago, Ryanair reduced the number of flights from London's Stansted Airport to avoid the high airport charges and extra tourist taxes that must be factored into ticket prices from Stansted. Some of these flights were switched to European airports where taxes and fees are lower. During the economic downturn, Ryanair's marketing plan focused on opportunities to attract large numbers of price-conscious travellers looking for bargain airfares. To capture market share from competing carriers, Ryanair periodically sells seats on selected flights for £1 – a pricing decision that can be implemented only because of the carrier's unusual strength in managing costs.[5]

Once you've assessed your main strengths and weaknesses and your main opportunities and threats, summarise and document the results in your marketing plan.

ANALYSING THE INTERNAL ENVIRONMENT

During an internal audit, you will scan and analyse five main factors: the organisation's resources and capabilities, current offerings, previous performance, business relationships and key issues. You are looking for information that can help you understand your organisation's current situation and the strengths you can rely on when implementing a marketing plan.

Organisational resources and capabilities

As noted in Chapter 1, core competencies are internal capabilities that contribute to competitive superiority yet are not easily duplicated. Such capabilities are traced to the organisation's human, financial, informational and supply resources (see Table 2.2).

One reason Reckitt Benckiser has boosted annual turnover beyond £6 billion – despite competition from such major players as Unilever and Procter & Gamble – is its competency in managing human resources around the world.

MARKETING IN PRACTICE: RECKITT BENCKISER

In addition to marketing prescription pharmaceutical products, Reckitt Benckiser – now known as RB – has 17 power brands that are well known by consumers in 180 nations. These include Vanish and Woolite fabric-care products, Dettol soaps, Airwick air fresheners, Clearasil face cleansers, Nurofen painkillers and French's mustard. RB's 23,000 employees are encouraged to develop their skills, knowledge and experience by transferring to different RB jobs and locations during their career. In the process, they uncover innovative ideas for new products and find fresh ways of marketing RB's existing products. In fact, products introduced in the past three years now account for 40 per cent of RB's turnover.

Although RB's marketers plan carefully for new products, a few – such as the Harpic Ready Brush, a battery-operated toilet cleaner – are delisted when actual sales don't match expectations. Yet the plan that led to marketing Dettol germ-protection soap in small, low-priced packages in India enabled RB to increase market share even during a difficult economic period. RB's commitment to company-wide entrepreneurial spirit starts at the top: 'I see my role as to provide the overall strategy and direction, to set clear targets and make sure that we focus on the right priorities,' explains the chief executive.[6]

Table 2.2	Analysing organisational resources

Human resources: Does your company have the people, commitment, rewards to successfully implement your marketing plan? Specifically examine:	**Informational resources**: Does your company have the data, tools and access to information to successfully implement your marketing plan? Specifically examine:
<ul><li>workforce knowledge, skills, morale, turnover</li><li>top management support</li><li>individual commitment, initiative, entrepreneurial spirit</li><li>recruitment, training, rewards</li></ul>	<ul><li>data capture, storage, reporting systems</li><li>analysis tools</li><li>access to timely, accurate, complete information</li></ul>
Financial resources: Does your company have the money to successfully implement your marketing plan? Specifically examine:	**Supply resources**: Does your company have the supplies, supply systems and relationships to implement your marketing plan? Specifically examine:
<ul><li>funding for marketing activities</li><li>funding for research and testing</li><li>funding for internal support</li><li>anticipating funding for multi-year programmes</li></ul>	<ul><li>ample availability of materials, parts, components and services</li><li>supply chain relationships</li><li>inventory management</li><li>transportation alternatives</li></ul>

When planning for marketing, you and your managers must balance the investment and allocation of resources. The organisation's values, ethical standards and social responsibility position also affect this balancing act. From a practical standpoint, the internal audit helps managers determine the resources they have, the resources they can obtain and where their resources are currently committed. This is the starting point for identifying any resource gaps and determining how best to allocate resources in support of the marketing plan.

Outsourcing, strategic alliances and supply chain realignment are three ways that organisations can gain or supplement resource arrangements to bridge any gaps for added strength. GlaxoSmithKline (GSK), for example, has arranged a strategic alliance with the generic drug manufacturer Dr Reddy's, based in India. GSK now has immediate access to dozens of additional drug products as its marketers implement plans to expand in Africa, Latin America and the Asia Pacific.[7]

Current offerings

In this part of the internal audit, you review and analyse the goods and services currently offered so you know where you stand before making plans to move ahead. Also understand how your organisation's offerings relate to the mission and to your resources. If records are available, review the following data and observe historic and current trends:

- composition, sales and market share of product mix and ranges
- customer needs satisfied by features and benefits
- product pricing and profitability, contribution to overall performance
- product age and position in product life cycle
- links to other products.

Previous performance

Although past performance is never a guarantee of future performance, looking at previous results can reveal insights about internal strengths and weaknesses. The purpose is to build on past marketing experience in planning new marketing activities. At a minimum, you should analyse these performance indicators:

- prior year sales (in units and monetary terms)
- prior year profits and other financial results
- historic trends in sales and profits by product, geographic region, customer segment, etc.

- results of previous marketing plans

- customer acquisition, retention and loyalty trends and costs.

Some companies use **data mining**, sophisticated analyses of database information to uncover customer behaviour patterns and relate these to marketing activities. Marketers for Tesco, the world's third-largest grocery retailer, look particularly closely at shopper data to determine which brands, products and ranges are selling well, to which customer segments and at what price points.

MARKETING IN PRACTICE: TESCO

With £59 billion in yearly turnover and 4,300 stores in 14 countries, Tesco has already achieved the long-term goal of becoming a successful international retailer. Now its marketing plans have the objective of increasing share, boosting turnover and selling as many non-food items as food items. Tesco's Clubcard, implemented as a loyalty scheme to reward frequent shoppers, has become so popular that today it serves 15 million UK participants and is well on its way to adding another 1 million cardholders.

By offering Clubcard points, Tesco's marketers are able to encourage purchasing of featured products and support recycling of carrier bags and mobile phones. Not only does the Clubcard help Tesco reward its shoppers and compete more effectively, it is also a valuable source of data about customer responses to marketing activities. When Tesco considered delisting a bread brand that didn't sell well, data mining convinced marketers to retain the brand because loyal customers liked it and would shop elsewhere if they couldn't find it at Tesco. Research based on Clubcard data has also suggested that the high number of price promotions in certain categories is causing shoppers to shift from brand to brand depending on price deals, eroding brand loyalty. Such analyses help Tesco and its suppliers plan for marketing activities to strengthen connections with customers.[8]

Business relationships

Good business relationships can act as strengths, helping organisations make the most of opportunities or defend against threats and profitably satisfy customers. Among the areas of business relationships to be examined during an internal audit are:

- value added by suppliers, distributors and strategic alliance partners

- internal relationships with other units or divisions

- capacity, quality, service, commitment and costs of suppliers and channel members

- changes in business relationships over time

- level of dependence on suppliers and channel members.

The existence of a business relationship is not in and of itself a strength. Moreover, not having strong connections with vital suppliers or channel members can be a definite weakness when an organisation is seeking aggressive growth or simply struggling to survive. Yet close connections with key channel members and suppliers can be an important competitive advantage. This is why small businesses such as Fair Oaks Farms, a US dairy that specialises in gourmet cheeses and other farm-fresh foods, compete to become suppliers to powerful chains such as Wal-Mart.[9]

Key issues

What specific issues could interfere with the firm's ability to move toward the mission and goals, and what are the warning signs of potential problems? What specific issues are pivotal for organisational success? Take a broad look at the key issues and then dig deeper to understand the implications for your targeted customer segments, markets and products.

Ecological concerns are a key issue for many organisations. Unilever, for instance, has a multi-year strategy for reducing ecological impact by making manufacturing, distribution and other operations more environmentally friendly and less energy-intensive. Still, Unilever's managers recognise that going greener over time means encouraging consumers to change the way they use the company's products. Unilever's research centres have testing areas to observe the way consumers use household products such as Persil. In addition, the researchers have developed 'loggers' to monitor the amount of laundry powder or liquid used by research participants in their home washing machines, as well as the water temperature and the power consumed during each wash. Such research helps Unilever's marketers plan for new ways to handle this key issue.[10]

ESSENTIAL MARKETING PLAN CHECKLIST NO. 3:
THE INTERNAL ENVIRONMENT

To formulate a realistic marketing plan, you must be knowledgeable about what your organisation has, where it has been and what it can leverage. Continue your marketing planning effort by adding a tick next to each question after writing answers in the spaces provided. If you are planning for a start-up or a hypothetical company, use this checklist to note ideas about potential weaknesses you should counter and internal strengths you'll need to support your marketing plan.

☐ Do you have appropriate human, informational, financial and supply resources for marketing?

☐ What do trends in marketing results and organisational performance suggest about the effectiveness of previous plans and the content of future plans?

☐ What goods and services are currently offered and how do they contribute to turnover and profits?

☐ How do your offerings provide value to customers – and is this value competitively superior?

☐ Are the offerings suitable for your firm's mission, goals and resources?

☐ What are the trends in customer needs, acquisition, retention and loyalty?

☐ How do business relationships affect capacity, quality, costs and availability?

☐ What marketing research does the organisation need to support marketing planning?

☐ What lessons can be applied to the marketing plan, based on the internal audit?

ANALYSING THE EXTERNAL ENVIRONMENT

In contrast to the factors in the internal environment, which offer clues to strengths and weaknesses, the factors in the external environment offer clues to opportunities and threats (see Figure 2.2). These factors also suggest additional lines of inquiry for researching and analysing markets and customers, as discussed in Chapter 3. Remember, your external audit is intended to help you identify trends or situations that you can exploit through marketing planning – and issues or circumstances that you should defend against through marketing planning. When you write your marketing plan, you'll summarise the most important point or points about each of these factors as you explain your organisation's current marketing situation. The following sections look at PESTLE and competitive factors in more detail. The checklist at the end of this section includes specific questions to ask when analysing the external environment.

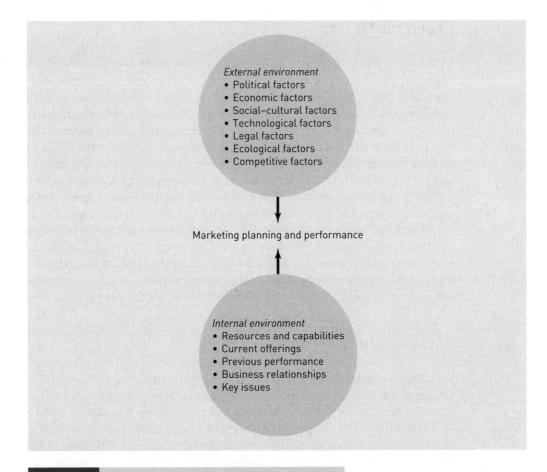

External environment
- Political factors
- Economic factors
- Social–cultural factors
- Technological factors
- Legal factors
- Ecological factors
- Competitive factors

Marketing planning and performance

Internal environment
- Resources and capabilities
- Current offerings
- Previous performance
- Business relationships
- Key issues

FIGURE 2.2   Factors in the external and internal environment

Political factors

Depending on where your organisation is based and where it does business, political factors can lead to profitable opportunities or potential threats (or both). Political instability, as one example, can pose a threat to ongoing operations. Changes such as new political leaders or new political initiatives can also result in opportunities or threats. Your analysis should look at how the various political factors might affect the current marketing plan (such as in your choice of markets) and your future plans (to continue in a particular market, for instance). Political factors are often closely linked to legal factors, which are discussed on page 40.

Economic factors

In the interconnected global economy, recession or recovery in one region can have a cascading effect on the purchasing patterns of consumers and businesses near and far. Economic factors influence customer buying power because of the effect on consumer and business income, debt and credit usage. Economic slowdowns often discourage businesses from spending heavily on upgrading their plants, for instance, or government agencies from proceeding with infrastructure improvements. Even if the home country economy is growing slowly, however, a company may create a marketing plan around opportunities in countries where the economic outlook seems more favourable.

To illustrate, the German retailer Metro has opened nine cash and carry superstores in Vietnam because that nation's economy has been expanding and the average per capita income has also been rising. The government encourages retail expansion, knowing that new stores help Vietnamese suppliers gain market share domestically and reach new markets abroad – which, in turn, strengthens the local economy.[11] Be alert for these kinds of opportunities based on economic factors. Also be aware of economic factors when you set your marketing plan objectives (see Chapter 5).

Social–cultural factors

Social–cultural factors are among the most dynamic in the external environment, affecting the size and composition of markets and segments as well as customers' requirements, characteristics, attitudes and perceptions. Population shifts due to higher or lower birth rates, longer life spans and immigration can create, expand or shrink markets. Along with these shifts come changes in demand and usage of different goods and services – key changes that must be considered in marketing planning.

During your planning, examine demographic details such as gender, education, occupation, ethnic and religious composition, household size, household composition and household income, any or all of which can affect purchasing and usage. Although such statistics are helpful, remember that customers are real people, not numbers; they have distinct feelings and attitudes toward companies, brands, products and buying situations, which in turn influence how they think, feel and act. Companies that market to businesses look closely at trends such as the size and growth of targeted industries as measured by number of firms, number of locations or outlets, workforce size, turnover and profitability.

Because 'word of mouse' (the electronic version of word of mouth) is often more credible than paid promotions, charities and businesses of all sizes are taking a careful look at the social and cultural implications of social media.

MARKETING IN PRACTICE: SOCIAL MEDIA

PDSA, the leading UK veterinary charity, has noticed animal lovers flocking to such social media sites as Bebo, YouTube, Flickr, Facebook and Twitter – and so the charity joined all of those conversations. Although much of the organisation's funding comes from seniors, PDSA wants 'to engage with younger people to encourage their involvement, both as pet owners and as future supporters of the charity', says an official. 'As social media grow in popularity, we have benefited from being involved with them.'[12] For example, PDSA's Facebook page has attracted more than 26,000 fans who post messages, videos and photos about pets; the page has also helped PDSA fans to coordinate contributions linked to special events such as the London Marathon.

Marketers for First Direct, the UK financial services firm, tweet and blog to understand what customers care about and to publicise activities that put the organisation in a positive light. Employees of Confused.com, a price-comparison website, tweet about news stories and special offers. They also watch for Twitter mentions of the company and rush to answer any customer complaints. 'A tweet can be as devastating as a negative review in more traditional media,' notes the PR manager. 'You can nip it in the bud and the customer sees that the company is responding.'[13]

Technological factors

Fast-changing technology has an effect on customers, suppliers, competitors, channel members, marketing techniques and organisational processes. Moreover, competing technology standards (sometimes coupled with government-imposed standards) are major factors in certain product categories. And although the Internet has opened opportunities for consumer and business marketing worldwide, it has also raised serious questions about privacy and security. Still, technology touches virtually every element of marketing, from digitally enhanced advertisements to packaging, research, distribution, pricing and beyond.

When examining technological factors to understand potential threats and opportunities, look at how rapidly innovations are spreading or evolving, how technology is affecting customers and others in the marketing environment, how technology is affected by or affecting standards and regulations, what and when technology is prompting substitute or improved products, how much the industry and key competitors are investing in research and development, and how technology is affecting costs and pricing.

Legal factors

Legal factors such as legislation, regulation and governmental actions can affect product purity and labelling, communications, data mining, pricing, distribution, competitive behaviour and consumer choices. In recent years, the European Commission has pursued antitrust cases against French glassmaker Saint-Gobain, US chip maker Intel, US software giant Microsoft and other businesses – legal cases that have affected the companies' marketing as well as their finances.

When Microsoft was preparing to introduce its Windows 7 computer operating system, for example, it changed the product so users in Europe could select web browsers other than the company's own Internet Explorer. This change was made after the EC charged the firm with monopoly abuse for bundling its browser with its Windows system.[14] In short, you must understand the legal environment of every market in which you do business so you can comply with applicable laws and anticipate future legal requirements.

Ecological factors

Ecological factors can influence marketing in numerous ways. Manufacturers will be unable to achieve their objectives if vital raw materials such as water or minerals are unavailable for production. A steady source of non-polluting energy is problematic for businesses and non-governmental organisations in certain regions; in other areas, high energy costs pose a challenge. Further, government regulations and community attitudes are shaping how companies interact with the natural environment.

The world's largest retailer, Wal-Mart, has made sustainability a top priority and asks its 100,000 global suppliers 15 questions about such eco-issues as greenhouse emissions and water conservation.[15] In this way, the chain adds the weight of its considerable buying power to the public sentiment favouring sustainability. Even if you are not a Wal-Mart supplier, your organisation may want to pay closer attention to ecological concerns, especially as they relate to your products and your societal objectives. Many businesses already include sustainability goals and reports in their marketing plans. (See page 41).

Competitive factors

All organisations, not just businesses, face competition. Charities compete with other charities for a share of donors' contributions; governments compete with each other when trying to attract businesses to create jobs, for example. As a marketer, you should examine three sets of industry forces to gauge the competitive attractiveness of the industry before you prepare your marketing plan: (1) how easily competitors can enter or leave the market; (2) how much power buyers and suppliers have; and (3) whether substitutes are available for your products and the effect on industry rivalry (see Figure 2.3).

MARKETING IN PRACTICE: SUSTAINABILITY REPORTS

With marketing transparency, competitive standing, corporate responsibility and publicity in mind, a growing number of firms now publish online or printed sustainability reports. BSS Group, which distributes heating and plumbing supplies, uses its annual sustainability report to highlight future targets and recent accomplishments related to environmental improvements. The report also covers involvement in social issues and charities in the communities where BSS Group operates. The report – and recognition for sustainability initiatives from FTSE4Good and Prince's Trust – help enhance BSS Group's public image.

Marks & Spencer's sustainability reports examine the retailer's results in implementing what it calls Plan A, 'because there is no Plan B for the planet', in the words of the sustainable-development manager. Plan A, established in 2007, set 100 specific long-term targets such as reducing energy consumption, eliminating excess packaging and marketing additional Earth-friendly products. M&S's reports state that not only were many of these targets attained earlier than expected, the plan quickly became self-sustaining thanks to cost savings from higher productivity and lower fuel consumption.[16]

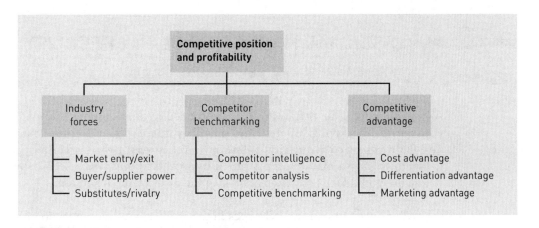

FIGURE 2.3   Competitive position and profitability

Source: Adapted from *BEST, ROGER J., MARKET-BASED MANAGEMENT: STRATEGIES FOR GROWING CUSTOMER VALUE AND PROFITABILITY, 2nd,©2000*. Prentice Hall, p.127. Reproduced by permission of Pearson Education, Inc., Upper Saddle River, New Jersey.

According to Michael Porter's model of competition,[17] when rivals can easily enter the market, the industry may suddenly and unpredictably become more competitive, which complicates the marketing planning process. When buyers and suppliers have relatively little power, the competitive environment is likely to be less pressured and the market may have more profit potential. When there are few rivals and few substitutes for the company's product, the company will feel less pricing pressure and be better positioned for profit potential. Keep this in mind as you think about pricing and other competitive issues.

Next, gather information on rivals, analyse the data and use benchmarking to set targets for equalling or exceeding what competitors do in key areas. Consider what your customers value as well as what your organisation needs to achieve its objectives and goals. Also be sure the measures you choose for monitoring your activities and competitors' activities can be tracked over time.[18]

The third set of competitive factors relates to how you plan for competitive advantage. Companies like Aldi (retailing) and Acer (computers) strive for cost advantage, minimising costs to keep their prices low. Companies like Luxottica (spectacles) derive competitive advantage from quality, style or another point of differentiation by positioning their offerings as superior in delivering features and benefits valued by customers. Companies like Shell (petrol and energy products) get a competitive edge from cost-effective marketing due to high brand awareness, extensive distribution and other efficiencies.

Many marketers tend to focus on current competitors that follow marketing plans similar to their own, typically within the same industry. However, you also need to scan the environment for trends that might change the future competitive situation and for companies that might soon be able to satisfy customer needs in an entirely new or different way.[19]

ESSENTIAL MARKETING PLAN CHECKLIST NO. 4:
THE EXTERNAL ENVIRONMENT

As you prepare your marketing plan, you need to analyse how external factors affect your current marketing situation and how they might influence future marketing activities. Put a tick by each question below as you note your answers in the space provided. If you're writing a marketing plan for a hypothetical business, use this checklist to list what you would focus on when analysing the external environment.

☐ What developments and changes in the political environment can or will affect the organisation and, specifically, its marketing decisions and actions?

_____

☐ How can local, regional, national and international economic conditions affect demand and customer buying power now and in the future?

_____

☐ In what ways are trends in demographics, social values, popular culture, customer attitudes and customer perceptions influencing demand, markets and segments?

_____

☐ How are technological innovations affecting customers, competitors, suppliers, channel partners, marketing and internal processes such as research and development?

☐ What emerging and ongoing ecological concerns may affect the organisation's materials, suppliers, energy access, processes, marketing programmes and public reputation?

☐ Which legal issues may have the most influence on your marketing activities in the short term? In the long term?

☐ What is the current competitive situation and how is it changing (or likely to change)?

☐ What are each main competitor's market share, strengths, weaknesses, opportunities, threats, resources and competitive advantages?

☐ What benchmarks can be used for competitive performance and on what basis can the organisation achieve competitive advantage?

☐ What lessons learned through the external audit can be applied to marketing planning?

 ## CHAPTER SUMMARY

Marketers use an internal audit to examine resources and capabilities, current offerings, past results, business relationships and key issues that affect marketing and performance. They use an external audit to understand how PESTLE (political, economic, social–cultural, technological, legal and ecological) factors as well as competitive factors might affect marketing. To gauge whether a market is competitively attractive, marketers look at ease of market entry and exit, power of buyers and suppliers, availability of substitutes, and the likely effect on industry rivalry.

After completing the internal and external audits, marketers analyse and distil the relevant data into a critique summarising the organisation's primary strengths, weaknesses, opportunities and threats, examined in the context of the mission and goals. Some marketers also prepare a SWOT analysis of key competitors. A SWOT analysis helps marketers match strengths with opportunities and understand how to guard against weaknesses and threats as they prepare the marketing plan.

CASE STUDY: CARREFOUR PLANS TO MEET MARKETING CHALLENGES

France's Carrefour relies on the key strengths of supplier contacts and customer knowledge when developing and implementing marketing strategy. Carrefour has €108 billion in yearly turnover and operates 1,530 hypermarkets, supermarkets, discount stores and convenience stores in 33 countries. Even though retailing is an intensely competitive industry, Carrefour's marketers have used these global strengths to great advantage when preparing marketing plans to address various opportunities and threats in Europe, Latin America and Asia.

For example, a few months after Carrefour moved its global sourcing office to Thailand, executives became aware that local farmers were producing an overabundance of fruits such as durian and mangosteens. In the past, these fruits had sold well in the 34 Thai Carrefour stores as well as in the chain's outlets in Taiwan, China and Indonesia. Identifying this as a marketing opportunity, Carrefour's marketing director in Thailand arranged to buy hundreds of additional tonnes of local fruits and created a plan to encourage the European stores to stock the fruits as a taste of Thailand at an attractive price.

Depending on the country, as much as 90–95 per cent of merchandise stocked in Carrefour stores is purchased from local suppliers. In markets such as India, where Carrefour's retailing model and distribution methods are not yet mainstream, local suppliers receive formal training in quality requirements and supply-chain management. The purpose is to make the most of the opportunity by establishing mutually beneficial connections with local suppliers for the long term.

When Carrefour's marketers analyse the internal environment, they use data mining to examine the results of previous marketing programmes across the entire chain and in individual stores. They have grouped the customer base of 14 million households worldwide into 60,000 customer segments for more relevant marketing attention; with data mining, they can target more precisely and measure the return on investment for each programme in the marketing plan. Carrefour also acts quickly when analyses point to unusual challenges or opportunities. For example, just a few months after opening hypermarkets in Moscow and Krasnodar, the retailer decided to halt expansion in Russia and sell the new stores because difficult economic circumstances had dimmed near-term growth prospects.[20]

Case questions

1. Given the global nature of Carrefour's operations, which external factors are likely to pose the greatest threats to its expansion in the coming years? Why?

2. How would you recommend that Carrefour's marketers plan to encourage European customers to buy Thai fruits?

 ## APPLY YOUR KNOWLEDGE

Research and analyse the forces shaping the industry of a company that is facing intense competitive pressure, such as a particular airline, food manufacturer or consumer electronics firm. Then prepare a brief oral or written report summarising your results.

- How powerful are suppliers to this industry? What are the implications for the company's business relationships?

- How powerful are buyers in this industry? What are the implications for the company's pricing decisions?

- Can customers substitute other goods or services for the company's offerings? What are the implications for customer loyalty to this company – and how can this be addressed through marketing?

- Can the company or competitors easily exit the industry? Can new rivals easily enter the industry? What are the implications for the company's marketing if environmental conditions threaten profitability?

- How do you think this competitive environment is likely to affect the chosen company's marketing plan for the coming year?

 ## BUILD YOUR OWN MARKETING PLAN

Continue the marketing planning process using the concepts and tools from this chapter, including the two checklists. Start with an internal audit of resources, offerings, previous performance, business relationships and key issues. If the organisation is a start-up, examine the recent performance of direct competitors and discuss what the trends might mean for your organisation. Next, look at relevant PESTLE and competitive factors in the external environment and analyse how these factors might affect your marketing decisions (and your competitors' marketing activities).

On the basis of your internal and external audits, prepare a SWOT analysis explaining how the main strengths and weaknesses relate to specific opportunities or threats and their implications for marketing strategy. Also consider how quickly you expect the marketing environment to evolve and how you plan to stay in touch with developments. Before you record your conclusions, think about how these latest ideas will help you develop a practical, successful marketing plan. Then enter this data in your marketing plan, with as much detail as needed to support your conclusions.

STOP ENDNOTES

1. 'Rolls-Royce considers legal action against £30,000 Chinese copycat', *Telegraph*, 23 April 2009, www.telegraph.co.uk/motoring; www.rolls-roycemotorcars.com; Nicolas Van Praet, 'Chinese eager to buy western car brands', *Vancouver Sun*, 9 September 2009, www.vancouversun.com/cars/Chinese+eager+western+brands/1979380/story.html; Prasad Sangameshwaran, 'Ghost to be the most driver focused Rolls-Royce car yet', *Economic Times*, 23 December 2009, http://economictimes.indiatimes.com.

2. David Williams, 'Rolls-Royce and Bentley hint at future of luxury', *Telegraph*, 12 June 2009, www.telegraph.co.uk/motoring/news; 'Keep on rolling: Rolls-Royce', *The Economist*, 9 May 2009, p. 64; 'For red-hot Rolls-Royce, will 2009 deliver a chill?', *Automotive News Europe*, 2 March 2009, p. 19; Diana T. Kurylko, 'Even Rolls is starting to feel the pinch', *Automotive News*, 30 March 2009, p. 10; 'Rolls on a roll', *Automotive Design & Production*, April 2009, p. 11; Erin Baker, 'Smaller Rolls-Royce nears production', *Telegraph*, 19 February 2009, www.telegraph.co.uk/motoring.

3. Stuart Read, Nicholas Dew, Saras D. Sarasvathy, Michael Song and Robert Wiltbank, 'Marketing under uncertainty: The logic of an effectual approach', *Journal of Marketing*, May 2009.

4. Mary K. Coulter, *Strategic Management in Action* (Upper Saddle River, NJ: Prentice Hall, 1998), Chapter 4.

5. Sarah Arnott, 'Profits soar at Ryanair in spite of price war as fuel costs fall', *Independent*, 28 July 2009, www.independent.co.uk; 'Ryanair reduces Stansted flights,' *BBC News*, 21 July 2009, http://news.bbc.co.uk/2/hi/business/8160923.stm; Amy Wilson, 'Ryanair vows to continue price war', *Telegraph*, 27 July 2009, www.telegraph.co.uk; Alistair Osborne, 'Ryanair ready for price war as Aer Lingus costs leap', *Telegraph*, 2 June 2009, www.telegraph.co.uk; Ben Leach, 'Ryanair to make passengers stand', *Telegraph*, 6 July 2009, www.telegraph.co.uk; Julia Kollewe, 'Ryanair downs talks with Boeing for 200 new aircraft', *Guardian*, 18 December 2009, www.guardian.co.uk/business/2009/dec/18/ryanair-boeing-talks-aircraft.

6. Quote from Josephine Moulds, 'Consumer champion', *CNBC European Business*, April 2009, pp. 19–20; http://www.reckittbenckiser.com; other sources: 'Reckitt Benckiser caves in on corporate identity and rebrands', *Daily Mail*, 15 July 2009, www.dailymail.co.uk/money; Ratna Bhushan, 'Dettol gains ground, Lux slips', 23 July 2009, http://economictimes.indiatimes.com.

7. Gill Plimmer, 'GSK in generic drug alliance', *Financial Times*, 15 June 2009, www.ft.com.

8. Noelle McElhatton, 'IPA report using Tesco data says brands risk long-term damage with price promotions', *Marketing*, 10 June 2009, www.marketingmagazine.co.uk/news; Joe Thomas, 'The

strategy behind the Tesco Clubcard relaunch', *Marketing*, 12 May 2009, www.marketingmagazine.co.uk/news; Burt Helm, 'Getting inside the customer's mind', *BusinessWeek*, 22 September 2008, p. 88; 'Tesco invests in Clubcard relaunch', *International Business Times*, 11 May 2009, www.ibtimes.co.uk; James Hall and Richard Fletcher, 'Planning test to safeguard competition could cost 25,000 supermarket jobs', *Telegraph*, 1 January 2010, 'http://www.telegraph.co.uk' http://www.telegraph.co.uk.

9. Emily Schmitt, 'The profits and perils of supplying to Wal-Mart', *BusinessWeek*, 14 July 2009, www.businessweek.com.

10. Steve Bush, 'Unilever develops suite of sensors for domestic washing machines', *Electronics Weekly*, 24 July 2009, www.electronicsweekly.com; 'Port Sunlight Unilever site safe despite job losses', *Liverpool Echo*, 2 December 2008, www.liverpoolecho.co.uk.

11. Quoc Hung, 'Distributors take long step to future', *The Saigon Times Daily*, 23 July 2009, http://english.thesaigontimes.vn/home/features/general/5590/; 'Metro eyes Pakistan', *MMR*, 24 April 2006, p. 15; 'Vietnam: competitor to go up against Big C, Metro', *Thai Press Reports*, 31 January 2006, n.p.; 'Metro Vietnam holds supplier conference', *Asia Africa Intelligence Wire*, 8 November 2005, n.p.

12. Carly Chynoweth, 'Warm hearts must be ruled by cool heads', *Times Online*, 21 June 2009, http://business.timesonline.co.uk.

13. Mark Frary, 'Twittering with the customers', *Times Online*, 17 June 2009, http://business.timesonline.co.uk; Carly Chynoweth, 'Warm hearts must be ruled by cool heads', *Times Online*, 21 June 2009, http://business.timesonline.co.uk.

14. Christine Seib, 'Microsoft Windows 7 users can choose browser', *The Times*, 24 July 2009, http://business.timesonline.co.uk/tol/business/industry_sectors/technology/article6727025.ece; David

Charter and Rory Watson, 'Anti-competitive Intel fined record 1bn', *The Times*, 14 May 2009, http://business.timesonline.co.uk/tol/business/industry_sectors/technology/article6283112.ece.

15. Stephanie Rosenbloom, 'At Wal-Mart, labeling to reflect green intent', *New York Times*, 16 July 2009, www.nytimes.com.

16. 'UK retailers Tesco, Marks & Spencer report progress in reducing carbon emissions', *GreenBiz*, 8 June 2009, www.greenbiz.com; Vivienne Walt, 'Charity crunch time', *Time International*, 30 March 2009, p. 43; Rachael Singh, 'Sustainability report gets public audit', *Computeractive*, 22 August 2008, www.computeractive.co.uk/2224571; www.bssgroup.com/sustainability.

17. Discussion based on theories in Michael Porter, *Competitive Advantage* (New York: Free Press, 1985), pp. 11–26; and Roger Best, *Market-Based Management*, 4th edn (Upper Saddle River, NJ: Pearson Prentice Hall, 2005), Chapter 6.

18. Companies may want to analyse competitors using some of the metrics they apply to their own performance. See Thomas J. Reynolds and Carol B. Phillips, 'In search of true brand equity metrics', *Journal of Advertising Research*, June 2005, pp. 171ff.

19. Craig S. Fleisher and Babette Bensoussan, *Strategic and Competitive Analysis* (Upper Saddle River, NJ: Prentice Hall, 2003), Chapter 11.

20. Lionel Laurent and Robin Paxton, 'Carrefour to exit Russia, hit by challenging markets', *Reuters*, 15 October 2009, www.reuters.com; Pitsinee Jitpleecheep, 'Carrefour aims to export Thai fruit glut to Europe', *Bangkok Post*, 12 June 2009, www.bangkokpost.com; 'Carrefour expands data warehouse', *Chain Store Age*, July 2009, p. 34; Writankar Mukherjee and Gulveen Aulakh, 'Cash & carry majors step up client training', *Economist Times*, 8 June 2009, n.p.; 'Carrefour starts hiring at first Russian hypermarket', *Russia & CIS Business and Financial Newswire*, 26 March 2009, n.p.; www.carrefour.com.

3 Analysing customers and markets

Comprehension outcomes

After studying this chapter, you will be able to:

- Understand why marketers examine markets according to definition, changes and share
- Explain the main influences on customer behaviour in consumer and business markets
- Describe how secondary and primary data are used in marketing planning

Application outcomes

After studying this chapter, you will be able to:

- Define and describe the market for a product
- Identify sources of information about consumer and business markets
- Calculate market share
- Analyse customer behaviour for marketing planning purposes

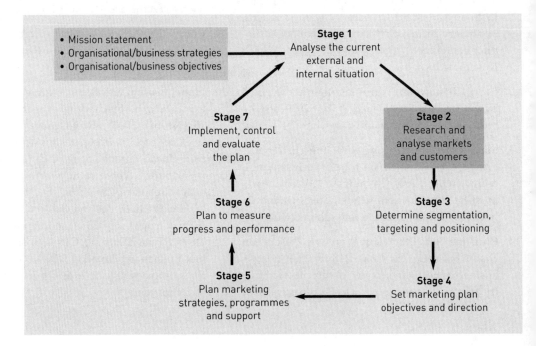

CHAPTER PREVIEW: NISSAN'S NEW LEAF

In the race to reduce harmful auto emissions and use alternative energy sources, auto-makers Toyota and Honda have taken the lead with their eco-friendly, fuel-efficient electric-petrol hybrid cars. Although all-electric cars have not yet gained the recognition and popular appeal of the Toyota Prius or the Honda Insight, Yokohama-based Nissan now has a marketing plan to change the situation. 'We don't see the electric car as a niche car,' says the chief executive. 'We see it as a mass-market car.'[1]

Nissan recently launched the Leaf (Leading, Environmentally friendly, Affordable Family), a hatchback with an electric motor and lithium-ion battery, as the first in an expanding range of all-electric vehicles for green-leaning car buyers. Once the battery is fully charged, the Leaf can travel 100 miles, a distance that Nissan's marketers say will meet the daily driving needs of 70 per cent of car owners. The Leaf's battery can be recharged in eight hours by plugging it into a household wall socket, but Nissan also wants petrol stations and car parks to install its 'quick charger' so owners can recharge Leaf batteries in only 30 minutes. Unless public recharging stations are available, drivers will be reluctant to buy any electric-only vehicle.[2]

Nissan and its partner Renault together hold more than 9 per cent of the global market for cars and trucks. This combined strength allows Nissan to draw upon considerable competitive power and brand recognition in introducing the range of Leaf electric cars to mainstream buyers. Nissan's marketing plan to build interest in Leaf vehicles includes the use of public relations and publicity, advertising, special events with dealers and a zero emissions website.[3]

This chapter takes you into Stage 2 of the marketing planning process, starting with a look at how and why markets are defined as a first step towards choosing specific markets and segments to be targeted. Next you'll see how market share is calculated and used. This discussion is followed by a discussion of how to analyse customer behaviour in consumer and business markets. The final section explores the use of secondary and primary data to inform marketing decisions. Use the two checklists in this chapter to analyse customers in consumer and business markets. Also examine the sample marketing plan in the Appendix for ideas about how to document your analyses and decisions.

ANALYSING CONSUMER AND BUSINESS MARKETS

People make a **market**, the group of potential customers for a good, service or other offering. The **consumer market** consists of individuals and families who buy goods and services for their own use. Nissan's marketers are aiming to sell Leaf electric cars to the consumer market. The **business (organisational) market** consists of companies, institutions, non-governmental organisations (NGOs) and government agencies that buy goods and services for organisational use.

However, when you're marketing to businesses, remember that you're not dealing with faceless organisations because buying decisions are, of course, made by people. Even when a company or institution develops an automatic system for reordering without human intervention, it still relies on a manager, employee or team to establish decision rules for when to buy, what to buy and from which supplier. As Figure 3.1 indicates, market analysis provides valuable background for understanding who might buy the product, what their needs are and what influences their buying behaviour – information you need to prepare an effective marketing plan.

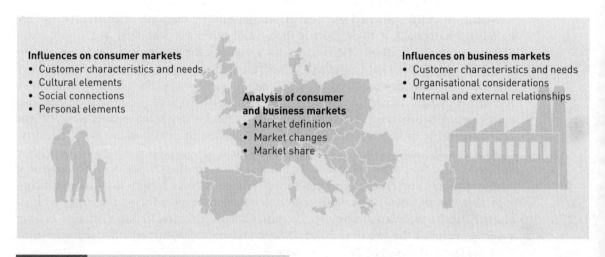

Influences on consumer markets
- Customer characteristics and needs
- Cultural elements
- Social connections
- Personal elements

Analysis of consumer and business markets
- Market definition
- Market changes
- Market share

Influences on business markets
- Customer characteristics and needs
- Organisational considerations
- Internal and external relationships

FIGURE 3.1   Consumer and business market analysis

During your preliminary analysis of consumer or business markets you'll examine three things: (1) market definition, (2) market changes and (3) market share.

Market definition

Defining the market helps you narrow the marketing focus to consumers or businesses that are qualified to be or already are buyers of a particular type of product. Within a given market, the broadest level of definition is the potential market, which has four subsets: the available, qualified available, target and penetrated markets. The **potential market** is all the customers who may be interested in that good or service. However, some customers in this market may be unaware of the product; some may have no access to it; some may not require its benefits; some may not be able to use it; and some may not be able to afford it. Thus, the potential market represents the *maximum* number of customers who might be interested in the product – but not the number who will *realistically* buy.

Part of the potential market is the **available market**, all the customers who are interested and have both adequate income and adequate access to the product. For Nissan's Leaf, the available market would be consumers who can afford the car and can get to a dealership to see and buy it. For Specsavers – a major UK optical retailer – the available market would be all customers who need spectacles or contact lenses to improve their vision.

A subset of that is the **qualified available market**, all the customers who are qualified to buy based on product-specific criteria such as age (for alcohol and other products that may not legally be sold to under-age consumers). Car buyers need not have a driver's licence, for instance, but they must be of age to sign the legal contract for buying and, if borrowing to buy, be sufficiently credit-worthy to obtain a loan. For Specsavers, the qualified available market would be all consumers who have a vision-correction prescription or want one of the chain's opticians to examine their eyes and provide a prescription.

The **target market** is the segment of customers within the qualified available market that an organisation decides to serve. For Nissan's Leaf, the target market would be car buyers who want and can afford a zero-emissions electric vehicle and who need to drive no more than 100 miles per day. Specsavers' target market is customers with vision-correction needs who want to save money on spectacles or lenses, want many style choices and want the convenience of consulting an in-store optician.

The smallest market of all is the **penetrated market**, all the customers in the target market who currently buy or have bought a specific type of product. At the time Nissan introduced the Leaf, the penetrated market for all-electric cars was much smaller than the penetrated market for hybrid cars. The penetrated market for Specsavers consists of all customers in the target market who have previously purchased vision-correction products. Figure 3.2 shows how a car-hire company might define its market according to these levels.

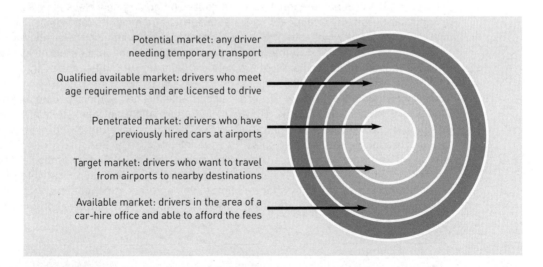

FIGURE 3.2   Five levels of market definition

Source: After Marian Burk Wood, *The Marketing Plan: A Handbook*, 4th edn, (Upper Saddle River, NJ: Pearson Prentice Hall, 2011), Chapter 3, Exhibit 3.3

For planning purposes, define your potential market by more than the product. Many organisations use geography and customer description in their market definitions. 'The UK consumer market for credit cards' is a general description of one potential market for Barclaycard. In plans to offer credit cards beyond UK borders, each new market would be defined geographically, such as 'the Western European consumer market for credit cards'. If marketers wanted to restrict Barclaycard's marketing to certain areas, they would describe each market more precisely: 'the London consumer market for credit cards' and 'the Manchester consumer market for credit cards'. If Barclaycard's marketers wanted to offer credit cards in a brand partnership with a well-known company such as Hilton Hotels, they would describe the market as 'the market for credit cards issued to loyal Hilton customers'.

Now narrow your focus by researching customer needs and buying behaviour within the potential market, yielding a more specific definition of the available and the qualified available markets. Research will help you understand what your customers value and what marketing decisions will best support competitive differentiation in a given market. Virgin Atlantic's marketers focus on understanding customers' needs, preferences and behaviour in a specific target market.

MARKETING IN PRACTICE: VIRGIN ATLANTIC

When Sir Richard Branson launched Virgin Atlantic Airways in 1984, he and his marketing team knew what trans-Atlantic travellers would value: first-class service at business-class fares, gourmet meals, roomy cabins, seat-back entertainment centres and other luxury touches. Over the years, Virgin Atlantic has increased market share by expanding beyond the original London–New York route and adding new classes of service such as premium economy to appeal to a broader target audience. Its marketers use Virgin's distinctive red-and-white colour scheme to identify and distinguish the airline and its aircraft from all competitors. Reinforcing the airline's classy image, its marketers regularly arrange star-studded media events to celebrate corporate milestones such as the airline's 25th anniversary.

Virgin Atlantic's mission is: 'To grow a profitable airline ... Where people love to fly ... And where people love to work.' Because customers and employees alike are attracted to companies with positive reputations, the airline's marketing plans support social causes through programmes such as 'Change for Children'. As another example, to celebrate the launch of the service to Nairobi, airline personnel and a number of frequent flyers worked together to refurbish a city school and restore running water to the area. Knowing that travellers enjoy sharing photos, tips and recommendations, Virgin Atlantic has created Vtravelled.com and invited the public to join the conversation online or via mobile access.[4]

Market changes

No market remains static for very long. Every day, consumers and business customers leave or enter an area; every day, consumers begin or stop buying a product. All the external factors in the marketing environment can influence market changes as well. For this reason, you will need to research expert projections and track overall market trends.

Two key changes that affect the size and nature of a market are:

- *Number of customers.* Is the consumer population (or number of businesses) increasing or decreasing, and by how much?

- *Purchases.* How many products are all companies in the industry estimated to buy in the next year and later years? How has the trend in purchases changed?

The purpose is to determine how changes, trends and projections are likely to affect customers in the market and the implications for your marketing decisions. For example, marketers for Philips India, a division of the Dutch corporation Philips, are projecting rapid population growth in India and, in particular, more consumers entering the middle class. Based on this population growth, they project that hospitals, clinics and individuals will boost purchases of health-care equipment and systems. Therefore, Philips India has invested heavily to market a range of medical technology products for diagnosing and managing heart ailments, sleep disorders and other conditions.[5]

Market share

Going beyond current and projected market size and trends, you will want to estimate your product's or brand's market share and the share held by competitors. Remember that your share will change as the market grows or shrinks and rivals enter, expand, reduce their presence or leave. Still, market share serves as a baseline against which you can track market dynamics and measure the progress of your marketing plan results.

Market share is defined as the percentage of sales within a market accounted for by a company, brand or product, as calculated in terms of units or money (or both, if the data can be obtained). The basic formula is: divide the company's or brand's unit or monetary sales by the entire market's unit or monetary sales of that type of product. Thus, if you sell 3 million units and overall market sales by all competitors selling that type of product are 12 million units, you hold a 25 per cent share. Your share would be 15 per cent if your product sales totalled £15 million or €15 million and overall sales of that type of product in that market totalled £100 million or €100 million.

Market share is one of the vital signs of a product or brand that you can track over time to spot potential problems and opportunities. You'll want to calculate or at least estimate the share for each product in each market on a regular basis to detect any significant shifts. In some industries, such as cars and mobiles, outside analysts regularly publish reports covering the market share of the top companies. Examining both market changes and market share changes can give you a better picture of what customers are doing, what rivals are doing and where the market is going so your marketing plan does not involve attracting an increasingly large share of an ever-shrinking, less profitable market. You can also identify less competitive markets and markets where purchases are projected to rise rapidly.

To understand market shifts in customer preferences and competitive activities, Cadbury's marketers closely track share for each of their three product ranges. They recently reported that Cadbury's share of the global market for chocolate is 7.5 per cent; for chewing gum, 28.9 per cent; and for sweets, 7.2 per cent.[6] Heinz's marketers are particularly attentive to market share because they're trying to reinforce loyalty to the Heinz brand despite intense competition from private-label ketchup and baked beans marketed by grocery chains.[7] Bear in mind that changes in share are not the only indicators – or the most important indicators – of competitive standing, nor do they necessarily warrant immediate attention. Companies usually include share among the standards for measuring progress in marketing programme implementation and to signal the need for adjustments, as discussed in Chapters 11 and 12.

ANALYSING CUSTOMERS IN CONSUMER MARKETS

Once you have a preliminary definition of the market, understand market changes and know your market share (or that of your main competitors), you're ready to look more closely at customer demographics, needs, buying behaviour and attitudes. For example, marketers for the UK-based fashion retailer New Look analyse their customers from many perspectives.

MARKETING IN PRACTICE: NEW LOOK

New Look, which operates more than 900 high-street apparel stores in Europe, the Middle East and Russia, has given its marketing plans a makeover based on in-depth customer research. New Look's researchers asked 4,000 customers about their shopping habits, their fashion likes and dislikes, and the way they view price and quality. Using this information to segment the market, they selected five specific segments for targeting and developed marketing plans to cater to those customers' needs and preferences. One change New Look made was to expand into larger stores wherever possible, with the long-term goal of doubling the amount of UK trading space to accommodate more merchandise. Another was to promote multichannel marketing so shoppers can choose when and where to buy, in a New Look store or from the New Look website.

Marketers for the chain also began tailoring the fashion range in each store for local shoppers' tastes. In addition, they created MyLookFashion as an online fashion community and a source of quick feedback about the retailer's merchandise and marketing. To encourage a feeling of exclusivity and engagement, New Look limited the community to no more than 5,000 participants. 'First and foremost it's an environment where the customer is empowered and can freely express opinion,' says the head of brand planning and insight. 'We would like to think that through this they have the opportunity to shape the brand.'[8]

What customers buy and how many customers buy can be influenced by different factors and experiences. Although you may start out with aggregated data to form a picture of the average customer, technology is available to help you identify and understand customer behaviour at the individual level. To understand consumers as a prelude to developing market targeting and programmes, you should analyse characteristics and needs as well as cultural elements, social connections and personal and psychological elements (see Table 3.1).

Table 3.1	Understanding behaviour in consumer markets
Customer characteristics and needs ● Demographics such as age, occupation, family status ● Problem that product will solve ● Changes in stated/unstated needs ● Customer-perceived value	**Social connections** ● Family and friends ● Work associates ● Organisations ● Opinion leaders
Cultural elements ● Culture ● Subculture ● Class	**Personal and psychological elements** ● Life cycle ● Lifestyle, psychographics ● Motivation and attitudes

Characteristics and needs

Often some characteristic, such as gender, family status, age, education or ethnic background, affects what consumers need and buy. Gender, for example, is a key factor in Unilever's marketing of Dove skin-care products for women. Similarly, Huggies and other disposable nappies are marketed to families with babies. Before conducting extensive marketing research, try to learn more about the characteristics of particular consumer markets from a variety of secondary sources.

As you assess consumers' needs, ask: What problem do customers want to solve by buying a particular product? What are customers requesting now that they haven't requested in the past? What changes in need are suggested by developments revealed through internal and external audits? Do customers have unstated needs and wants (such as boosting status or looking stylish) that can be uncovered through marketing research and satisfied through marketing?

When Daimler created a marketing plan to test a new car-sharing service in Ulm, Germany, it learned that more than 40 per cent of city residents don't own a car, yet these consumers occasionally want or need to drive somewhere. Daimler's Car2go meets that need by offering small, stylish Smart cars on hire by the minute without advance reservation. During the first year, nearly 10 per cent of Ulm's driving population hired a car through Car2go; Daimler's analysis showed that 60 per cent of these customers were aged 18–35. Based on this success, Daimler's next move was to open a branch of Car2go in Austin, Texas, a US city with 55,000 university students, and to plan for future expansion in Asia.[9]

Closely related is the value that consumers receive when they buy products to satisfy their needs. **Value** is defined as the difference customers perceive between the benefits they derive from a product and the total price they pay for the product. Customers perceive more value from a good or service that seems to deliver more or unique benefits for the money. *Virtual products* that exist in electronic form only – not the actual software but as digital accessories purchased for personal avatars for Gaia Online users or digital gifts purchased for Facebook users – have value to the buyers because of their novelty and symbolism. When customers buy, these products also bring monetary value to their marketers.[10]

Cultural elements

The beliefs, customs and preferences of the culture in which consumers were raised – and the culture where they currently live – can have an influence on consumer buying behaviour. Don't make the mistake of assuming that customers everywhere have the same wants, needs and buying patterns as you do. Marketing research is a crucial way for marketers to avoid this misconception.

Within a larger culture are **subcultures**, each a discrete group that shares a particular ethnicity, religion or lifestyle. These groups can affect buying behaviour. As an example, many marketers see teens as a distinct global subculture. Consumers in this age group have much in common regardless of geography, including a shared interest in pop music and fashion. Television, social media such as YouTube and the popularity of mobiles have only intensified the commonalties of this subculture, which has an immense collective spending power.

MARKETING IN PRACTICE: TEENS, MOBILES AND MARKETING

Whether buying for themselves or influencing the purchases of their parents, teens are a lucrative target market for companies that understand their preferences and priorities. In a recent UK promotion, Coca-Cola printed special codes for free mobile credits on bottles and cans of Fanta, Dr Pepper and Sprite soft drinks. A Coca-Cola marketing executive explained that this promotion targeted teens in particular because: 'We know mobiles are integral to their lives and we wanted to bring them both value and a point of difference that will fully engage them with the promotion.'

Orange, the UK mobile operator, created the Monkey music package to appeal to its millions of teen mobile customers. Knowing that teens frequently share music digital files, Orange arranged a tie-up with Channel 4 and Universal Music to offer free music to customers who top up their talk time by £10 or more during a month. Unlike music services that require costly wireless network downloads, Monkey customers need only dial 247 on their mobiles to listen to playlists. They can also access exclusive content and share playlists with friends on a special Monkey website, features that further enhance the value of the service.[11]

Class distinctions – more subtle in some cultures than in others – are yet another influence on consumer behaviour. Consumers in a certain class tend to buy and use products in similar ways. At the same time, consumers who want to emulate a different class – such as those who strive to move into a higher class – may adopt that class's buying or usage behaviours.

Social connections

Social connections such as family members, friends, work associates and non-work groups can influence how, what and when consumers buy. You will want to determine whether any of these connections are relevant to a particular product's purchase or usage and how they affect buying behaviour. Just as some consumers follow the buying behaviour of another class to which they aspire, others follow the buying behaviour of the social groups to which they aspire. Youngsters often imitate the clothing and accessory choices of their older siblings; employees seeking job advancement may imitate the attire of higher-level managers.

People who are especially admired or possess special skills may be seen as **opinion leaders** in a social group and therefore exert more influence over the purchasing decisions of others. Not surprisingly, marketers often single out opinion leaders for special marketing attention to promote their brands through key social connections. Sports figures are viewed as opinion leaders for athletic clothing, footwear and equipment; this is why the sportswear brand Puma sponsors the Irish Rugby Football Union, as well as sponsoring national football teams in many countries.[12] Athletes, pop singers and actors are also considered opinion leaders for fashion products and beverages, among other product categories.

Many businesses, NGOs and government agencies are building social connections with their publics through social media such as **blogs** (short for *web logs*), informal online journals where people can exchange ideas and opinions, and very short messages on *microblogs* such as Twitter (see Table 3.2). Zappos, a fast-growing US online retailer of shoes and accessories, was a pioneer in using Twitter to communicate with customers; most of its employees tweet, and the chief executive has more than 1 million Twitter followers. Some marketers are combining the clout of opinion leaders and the power of social media by offering pay or products in exchange for mentions by influential independent bloggers or Twitter users, a practice known as *sponsored conversations*. Following the principle of marketing transparency, such sponsorship should be clearly disclosed to avoid any misunderstandings.[13]

Table 3.2 Dove and social media

Social media activity	Marketing use
Dove website (www.dove.co.uk)	To inspire brand loyalty; to communicate product features and benefits; to offer samples and vouchers to attract new customers
Dove blogs	To build a sense of community through online conversations between opinion leaders and customers
Dove videos	To share insights about beauty and self-esteem; to encourage positive brand attitudes
Dove Facebook page (www.facebook.com/dove)	To promote positive self-esteem and communicate about Dove products

Personal elements

The fourth category of influences in consumer markets relates to personal elements such as life cycle, lifestyle, motivation and attitudes. An adult's *life cycle* is his or her changing family status over time. People may be single, single parents, single but co-habitating, engaged, married, married with children, divorced, divorced with children and so on. Consumers have different needs, behaviour patterns and buying priorities in each of these life-cycle phases – which, in turn, translate into marketing opportunities.

Lifestyle is the pattern of living reflecting how consumers spend their time or want to spend their time. Through research, you can learn more about how lifestyle influences what and when purchases are made in your market, how purchase transactions are planned and completed, who is involved in the purchase and other aspects of consumer buying behaviour. By analysing consumer behaviour using a complex set of lifestyle variables related to activities, interests and opinions – collectively known as **psychographic characteristics** – you can learn more about what drives consumer behaviour.

Psychological factors such as motivation and attitudes are also important influences on consumer buying. **Motivation** is the internal force that drives a consumer to act in a certain way and make certain purchases as a way of satisfying needs and wants. **Attitudes** are the consumer's assessment of and emotions about a product, brand or something else, which can affect actions. Understanding how such factors drive consumer behaviour gives you a solid foundation for making decisions about who to target, where a product should be distributed and so on.

ESSENTIAL MARKETING PLAN CHECKLIST NO. 5:
ANALYSING CUSTOMERS IN CONSUMER MARKETS

This checklist will guide you through the stage of marketing planning in which you must research and analyse information about consumers. Answer the questions in the spaces provided, putting a tick next to each as you finish it. If your marketing plan is for a start-up or a hypothetical company, use this checklist to note where you might obtain the information you need and ideas about how to research appropriate details.

☐ What consumer needs must the product and product category address?

☐ How can customers in each consumer market be described (by demographics, geography, etc.)?

☐ How is customer behaviour affected by cultural elements such as subculture and class?

☐ How is customer behaviour affected by social connections such as family, friends and online communities?

☐ How is customer behaviour affected by personal elements such as lifestyle, motivation and attitudes?

☐ What do these influences mean for segmentation, targeting and marketing decisions?

ANALYSING CUSTOMERS IN BUSINESS MARKETS

Individuals or groups make buying decisions for businesses, government agencies and non-governmental organisations. Sometimes these decisions involve huge sums of money and months of internal review spanning multiple management layers. Business buying behaviour is generally influenced by the organisation's characteristics and needs, relationships inside and outside the organisation, and considerations unique to each organisation and its environment (see Table 3.3).

Table 3.3	Understanding behaviour in business markets

Customer characteristics and needs	Internal and external relationships	Organisational and environmental considerations
● Industry classification ● Turnover ● Workforce size ● Facilities location ● Geographic focus ● Customer-perceived value	● Buying centre participants ● Decision process ● Supplier relations ● Customer relations	● Objectives ● Budgets and buying cycle ● Buying policies and procedures ● Share and growth ● Competitive situation ● Other environmental factors

Characteristics and needs

For your marketing plan to be successful, you need to understand the unique characteristics, buying requirements and challenges of the organisations in the business markets you are considering. Try to determine the common needs and concerns of organisations in each industry and see which characteristics affect these needs (and how). One way to do this is by categorising organisations according to characteristics such as type of industry, annual turnover, number of employees, location of facilities and geographic focus.

Small businesses frequently have different needs (and smaller budgets) than large businesses, for example; companies that serve localised markets have different needs than multinational corporations. Industries that are closely tied to economic conditions, such as automotive manufacturing, have different buying patterns depending on the strength of the economy. Marketers for Michelin, the French tyre manufacturer, have studied the different characteristics and needs of companies that make cars, trucks, motorcycles, aircraft and tractors. They also recognise that these customers generally buy in higher volume during periods of economic expansion and place fewer or smaller orders during economic downturns. Understanding these patterns helps Michelin prepare marketing tyres to customers in different industries and different economic situations.

The European Community's Eurostat system provides a standardised method for researching, describing and categorising statistics by industry. Similarly, the North American Industry Classification System (NAICS) provides a method for researching the characteristics of companies in specific industries in the United States, Mexico and Canada. Data organised according to UN industry standard classifications and other international and national industry standards systems are available as well.

To gather more data about industries, characteristics of businesses, non-profit organisations or government agencies and business products, you can consult numerous sources, including national and international trade organisations, country consulates, multinational banks, university sources, magazines, newspapers and other publications that follow international business developments.

Organisational and environmental considerations

Although a few organisations buy without budgets, most plan ahead by budgeting for certain purchases during a specified period. Thus, after gathering and analysing general data about a business market, your next step is to learn something about the size of each organisation's budget and the timing of its purchases, which can vary widely within an industry. New and fast-growing businesses are likely to make more frequent purchases than businesses that are retrenching, for instance.

Think about the company's environmental influences, including its market share situation, its objectives and its competitive situation – all of which can influence what, when and how much the organisation buys. Also research the buying policy and proce-dure, buying cycle and policies. If a multinational corporation's policy is to encourage decentralised or local buying, for example, you will have to plan for communicating with more buyers than if the policy is to centralise buying at the headquarters level. If a business insists on online buying, that policy must also be taken into account during the marketing planning process.

Budgeting and buying cycles are particularly important factors for business-to-business (B2B) marketers that sell to non-governmental organisations and government agencies. Meanwhile, growing cities and countries tend to increase their annual budgets for infrastructure improvements, creating opportunities for construction companies, telecommunications firms and other suppliers.

Budget cycles and international commerce are key issues for Inmarsat, the London-based provider of mobile satellite communications for government agencies and businesses in the maritime, media, energy construction and aeronautical industries. During the recent economic slump, lower demand for global shipping meant that many vessels remained parked in ports for weeks or months at a time. Yet Inmarsat experienced higher demand and profits during this period because customers with ships at sea budgeted for more data services than in the past as their crew members accessed the latest navigational informa-tion and checked e-mail. Inmarsat's marketers are planning for further expansion as they introduce their first hand-held satellite phone for the company's network and provide enhanced data communications for lorry fleets and railroad operations.[14]

Internal and external relationships

Many internal and external relationships can affect an organisation's buying patterns. Particularly in large organisations, a group of managers or employees may be responsi-ble for certain purchases. Different individuals within this **buying centre** play different roles in the buying process, as shown in Table 3.4. To illustrate, when marketing their PCs and laptops, Lenovo and Fujitsu recognise that information technology managers are generally the deciders for such corporate purchases, although the businesspeople who use the computers may influence brand choice. However, not every member of the buying centre will participate in every purchase.

Table 3.4	How buying centre participants influence purchases
Buying centre participant	**Influence on purchases**
Users	Often initiate the buying process and help define specifications.
Influencers	Often define specifications and provide information for evaluating alternatives.
Buyers	Have the formal authority to select suppliers and negotiate purchases.
Deciders	Have the formal or informal power to select or approve suppliers.
Gatekeepers	Control the flow of information to other buying centre participants.

Source: Adapted from Philip Kotler, Veronica Wang, John Saunders and Gary Armstrong, *Principles of Marketing*, 4th European edn (Harlow: Pearson Education, 2005), p. 309. Reproduced with permission from Pearson Education Ltd.

Each participant's individual situation (age, education, job position and so forth) also affects the buying decision. Thus, you should investigate relationships within the buying centre, understand the participants and the decision process so you can market to the right participants at the right time. This is especially vital when the purchase represents a major commitment of money, time and changeover for a business customer.

Check the organisation's relations with current suppliers to find out whether long-term contracts are the norm, whether certain future purchases are already committed to current suppliers, what standards suppliers are expected to meet and how suppliers are evaluated. In some cases, a company cannot become a supplier until it has met certain criteria and been approved. Even if prior approval is not needed, you should determine what criteria the business customer uses to select suppliers so you can plan accordingly.

Clearly, cost is not the only criterion in a B2B buying decision. Staff expertise, quality, reliable delivery and other considerations can be important criteria by which buying centre participants choose among competing suppliers. In addition, by looking at how an organisation deals with its customers, you can get a sense of the value you can add to help satisfy your customers' customers.

ESSENTIAL MARKETING PLAN CHECKLIST NO. 6:
ANALYSING CUSTOMERS IN BUSINESS MARKETS

If you're preparing to target a business market, this checklist will guide you through the planning in which you research and analyse information about business customers. Simply put a tick by each question, one by one, as you write answers in the spaces provided. If your marketing plan is for a start-up or a hypothetical company, use this checklist to note information you can obtain and ideas about how to research additional details, including possible data sources.

☐ What customer needs must the product and product category address?

_____

☐ How can customers in each business market be described (by demographics, buying policies, etc.)?

_____

☐ Who participates in the buying centre and what is each participant's role?

_____

☐ How does each business customer solicit, qualify and assess suppliers?

_____

☐ How do current supplier arrangements affect competition for orders?

_____

☐ What other relationships and considerations affect buying behaviour in this business market?

_____

☐ What do these influences mean for your segmentation, targeting and marketing activities aimed at the business market?

_____

RESEARCHING MARKETS AND CUSTOMERS

When researching markets and customers, you will usually start by consulting **secondary data**, information previously collected for another purpose. You can glean basic facts and figures from secondary research more quickly and cheaply than through **primary**

data, data from studies undertaken to address specific marketing questions or situations. When using secondary research, check that the information is current, comes from a legitimate and unbiased source, can be verified through another source and can be clarified (if necessary) through contact with sources.

Primary research is particularly useful for gaining detailed knowledge about issues of great concern to customers. W.W. Grainger, a US-based global distributor of facilities management supplies that serves business and institutional customers, recently conducted a research programme in which its employees visited 80 customers in the manufacturing industry. The objective was to learn first-hand about these manufacturers' needs and ask how Grainger could help them be more effective in meeting the needs of *their* customers. As a result of this research, Grainger changed its website to highlight offerings geared to the specific needs of manufacturers. The company has also hosted networking and training meetings to enable its customers to share information about challenges such as implementing strategic criteria for purchasing decisions.[15]

Online research, conducted via the Internet, is increasingly popular because it's not costly, it can be implemented easily and it yields results quickly. Asda e-mails members of its Pulse of the Nation consumer panel when it wants speedy answers to questions such as 'Would you like to see this product in your local Asda store?'.[16] Remember, however, that the results will not be entirely representative of a product's market. Why? Because many consumers and businesses don't use the Internet or prefer not to answer online surveys, their views are excluded from online research. Still, online surveys and analyses of unsolicited consumer comments posted on Twitter and other social media can give marketers clues to attitudes, brand reactions and purchase intentions.

Ethnographic research – observing customers' behaviour in real situations rather than in experimental surroundings – has become increasingly important for learning about needs and preferences not easily articulated. Advertising expert Joseph Plummer notes that ethnography can lead to new customer behaviour insights, generate learning across cultures and spark product design ideas as well as advertising creativity.[17] China's Lenovo Group, for example, uses ethnographic software to interpret large quantities of visual and written observations of how consumers around the world use personal computers and laptops.[18]

A related technique is **behavioural tracking,** monitoring what consumers and businesspeople do online as they visit websites, click on ads and fill virtual shopping trolleys. The purpose is better targeting and more personalised communications. Google's software, for instance, tracks how people search and move around the web, analyses behaviour patterns and chooses to display specific ads based on the interests revealed by individuals' behaviour.[19] Marketers should be aware that questions have been raised about whether behavioural tracking invades Internet users' privacy, which could lead to new regulatory guidelines in the near future.[20]

Marketers for major corporations are beginning to apply **neuromarketing**, using brain science and body responses to investigate and understand consumer reactions to marketing activities.[21] Here's how two marketers are using neuromarketing for consumer research.

MARKETING IN PRACTICE: NEUROMARKETING

Honda and Frito-Lay are two of the growing number of companies using neuromarketing to understand what consumers might think and feel as they pass products on display, are exposed to advertising and make buying decisions.[22] Honda UK, for example, recently asked research participants to wear a special 'vest' and look at cars in a Honda dealership. The vest is equipped to measure heart rate, breathing and other physical reactions. 'Conventional research only gets you so far because it's rationalisation after the event, and most decision-making is done subconsciously,' explains the manager of customer communications. 'We set out to measure physical changes people cannot consciously control.'[23]

Frito-Lay, which markets Doritos and other snacks, has used neuromarketing to understand how and why men and women react differently to various marketing activities. In particular, the company's researchers want to gauge reaction to advertising, packaging and flavours. Based on brain studies, they believe that women can more effectively process complicated advertising messages, compared with men; this suggests new approaches to advertising messages and placement. In addition, they have concluded that women want to be reminded of the health benefits of the snacks they choose. Therefore, Frito-Lay has changed the packaging of its Baked Lay's crisps to emphasise the healthy ingredients.[24]

Indicate any need for primary research in your marketing plan and allow for the time and money in your schedules and budgets. Also plan for research to test programmes and track marketing progress, including customer satisfaction surveys, market-share studies and promotion pre- and post-tests. These kinds of studies can yield insights to help you make decisions about segmentation, targeting, positioning and the marketing mix.

CHAPTER SUMMARY

Marketers examine markets to narrow their focus to a subset of customers qualified to buy (or currently buyers of) a particular type of good or service. The overall market consists of the potential market (all customers who may be interested in that product) and, inside that, the available market (those with income and access). A narrower definition is the qualified available market (those who meet product-related criteria for buying); narrower still is the target market (which the organisation wants to serve) and, narrowest of all, the penetrated market (customers who buy or have bought that type of product). Then marketers dig deeper to research and analyse market changes and market share.

During marketing planning for consumer markets, look at (1) needs stemming, in part, from characteristics such as age; (2) national or regional culture, subculture and class; (3) social connections; (4) personal and psychological elements. Three main influences on business markets are (1) organisational characteristics; (2) organisational and environmental considerations; (3) internal and external relationships. Secondary data is information previously collected for a different purpose; primary data is collected to address specific questions or situations relevant to the marketing plan.

CASE STUDY: UNILEVER PLANS FOR WINNING HEARTS, MINDS AND MARKET SHARE

Unilever's mission is to 'meet everyday needs for nutrition, home hygiene and personal care with brands that help people feel good, look good and get more out of life'. The company is active in 100 countries and markets tens of thousands of products. Among its many well-known brands are 13 that each achieve more than £1 billion in turnover every year, including Axe, Dove, Lipton, Lux and Omo. Yet because its products face strong competition from brands sold by multinationals like Procter & Gamble and Nestlé, Unilever's marketers are always conducting research to get to the heart of what customers want, need, like and dislike. For example, in Unilever's research centres, marketers learn about how consumers use Persil by observing them using washing machines in a simulated home-laundry environment. With permission, they set up devices in consumers' homes to measure the amount of detergent, water and energy used in washing machines for different types of laundry. Unilever's researchers also study how clothes get dirty as children play, which led to the company's adoption of the theme 'Dirt is good' for marketing its detergents worldwide.

The 'Dirt is good' theme, used in advertising for Persil, Omo, All and other Unilever laundry powders and liquids, expresses the positive value of play for child development – a value that's important in nearly every culture. When Unilever began this campaign in Brazil, it increased its market share by six points. When the campaign began in Pakistan, Unilever increased its market share by nine points. In all, 'Dirt is good' has helped Unilever increase its detergent sales to £2.2 billion yearly.

Unilever has set global goals for reducing the amount of salt in its food products to meet the World Health Organisation guidelines for daily salt intake. It has also changed its food packaging to highlight nutritional value and help buyers make healthy choices. To engage customers and encourage dialogue, Unilever's marketers have set up branded websites where visitors can view how-to videos, share ideas, check products' environmental impact and learn more about the company. Digital marketing activities are increasingly important because 'brands are now becoming conversation factors where academics, celebrities, experts and other key opinion formers discuss functional, emotional and, more interestingly, social concerns', says Unilever's chief marketing officer.[25]

CASE QUESTIONS

1. How would you define the qualified available market for Persil laundry powder? What are the key qualifying criteria for this market definition?

2. What specific questions about the influence of personal elements on detergent preference would you suggest that Unilever's marketers seek to answer through primary research? How would such research help Unilever market Persil detergent?

 ## APPLY YOUR KNOWLEDGE

To reinforce your knowledge of Stage 2 of the marketing planning process, research the general definition of a particular market. You might focus on the consumer market for spectacles or mobile phones, for instance, or the business market for office furniture or specialised software. Prepare a brief oral or written report summarising your thoughts.

- How can your chosen market be described broadly in terms of product, geography and demographics?

- What characteristics relevant to the product might influence the behaviour of consumers or organisations in this market?

- What, specifically, are the main influences on buying behaviour in this market? Refer to the checklists in this chapter as you answer this question.

- How much influence do opinion leaders have on buyers in this product category? Which social media are important for influencing buyers in this market?

- What have you learned that would affect your decisions if you were preparing a marketing plan for this market?

 ## BUILD YOUR OWN MARKETING PLAN

Continue the marketing planning process for a hypothetical organisation or an actual organisation you have chosen by broadly describing the market and the influences on customer buying behaviour. Use the two checklists in this chapter as you build your marketing plan. First, identify the five levels of market definition that apply, from the potential market to the penetrated market. Also determine the criteria by which you would consider customers to be in the available market and in the qualified available market.

Next, research the most important changes affecting this market. Also look at market share trends and the major influences on customer needs and behaviour in this consumer or business market. How do cultural elements, social connections, personal elements or psychological elements affect the consumer's buying behaviour? What social media do opinion leaders and customers in your product category typically use? If your plan is for a business market, how do customer characteristics and needs, internal and external relationships and organisational/environmental considerations affect buying behaviour? Finally, list any primary and secondary data you would like to have to better understand your markets and look for recent, reliable online sources of information about customers such as yours. Be sure to document what you have learned and the implications for your marketing-plan decisions.

(STOP)   ENDNOTES

1. Quoted in Jonathan Soble, 'Nissan to 'mass market' electric cars', *Financial Times*, 2 August 2009; www.ft.com.

2. Andrew English, 'Tokyo motor show: Nissan Leaf joins wacky concepts', 9 October 2009, www.telegraph.co.uk/motoring; Ken Gibson, 'New Nissan has a mains dealership', *The Sun*, 3 August 2009, www.thesun.co.uk; Chang-Ran Kim, 'Nissan unveils zero-emission hatchback Leaf', *Reuters*, 2 August 2009, www.reuters.com; Tim Webb, 'Nissan unveils its electric car, the Leaf', *The Guardian*, 2 August 2009, www.guardian.co.uk/business; Andrew Charlesworth, 'Going electric: on the road to decarbonisation', *Telegraph*, 24 December 2009, www.telegraph.co.uk.

3. www.nissan-zeroemission.com/EN/index.html; www.nissan-global.com/EN/index.html.

4. 'Virgin works with vexed to take Vtravelled site onto mobile', *New Media Age*, 2 July 2009, www.nma.co.uk; Simon Calder, 'Branson's flights of fancy', *The Independent*, 6 June 2009, www.independent.co.uk; David Quainton, 'Case study: Virgin Atlantic', *Event*, 3 March 2009, www.eventmagazine.co.uk; www.virgin-atlantic.com.

5. 'From chulhas to defibrillators: can Philips India be all things to all people?', *India Knowledge@*

Wharton, 30 July 2009, http://knowledge.wharton.upenn.edu/india; Writankar Mukherjee, 'Philips to make India hub for medical equipment manufacturing', *The Economic Times*, 8 April 2009, http://economictimes.indiatimes.com.

6. Cadbury financial fact-sheet: Q1 2009, from www.cadbury.com.

7. Jenny Wiggins, 'Heinz finds new outlets to fight own-label sales', *Financial Times*, 26 July 2009, www.ft.com.

8. Morag Cuddeford-Jones, 'Socially acceptable; case study: New Look', *Marketing Week*, 27 July 2009, www.marketingweek.co.uk; Amy Shields, 'New Look to rival fashion giants as it aims to double trading space', *RetailWeek*, 1 May 2009, www.retail-week.com; *New Look Annual Report 2009*, www.newlook.co.uk; www.mylookfashion.co.uk; Mark Foxwell, 'New Look considers a float or sale', *Daily Mail Online*, 29 December 2009, www.dailymail.co.uk.

9. 'Get smart about car use', *Fast Company*, September 2009, p. 18; Michael Taylor, 'Car2go coming down under?', *CarPoint*, 22 April 2009, www.carpoint.com/au.

10. Michael Fitzgerald, 'Boomtown: the real money behind virtual goods', *Fast Company*, 1 July 2009,

www.fastcompany.com/magazine/137/boom-town.html.

11. Jo Roberts and Sarah Scott, 'The teen commandments', *Marketing Week*, 20 May 2009, www.marketingweek.co.uk/home/the-teen-commandments/2065514.article; James Quilter, 'CCGB offers free mobile credits in teen promotion', *Marketing Promotions & Incentives*, 15 July 2009, www.promotionsandincentives.co.uk; Camille Alarcon, 'Orange's youth push no monkey business', *Marketing Week,* 30 July 2009, www.marketingweek.co.uk; Richard Wray, 'Orange, Universal and C4 woo youth music market on mobiles', *The Guardian*, 29 July 2009, www.guardian.co.uk.

12. Margareta Pagano, 'So hip, it hurts. Can Puma leave the recession for dead?', *The Independent*, 1 February 2009 www.independent.co.uk; 'Puma strikes Irish rugby kit deal', *Sport Industry Group*, 31 March 2009, www.sportindustry.biz/news.

13. Josh Bernoff, 'When and how to pay a blogger', *Advertising Age*, 26 May 2009, http://adage.com/digitalnext/post?article_id=136852; Kunal Dutta, 'Will blog for cash', *Revolution Magazine,* 26 June 2009, www.revolutionmagazine.com.

14. Maija Palmer, 'Inmarsat mulls European mobile services', *Financial Times*, 6 August 2009, www.ft.com; 'Inmarsat completes SkyWave mobile investment', *Satellite Today*, 7 July 2009, www.satellitetoday.com; www.inmarsat.com.

15. Kate Maddox, 'Marketers 'unlearn' at BMA conference', *BtoB*, 20 July 2009, www.btobonline.com; Susan Avery, 'Strategic MRO sourcing takes centre stage at Grainger event', *Purchasing*, 12 February 2009, p. 22; www.grainger.com.

16. Chloe Smith, 'Asda's Chinese democracy lets shoppers vote on new products', *The Grocer*, 7 July 2009, www.thegrocer.co.uk; Karen Talley, 'Wal-Mart's Asda to let customers help choose what stores sell', *Dow Jones Newswires*, 6 July 2009, www.wsj.com.

17. Joseph T. Plummer, 'Up close and personal: the value of ethnography', *Journal of Advertising Research*, September 2006, p. 245.

18. Robert Berner, 'Design visionary', *BusinessWeek Innovation*, June 2006, pp. 102–14.

19. Claire Beale, 'Time the online watchers were being watched', *The Independent*, 16 March 2009, www.independent.co.uk/news/media/advertising.

20. Maija Palmer, 'A deeper peeper', *Financial Times*, 14 April 2009, www.ft.com.

21. 'Market research: It's all in the mind', *Marketing Week*, 2 April 2009, p. 29.

22. Elisabeth A. Sullivan, 'Pick your brain', *Marketing News*, 15 March 2009, p. 10; Cheryl Lu-Lien Tan, 'The neuroscience of retailing', *Wall Street Journal*, 15 May 2008, www.wsj.com; 'The way the brain buys', *The Economist*, 20 December 2008, pp. 105–7.

23. Meg Carter, 'Neuromarketing is a go', *Wired UK*, 24 June 2009, www.wired.co.uk/wired-magazine.

24. Stephanie Clifford, 'Frito-Lay tries to enter the minds (and lunch bags) of women', *New York Times*, 25 February 2009, p. B3.

25. Elizabeth Rigby and Jenny Wiggins, 'Chief sets out strategy for consistent growth', *Financial Times*, 7 May 2009, p. 24; 'Unilever makes impact on diverse fronts', *Chain Drug Review*, 29 June 2009, p. 118; 'Port Sunlight Unilever site safe despite job losses', *Liverpool Echo*, 2 December 2008, www.liverpoolecho.co.uk; Elaine Wong, 'Unilever's true grit', *Adweek*, 25 May 2009, p. AM8; Jack Neff, 'Lever's CMO throws down the social-media gauntlet', *Advertising Age*, 13 April 2009, p. 1; 'Can Unilever's brand fit all?' *Marketing*, 21 January 2009, p. 14; Steve Bush, 'Unilever develops suite of sensors for domestic washing machines', *Electronics Weekly*, 24 July 2009, www.electronicsweekly.com.

4

Planning segmentation, targeting and positioning

Comprehension outcomes

After studying this chapter, you will be able to:

- Explain the benefits of segmentation, targeting and positioning
- Identify segmentation variables for consumer and business markets
- Describe undifferentiated, differentiated, concentrated and individualised target marketing
- Discuss the criteria for effective positioning

Application outcomes

After studying this chapter, you will be able to:

- Apply segmentation variables in consumer and business markets
- Evaluate segments for marketing attention in your plan
- Choose a targeting approach for market coverage in your plan
- Develop a meaningful positioning for marketing planning purposes

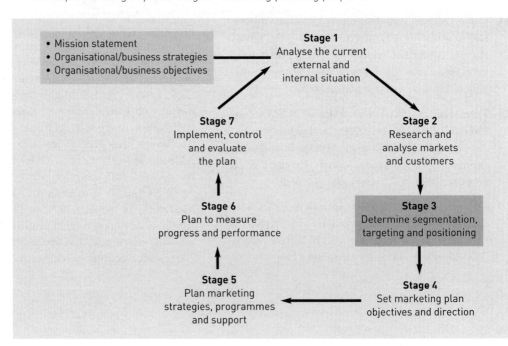

- Mission statement
- Organisational/business strategies
- Organisational/business objectives

Stage 1
Analyse the current external and internal situation

Stage 7
Implement, control and evaluate the plan

Stage 2
Research and analyse markets and customers

Stage 6
Plan to measure progress and performance

Stage 3
Determine segmentation, targeting and positioning

Stage 5
Plan marketing strategies, programmes and support

Stage 4
Set marketing plan objectives and direction

CHAPTER PREVIEW: NESTLÉ'S PURINA PETCARE DIVISION TARGETS PET OWNERS

How much do consumers pamper their pets? UK pet owners alone spend more than £1.25 billion annually on food for their dogs and cats; the global market for pet food is similarly large and lucrative. Marketers at Nestlé's Purina Petcare division have identified this market as a major profit opportunity and are using their knowledge of consumer behaviour to market different brands to different customer segments, such as Purina One dog food and Felix cat food.

Even during the recent recession, sales of Purina Petcare's products increased as the company focused on communicating the nutritional benefits of its premium pet foods. The company offers special formulas for younger pets, older pets, overweight pets and pets with sensitivities to certain ingredients. Yet Purina Petcare also faces growing competition from private-label pet foods offered by the big grocery chains, which are attracting value-conscious buyers who want to save money. Still, with pet-food sales on the rise in many countries, the company is seeking to influence brand selection through advertising, celebrity appearances, online newsletters and videos, and other activities that appeal to specific groups of pet owners in targeted geographic areas.[1]

Purina Petcare's marketing plan is not to reach out to every customer, everywhere. Instead, the company studies the needs, attitudes, behaviour and buying patterns of different customer groups, then selects specific groups for marketing attention – as in Stage 3 of the marketing planning process. You'll learn about the benefits of market segmentation, targeting and positioning in this chapter, starting with an understanding of how the segmentation process works. Next, you'll learn about how and why marketers use targeting today. Finally, you'll see how to apply positioning for competitive power. Use this chapter's checklist as you prepare to evaluate segments for marketing attention. In addition, learn how marketers document their segmentation, targeting and positioning ideas by looking at the sample marketing plan in the Appendix.

BENEFITS OF SEGMENTATION, TARGETING AND POSITIONING

Market segmentation involves grouping consumers or business customers within a market into smaller segments based on similarities in needs, attitudes or behaviour that marketing can address. Purina Petcare segments its markets on the basis of similarities in consumers' attitudes, lifestyles and behaviour, including pet ownership. By eliminating inappropriate markets (such as consumers who don't own pets) and identifying promising segments for more thorough research, the company can better understand customers and more effectively respond to their needs. Because local, national and global markets are increasingly competitive these days, marketers of all sizes must know how to distinguish between different customer groups in preparation for meeting stated and unstated needs through marketing.

Segmentation also helps Purina Petcare decide which segments to target for marketing activities, and in what order. Having a process for determining which customer groups should be given priority marketing attention is especially important in light of the budget pressures most marketers face today. Finally, the knowledge gained during segmentation helps the firm determine how to create a meaningful and competitively distinctive position in the minds of the targeted customers (see Figure 4.1).

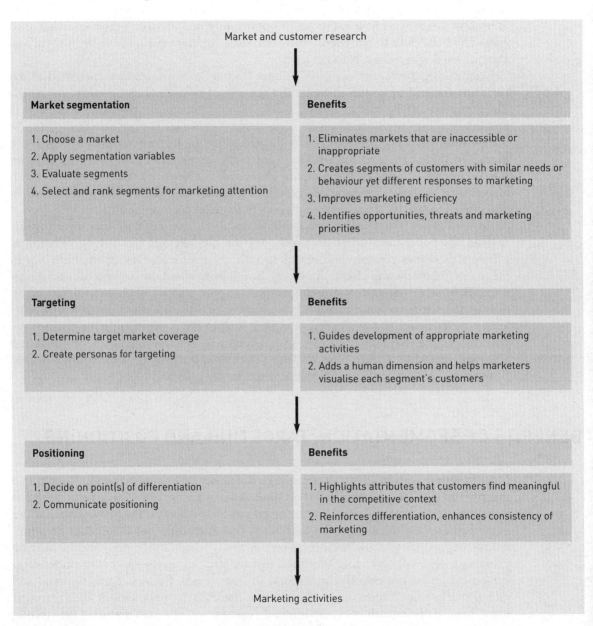

FIGURE 4.1   Applying segmentation, targeting and positioning

Segmentation is useful for marketing planning when:

- the customers within each segment have something identifiable in common
- different segments have different responses to marketing efforts
- the customers in segments can be reached through marketing
- competitive advantage can be gained by focusing on segments
- segments are sufficiently large or potentially profitable to warrant attention.

A segment may consist of millions of people, yet still be a select subset of a much larger market. Customers within each segment will have similar behaviour and needs or be seeking the same benefits from a product. Taking segmentation one step further, you may be able to distinguish **niches**, small subsegments of customers with distinct needs or requirements. Consider the success that companies such as Daas Organic Beer enjoy by focusing on niches.

MARKETING IN PRACTICE: DAAS ORGANIC BEER

Daas Organic Beer, with its Belgium-based microbrewery and London-based marketing, is focusing on the niche of eco-conscious beer connoisseurs. The company special-ises in premium beers such as Daas Witte and Daas Blond, which are brewed in small batches using only organic ingredients. To reach UK consumers in the niche it tar-gets, Daas distributes its beers through Waitrose, Ocado and independent grocers. It also offers its products through wine distributors that serve specific UK areas. Daas's niche marketing activities include publicity about its organic certifications, promotions that reinforce upmarket associations, a blog and a Twitter presence, all guided by the philosophy of quality, luxury and environmental responsibility.[2]

Taken to the extreme, you may be able to segment a market to create niches of one. In the past, marketing to such small niches would not be profitable. Now you can use technology to discern the specific needs, behaviours and responses of individual con-sumers or business customers. In some industries, the potential size of and profit from a single order make it worthwhile to segment and target single-customer niches or, in large markets, to individualise marketing on a mass basis.

THE MARKET SEGMENTATION PROCESS

As you create your marketing plan, you'll follow three steps to segmenting a market, as Figure 4.1 indicates. The first is to choose the market to be segmented, the second is to apply appropriate segmentation variables and evaluate segments for marketing attention and the third is to select your coverage approach for targeting chosen segments. Your decisions in all three steps depend on understanding your mission and long-term goals as well as on detailed, current information drawn from internal and external audits (see Chapter 2), plus your analyses of markets and customers (see Chapter 3).

Choose the market

With your market definitions as a starting point, you begin the segmentation process by determining which markets you will investigate further and which you will eliminate. Although the specific criteria differ from organisation to organisation, you may want to consider eliminating markets based on:

- formidable legal, political, social or competitive pressures
- extreme logistical difficulties
- lack of purchasing power or other serious economic challenges
- troubling ethical controversies
- persistent ecological concerns.

For years, many marketers eliminated Vietnam from their list of viable markets because of trade barriers and other political and legal difficulties. However, once Vietnam simplified its business laws, joined the World Trade Organisation, improved its transportation infrastructure and lowered trade barriers, the country rejoined the list of markets being considered by companies around the world. Vietnam's economy has managed to grow even when other nations were experiencing economic downturns. Consumer buying power has been increasing year by year and the government is offering tax incentives for investment. As a result, multinational firms are now targeting Vietnamese consumers with a wide variety of goods and services, including personal care products marketed by the UK's Unilever, savings accounts marketed by Australia's Commonwealth Bank, cars and trucks marketing by the US's Ford Motor and luxury accessories by France's Cartier.[3]

Once you have eliminated inappropriate markets, look for ways to distinguish meaningful segments in your chosen markets. The point is to form consumer or business segments that are internally homogeneous yet exhibit some differences (compared with other segments) that can be addressed through marketing. If you find no differences, segmentation is pointless, because you will not need to vary your marketing approach for each segment.

Apply segmentation variables in consumer markets

In consumer markets, customer characteristics and product-related behavioural variables can be used to identify segments for planning purposes (see Table 4.1). For more specific segment definition, you should apply a combination of appropriate variables. Many customer characteristics are relatively easy to identify and apply. However, behaviour-based, product-related approaches, which can be challenging to isolate and analyse, typically give you more insight into potentially effective marketing approaches for each consumer segment.

Table 4.1 Variables for segmenting consumer markets

Customer characteristics – a user-based approach that asks: 'Who purchases what?'

Demographic	**Socioeconomic**
● Age	● Income
● Family size	● Class
● Marital status	● Vocation
● Gender	● Education
	● Religion
	● Ethnicity

Geographic	**Lifestyle/personality**
● Global, hemispheric, national, state, city, postal code	● Attitudes/opinions
● Climate	● Interests
● Rural vs. urban	● Avocations
	● Tastes and preferences

Product-related approaches – a behavioural approach that asks: 'Why do they purchase?'

User types	**Price sensitivity**
● Regular	● Low-cost orientation
● Non-user	● Higher-cost quality/differentiation focus
● First-time	
● Potential	

Purchase and consumption patterns	**Perceived benefits**
● Purchase occasion	● Performance
● Buying situation	● Quality
● Low, medium, high consumption	● Image enhancement
● Application	● Service

Brand loyalty	**Media exposure and usage**
● Loyal/satisfied	● Preferred media
● Experimenters	● Multiple media usage
● Unsatisfied/defectors	● Time, day, occasion
● Unaware	

Source: Adapted from *FLEISHER, CRAIG S.; BENSOUSSAN, BABETTE, STRATEGIC AND COMPETITIVE ANALYSIS: METHODS AND TECHNIQUES FOR ANALYZING BUSINESS COMPETITION, 1st,©2003*. Prentice Hall, p.173. Reproduced by permission of Pearson Education, Inc., Upper Saddle River, New Jersey.

You can also apply geographic variables when you want to enter or increase sales in specific regions or climates, avoid specific countries or regions because of competitive challenges or other threats, or leverage your organisation's strengths for competitive advantage in those areas. Remember, however, that people are more complex and buying is motivated by numerous factors; even those who share a particular characteristic will not necessarily respond in the same way to the same marketing activities. Thus, applying non-geographic variables such as gender or vocation can reveal viable segments across geographic boundaries. Marketers for Burberry use a variety of variables to segment the global market for one of the UK's oldest and most recognisable brands.

MARKETING IN PRACTICE: BURBERRY

Burberry's marketers rely on more than socioeconomic characteristics such as class and income to segment the market for the company's clothing and accessories. The company's British roots, iconic fashion status and associations with royalty and celebrity enhance its global appeal to brand-conscious consumers. In Japan, where consumers are particularly status conscious, Burberry has launched the Blue Label collection for women and the Black Label collection for men to target younger, price-sensitive buyers who aspire to the brand's traditional cachet. Burberry is also using geography, fashion affinity, desire for quality, gender, brand loyalty and lifestyle to segment the market for its upmarket products across Europe, the Americas, the Middle East and Asia.

With annual turnover of £1.2 billion, Burberry restricts distribution to upmarket department stores and more than 100 branded stores worldwide in fashionable shopping districts such as Knightsbridge in London and Beverly Hills in Los Angeles. To reach out to younger consumers, Burberry has featured actress Emma Watson, of *Harry Potter* fame, in advertising campaigns and increased its online activity, especially targeting consumers who visit the websites of high-fashion magazines.[4]

One advantage to applying variables such as consumption patterns and purchase occasion is that they are easily observed, measured and analysed. For example, McDonald's sees significant profit potential in selling breakfasts, especially for takeaway. McDonald's has opened more than 1,000 McCafés in its European restaurants to attract consumers who regularly buy coffee or espresso in the morning on their way to work. McDonald's is also targeting price-conscious buyers with a 'saver menu' of bargain-priced items.[5] Domino's uses behavioural variables such as frequency of purchase to segment the British market for takeaway pizza. This has enabled the firm to identify segments such as 'hard-core loyals' that have a high long-term profit potential.[6]

Because consumer reactions are often heavily influenced by one or more of the product-related variables listed in Table 4.1, you should apply those in addition to characteristics and other variables during your marketing planning. In many cases, understanding how and why a consumer uses or does not use a product can help you identify signs of underlying wants or needs that you will then be able to address through marketing strategies. Note that different segmentation variables are appropriate for different markets and products. Nokia is applying a variety of segmentation variables as it puts a major marketing push behind its multifunction smartphones, the next generation of networked mobiles.

MARKETING IN PRACTICE: NOKIA

Although more than 1 billion mobiles are purchased every year, sales of multifunction smartphones are growing much faster than overall sales of mobiles worldwide. Based on market and customer analysis, Nokia, which is based in Finland, forecasts especially strong demand for popularly priced smartphones in rural areas of India and China. Because electricity isn't always available in these areas, local consumers frequently rely on mobiles for communication, Internet access and more. In India, Nokia's objective is to increase its share of market beyond the 60 per cent it currently holds as the dominant player. It is also aiming for higher market share in China, where it already has mobiles for sale in 30,000 shops.

To achieve these objectives, Nokia has segmented the market for smartphones according to geography, mobile communication preferences, interest in music, interest in games and many other variables. Just as important, the company has segmented the market by price sensitivity and designed dozens of new smartphones for affordability. To meet the specific needs of customers in selected segments, it markets keyboard-equipped smartphones for consumers who are frequent users of social networking and e-mail, speedy smartphones for heavy users of mobile-based games and memory-enhanced smartphones for those who download lots of music.[7]

Apply segmentation variables in business markets

As in consumer markets, business markets can be segmented using both customer characteristics and product-related approaches that probe behaviour (see Table 4.2). Customer characteristics describe the organisation from the outside, whereas behavioural variables look at activities and dynamics below the surface. Generally marketers apply both types of variables to form segments of organisational customers that are internally homogeneous but have different needs or different responses to marketing when compared with other segments.

Table 4.2	Variables for segmenting business markets

Customer characteristics – a user-based approach that asks: 'Who purchases what?'

● Industry type	● Company size
● Geographic	● Technology employed
● Industry position	● Business age
	● Ownership structure

Product-related approaches – a behavioural approach that asks: 'Why do they purchase?'

● Consumption patterns/usage frequency	● Relationship between seller/purchaser
● End-use application	● Psychodemographics of purchaser
● Perceived benefits	● Purchasing policies
● Goals	
● Size of purchase	

Source: Adapted from *FLEISHER, CRAIG S.; BENSOUSSAN, BABETTE, STRATEGIC AND COMPETITIVE ANALYSIS: METHODS AND TECHNIQUES FOR ANALYZING BUSINESS COMPETITION, 1st,©2003.* Prentice Hall, p.174. Reproduced by permission of Pearson Education, Inc., Upper Saddle River, New Jersey.

You can apply demographics such as industry type, geography and annual turnover to narrow the dimensions of a business market before you apply behavioural variables. Business customers typically have different needs and responses from those of non-profit organisations and government agencies; likewise, larger or older organisations tend to have different needs and responses from those of smaller or newer organisations. Some organisations rely more heavily than others on certain technologies (such as e-commerce or customer contact software), another indicator that can help you segment your market. In general, look carefully at how certain characteristics reveal differences that you can build on when planning marketing activities.

You can use frequency, size, timing and method of purchasing to segment business markets, along with variables reflecting purchasing policies and authorised buyers. When you segment a business market by product-related variables, especially in combination with customer characteristics, you can uncover important customer needs and buying patterns. Here's how the German multinational corporation BASF segments the business market for chemical products.

Evaluate and select segments for targeting

The next step in the segmentation process is to assess the attractiveness of each segment in terms of opportunity, environment, reach and response and see how each fits with internal considerations such as mission, image, strengths, core competencies, resources and performance. The purpose is to eliminate undesirable segments and evaluate the possible opportunities inherent in the remaining segments. Ideally, you want to be active in segments that play to your organisation's strengths and capabilities, but take care not to stretch your resources too thin. At this point, you can screen out segments with insufficient profit potential, intense competition or other complications.

MARKETING IN PRACTICE: BASF

BASF's long-term goal is to 'remain the world's leading chemical company'. With annual turnover of €62 billion, it makes industrial chemicals, plastics, coatings, additives, crop-protection and oil and gas products. BASF's marketers use customer characteristics such as industry type, geography and production process employed to segment the business market for its products.

In addition to focusing on agribusiness, a profitable and growing segment in Asia and other regions, BASF's marketers have chosen to serve manufacturers of products such as cars and trucks, packaging, construction, plastics, personal care items, pharmaceuticals and cleaners for commercial and household use. They also study buying behaviour industry by industry to understand differences and similarities in consumption patterns, end-use applications and perceived benefits so they can plan the most effective marketing approach for each segment. In some cases, BASF collaborates with key customers to research and develop new offerings tailored to each customer's unique needs and challenges – in effect, niche marketing geared to the requirements of a single customer.[8]

After you drop unattractive or unsuitable segments from consideration, you are ready to rank the remaining segments in priority order for marketing attention, on the basis of research and analysis. You can do this in several ways. For example, you might assign relative weights to each of the evaluation criteria and calculate the total scores segment by segment. The sample ranking shown in Table 4.3 shows how you might score three segments based on the five criteria categories, along with a total score per segment. As in this sample, a segment may merit a high score for opportunity yet have a much lower score for environmental factors or another of the criteria.

Table 4.3　Sample segment ranking

	Segment A	Segment B	Segment C
Opportunity	8	6	5
Environmental factors	3	5	5
Reach and response	6	4	7
Competitive advantage	7	5	3
Internal considerations	9	9	4
TOTAL SCORE	33	29	24

Note: Weighted scores range from 1 (extremely unattractive) to 10 (extremely attractive).

To decide which segment should be your top priority, look at the total score and, if necessary, set minimum scores for individual criteria. In the sample ranking, Segment A has the highest total score and, if the organisation does not require a minimum score of 5 or higher on all criteria, would be the highest priority. Note that Table 4.3 is a very simplified, fictitious example; organisations vary widely in their evaluation criteria, weighting and ranking systems.

Different companies use different criteria to rank segments. One criterion used by some marketers is **customer lifetime value**, the total net revenue (or profit) a particular customer relationship represents to the organisation over time. Why? Because research indicates that focusing marketing activities on customers in segments with the potential for higher lifetime value can significantly increase revenue.[9]

The choice of criteria depends on your unique situation, your chosen market and your customer knowledge. If possible, use sensitivity analysis to adjust criteria weights under differing forecasts and confirm priority rankings by testing prospective strategies before moving ahead with full-scale marketing plans. Among the criteria you can use to select and rank segments for marketing attention are:

- fit with the firm's goals, strengths, resources and core competencies
- competitive advantages
- advantageous pricing or supply costs due to relative power of buyers or suppliers
- sizeable profit and growth potential
- ecological impact
- significant potential for building long-term customer relationships.

The checklist for this chapter offers specific questions to ask when evaluating and selecting segments for marketing attention.

ESSENTIAL MARKETING PLAN CHECKLIST NO. 7:
EVALUATING MARKET SEGMENTS

Before you can set objectives and plan marketing programmes, you must determine which customer segments you want to reach. This checklist will help you evaluate the various segments identified within the overall market. After you write your answers in the spaces provided, put a tick next to the questions you've answered. If your marketing plan is for a hypothetical firm, you can use this checklist as a guide to the data you'll need to gather to be able to evaluate segments.

☐ What is the current size of the segment and how is it changing?

☐ What current and future sales and profit potential do you see for this segment?

☐ Would marketing to this segment yield an acceptable or superior payback in customer lifetime value?

☐ What is the competitive situation in this segment?

☐ Can the organisation realistically capture or defend market share in this segment?

☐ How much power do buyers and suppliers in this segment have?

☐ What threats exist or could emerge to prevent success in this segment?

☐ Can customers in the segment be reached through appropriate marketing activities?

☐ Does the organisation have the strengths, competencies and resources to serve this segment?

☐ Does the segment fit with the organisation's mission, image, overall goals and sustainability situation?

Once you've selected segments for marketing attention, you're ready to make decisions about targeting.

THE TARGETING PROCESS

To plan for targeting, you must consider the market coverage approach you want to take. As shown in Figure 4.2, you can use one of four coverage approaches: undifferentiated marketing, differentiated marketing, concentrated marketing or individualised marketing.

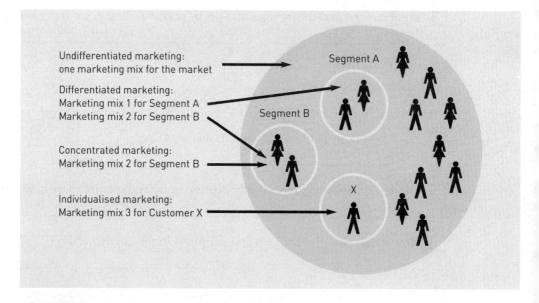

FIGURE 4.?   Segment targeting coverage strategies

Undifferentiated marketing

Essentially a mass-marketing approach, **undifferentiated marketing** means target-ing the entire market with the same marketing mix, ignoring any segment differences. This assumes that all customers in a particular market, regardless of any differences in characteristics or behaviour, will respond in the same way to the same marketing atten-tion. Undifferentiated marketing is less expensive than other coverage strategies, due to the lower costs of developing and implementing only one marketing mix. However, today's markets are rarely so homogeneous; even slight differences can serve as clues to underlying needs in segments where an organisation can gain competitive advantage, encourage customer loyalty and ultimately return profits.

Consider the market for salt, discussed in the box on the next page.

Differentiated marketing

With **differentiated marketing**, you formulate a separate marketing mix for the two or more segments you choose to target. You may not target all segments in a given market, but for those you rank as priorities, you will need different marketing mixes geared to each segment's unique characteristics and behaviours. The assumption is that you can provoke a different response from each segment by using different marketing mixes. Customers benefit because their specific needs are being addressed, which increases sat-isfaction and encourages customer loyalty. Moreover, you can compete more effectively by tailoring the marketing mix for each segment, although this is much more costly than undifferentiated marketing and may overburden resources if not carefully managed.

MARKETING IN PRACTICE: THE FRAGMENTED SALT MARKET

Industry giants Morton (owned by K+S) and Diamond Crystal (owned by Cargill) are two of the growing number of marketers segmenting what was once assumed to be a homogeneous market for salt. Today the salt market can be segmented according to type of customer (consumers, restaurants, institutional and municipal customers) and specific uses and occasions (such as for cooking, for melting ice on roadways and as a water-softening agent). As a result, products such as sea salt, coarse crystal salt, natural mineral rock salt, low-sodium salt and other variations are being marketed differently to different segments.

Meanwhile, major retailers such as Sainsbury's also offer their own private-label brands of salt. Celebrity chef Jamie Oliver offers a variety of gourmet sea salts. The family-owned Maldon Crystal Salt Company in Maldon, Essex, is known around the world for its speciality salts. With all this competition – and increased buyer knowledge and power – it is clear that salt marketers should avoid undifferentiated marketing because the mass market for salt no longer exists.[10]

At Nike, where the well-known swoosh appears on thousands of new athletic shoes and apparel products every year, marketers understand that consumers in different segments have different needs, interests, lifestyles, buying behaviours and media consumption patterns. After segmenting the market, they develop separate marketing mixes for targeted segments. These include consumers who participate in or are fans of particular sports (football, golf, tennis and so on), consumers who want the latest sportswear styles and consumers who care about the environment (and would appreciate the recycled materials fashioned into Trash Talk basketball shoes).

Depending on the segment, Nike will convey the brand's image and benefits using a variety of adverts, billboards, online and in-store videos, bespoke microsites, social media such as Facebook, celebrity appearances and special events. In the year leading up to FIFA World Cup matches, Nike's marketing plans include sponsoring national football teams, introducing new boots and apparel, creating event-specific advertising and websites and other activities that appeal to the targeted segment of World Cup fans.[11]

Concentrated marketing

As you saw in Figure 4.2, **concentrated marketing** involves targeting one segment with one marketing mix. The idea is to compete more effectively and efficiently by understanding and satisfying one sizeable set of customers, rather than spreading organisational resources across multiple marketing activities for multiple segments. As long as the targeted segment remains attractive, this can be a profitable coverage approach. However, be aware that uncontrollable and unexpected factors such as new competition or changes in customer needs can make the targeted segment less attractive or even unfeasible over time.

EasyJet has profited from its concentrated marketing approach to targeting.

MARKETING IN PRACTICE: EASYJET

Based at Luton Airport in Bedfordshire, EasyJet targets one major segment: price-sensitive travellers who respond to bargain airfares. The airline's goal is to become a pan-European airline by continually expanding beyond the United Kingdom to major cities such as Milan, Geneva and Paris. It keeps costs down by offering few frills and charging passengers for every extra, including priority boarding and check-in. Especially during the recent global recession, when both consumers on holiday and travellers on business were eager to save money, EasyJet attracted customers in its targeted segment by promoting low, low fares.

Now in its second decade of operation, EasyJet carries more than 44 million passengers yearly and continues to expand its fleet with efficient jumbo jets that reduce its fuel costs. In competition with the low-fare carrier Ryanair and the full-service carrier British Airways, EasyJet uses a combination of online and traditional marketing communications to highlight its budget-friendly fares, reinforce loyalty and maintain its brand image.[12]

Individualised marketing

You may be able to tailor marketing offers to individuals within certain targeted segments, a coverage approach known as **individualised** (or **customised**) **marketing**. Airbus, for example, can identify all the potential buyers for passenger jets and cargo planes, get to know their needs and specifications, then develop a separate marketing mix for each. The markets for commercial passenger jets and cargo planes are not so large that this is impractical, and the potential profit from each order is so great that individualised marketing makes sense for Airbus. Individualised marketing is especially important to Airbus in its competitive battle to win orders for its new A380 super-jumbo jet while arch-rival Boeing promotes its forthcoming 787 Dreamliner jet.[13]

If you have the right technology, you can opt for **mass customisation** and create products and/or communications tailored to individual customers' needs on a larger scale. New Zealand, Canada and the United States are doing this with personalised postage stamps. Not long ago, Moet & Chandon opened a temporary pop-up store in London where buyers could order bottles of champagne decorated to their taste with Swarovski crystals. The limited-time customisation offer further enhanced the product's upmarket image and sense of exclusivity.[14]

Segment personas

Ford and other marketers are adding a human dimension to targeting by constructing **personas,** fictitious yet realistic profiles representing how specific customers in targeted segments would typically buy, behave and react in a marketing situation. The idea is to think about how customers actually interact with a product (and competing products), what influences and motivates those customers and how their needs and preferences affect their buying and consumption behaviour. Here's how Ford uses personas to more effectively target customers in specific market segments.

MARKETING IN PRACTICE: FORD

When Ford's marketers began a redesign of the Fiesta model for European markets, they researched the interests, lifestyles and preferences of 20- to 30-year-old consumers who favour small cars. They even went shopping with young women in this segment to better understand their likes, dislikes and brand attitudes. What they learned helped them create personas that brought to life the personality traits, feelings, interests and behaviour of consumers in the Fiesta's targeted segment.

Isabella, one of the personas dreamed up by Ford, is a style-conscious university graduate living near Milan who has a moderate income and is a heavy user of social media. Antonella and Anton, two additional personas based on Ford's research, live in Rome, enjoy going to parties and clubs, and are both tech savvy and brand conscious. With these personas as a guide, Ford's marketers could really envision the way consumers in the targeted segment think and feel about their cars. 'We had done lots of models based on rationality, but now we are recognising that emotions play a much more dominant role than we ever admitted,' says Ford's director of global advanced product strategy. 'We now focus quite a bit on aspirations and dreams.' The redesigned Fiesta quickly became Ford's best-selling model in Europe and helped the company gain market share.[15]

THE POSITIONING PROCESS

With positioning, you use marketing to create a competitively distinctive position for your product in the minds of targeted customers. You need marketing research to understand how your targeted customers perceive your organisation, product or brand and your competitors. Research can also help determine which attributes matter most to the targeted customers. Regardless of how you see your products, it is the customer's view that counts. For example, US-based Zappos was founded as an online shoe store differentiated by fast, friendly customer service and extensive selection. Extras such as free shipping helped the company increase annual turnover from less than £1 million to more than £606 million in only eight years.[16]

Altering a brand's positioning, even slightly, can be difficult. **Repositioning** means using the marketing plan to change the competitively distinctive positioning of its brand in the minds of the targeted customers. Zappos, which was acquired by e-tail pioneer Amazon, has in recent years adopted the goal of being 'the company that provides the absolute best service online – not just in shoes, but in any category'. Now its inventory includes clothing, accessories, sunglasses and other products in addition to shoes. To support this repositioning, Zappos uses online, print and television advertising, as well as its website home page and social media such as Twitter, to reinforce its differentiation on the basis of superior service while suggesting the wider selection of product categories.[17]

Deciding on differentiation

Zappos and other successful marketers understand the importance of deciding on points of difference that are not only competitively distinctive but also relevant and believable. Zappos differentiates itself from rivals on the basis of two points that its targeted customers find advantageous, credible and relevant: top-notch service and extensive merchandise selection.

In general, you can differentiate your offering along the lines of quality, service, image, personnel or value. Whatever your choice, a product's positioning must be based on criteria that are meaningful and desirable from the customer's perspective yet competitively distinctive. Here are three examples of effective positioning based on desirable differentiation criteria:

- Specsavers: affordable, stylish spectacles (value differentiation)

- Mercedes-Benz: well-engineered, well-appointed luxury vehicles (quality differentiation)

- Ocado: convenient online grocery shopping with home delivery (service differentiation).

Applying positioning

Your marketing plan must show how you'll actually carry through the positioning in your product's marketing and performance. Determine first whether your organisation can, realistically, develop and market a product that will live up to the meaningful points of difference you've chosen. Second, consider whether the points of difference can be communicated to the targeted segments. And third, determine whether you can sustain the product's performance and continue to communicate the points of difference over time.

Positioning is basically the driver behind all the marketing activities you will include in your marketing plan. With differentiated marketing, you develop a positioning appropriate to each segment and apply that positioning through your marketing decisions for each segment. With concentrated marketing, you establish one positioning for the single segment you target. Remember that positioning is not a one-time decision: as markets and customers' needs change, you must be prepared to reposition a product, if necessary, for desirability and deliverability.

CHAPTER SUMMARY

Segmentation helps marketers rule out inappropriate markets, identify specific segments for more study and better understand customers in those segments so the organisation can more easily respond to their needs by providing value. Evaluating segments enables the organisation to decide which groups of customers to target and in what order. The process also provides a basis for creating a meaningful and competitively distinctive position in the minds of each target segment's customers.

Marketers can segment consumer markets by user-based characteristics (demographic, geographic, socioeconomic and lifestyle/personality) and product-related behavioural variables (user types, consumption patterns and usage frequency, brand loyalty, price sensitivity, perceived benefits and more). Business markets can be segmented using customer characteristics (industry type, geographic, industry position, company size and more) and product-related behavioural variables (consumption patterns/usage frequency, end-use application, perceived benefits and more). Target-market coverage strategies include undifferentiated, differentiated, concentrated and individualised (customised) marketing. Effective positioning and repositioning must be competitively distinctive, relevant and credible as well as feasible, able to be communicated and sustainable.

CASE STUDY: HOTEL CHOCOLAT'S SWEET SEGMENTATION, TARGETING AND POSITIONING

Hotel Chocolat was founded in 1993 as the Choc Express catalogue, selling gourmet chocolates by post and by phone. In 2003, it rebranded itself as Hotel Chocolat to better convey the positioning, which blends the romance of premium chocolate, the fun of British wit and the ethics of 'no nasties'. 'We wanted a brand name that more accurately reflected the aspirations and quality of the brand,' says co-founder Angus Thirlwell.[18] To explain that the name was changing, but not the product or its high quality, Hotel Chocolat communicated with its customer base before launching a campaign to promote the new brand and attract new customers.

The company, headquartered just north of London, knows that customers in its targeted segments are 'quite cosmopolitan, concerned with where their food comes from and willing to pay extra to make sure it's ethically sound and made only with the good stuff', says the chief operating officer.[19] Through its Engaged Ethics programme, Hotel Chocolat imports cocoa from its own Rabot Estate in St Lucia as well as from Ghana, providing its cocoa farmers with fair pay and improving local communities in both regions.

Hotel Chocolat segments the consumer and business markets for luxury chocolate by occasion (i.e. birthdays, weddings, holidays, etc.), person (i.e. man, woman, child, business associate, vegan, etc.), product (i.e. hampers, packaged chocolates, etc.)

product attribute (i.e. milk, dark, alcohol-free, etc.) and price (i.e. less than £25, more than £25). It constantly tests in-store innovations and experiments with tasty new chocolates, requesting feedback from the 100,000 members of its Tasting Club before putting new products into production. To tempt the palates of loyal buyers and attract new customers, Hotel Chocolat changes more than 25 per cent of its range every year.

It reaches out to its targeted segments through printed catalogues, a retail website, dozens of company-owned UK stores, a US store in Boston and business links with high-street retailer John Lewis and World Duty Free airport shops. This multichannel strategy allows customers the convenience of buying when, where and how they prefer. With annual turnover of £50 million, more growth is on the menu as Hotel Chocolat expands cocoa production and plans to enter new geographic markets in the coming years.[20]

Case questions

1. Identify Hotel Chocolat's points of differentiation. What can the company do to reinforce the distinctiveness, believability and relevance of these points through its marketing plan?

2. Is Hotel Chocolat using undifferentiated, differentiated or concentrated marketing? What are the implications for its marketing communications? For its multichannel strategy?

 **APPLY YOUR KNOWLEDGE**

Research the segmentation, targeting and positioning of a particular company active in consumer or B2B marketing, using its products, advertising, website and other activities as clues. Prepare a brief oral or written report summarising your thoughts after completing this exercise.

- Based on the organisation's marketing, what market(s) and segment(s) appear to be targeted?

- Is this company using differentiated, undifferentiated, concentrated or customised marketing? How do you know?

- What benefits are featured in the company's marketing and what customer needs are they designed to satisfy? How might the targeted segments be described in terms of needs?

- Analysing the marketing clues you have observed, what product-related variables do you think this company is using to segment its market(s), apart from benefits sought?

- In one sentence, how would you summarise the positioning this company is trying to reinforce in one of the targeted segments?

BUILD YOUR OWN MARKETING PLAN

Proceed with the marketing plan for a hypothetical organisation or an actual organisation that you have chosen. During the segmentation process for this organisation, what markets would you eliminate from consideration and why? What specific segmentation variables would you apply to the remainder of the market, and how would you expect them to create segments that make sense from a marketing perspective? What further research would support this segmentation?

What criteria would you use to evaluate the segments you identify? Given the organisation's overall goals, strengths and resources, what targeting approach would you choose? If you were constructing a persona for one of your segments, how would you describe that customer? Finally, what positioning or repositioning would you want to reinforce for the customers in each targeted segment? Be sure that these ideas are appropriate in light of your earlier decisions, then document your choices (and explain how they affect your strategy) in a written marketing plan.

ENDNOTES

1. 'Nestlé Purina PetCare names CMO', *St. Louis Business Journal*, 21 September 2009, http://stlouis.bizjournals.com/stlouis/stories/2009/09/21/daily7.html; Catherine Boyle, 'Nestlé finds fizz has gone out of bottled water', *Times Online*, 13 August 2009, www.business.timesonline.co.uk; Goran Mijuk and Anita Greil, 'Nestlé finds pet owners more willing to spend', *Wall Street Journal*, 13 August 2009, www.wsj.com; 'Purr-fect feast for felines', *New Straits Times*, 21 July 2009, n.p.; 'Pack leaders struggle for pet-food power', *Grocer*, 20 December 2008, p. 109; Joe Fernandez, 'Nestlé to launch new campaign for Friskies cat food', *Marketing Week*, 17 December 2009, www.marketingweek.co.uk.

2. 'A little taste of Belgium', *Europe Intelligence Wire*, 15 May 2009, n.p.; 'UK launch for Daas Witte Wheat Beer', *Grocer*, 28 March 2009, p. 30; www.thepureindulgence.com.

3. 'Vietnam's chronic currency weakness takes toll on firms', *Reuters*, 12 October 2009, www.nytimes.com/reuters/2009/10/12/world/international-uk-vietnam-currency.html; Don Lee, 'Multinationals take a longer view of Vietnam', *Los Angeles Times*, 11 April 2009, www.latimes.com; Michael Sheridan, 'Brits ride the Vietnam tiger', *Sunday Times*, 27 January 2008, p. 1; Ben Stocking, 'Vietnam officially becomes WTO member', *Associated Press*, 11 January 2007, www.businessweek.com; Clay Chandler, 'Vietnam vroooom', *Fortune*, 11 December 2006, pp. 147ff.

4. Andrea Felsted, 'Tourists provide fillip for Burberry', *Financial Times*, 16 July 2009, p. 17;

Olivia Bergin, 'Emma Watson as the new face of Burberry', *The Telegraph*, 9 June 2009, www.telegraph.co.uk; Haig Simonian, 'Slimming all the rage as belts tighten', *Financial Times*, 15 June 2009, p. 1; 'Burberry joins push online by luxury brands', *New Media Age*, 7 May 2009, p. 1; 'What it's really like inside – Burberry', *Marketing*, 25 February 2009, p. 71; Johnny Davis, 'Comes to town: Tastemaker', *The Times*, 28 February 2009, p. 12; www.burberry.com; Imogen Fox, 'Burberry named British designer of the year and wins best brand', *Telegraph*, 9 December 2009, www.guardian.co.uk.

5. Chris Irvine, 'McDonald's McCafes set to take on Starbucks', *The Telegraph*, 28 May 2009, www.telegraph.co.uk; Simon Bowers, 'Europe loving McD's again', *The Observer*, 25 January 2009, www.guardian.co.uk.

6. Noelle McElhatton, 'Britain's got Domino's', *Marketing Direct*, 12 August 2009, www.marketingdirectmag.co.uk/news.

7. Nic Fildes, 'Nokia is hit by big writedown despite increase in handset sales', *The Times*, 16 October 2009, http://business.timesonline.co.uk/tol/business/industry_sectors/technology/article6877154.ece; Adam Smith, 'Nokia plays it (not too) smart', *Time*, 24 August 2009, pp. G1–G2; Ian Grant, 'Smartphones save Nokia and Apple as mobile sales surge', *ComputerWeekly*, 12 August 2009, www.computerweekly.com; Mikael Ricknas, 'Cheap smartphones set to boom in the pre-paid market', *PC World*, 10 August 2009, www.pcworld.com; Masa Serdarevic, 'Nokia rises after Apple complaint', *Financial Times*, 30 December 2009, www.ft.com.

8. Peter Stiff, 'BASF to cut 3,700 jobs after CIBA takeover', *Times Online*, 6 July 2009, http://business.timesonline.com; Graeme Wearden, 'BASF to cut more than 2,000 jobs worldwide', *The Guardian*, 30 April 2009, www.guardian.co.uk; 'Green shoots', *The Economist*, 19 March 2009, www.economist.com.

9. V. Kumar and Bharath Rajan, 'Profitable customer management: measuring and maximizing customer lifetime value', *Management Accounting Quarterly*, Spring 2009, pp. 1ff.

10. Alex Renton, 'Designer salt? Take that with a pinch of you-know-what', *Times Online*, 8 May 2009, www.timesonline.co.uk; Gerrit Wiesmann, 'K+S to buy Morton Salt for $1.7 bn', *Financial Times*, 3 April 2009, p. 15; 'Morton has solutions for drug chains', *Chain Drug Review*, 29 June 2009, p. 146; www.maldonsalt.co.uk; www.jamieoliver.com.

11. John Sarkar, 'Sportswear firms kick off merchandising plans for 2010 FIFA World Cup', *Economic Times*, 16 August 2009, www.economictimes.indiatimes.com; 'Nike promotes Air Max 1 reissue with pan-Euro campaign', *New Media Age*, 23 July 2009, p. 3; Venessa Wong, 'Best in show: Nike's scrappy Trash Talk Shoes', *BusinessWeek Online*, 30 July 2009, www.businessweek.com.

12. 'Forget those no-frills frequent-flyer deals', *Sunday Times*, 16 August 2009, p. 2; Rebecca O'Connor, 'EasyJet resolves dispute with airline founder', *Times Online*, 27 July 2009, http://business.timesonline.co.uk; David Robertson, 'Rising first-half losses turn up pressure on EasyJet over plans to buy 91 aircraft', *The Times*, 7 May 2009, p. 47; www.easyjet.com.

13. Paul Betts, 'Boeing and Airbus dream on as big birds fail to fly', *Financial Times*, 25 June 2009, p. 16; Dominic O'Connell, 'Touchdown nears in air trade battle', *Sunday Times*, 26 July 2009, p. 3.

14. Carol Lewis, 'First in line: Pop-up stores', *Times Online*, 8 December 2008, http://business.timesonline.co.uk; 'New Zealand post tries personalized stamps', *ePostal News*, 10 October 2005, p. 2.

15. 'Ingvar Sviggum', *Automotive News*, 6 July 2009, p. 28; David Kiley, 'One Ford for the whole wide world', *BusinessWeek*, 15 June 2009, pp. 58–9; Phil Patton, 'Before creating the car, Ford designs

the driver', *New York Times*, 19 July 2009, www.nytimes.com; David Kiley and Jack Ewing, 'A magic moment for Ford of Europe', *BusinessWeek*, 6 July 2009, p. 46; 'Fiesta: the next fashion icon?', *Autocar*, 10 April 2008, www.autocar.co.uk.

16. Lisa Berwin, 'Amazon takeover to open Zappos up to new markets', *RetailWeek*, 31 July 2009, www.retail-week.com; Brad Stone, 'Amazon expands with deal for Zappos', *New York Times*, 23 July 2009, p. B3.

17. See www.zappos.com.

18. Quoted in Glynn Davis, 'On the shop floor with . . . Hotel Chocolat founder Angus Thirlwell', *The Retail Bulletin*, 29 June 2009, www.theretailbulletin.com/news.

19. Quoted in Beth Negus Viveiros, 'Hotel Chocolat checks into US market', *Chief Marketer*, 1 June 2009, www.chiefmarketer.com.

20. Sam Williams, 'A recipe for growth', *Eastern Daily Press (Norfolk)*, 16 October 2009, www.edp24.co.uk/content/edp24/business/story.aspx?brand=BIZOnline&category=Features&tBrand=EDPOnline&tCategory=xBusiness&itemid=NOED15%20Oct%202009%2017%3A05%3A18%3A023; 'Profile: Fredrik Ahlin', *Design Week*, 5 August 2009, www.designweek.co.uk; Viveiros, 'Hotel Chocolat checks into US market'; Beth Negus Viveiros, 'Hotel Chocolat has no reservations about US launch', *Chief Marketer*, 15 June 2009, www.chiefmarketer.com; Kate Pritchard, 'Angus Thirlwell takes Hotel Chocolat stateside', *Real Business*, 3 September 2008, www.realbusiness.co.uk/news; www.hotel-chocolat.co.uk.

5

Planning direction, objectives and strategy

Comprehension outcomes

After studying this chapter, you will be able to:

*   Explain the three broad directions that can shape a marketing plan
*   Describe the characteristics of effective objectives
*   Understand how financial, marketing and societal objectives work together in a marketing plan

Application outcomes

After studying this chapter, you will be able to:

*   Set a direction for your marketing plan
*   Formulate your marketing plan objectives

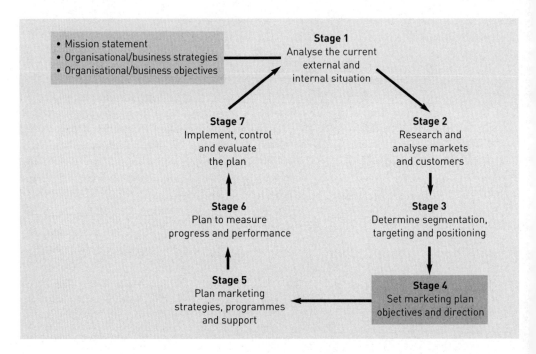

CHAPTER PREVIEW: REACHING FOR INTERDEPENDENT GOALS AT JOHN LEWIS

The John Lewis Partnership, UK owner of the John Lewis department stores, Waitrose grocery chain and a new chain of John Lewis at Home speciality stores, has an ambitious set of three interrelated goals for long-term success. The first goal of this £7 billion business is for its employee-owners to gain personal satisfaction from worthwhile, secure and fulfilling work. The second goal is to build customer loyalty by winning the trust and confidence of shoppers who seek value, choice, service, honesty and good corporate citizenship. And the third goal is to achieve sufficient profit to retain the company's distinctive character and continued growth, with employee-owners sharing in the rewards.[1]

During the recent economic downturn, while many retailers struggled and a few failed, John Lewis's marketing plans called for expansion. According to the department store's managing director: 'When we saw the recession coming, the thing we said right from the beginning was: Let's not worry about the short-term numbers; let's worry about how strongly the brand comes out of it at the end of the recession.'[2] Management created marketing plans to achieve financial and marketing objectives by opening the new Home stores, adding 'value' products to Waitrose's range, improving the John Lewis Direct website, developing new apparel ranges and taking other steps to support ongoing growth. The marketing plans also guided the company's social responsibility and sustainability activities, with objectives such as conserving energy and water, buying from socially responsible suppliers and reducing excess packaging.

By following these marketing plans and making adjustments for external factors such as increased competition, John Lewis has gained market share and earned public admiration and affection despite the challenging economic situation.[3]

In this chapter you'll learn about marketing plan objectives and direction, which make up the fourth stage in the marketing planning process. First, the chapter examines how direction and objectives guide the marketing plan and help the organisation achieve longer-term goals. Next is a discussion of marketing plan direction, covering both growth and non-growth strategies. Finally, the chapter explains how to set effective marketing, financial and societal objectives. Use this chapter's checklist to evaluate your objectives; also look at the objectives in the sample marketing plan, located in the Appendix, for ideas about how to document your objectives.

DIRECTION AND OBJECTIVES DRIVE MARKETING PLANNING

Your marketing plan is not the only plan created to guide your organisation forward. As noted in Chapter 1, corporate-level plans are supported and implemented by business-level plans and, in turn, supported and implemented by functional-level plans for marketing, operations and so forth. As a marketer, you will formulate strategy, determine the optimal marketing-mix tools, and make programme-level decisions based on the direction and objectives of your marketing plan.

If the objectives in your marketing plan are explicit and clearly connected to higher-level objectives and long-term goals, the plan is more likely to produce the desired performance.[4] Thus, each objective, marketing strategy and marketing programme must be consistent with the plan's direction as well as with both organisational and business objectives, as Heinz's marketers are aware.

MARKETING IN PRACTICE: HEINZ

Heinz, well known for its beans, ketchup, baby food and salad cream, uses its marketing plans to pursue growth, even during difficult economic periods. Year after year, the corporation seeks to increase turnover by 4 per cent or more worldwide; within a few years, fast-developing markets such as Latin America and Russia are expected to account for as much as 20 per cent of Heinz's overall sales. Already, 15 power brands (including Heinz, WeightWatchers and Ore-Ida) account for 70 per cent of the firm's £6 billion in annual turnover, with most of the purchases made in grocery and discount store chains. Building on this brand and channel strength, Heinz's marketing plans call for introducing at least 30 new products every year and using media advertising to send customers into stores in search of its brands.

To support global growth and brand profitability, Heinz's managers are cooking up a variety of innovative new marketing plans. Recently they arranged to have Heinz's barbecue sauces distributed through Wyevale Garden Centres and its baby foods distributed through Mothercare stores, allowing consumers to make additional purchases outside the usual supermarket channels. Heinz's marketers have also been using social media such as online videos to engage customers, communicate brand personality and build brand preference. With new labels, new packaging and new advertising messages on the way, Heinz continues to seek higher sales in every season.[5]

MARKETING PLAN DIRECTION

Heinz, like many companies, has set growth as the direction for its marketing plans. Not all organisations pursue growth. Some seek to maintain their current position, postponing growth because of adverse economic conditions, fierce competition, financial problems or for other reasons. Others retrench by selling off units or products, exiting particular markets or downsizing in other ways – often for survival purposes or to prepare for later growth. Growth and non-growth strategies, summarised in Figure 5.1, are discussed next.

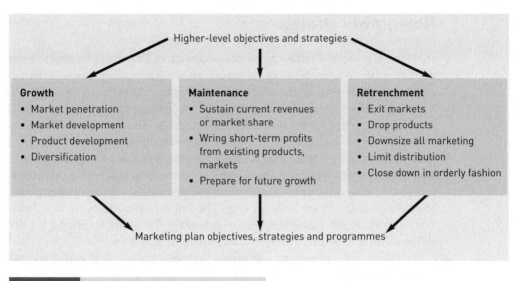

FIGURE 5.1 Choices of marketing plan direction

Growth strategies

If your organisation wants to grow, you will choose among the four main growth strategies proposed by H. Igor Ansoff: market penetration, product development, market development and diversification.[6] With **market penetration**, you offer existing products to customers in existing markets. This increases unit and/or monetary sales and simultaneously reinforces the brand or product's strength in each market. It also strengthens relationships by connecting customers to the organisation with more product ties. When Heinz put its barbecue sauces onto store shelves at Wyevale Garden Centres, it was using market penetration to spur growth.

With **product development**, you market new products or product variations to customers in existing markets. This works only when you can develop a steady stream of product innovations appropriate for the needs of customers in those markets. Heinz developed Snap Pots, for example, as convenient heat-and-eat single servings of beans for on-the-go snacks or for children. Now the range is established, attracting new customers and adding to Heinz's bottom line year after year.[7]

With **market development**, you pursue growth by marketing existing products in new markets and segments. Such a strategy builds on the popularity of established products and allows firms to expand their customer base either geographically or by segment, the way Heinz has brought its ketchup, beans and baby foods to new markets and customer groups.

The fourth growth strategy is **diversification**, which means marketing new products in new markets or segments. You can diversify by (1) distributing new products in new markets through existing channel arrangements, (2) initiating new marketing activities in new markets or (3) acquiring companies to gain access to new products and new markets. Heinz did this when it acquired Golden Circle fruit juices, marketed in Australia and New Zealand, and formulated plans to expand distribution in additional markets.[9]

Non-growth strategies

Sometimes growth is not an appropriate direction. Pressured by severe economic or competitive conditions, insufficient resources, ambitious expansion, lower demand or stagnant revenues and profits, organisations may follow a maintenance strategy or even retrench. You might therefore create a maintenance marketing plan to keep revenues, market share or profits at current levels, if possible, or at least defend against deterioration.

Rather than invest heavily in improving products, targeting new markets, developing new promotions or other marketing activities, your organisation could try to harvest short-term profits from existing products or markets and retain relationships with customers. In this way, you would conserve resources while simultaneously building a stronger foundation for later growth. The important point here, says Professor Michael Porter of Harvard University, is 'to integrate the short term and the long term, and think about the two together'. In fact, taking a long-term view when reacting to short-term threats can present opportunities 'to make moves that you could never dream of making before'.[9]

Organisations that cannot maintain their current levels may be forced into making marketing plans to retrench or, in the extreme, to shut down entirely. As shown in Figure 5.1, some common choices here are to withdraw from certain markets, eliminate particular products, downsize all marketing efforts, shrink distribution or go out of business. And, if the retrenchment goes well, the company will soon be able to start planning for a turnaround through a new growth strategy.

During the recent economic downturn, the US motorcycle manufacturer Harley-Davidson switched from a growth to a non-growth strategy to establish a foundation for future profits.

MARKETING IN PRACTICE: HARLEY-DAVIDSON

With $6 billion in global sales, Harley-Davidson holds a 10 per cent share of the European market for heavyweight motorcycles and a 46 per cent share of the US market. As the global economic crisis continued, Harley-Davidson announced that its quarterly retail sales had slipped by 30 per cent worldwide (35 per cent in the United States) during one particularly challenging period. The company quickly began conserving financial resources, cutting production by 25 per cent and laying off 1,000 employees, with the objective of remaining a strong competitor after the economy rebounded.

Although Harley-Davidson's marketing plan wasn't geared towards growth in the immediate future, it included a number of steps necessary to strengthen the firm's ability to expand in the coming years. For example, the company took this time to retool its new product development process so its marketers would be able to introduce new motorcycles and accessories more quickly than in the past. The marketing plan also included special activities for attracting first-time buyers among women and younger adults as the loyal customers of the future. The company sought to maintain an overall gross profit margin of more than 30 per cent so it would have the means to invest in tomorrow's marketing plans for growth. Finally, it prepared for entry into India by planning dealerships in major cities and arranging special events to show off Harley bikes.[10]

Clearly, the marketing plan for Harley-Davidson's non-growth strategy will be completely different from the marketing plan for any growth strategy. Guiding the organisation in a particular direction requires specific marketing plan objectives keyed to that situation, which in turn will lead to different marketing strategies and programmes.

MARKETING PLAN OBJECTIVES

Marketing plan objectives are short-term targets that, when achieved through implementation of appropriate action programmes, will bring the organisation closer to its longer-term goals. Some companies use the **Balanced Scorecard**, broad performance measures used to align strategy and objectives as a way to manage customer relationships, achieve financial targets, improve internal capabilities, prepare for future innovation and attain sustainability. In such cases, the marketing plan objectives have to be structured appropriately to support these broader measures of performance.[11]

Characteristics of effective objectives

To be effective, your marketing plan objectives should be:

- *Relevant*. Be sure your objectives relate to the chosen direction and higher-level strategies and goals. Otherwise, the programmes you implement to achieve your plan's objectives will not support organisational needs. Although most businesses set objectives for revenues and profits, non-financial objectives such as those relating to corporate image are also important because they build and strengthen connections with other stakeholders. After South Korea's LG Electronics committed to a three-year goal of dominating Europe's electrical appliance market, its plans included relevant objectives such as increasing market share by 10 per cent per year in each appliance category and increasing new product introductions.[12]

- *Specific and measurable*. Vague targets will not help you determine what you need to accomplish and how. Simply calling for 'growth' is not enough. To be effective, your objectives should indicate, in quantitative terms, what the marketing plan is being developed to achieve. To illustrate, Ryanair has a five-year goal of doubling its airline profits and the number of passengers it carries. Its marketers must set specific year-by-year objectives in each marketing plan to ensure that they're making progress towards the five-year goal and allow for measuring interim results along the way.[13]

- *Time defined*. What is the deadline for achieving the objective? You will plan differently for objectives that must be achieved in six months compared with objectives to be achieved in 12 months. Setting an open-ended objective is like setting no objective at all, because you will lack a schedule for showing results – and will not be accountable. Highland Spring's marketers want to achieve the objective of becoming the

UK's top-selling bottled water within two years. When they set this objective, Evian was the UK's number one bottled-water brand, with a market share of nearly 10 per cent; Highland Spring's share was slightly less than 9 per cent. Highland Spring is launching a new ad campaign and revamping its website to help achieve its objective on schedule.[14]

- *Realistic.* A marketing plan geared to attaining market dominance in six months is unlikely to be realistic for any business – especially for a start-up. Thus, your marketing plan objectives should be realistic to provide purpose for marketing and to keep organisational members motivated. When Plum Baby, which makes premium organic baby food, decided to introduce a new range of chilled baby foods, its marketers set an objective of achieving 5 per cent market share within two years. Although the baby-food industry is extremely competitive, this objective was realistic because the company had achieved a similar market-share objective with its original baby-food range.[15]

- *Challenging.* Realistic objectives need not be easy to attain. In fact, many marketers set aggressive yet realistic marketing plan objectives so they can expand more quickly than if their objectives resulted in incremental growth. Objectives that are too challenging, however, may discourage the marketing staff and tie up resources without achieving the desired result. Cisco Systems, which makes networking equipment such as routers and servers for homes and businesses, sets objectives for entering new product markets 'with a speed nobody has ever attempted', the chief executive points out. Attaining such objectives requires extra effort, but it also helps Cisco keep its competitive edge and provide customers with a wider range of offerings.[16]

- *Consistent.* Is the objective consistent with the organisation's mission, goals, strengths, core competencies and interpretation of external opportunities and threats? Are all objectives consistent with each other? Inconsistent objectives can confuse staff members and customers, detract from the marketing effort and result in disappointing performance.

Types of objectives

You can set marketing plan objectives in three categories. **Financial objectives** are targets for achieving financial results through marketing strategies and programmes. **Marketing objectives** are targets for achievements in marketing relationships and activities, which in turn directly support attainment of financial objectives. **Societal objectives** are targets for accomplishing results in areas related to social responsibility; such objectives indirectly influence both marketing and financial achievements.

The choice of marketing plan objectives and specific targets will, of course, be different for every organisation. No matter what objectives you set, however, be sure you can measure progress towards your targets after you implement your plan. During the economic downturn, marketers for Procter & Gamble, the US-based marketer of personal care and household brands such as Tide (detergent) and Olay (beauty products), assessed their market-share situation on a daily basis to determine how well brands were faring. They also kept a close eye on competition and pricing as they moved towards their profitability objectives. Yet despite the challenging business environment, P&G set even higher societal objectives for addressing issues such as providing safe drinking water to children in impoverished areas.[17]

Financial objectives

Companies usually set objectives for external results such as unit, monetary, product and channel sales plus internal requirements such as profitability, return on investment and break-even deadlines. Table 5.1 shows the focus and purpose of financial objectives commonly used by businesses. Non-governmental organisations typically set objectives for short-term and long-term fundraising as well as other financial targets. To achieve the organisation's financial objectives, you will need to coordinate other compatible objectives dealing with relationships between buyers and sellers as well as suppliers and distributors.

Table 5.1   Focus and purpose of financial objectives

Focus of financial objective	Purpose and examples
External results	To provide targets for outcomes of marketing activities such as: ● increasing unit or monetary sales by geographic market ● increasing unit or monetary sales by customer segment ● increasing unit or monetary sales by product ● increasing unit or monetary sales by channel ● other objectives related to external results
Internal requirements	To provide targets for managing marketing to meet organisational requirements such as: ● achieving break-even status ● achieving profitability levels ● achieving return on investment levels ● other objectives related to internal requirements

A company might set a financial objective for external results such as: *to achieve a minimum weekly sales volume of £1,000 for each new product*. Notice that this objective is relevant (for a profit-seeking organisation), specific, time defined and measurable. Whether it is realistic, challenging and consistent depends on the company's particular situation. A financial objective related to internal requirements might be: *to achieve an average annual profit margin of 13 per cent across all products*.

Because such objectives are measurable and time defined, you can check progress, adjust your targets or change your marketing if necessary. Nokia, the world's largest marketer of mobiles, decided to change its profit-margin objectives after checking mid-year results during the economic downturn. Its full-year marketing plan originally called for achieving mobile margins of 13 per cent or higher. However, after determining that Nokia's actual margin on mobiles for the first six months was 11.3 per cent – the result of sharply lower demand and sharply higher competitive pricing pressure – management announced that for the rest of the year, its target for mobile margins would be similar to the actual margins achieved in the first half.[18]

Marketing objectives

Connections with customers and channel members are particularly critical to organisational success, which is why every marketing plan should include objectives for managing these external relationships. Looking at the life cycle of a customer relationship, the organisation would begin by approaching the customer to explore a possible relationship, establishing a relationship and adding more ties to strengthen it; reigniting customer interest if purchases plateau or loyalty wavers, saving the relationship if the customer signals intention to switch to another product or brand, and restarting the relationship if the customer is open to switching back. This life cycle applies to relations with channel members as well.[19]

Many businesses establish explicit objectives for building their customer base, enhancing customers' perceptions of the brand, product or company, holding on to existing customers, increasing customer loyalty, boosting or defending market share, strengthening ties with key distributors, improving customer satisfaction, and so on, as in Table 5.2.

Table 5.2 Focus and purpose of marketing objectives	
Focus of marketing objective	**Purpose and examples**
External relationships	To provide targets for managing relations with customers and other publics such as: ● enhancing brand, product, company image ● building brand awareness and preference ● stimulating product trial ● acquiring new customers ● retaining existing customers ● increasing customer satisfaction ● acquiring or defending market share ● expanding or defending distribution ● other relationship objectives
Internal activities	To provide targets for managing specific marketing activities such as: ● increasing output or speed of new product development ● improving quality of goods or services ● streamlining order fulfilment ● managing resources to enter new markets or segments ● conducting marketing research ● other objectives related to internal activities

In practice, you need to avoid conflicts between your marketing objectives and your financial objectives. It can be difficult to dramatically increase both market share and profitability at the same time, as one example. Therefore, determine your organisation's priorities and formulate your marketing plan accordingly. In conjunction with objectives aimed at external relationships, you may formulate objectives covering internal activities such as increasing the accuracy or speed of order fulfilment, adjusting the focus, output or speed of new product development, and arranging the resources for entering new segments or markets.

Planning for these activities helps lay the groundwork for achieving relationship objectives and the financial objectives that depend on those relationships, as marketers at Samsung Electronics are doing.

MARKETING IN PRACTICE: SAMSUNG ELECTRONICS

Samsung Electronics, based in South Korea, is known all over the world for its televisions, mobiles and other consumer electronics products. The firm's top marketing priorities for external relationships include: building brand preference, enhancing the brand's premium image, acquiring market share, increasing customer satisfaction, and expanding distribution. 'Brand preference is created through emotional engagement,' explains the marketing director of Samsung Electronics UK. 'It's the starting point of dialogue with consumers and introduces a first level of desire.'[20] Thus, Samsung's marketing plans call for communications that show how products such as the Jet smartphone deliver meaningful benefits for today's busy lifestyles.

Samsung's top marketing priorities for internal activities include increasing the pace and output of innovative product development, using product reviews and other data to better understand and respond to consumer needs and wants, working with channel partners to improve the shopping experience and nurture brand loyalty. With the mobile market changing so rapidly, Samsung's marketing plans focus on product introductions that capture the public imagination while providing a balance of value for money and break-through technology. As a result, the company has achieved its global market share objective, approached its target of selling more than 200 million mobiles in a year and boosted turnover.[21]

Societal objectives

Because businesses are increasingly mindful of their responsibilities to society – and the way their actions are viewed by stakeholders – a growing number are setting societal objectives to be achieved through marketing. Such objectives are addressed in marketing plans because they indirectly help the company strengthen ties with customers (achieving marketing objectives) and increase or maintain sales (achieving financial objectives). As shown in Table 5.3, societal objectives may relate to ecological protection or to social responsibility and stakeholder relations.

Table 5.3	Focus and purpose of societal objectives

Focus of societal objective	Purpose and examples
Ecological protection	To provide targets for managing marketing related to ecological protection and sustainability, such as: ● reducing carbon footprint with eco-friendly processes, products and activities ● doing business with 'green' suppliers and channel members ● reducing waste by redesigning products and processes for recycling and other efficiencies ● conserving natural resources ● other objectives related to ecological protection
Social responsibility and relations with publics	To provide targets for managing marketing related to social responsibility and relations with publics, such as: ● building a positive image as a good corporate citizen ● supporting designated charities, community projects, human rights groups, and others, with money and marketing ● encouraging employees, customers, suppliers and channel members to volunteer ● engaging publics in two-way dialogue to share concerns and explain societal initiatives ● other objectives related to social responsibility and relations with publics

Many businesses fulfil their societal objectives by donating money, goods or services to charities or good causes. This helps polish their image and demonstrates their commitment to the community and to society at large. Others integrate societal and marketing objectives. For example, in developing nations, the marketing plans for Unilever's Lifebuoy soap brand include societal objectives for reducing the number of diarrhoea-related deaths by promoting hand-washing. During the past five years, Lifebuoy has brought this message to 120 million people through mobile marketing, contests, special packaging and other marketing activities. Sales of Lifebuoy soap have also increased as the clean-hands message reaches a wider audience. 'It's a marketing programme with social benefits,' explains Unilever's chief marketing officer.[22]

Some companies set specific societal objectives for **cause-related marketing**, in which the brand or product is marketed through a connection to benefit a charity or other social cause. Experts say the chosen cause should have value for both stakeholders and the company. Properly implemented, such marketing initiatives have a positive effect on the cause, customer satisfaction and the company's market value.[23] However, both the charity and the company must be transparent about exactly how the cause will benefit from the connection, to avoid the public perception that the programme is merely a gimmick. And, to protect their reputations, the charity and the company should choose carefully when partnering for marketing purposes.[24]

Marks & Spencer has teamed with Oxfam on a cause-related marketing programme with societal, marketing and financial benefits.

MARKETING IN PRACTICE: MARKS & SPENCER AND OXFAM

The UK retailer Marks & Spencer established Plan A in 2007, when it set 100 long-term goals for improved sustainability through reduced waste, greener operations and other eco-friendly activities. Each year, the retailer's marketers set societal objectives to move the store chain closer to those Plan A goals. Concerned about keeping clothing purchased at its stores from eventually winding up in landfills, Marks & Spencer's marketers recognised an opportunity to partner with Oxfam, the charity that operates hundreds of UK outlets selling used goods to raise money for fighting poverty worldwide.

At the time, Oxfam was looking to increase donations of clothing, furniture and other household items so it could maintain financial support for programmes such as providing clean drinking water to rural regions and donating emergency shelters for homeless people. The retailer and the charity worked together to create the Marks & Spencer and Oxfam Clothes Exchange. Now consumers who bring used Marks & Spencer clothing to any Oxfam shop receive a voucher for £5 off any £35 purchase of new clothing or home products at Marks & Spencer. In the first year alone, this cause-related marketing scheme kept 3 million pieces of apparel from landfills, raised nearly £2 million for Oxfam's charitable activities and helped half a million consumers save a total of £2.5 million off their Marks & Spencer purchases. According to the director of Plan A, the programme is successful because it's 'important to our customers to do the right thing – and here you're helping to save the planet as well as your wallet'.[25]

To communicate their societal objectives, activities and results to stakeholders, some companies distribute information to the media and post social responsibility and sustainability reports on their websites. See Table 5.4 for a brief listing of online sources of more information about these issues.

Table 5.4 Societal objectives, sustainability and social responsibility: online resources

Website	Focus
CSR Europe (www.csreurope.org)	Online business network for sharing social responsibility and sustainability objectives, practices and successes
Envirowise (www.envirowise.gov.uk)	Ideas and tools for reducing business's ecological impact by reducing waste and conserving natural resources
Third Sector (www.thirdsector.co.uk)	Publication covering charities, social enterprise and voluntary organisations
Business Link (www.businesslink.gov.uk)	Guide to planning for future sustainability and social responsibility actions
ENDS Europe (www.endseurope.com)	News about the latest developments in environmental issues and resource conservation for businesses
Centre for Business Relationships, Accountability, Sustainability and Society (www.brass.cf.ac.uk)	Research and information to help businesses plan for sustainability, social responsibility and stakeholder relations

ESSENTIAL MARKETING PLAN CHECKLIST NO. 8:
EVALUATING OBJECTIVES

You must set appropriate objectives if you are to develop suitable marketing programmes for your organisation's chosen direction and current situation. This checklist will help you evaluate the marketing, financial and societal objectives you have formulated for your marketing plan. Note your responses in the spaces provided, then put a tick next to the questions as you answer each one.[26]

☐ Is the objective relevant to the organisation's direction and long-term goals?

☐ Is the objective consistent with the organisation's mission, strengths and core competencies?

_____

☐ Is the objective appropriate for the market's opportunities and threats?

_____

☐ Is the objective specific, time defined and measurable?

_____

☐ Is the objective realistic yet challenging?

_____

☐ Is the objective in conflict with any other objective?

_____

FROM OBJECTIVES TO MARKETING-MIX DECISIONS

The objectives you set during this stage of the marketing planning process are the targets to be achieved by implementing the decisions you make about the various marketing-mix elements. This is the point at which your earlier work comes together: on the basis of your situational analysis, your market and customer research and your segmentation, targeting and positioning decisions, you will be creating product, place, price and promotion strategies and action programmes for the who, what, when, where and how of marketing. Be aware that designing programmes to achieve some of your objectives may require marketing research support. Also note that your objectives will guide the development of customer service and internal marketing strategies to support your marketing mix.

Hyundai Motor Company, based in South Korea, creates market-by-market and product-by-product marketing plans to sell vehicles around the world. The exact marketing-mix choices documented in each plan depend on the objectives set for that market, product and time period.

MARKETING IN PRACTICE: HYUNDAI MOTOR COMPANY

Hyundai Motor Company coordinates the financial objectives in every marketing plan with business-level objectives and long-term corporate goals. Several years before the South Korean car company decided on a target of selling 500,000 cars in Europe during 2012, it began working towards the goal by setting and achieving quarterly and yearly objectives for unit sales in European countries. Hyundai also balances its financial objectives with marketing objectives such as increasing brand awareness, boosting market share and introducing new vehicles. As an example, to improve brand recognition among younger UK car buyers, Hyundai's marketing mix included a contest inviting YouTube users to make a video from samples of the i30 hatchback's sounds, such as its horn and its electric windows sliding up or down.

In particular, one objective for external relationships in Hyundai's marketing plans is to reinforce the brand's credentials for quality, value, technical innovation and sustainability. A related objective for internal activities is to develop green vehicles, such as the world's first hybrid car powered by liquefied petroleum gas, to help Hyundai compete with Toyota, Honda and other major rivals. Its marketing plan for introducing the Elantra hybrid in South Korea included marketing-mix activities such as media previews, dealership training and advertising to support the new-product launch. 'We are moving with 'Hyundai speed' to achieve our goal of environmental leadership in our industry and redefining the Hyundai brand as a technological innovator,' explains a Hyundai executive.[27]

Chapters 6, 7, 8 and 9 discuss planning for the four marketing-mix elements; Chapter 10 covers customer service and internal marketing. These are all part of Stage 5 in the marketing planning process.

CHAPTER SUMMARY

Higher-level strategies and goals set the direction for marketing plans that outline objectives to be achieved through marketing strategies, tactics and programmes. Many organisations prepare marketing plans for growth through market penetration (offering existing products to existing markets), product development (offering new products or variations to existing markets), market development (offering existing products to new markets or segments) or diversification (offering new products to new markets or segments). Non-growth strategies include maintenance (to sustain current levels of revenues, share or profits) and retrenchment (to prepare for a turnaround into growth or to close down entirely).

Effective objectives must be relevant, specific, time defined, measurable, realistic yet challenging, and consistent with the current situation. Financial objectives are targets for attaining financial results such as profitability through marketing strategies and programmes. Marketing objectives are targets for achievements in marketing relationships and activities. Societal objectives are targets for ecological protection or other areas of social responsibility. These objectives indirectly support the organisation's ability to achieve financial and marketing objectives.

CASE STUDY: APPETITE FOR GROWTH AT MCDONALD'S EUROPE

With 6,600 fast-food restaurants in 40 nations, McDonald's Europe has profited from the recent trend towards lower-priced, more casual dining. During the economic crisis, competitors such as Starbucks were closing European outlets – yet McDonald's Europe was following marketing plans for opening hundreds of new restaurants in France, Italy, Spain and other nations. The marketing plans also called for opening more than 1,000 McCafé gourmet coffee counters in or adjacent to existing McDonald's restaurants across Europe.

Pursuing growth in turnover and profits by opening new restaurants and coffee bars represents a strategic shift for McDonald's Europe. From 2003 to 2008, the company focused on growth through market penetration, taking steps such as redesigning its stores and introducing new menu items to bring customers back again and again. It also repositioned its in-store play areas as Ronald Gym and Fun Clubs to reflect the benefit of keeping children fit and to encourage family visits to neighbourhood McDonald's restaurants.

Since 2009, however, McDonald's Europe has been using its marketing plans to support a major expansion initiative. Its saver menu has made the restaurants more popular than ever among price-conscious consumers, and the seasonal specials help McDonald's broaden its appeal beyond hamburger fans. The McCafés add an upmarket option for consumers seeking fresh-brewed espresso and mochas – and give customers another reason to choose McDonald's for takeaway breakfasts.

Today the marketing plans for McDonald's Europe aim to achieve financial objectives such as increasing overall turnover and profitability, selling more of specific menu items, increasing sales during certain times of the day and achieving a 20 per cent return on investment in new restaurant openings within ten years. Marketing objectives include adding to market share, polishing the brand image, stimulating trial of new menu items geared to local and regional tastes and reinforcing customer loyalty. Societal objectives include supporting sustainable agricultural practices, reducing greenhouse-gas emissions, using renewable materials in food packaging and increasing recycling within its communities. In the long run, the McCafés could be a major factor in the company's expansion. 'We can become the biggest seller of coffee in Europe,' observes one executive.[28]

Case questions

1. To set consistent and realistic yet challenging objectives, what internal and external factors should the marketers at McDonald's Europe consider when preparing marketing plans?

2. If McDonald's Europe adopts the long-term goal of becoming the biggest seller of coffee in Europe, what are the implications for its yearly marketing plans?

 **APPLY YOUR KNOWLEDGE**

Research the direction, marketing, financial and societal objectives of a particular company by examining its website, media coverage, products, advertising, packaging, financial disclosures, social responsibility reports and other aspects of its operation. Based on your findings, write a brief report or make a brief oral presentation to the class.

- Is the company pursuing a growth, maintenance or retrenchment strategy? How do you know?

- Does the company disclose any specific objectives? If so, what are they and how do they relate to the company's direction?

- Identify one specific marketing, financial or societal objective that this company has set and compare it to the characteristics in this chapter's checklist. What changes would you recommend to make this objective more effective as a target for performance?

- Look for clues about whether the objective you have identified was actually achieved (and if not, why).

 **BUILD YOUR OWN MARKETING PLAN**

Continue working on your marketing plan. Examining the organisation's current situation, environment, markets, customers and mission statement, what is an appropriate direction for your marketing plan? What marketing, financial and societal objectives will you set to move in the chosen direction? If any of these objectives conflict, which should take priority, and why? How will these objectives guide your planning for the marketing mix and marketing support? What might cause you to rethink your objectives? Take a moment to consider how the direction and objectives fit with the information already in your marketing plan and how practical they are in terms of marketing implementation. Then record your thoughts in your marketing plan.

ENDNOTES

1. John Lewis Partnership website, www.johnlewis-partnership.co.uk.

2. Quoted in Martin Hickman, 'Streets ahead: Does John Lewis offer a revolutionary way forward for big business?', *The Independent*, 20 August 2009, www.independent.co.uk/news/business/analysis-and-features/streets-ahead-does-john-lewis-offer-a-revolutionary-way-forward-for-big-business-1774510.html. Other sources: 'John Lewis to revamp online fashion area in major web repositioning', *New Media Age*, 30 April 2009, p. 5; Hillary Alexander, 'John Lewis announces first designer menswear collaboration', *The Telegraph*, 16 October 2009, www.telegraph.co.uk/fashion.

3. Marcus Leroux, 'Sought after and elusive, yet John Lewis may soon come to a town near you', *The Times*, 17 August 2009, p. 42; 'Wine and beds bucking the John Lewis downward trend', *Evening Standard*, 21 August 2009, n.p; James Hall, 'John Lewis has come out of the recession fighting', *Telegraph*, 19 December 2009, www.telegraph.co.uk.

4. Tim Ambler, 'Set clear goals and see marketing hit its target', *Financial Times*, 29 August 2002, p. 8.

5. Alan Rappeport, 'Home dining boosts Heinz and Hormel', *Financial Times*, 20 August 2009, www.ft.com; Bill Bruce, 'Heinz chairman reviews record 2009 results', *FoodBev.com*, 12 August 2009. www.foodbev.com; David Goetzl, 'Heinz to raise spending cap to keep ketchup flowing', *Media Post*, 21 August 2009, www.mediapost.com; Gemma Charles, 'Heinz looks beyond the supermarket shelf', *Marketing*, 4 August 2009, www.marketingmagazine.co.uk; www.heinz.com.

6. H. Igor Ansoff, 'Strategies for diversification', *Harvard Business Review*, September–October 1957, pp. 113–25; Philip Kotler, *Kotler on Marketing* (New York: Free Press, 1999), pp. 46–8.

7. 'Heinz Snap Pots celebrate first birthday', *Talking Retail*, 6 January 2009, www.talkingretail.com.

8. Teresa F. Lindeman, 'Heinz: Buyers still loyal despite recession', *Pittsburgh Post-Gazette*, 13 August 2009, www.post-gazette.com/pg/09225/990496-28.stm#ixzz0PEARobH7; 'Heinz keen to grow Golden Circle brand', *International Business Times*, 2 March 2009, www.ibtimes.com.au.

9. 'Sound long-term strategy is key, particularly in a crisis: Harvard's Michael Porter', *Insead Knowledge*, 1 July 2009, http://knowledge.insead.edu.

10. John Reed, 'Harley-Davidson sees rocky road ahead', *Financial Times*, 16 July 2009, www.ft.com; Rick Barrett, 'Keeping ingenuity rolling: As Harley cuts staff, the key is not to hurt product development', *Milwaukee Journal Sentinel (Wisconsin, USA)*, 22 August 2009, n.p.; Eric Bellman, 'Harley to ride Indian growth', *Wall Street Journal*, 28 August 2009, p. B1; Ilan Brat, 'Harley picks outsider for chief amid downturn', *Wall Street Journal*, 7 April 2009, p. B4; www.harley-davidson.com; Sumit Chaturvedi, 'Super bikes to get "affordable"', *Economic Times*, 29 December 2009, http://economictimes.indiatimes.com.

11. For more information, see: Aaron Toogood, 'Management accounting – business strategy', *Financial Management (UK)*, June 2009, pp. 50ff; and 'Linking strategy to operations', *Journal of Accountancy*, October 2008, pp. 80ff.

12. 'LG Electronics states aim to dominate appliances market', *London Evening Standard*, 2 September 2009, www.thisislondon.co.uk/standard-business; Kim Tong-hyung, 'LG has white goods going green', *Korea Times*, 2 September 2009, www.koreatimes.co.kr.

13. Kevin Done, 'O'Leary looks to skies as he keeps throttle open', *Financial Times*, 2 June 2009, www.ft.com.

14. 'Highland Spring plots to topple Evian as UK's no. 1', *Marketing Week*, 16 April 2009, p. 3.

15. Gemma Charles, 'Plum baby food brand enters chilled market', *Marketing,* 14 January 2009, www.marketingmagazine.co.uk; Martin Waller, 'Posh organic cookery leads to plum job', *Times Online,* 3 May 2008, http://business.timesonline.co.uk.

16. Peter Burrows, 'Cisco's outlook: Clearing, but still overcast', *BusinessWeek Online,* 7 August 2009, www.businessweek.com; Peter Burrows, 'Cisco seizes the moment', *BusinessWeek,* 25 May 2009, pp. 46–8.

17. Jonathan Birchall, 'Procter & Gamble loses sales volume as consumer demand drops', *Financial Times,* 6 August 2009, www.ft.com; Roger O. Crockett, 'Household chores for P&G's incoming CEO', *BusinessWeek,* 5 August 2009, www.businessweek.com; www.pg.com.

18. Mike Harvey, 'Nokia eyes netbook market with 'mini-laptop'', *Times Online,* 24 August 2009, http://business.timesonline.co.uk; Andrew Parker and Andrew Ward, 'Nokia shares fall as expansion put on hold', *Financial Times,* 16 July 2009, www.ft.com.

19. See Sandy D. Jap and Erin Anderson, 'Testing the life-cycle theory of inter-organisational relations: do performance outcomes depend on the path taken?', *Insead Knowledge,* February 2003, http://knowledge.insead.edu.

20. Quoted in Mikah Martin Cruz, 'Brand-led marketing: Samsung viewpoint', *Marketing Week,* 2 July 2009, p. 18.

21. Mikah Martin Cruz, 'Brand-led marketing: Samsung viewpoint', *Marketing Week,* 2 July 2009, p. 18; Abbey Klaasen, 'Forget Twitter', *Advertising Age,* 29 June 2009, p. 1; Moon Ihlwan, 'Samsung's plan to widen its range', *BusinessWeek,* 24 August 2009, p. 30; Moon Ihlwan, 'Samsung earnings soar thanks to TVs', *BusinessWeek Online,* 27 July 2009, www.businessweek.com.

22. Jack Neff, 'Lever's CMO throws down the social-media gauntlet', *Advertising Age,* 13 April 2009, www.adage.com; Rob Walker, 'Cleaning up', *New York Times,* 10 June 2007, http://www.nytimes.com/2007/06/10/magazine/10wwln-consumed-t.html.

23. Xueming Luo and C.B. Bhattacharya, 'Corporate social responsibility, customer satisfaction and market value', *Journal of Marketing,* October 2006, pp. 1–18.

24. 'Consuming for a cause', *Choice (Australian Consumers' Association),* October 2008, pp. 24ff.

25. 'Golden Jubilee Awards 2009: Cause-related marketing', *Marketing,* 10 June 2009, p. 28; 'Oxfam plea as donations fall 12 per cent', *BBC News,* 7 May 2009, http://news.bbc.co.uk; www.oxfam.org.uk.

26. *Source*: After Marian Burk Wood, *The Marketing Plan Handbook,* 4th edn (Upper Saddle River, NJ: Pearson Prentice Hall, 2011), Chapter 5.

27. Quoted in Song Jung-a, 'Hyundai launches first hybrid in S Korea', *Financial Times,* July 2009, www.ft.com; Moon Ihlwan, 'Korea's Hyundai begins its hybrid push', *BusinessWeek Online,* 9 July 2009, www.businessweek.com; 'Top warranty wins admirers', *Europe Intelligence Wire,* 21 August 2009, n.p.; Chang-Ran Kim, 'Autoshow: Hyundai Europe sees market share gains', *Reuters,* 3 March 2009, www.reuters.com; 'Hyundai dips a toe into social media for i30 campaign', *New Media Age,* 6 August 2009, p. 6; Choe Sang-Hun, 'Hyundai sets record for profit in quarter', *New York Times,* 24 July 2009, p. B4.

28. Quoted in Chris Irvine, 'McDonald's McCafés set to take on Starbucks', *The Telegraph,* 28 May 2009, www.telegraph.co.uk. Other sources: Leona Liu, 'Europe's new McCafé culture', *BusinessWeek,* 5 October 2009, p. 70; Jenny Wiggins, 'McCafé concept helps fast food chain', *Financial Times,* 11 August 2009, www.ft.com; Nigel Hunt, 'McDonald's Europe seeks to raise farming standards', *Reuters,* 18 June 2009, www.reuters.com; 'McDonald's Europe promotes sustainable farming', *Environmental Leader,* 22 June 2009, www.environmentalleader.com; Jonathan Birchall and Jenny Wiggins, 'McDonald's defies downturn with plans for 240 more restaurants', *Financial Times,* 24 January 2009, p. 1; Jill Park, 'McDonald's aims for 100 per cent sustainable packaging by 2010', *Packaging News,* 22 May 2009, www.packagingnews.co.uk; Kerry Capell, 'A golden recipe for McDonald's Europe', *BusinessWeek,* 17 June 2008, www.businessweek.com; www.mcdonalds.com; www.mcdonalds.co.uk.

6 Planning for products and brands

Comprehension outcomes

After studying this chapter, you will be able to:

- Explain how product mix, product line and product life cycle affect product planning
- Understand the steps in new product development
- Discuss how product attributes provide value for customers
- Describe how to analyse and enhance brand equity

Application outcomes

After studying this chapter, you will be able to:

- Analyse a product's position in the product mix and the life cycle
- Make planning decisions about products
- Make planning decisions about brands

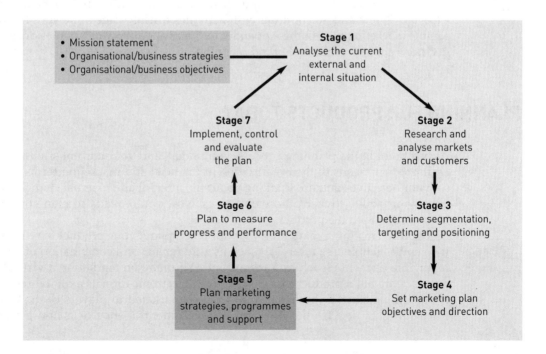

CHAPTER PREVIEW: ADIDAS RACES TOWARDS HIGHER MARKET SHARE

Germany's Adidas Group is racing towards higher market share and increased turnover in its mission to be the leading sports brand in the world. Founded in 1949, Adidas now markets sports footwear, apparel and accessory products under three main brands: Adidas, Reebok and TaylorMade. By putting its brands in the spotlight and introducing products that combine performance and style, the company seeks to overtake global market leader Nike, dominate the women's fitness segment and gain share in the men's sports segment.

Adidas's partnership with FIFA and outfitting deals with many national football teams and sports stars give its brands significant exposure during popular events such as the football World Cup and the European Championship. Facebook fan pages for its Adidas Originals have attracted 2 million fans for localised brand-related content based on where the user is located. Through collaboration with Cirque du Soleil, Adidas has created a new range of co-branded gym workout equipment and apparel for women. Finally, having Stella McCartney to design women's sportswear and trainers made from non-leather materials reinforces the brand's association with the fashion world.[1]

Adidas is seeking to achieve financial, marketing and societal objectives through product and brand planning, part of stage 5 in the marketing planning process. This chapter opens with a discussion of product mix, product lines and the product life cycle, followed by an examination of new product development. Next, you'll learn how to use different attributes in devising a tangible good or intangible service that will meet your customers' needs, your organisational targets and the marketplace realities. The final section looks at what you should consider when you plan for brands and brand equity.

The two checklists in this chapter will help you plan for products and branding. Chapters 7, 8, 9 and 10 continue with activities during stage 5. Be sure to browse the sample marketing plan in the Appendix for ideas about how companies document their decisions about product and brand planning.

PLANNING FOR PRODUCTS TODAY

At this point in the planning process, you understand your current situation and what each product means to the organisation in financial and marketing terms. You've also set your objectives and are thinking about the internal and external changes that might affect your ability to reach those objectives. Now you're ready to plan your marketing mix, starting with the product.

If you're creating a marketing plan for a company, your product may be a physical item (such as trainers), a service (such as auto repair) or a combination of tangible and intangible elements (such as a restaurant). You may be marketing a **virtual product,** not software but a product that exists only in electronic form as a digital representation of something, such as a virtual Mini Cooper marketed to players of the Crazyracing KartRiding game.[2] If you work for a government agency or a non-governmental organisation, your product may be an idea such as better health; if you're marketing a geographic region, your product may be a place such as a tourist destination.

For any specific product you market or plan to market, look closely at:

- the customer segment being targeted
- the needs satisfied and value provided
- trends in pricing, unit sales, market share, revenues and profits
- age and performance over time, by segment, channel and geography
- sales connections between products
- current or potential opportunities and threats related to each product
- competitive strengths, weaknesses, position
- customers' perceptions of competing products.

The point of these analyses is to determine how each product provides value to customers and your organisation. As a visual summary, create a grid matching each product to the intended target market, detail the need each product satisfies and indicate the value delivered from the customer's and organisation's perspectives (see Table 6.1). In addition, you may want to include information about each product's competitive position and strength – with the understanding that competitive circumstances can change at any time, given the volatility of today's marketplace.

Table 6.1   Product/segment analysis grid

	Customer segment A (briefly describe)	Customer segment B (briefly describe)	Customer segment C (briefly describe)
Product 1 (identify)	Customer need: Value to customer: Value to organisation: Competitive situation:	Customer need: Value to customer: Value to organisation: Competitive situation:	Customer need: Value to customer: Value to organisation: Competitive situation:
Product 2 (identify)	Customer need: Value to customer: Value to organisation: Competitive situation:	Customer need: Value to customer: Value to organisation: Competitive situation:	Customer need: Value to customer: Value to organisation: Competitive situation:
Product 3 (identify)	Customer need: Value to customer: Value to organisation: Competitive situation:	Customer need: Value to customer: Value to organisation: Competitive situation:	Customer need: Value to customer: Value to organisation: Competitive situation:

Today, many companies use **crowdsourcing** to generate new product ideas or marketing materials from concepts, designs, content or advice submitted by customers and others outside the organisation. Cisco Systems recently used crowdsourcing to obtain more than 1,000 promising new technology product ideas during a contest it called the I-Prize. The winning idea, a sensor-enabled smart-electricity grid, is in development for introduction in the near future.[3] Here's how Walkers has used crowdsourcing to its advantage in planning products for consumers.

MARKETING IN PRACTICE: WALKERS

Although the Walkers brand already holds 23 percent of the UK market for crisps, its marketers are planning for new ways to gobble up additional share and increase turnover. Understanding snacking attitudes and behaviours, flavour preferences and buying patterns helps them plan to satisfy needs and wants through a variety of product innovations that customers value. In addition to the original crisps range, Walkers' marketers have introduced light crisps, deep-ridged crisps and low-fat baked crisps in several flavours and package sizes to give customers more choices as they please their palates and fit their lifestyles. They've also relaunched the Sensations brand of upmarket crisps with special flavour combinations, new packaging and new advertising.

Knowing that snackers value novelty, Walkers challenged customers to suggest unusual flavours for new crisps. This crowdsourcing campaign brought in more than 1 million ideas, including chilli and chocolate, onion bhaji and Cajun squirrel. A panel of judges chose six flavours to introduce for a limited time and then invited consumers to vote for their favourites online, by mobile messaging, on Facebook and by e-mail. Builder's Breakfast, which tastes like egg and beans, was the winning flavour – and Walkers was the big brand winner, having stirred up much word-of-mouth excitement about itself and its snacks.[4]

After analysing your products, you'll face decisions about managing the product mix and product lines, product attributes including quality and performance, features and benefits, design, packaging and labelling and branding, the product life cycle, and new product development. Table 6.2 shows these four categories of product planning decisions.

Product mix and product line decisions

When you manage the **product mix**, you're determining the assortment of product lines offered by your organisation. **Product line length** is the number of individual items in each line (or range) of related products; **product line depth** refers to the number of variations of each product within one line. Your marketing plan can cover one or more of the following activities:

| Table 6.2 | Product planning decisions |

Product mix and product lines	Product attributes
• Change product line length or depth • Change product mix width • Manage product cannibalisation	• Plan level of quality, performance • Provide valued benefits through features • Design for functionality, differentiation • Create packaging and labelling • Build brand equity
Product life cycle	**New product development**
• Locate product in cycle by segment and market • Change progression through life cycle • Balance life cycles of multiple products	• Add new product categories • Expand existing lines or brands • Manage steps in process • Address ecological, ethical concerns

- introduce new products in an existing line under the existing brand name (line extensions that lengthen the line)

- introduce variations of existing products in a product line (deepening the line)

- introduce new brand names in an existing product line or category (**multibrand strategy**)

- introduce new products under an existing brand (**brand extensions** that widen the mix)

- introduce new lines in other product categories (**category extensions** that widen the mix)

- eliminate a product (shortening the line)

- eliminate or add a product line (narrowing or widening the mix).

Each decision about the product changes the way you satisfy customers in targeted segments, address opportunities, avert threats, allocate marketing resources and achieve marketing objectives. Adding new products by extending a familiar, established line or brand can minimise the risk that customers and channel partners may perceive in trying something new. Because of this familiarity, the product's introductory campaign is likely to be more efficient and may even cost less than for an entirely new brand or product in a new category. Your development costs may also be lower if you base a new product on an existing product. L'Oréal, the French beauty-products firm, is using its marketing plans to add new products under established brand names and expand distribution of its current products.

MARKETING IN PRACTICE: L'ORÉAL

L'Oréal, the world's largest cosmetics company, markets beauty products under luxury brands such as Lancôme and Biotherm, mainstream brands such as Maybelline New York and Garnier, professional brands such as Matrix, and speciality skin-care brands such as Vichy. It also owns the Body Shop retail chain. With €17.5 billion in annual turnover, L'Oréal is pursuing a growth strategy by introducing new products and marketing existing products to additional segments and additional markets. 'The idea is to broaden consumer targets, in terms of price, categories and geography,' explains the chief executive. 'Having several different levels of price and offers can help us compete.'[5]

L'Oréal has therefore created Basics from Garnier as a more affordable mainstream brand and introduced smaller packages of some premium skin-care items. It now markets some of its beauty brands in Egypt, Pakistan and Kazakhstan, where it previously had no market presence, and has launched new cosmetics products in China, Brazil and India. Currently L'Oréal's product experts are working on scientific breakthroughs to develop new anti-ageing skin creams geared to the needs of targeted consumer segments. Both new products and existing ranges are receiving strong advertising and promotional support to highlight their competitive differentiation and communicate important benefits.[6]

Extensions that are well received will reinforce the brand, capture new customers and accommodate the variety-seeking behaviour of current customers. Extensions are not without risk, however. If you extend a line or brand, customers or channel members may become confused about the different products you offer. Remember that channel members with limited shelf or storage space may be reluctant to carry additional products. And if the product does not succeed, perceptions of the brand or the remaining products in the line may be affected.

In particular, look closely at whether you are spreading your resources too thinly and at how each product or line will contribute to organisational objectives. Be ready to cut products or lines that do not perform as desired. Also manage your products with an eye towards minimising product **cannibalisation**, which occurs when one of your products takes sales from another of your products. A line extension may attract customers who previously purchased other products in the same line, for example. Still, marketers sometimes decide they can attract new customers, retain current customers or achieve other objectives only by cannibalising their own products rather than risk competitors luring customers away.

Product life-cycle decisions

As you plan, you must make decisions about how to manage the **product life cycle**, a product's movement through the market as it passes from introduction to growth, maturity and eventual decline. Although no individual product's life cycle is entirely predictable or even necessarily sequential, the typical life cycle pictured in Figure 6.1 shows how sales and profitability can change in each part of the cycle. Corporate giants such as L'Oréal and Unilever tend to have numerous products in targeted markets at one time, and each could very well be in a different part of its life cycle. Be aware that product life cycle can vary by segment and by market.

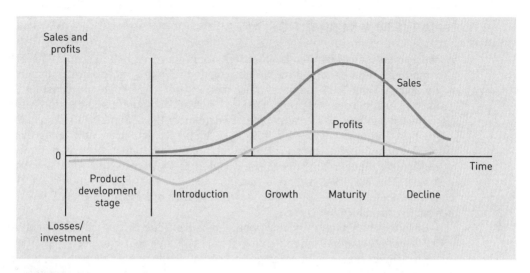

FIGURE 6.1 Product life cycle

Source: Philip Kotler, Veronica Wang, John Saunders and Gary Armstrong, *Principles of Marketing*, 4th edn (Harlow: Pearson Education, 2005), p. 604. Reproduced with permission from Pearson Education Ltd.

Analysing a product's life-cycle situation and using marketing activities to manage the cycle can help you plan to take advantage of anticipated ups and downs. Where is the product within its life cycle, how quickly is it progressing through each part of the cycle and what can marketers do either to alter the cycle or to get the most out of each part? As Figure 6.1 suggests, profitability is highest during the growth part of the life cycle and tends to decrease with maturity. This is why many companies, including Apple, plan strategies to extend and reinvigorate products in the growth and maturity stages. (See Marketing in Practice on page 118).

Some products are reaching maturity much faster, compressing their life cycle and creating additional marketing challenges. The DVD player, for instance, matured extremely quickly because of standardised components and technology; as more competitors entered the market and volume skyrocketed, the average price dropped to little more than 10 per cent of the introductory price in only six years. Now manufacturers are extending the life cycle by introducing Blu-ray DVD players with recording capabilities and other special features. Looking ahead, will wider availability of downloadable movies and free or advert-supported online entertainment programming push DVD players into decline?[8]

Companies are learning to use mass customisation to extend the life cycle for products that have been mature for some time. Marks & Spencer now offers personalised greeting cards for customers to design and order online.[9] Adidas invites buyers to choose custom colours for their trainers; BMW's Mini Cooper offers customised colours and accessories for its cars. Ucodo.com allows buyers to custom-design everyday items such as pens and mugs to their own specifications.[10]

MARKETING IN PRACTICE: APPLE

Apple, a pioneer in personal computers, markets three main product lines: Macintosh computers, iPod handheld media devices and iPhone smartphones. Since introducing the original Macintosh computer more than 25 years ago, Apple has constantly expanded and updated this product line to include notebook computers and desktop computers for home and business use. In all, Apple has sold more than 37 million iPod and iPhone units. The first iPod was launched in 2001 as a digital music player; now Apple has extended and deepened its line of 'pocket products' to include tinier versions and touch-screen multimedia models, among others, updated every year in time for the holiday selling season. The iPhone smartphone was introduced in 2007 and is regularly refreshed with new technology, new styling and an ever-expanding array of downloadable applications from the App Store.

Despite increasingly intense competition and products in various stages of late growth or maturity, Apple has managed to maintain healthy profit margins. It is not only investing heavily in research and design to keep a steady flow of innovative variations in its product pipeline, it's also boosting sales by bringing its products to new markets. For example, through a deal with China Unicom, Apple now sells millions of iPhones in China every year. Such marketing moves are helping Apple manage the product life cycle on a global basis.[7]

New product development decisions

Having discovered promising opportunities during earlier stages of the planning process and analysed the life cycle of current products, you may decide to change your product mix by developing new products for targeted customer segments. Some products may open up new categories for your organisation; other products may extend existing lines or brands. Either way, product development details are usually shown in an appendix or separate document, not in the main marketing plan. However, your plan should outline the major decisions, include research or other evidence, highlight key actions and outline the product development schedule.

Here's an overview of the new product development process:

1. *Generate ideas* from inside the organisation and from customers, sales representatives, channel partners, suppliers, competitive materials and other sources. UK-based Reckitt Benckiser, which makes Dettol and other household products, set up the RB-Idealink website in 2006 to tap the power of crowdsourcing for new-product ideas. RB encourages consumers, inventors and businesses to submit ideas for new goods or for technologies and processes that can lead to new products.[11]

2. *Screen ideas* to eliminate those that are inappropriate or not feasible, given the organisation's strengths, core competencies and resources. Reckitt Benckiser has a panel of experts to evaluate the technical aspects and market potential of crowdsourced ideas within three months of submission.

3. *Develop and test product concepts* to find out whether customers (and perhaps influential channel members) perceive value in the remaining ideas and respond positively to them. The point is not just to innovate but to differentiate your products from those of competitors.

4. *Develop the marketing strategy* to clarify targeting, positioning and specific marketing plan objectives for the new product. Also outline the proposed marketing mix and project sales and profits. Reckitt Benckiser's marketers include planning for advertising and other marketing communications to support the launch of new products.

5. *Analyse the business case* for introducing each new product, including associated costs, sales and profits, to gauge the contribution towards achieving organisational objectives such as profitability. On occasion, a particular new product idea may not be profitable on its own, but may be valuable to the organisation for other reasons. One product may lead to the purchase of other products (the way printers lead to the purchase of ink cartridges), or a product may demonstrate the firm's commitment to going green. Consider such motivations when evaluating the overall business case for a new product.

6. *Develop the product* to see whether the concept is practical, cost effective and meets customers' needs and expectations. Sometimes this step means reinventing the way a firm has always produced and marketed its goods or services.

7. *Test market the product*, with associated marketing strategies, to assess the likelihood of market acceptance and success. Try different marketing activities, evaluate customer response, anticipate competitors' reactions and adjust the product and marketing as needed.

8. *Launch the product commercially*, applying the lessons learned from test marketing and from previous product introductions. Reckitt Benckiser's marketers get new products to market quickly and are accountable for achieving the expected performance from each product and range.[12]

New product development doesn't end with commercialisation. You must monitor market response, including the reactions of customers, channel members and competitors. If you see that the product is not selling as well as projected, you will want to change the product or other elements of the marketing mix as needed. Research shows that the most successful new product innovations result from need identification, solution identification and marketing research. At the same time, the rate of new product failure is so high that you must carefully screen ideas to avoid investing in unpromising or unneeded products.

Don't forget the ecological and ethical issues related to your product. Can ecofriendly supplies and processes be incorporated? Will the product's production or use adversely affect the natural environment? How will the new product serve your organisation's societal objectives? What ethical questions might arise (such as whether to test products on animals) and how can you address these in a satisfactory way?

Here's how Belu is using new product development to create eco-friendly bottled waters that can be marketed to meet its key societal objective.

MARKETING IN PRACTICE: BELU

Belu (pronounced 'blue') began with a single product, a 750 ml glass bottle of spring water, and the goal of building an ecologically sustainable UK business to raise money for funding clean-water projects. 'I realised that the product itself – water – could be used to raise awareness and reach people who do not normally read environment magazines,' explains founder and chief executive Reed Paget.[13] Backed by investors interested in the societal objective, Paget located a water source in Shropshire and began selling Belu's first product to Waitrose and to posh London restaurants and caterers.

Wanting to make Belu's new products even greener, Paget pushed for research into new technologies for compostable bottles. The efforts paid off when Belu introduced a new range of spring water in bio-bottles manufactured from corn for faster biodegrading. Today Belu's waters are sold in many UK groceries and restaurants, and annual turnover tops £2.5 million, with all profits paying for clean-water projects in Africa and India. Once more factories are available to produce bio-bottles, Paget plans to switch away from glass bottles entirely and introduce new sizes to meet growing demand from customers who share Belu's social and ecological values.[14]

Product attribute decisions

Whether you're developing new products or improving existing ones, you'll seek the optimal combination of quality and performance, features and benefits, design, packaging and labelling (see Table 6.3). You'll also face important decisions about branding, as discussed later in this chapter. You want your product to be competitively distinctive, attractive and valuable to customers while returning profits to the organisation. Be sure your product is competitively superior on features and benefits valued by customers; also check that the product supports your marketing plan objectives.

Table 6.3 Planning product attributes

	Product 1	Product 2	Product 3
Quality (customers' view) and **performance** (objective measures)			
Features and **benefits** (to satisfy customer needs)			
Design (for performance and differentiation)			
Packaging (protect, store, facilitate use) and **labelling** (information, marketing communication)			
Brand (identify, differentiate, provoke response)			

Quality and performance decisions

Quality means different things to different people; this is why you should define a product's **quality** in terms of how well it satisfies the needs of your customers. From this perspective, a high-quality product is one that satisfies needs better than a poor-quality product. You can certainly use objective performance measures to demonstrate a product's functionality, reliability, sturdiness and lack of defects. Quality counts in services as much as it does in tangible products, although the measures may differ from service to service.

In the marketplace, customers are the final judges of quality and decide for themselves what level of quality they want and will pay for – a decision that can change depending on customers' economic situations and other factors. During the recent recession, many business travellers and holidaymakers opted for affordable luxury accommodations rather than pay the highest room rates for top-quality hotels. Noticing this price-conscious behaviour, a few upmarket hotels discontinued some of their expensive service touches and lowered room rates to increase occupancy rates.[15]

With demand for smaller cars increasing, Tata Motors has been carefully balancing quality and performance as it markets its low-priced Nano.

MARKETING IN PRACTICE: TATA'S NANO

Tata Motors markets the Nano as the cheapest car in the world, with a starting price of 100,000 rupees (about £1,400) in its home market of India. The tiny car offers basic transportation, with a single windscreen wiper, one side mirror, minimal cargo space, a small but highly fuel-efficient motor and a choice of three body colours. Seat belts are standard; heat, air-conditioning and power windows all cost extra. Still, the Nano's functionality meets the needs of so many consumers that the entire first-year production run sold out well in advance, despite well-publicised delays in delivering cars to buyers. In fact, many of the 200,000 orders were for better-kitted-out models.

Now Tata's plans call for bringing a redesigned, plusher Nano to the European market very soon and then, within a year or two, to the North American market. The Tata has already passed several crash tests mandated by the European Union, and its size and fuel efficiency continue to attract media attention worldwide. Down the road, Tata hopes to ship Nano components to partners who will then assemble and market the cars in local markets worldwide.[16]

B2B marketers are concerned with quality and performance as well. For example, Samsung's computer chips must meet Apple's quality and performance standards to provide the proper functionality for Apple's iPhones.[17] Before you introduce or even begin developing a new product, you have to ensure that the entire organisation is capable of consistently delivering the expected quality, given the available resources and schedule. This, too, is part of the marketing planning process.

Feature and benefit decisions

Customers buy a product not only for the **features** – specific attributes that contribute to functionality– but also for the **benefits** – the need-satisfaction outcomes they want or expect. To illustrate, Nokia's customers want mobiles to satisfy their communication needs with features for calling, texting and the Internet, all of which provide the benefit of exchanging information. When evaluating competing products, customers look at whether each model has the features that provide the benefits they value. In practice, you should plan for features that deliver the benefits that you know your customers value (based on marketing research).

Not all customers want or are willing to pay for the benefits provided by a particular product's features. In fact, too many features can make a product too complex or expensive for the targeted audience.[18] Different segments often have different needs and different perceptions of the value of features and benefits. Table 6.4 shows, in simplified form, how Groupe Michelin, the French tyre maker, might match features to benefits that satisfy the needs of specific customer segments. You can see how Michelin could offer value and differentiate its tyres from those of competitors such as Goodyear. Creating a similar matrix can help you pinpoint each segment's needs and identify features and benefits to satisfy those needs.

Table 6.4   Matching features and benefits to needs

Customer segment and need	Feature and benefit
Lorry fleet owners who need to monitor tyre pressure and track the location of all tyres	Sensor patch on each tyre electronically transmits pressure and identification data to owners
Farmers who need to drive tractors over fields and in uneven terrain	Large, deep tyre patterns provide more secure road grip
Professional sports car drivers who seek winning performance	Special composition tyres for speed and handling
Airlines that require durable, cost-efficient tyres	Special composition tyres for longer wear and lower maintenance costs

Features are as important for services such as hotels as they are for physical goods.

MARKETING IN PRACTICE: INTERCONTINENTAL HOTEL GROUP

As the world's largest operator of hotels, the UK-based InterContinental Hotel Group markets 630,000 rooms in 4,300 hotels in more than 100 nations under Holiday Inn, Crowne Plaza, Hotel Indigo and four other brands. The company carefully plans the features of each hotel to satisfy the needs of each targeted segment. For instance, Crowne Plaza hotels that target business customers are built with meeting rooms and offer special menus for group meals, features that deliver the benefits of convenience and customisation valued by this segment.

All Holiday Inn hotels are being upgraded to enhance the benefit of comfort with in-room features such as high-speed Internet access, flat-panel televisions and high-quality bedding. Although these features can easily be compared with those of competitors, Holiday Inn has other features that deliver more subtle benefits. It scents hotel lobbies and public areas with a proprietary fragrance that suggests a warm, airy feeling, and it combines lighting and landscaping to reinforce the welcoming impression that travellers experience when they visit. Holiday Inns that have been upgraded are already seeing a significant improvement in customer satisfaction and marketing performance.[19]

Design decisions

Directly or indirectly, customers' perceptions and buying choices are influenced to some degree by design. Moreover, your design decisions can affect the ecology as well as product performance. Therefore, as with all other product decisions, you should be sure that a product's design is consistent with your organisation's marketing, financial and societal objectives and that it fits with your other marketing mix decisions. Ideally, design decisions should create a bridge to your future vision of how the product will benefit the target market and set it apart from those of rivals. The distinctive bonnet ornaments of Rolls-Royce Motors and Jaguar are design elements that convey the cars' branding and have become associated with status, for instance.

Product design has become such a prime point of differentiation, especially for mature products like household appliances, that everyday products need not be ordinary looking. In fact, the pressure of global competition has prompted many marketers to devote more time and resources to product design. Not so long ago, personal computers were large, boxy products available only in dull beige or black; today, Apple, Lenovo, Dell, Acer and others offer light and compact models, brightly coloured cases and other design touches that buyers appreciate for their style, ease of use and portability. Panasonic's Toughbook laptops have been designed to withstand rugged conditions such as extreme weather, which differentiates them from competing laptops. How can you use design in your marketing plan to advance your objectives and satisfy your customers?

Packaging and labelling decisions

Good packaging protects tangible goods, makes their use or storage more convenient for customers and, ideally, serves societal objectives such as ecological protection. Think about how Walkers crisps are packaged to remain fresh and crispy for weeks; the company also offers packaging in various sizes for different customer needs, such as on-the-go snacks and family meals.

When planning for any product to be sold in a store, be sure to consider how labelling can serve marketing functions. Labels are more than informative: they can capture the shopper's attention, describe how product features deliver benefits, differentiate the product from competing items and reinforce brand image. For instance, Beck's uses limited-edition labels designed by pop stars such as Ladyhawke to call attention to its beers in shops and bars and generate brand buzz among consumers.[20]

Marketing functions aside, labels must meet applicable laws and regulations wherever your products are sold. In the UK, cigarette marketers are required to include graphic warning labels on every pack.[21] In Canada's Quebec province, multilingual labels must include a French equivalent for every word, printed in type that is as big as or bigger than the type used for other languages. In the United States, supermarkets must label fruits, vegetables and meats to indicate the country of origin.[22]

Use the following checklist as you proceed with planning product attributes, and be sure to consider brand planning, as discussed in the next section.

ESSENTIAL MARKETING PLAN CHECKLIST NO. 9:
PLANNING FOR PRODUCTS

Now that you've set specific objectives for your marketing plan, you need to begin planning for your products. This checklist will help you think through the main issues and decisions. Write your answers in the spaces provided and put a tick next to the questions as you complete each one. If your marketing plan is for a product not yet on the market, use this checklist to consider the key decisions you'll face in planning for a successful introduction.

☐ What is the current situation of each product within its line and the overall product mix?

_____

☐ Would customers' needs and the organisation's interests be served by changing the product mix, product lines or line depth?

_____

☐ Where is each product in its life cycle and what are the implications for product planning?

_____

☐ What new products can be developed to take advantage of promising opportunities in targeted segments?

_____

☐ If you're planning a new product, how can you improve the odds of success as you move through each step in the development process?

_____

☐ How might cannibalisation be minimised following new product introductions?

_____

☐ What are the ecological and ethical considerations associated with each product?

_____

☐ How can you change quality and performance, features and benefits, design, packaging or labelling to provide more value for customers and your organisation?

_____

PLANNING FOR BRANDS

Branding is a pivotal aspect of product planning because it provides identity and competitive differentiation to stimulate customer response. An unbranded product is just a commodity, indistinguishable from competing products except in terms of price. A branded product may have similar attributes to competitors' products yet be seen as distinctly different (and provoke a different customer response) because of the rational or emotional value the brand adds in satisfying the customer's needs and wants.[23]

In planning for a brand, you should identify ways to increase **brand equity**, the extra value customers perceive in a brand that ultimately builds long-term loyalty. Higher brand equity contributes to sustained competitive advantage, attracts new channel partners and reinforces current channel relationships. As you build brand equity, you educate your customers to the nuances of brand meaning among competitors in your product category. You also enhance your marketing power, allowing you to wring more productivity out of your marketing activities as customers (1) become aware of your brand and its identity, (2) know what the brand stands for, (3) respond to it and (4) want an ongoing relationship with it. The brand equity pyramid in Figure 6.2 illustrates these four levels leading to strong brand equity. At the lowest level, customers understand what your brand is about; at the peak, customers are strongly attached to the brand and interact with it.[24]

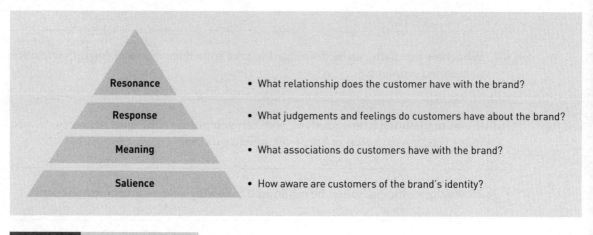

Resonance	• What relationship does the customer have with the brand?
Response	• What judgements and feelings do customers have about the brand?
Meaning	• What associations do customers have with the brand?
Salience	• How aware are customers of the brand's identity?

FIGURE 6.2   Brand equity pyramid

Source: After KELLER, KEVIN LANE, STRATEGIC BRAND MANAGEMENT, 2nd,©2003. Prentice Hall, p.76. Reproduced by permission of Pearson Education, Inc., Upper Saddle River, New Jersey.

Be aware that customers in the targeted segment may know the brand, understand what it stands for and respond to it – but not want the kind of ongoing relationship that the organisation would like. The ultimate objective of brand planning is to move customers upwards through the levels of brand equity and encourage them to remain at the top, where they are likely to be loyal and even act as advocates to bring new customers to the brand. This raises the customer's lifetime value to the organisation and helps achieve your objectives. It's important to remember that companies benefit financially from brand equity, but the identity, meaning, response and relationships all derive from customer interaction with the brand.[25]

Brand identity

Here, you want to make customers in the targeted segment aware of your brand's identity. A brand can consist of words, numbers, symbols and/or graphics to add salience, such as the Nike name combined with its swoosh symbol or the Nestlé name combined with the nesting bird logo. You can develop or license a brand using one or more of the approaches to naming shown in Table 6.5.

Table 6.5 Naming a brand		
Approach to naming	**Description**	**Example**
Company brand (also known as manufacturer's brand or national brand)	The company name becomes the brand, thus associating the company image with the product	Virgin puts its name on all products
Family or umbrella brand	Each product in one or more lines or categories is identified as belonging to that particular brand family (or being under that brand umbrella)	Toyota puts the Lexus name on its family of luxury vehicles
Individual brand	A product is identified with a brand not shared by other products	Plum Baby brand of baby foods
Private brand	Retailers and other channel members frequently brand their own products for differentiation from manufacturers' branded products	Tesco uses Finest as one of its private brands
Co-brand	Two or more companies put their brands on one or more goods or services	Hilton HHonors BarclayCard Visa credit card

If a product doesn't perform as it should or if it attracts negative reaction for some other reason, the brand will suffer – a particular risk when you use the company name as the brand or you're participating in a co-branding arrangement. Ideally, when you specify co-branding in a marketing plan, look for a partner whose brand identity fits well with your brand identity and whose values are similar to your firm's values.[26]

Bringing customers to this first level of brand equity involves decisions about the brand itself as well as other product attributes and marketing actions. For example, how can you use product packaging and labelling to convey a distinctive brand identity? Coca-Cola uses hourglass-shaped bottles and an easily recognised red-and-white logo to set its colas apart from other soft drinks. You can also build customers' awareness of the brand through advertising, in-store promotions, websites and other marketing activities that reinforce the differentiation. Customers who are unaware of a brand will not think of it when purchasing, which is why organisations often set marketing objectives for awareness. Establishing a brand identity and making customers aware of it is a prelude to creating brand meaning.

Brand meaning

The second level of brand equity is to shape the associations that customers have with your brand. What do you want the brand to stand for? What image or personality does the brand have, and is it the same as what you want to create? These are especially important points to consider when planning brand extensions, as Kraft Foods has done with its Oreo biscuit brand.

MARKETING IN PRACTICE: KRAFT FOODS AND OREO

Kraft Foods' Oreo creme sandwich biscuits have been American favourites for decades. In addition to the original biscuits, Kraft has extended the brand to include dozens of variations such as Golden Original Oreos, reduced-fat Oreos, bite-size mini-Oreos and Duo chocolate and vanilla Oreos. Tailoring Oreos to local tastes by reducing the sugar content helped Kraft build Oreos into China's most popular biscuit brand. Now Kraft's marketers are using Oreo to make a big brand statement in the UK.

Although Oreo biscuits had been available at Sainsbury's for some time, Kraft recently introduced the product to the full market with nationwide distribution and a long roll-pack more familiar to UK consumers. The company started an advertising campaign targeting parents of youngsters 6 to 12 years old with humorous messages conveying the brand's wholesome family fun image and promoting the idea of dunking Oreos in milk. Once UK shoppers were aware of the brand's meaning and personality, Kraft's marketers had a firm foundation for plans to offer brand extensions such as Oreo Chocolate Creme biscuits.[27]

As customers come to understand a brand's meaning, they rely on it as a shortcut when making buying choices, which expedites the buying process and reduces the perceived risk. You can mould brand meaning through positioning and through favourable associations backed up by product performance, features that deliver value through need satisfaction, distinctive design and so on. As with brand identity, other marketing activities are involved as well.

Brand response

The third level of brand equity relates to customer response. Once customers are aware of the brand's identity and understand its meaning, they can make up their minds about the brand. Ideally, you want your customers to believe in your brand, trust it and perceive it as embodying positive qualities. You also want customers to see the brand as competitively superior and, just as important, have an emotional connection to it. Determining customer response requires marketing research, followed up by action steps either to reinforce positive responses or to turn negative (or neutral) responses into positive ones through marketing activities.

Brand relationship

The fourth level of brand equity deals with customers' relationship to the brand. They know about the brand, know what it means to them and how they feel about it. But are they sufficiently attached to remain loyal buyers? You want to encourage strong and enduring brand relationships because loyal customers tend to buy more, resist switching to competing brands and be willing to pay a premium for the brand and recommend it to others.[28] The issue is therefore how you can use your product plan, along with other marketing-mix activities, to reinforce customers' brand preference and loyalty.

One approach is to improve or at least maintain product quality and performance to avoid disappointing customers, tarnishing the brand and discouraging customer loyalty. Another is to add products or features that better satisfy current customers' needs. A third is to continue introducing innovative or upgraded product designs, packaging and labelling consistent with the brand image. Finally, your marketing plan should allow for research to see how effective you have been in moving customers up the brand equity pyramid towards sustained customer loyalty. Use the following checklist as you plan for your brand.

ESSENTIAL MARKETING PLAN CHECKLIST NO. 10:
PLANNING FOR BRANDS

Planning for brands must be carefully coordinated with planning for products. This brief checklist can help you think about your branding decisions and about how your product will support your brand. Note your answers in the spaces provided, putting a tick next to the questions as you answer them.

☐ How is the brand identified and what are the implications for its image?

_____

☐ How is the brand positioned for competitive differentiation?

_____

☐ How do product attributes support the brand image?

_____

☐ Are customers aware of the brand? If so, what does it mean to them? How can brand awareness be expanded through marketing?

_____

☐ What do customers think and feel about the brand? What relationship do they have or want with it?

_____

☐ How can brand preference and loyalty be encouraged through marketing?

_____

Source: Adapted from Kevin Lane Keller, *Strategic Brand Management*, 2nd edn (Upper Saddle River, NJ: Prentice Hall, 2003), Chapter 2.

CHAPTER SUMMARY

Planning for products includes decisions about the product mix (the assortment of product lines being offered), product line length (the number of items in each line) and product line depth (the number of product variations within a line). The product life cycle is a product's market movement as it progresses from introduction to growth, maturity and decline. In new product development, you will: (1) generate ideas; (2) screen ideas; (3) research customer reaction to ideas; (4) develop the marketing strategy; (5) analyse the business case; (6) develop the product to determine practicality;

(7) test market the product; (8) commercialise it. After introduction, you'll monitor market response.

Decisions must be made about product quality and performance, features and benefits, design, packaging and labelling, and branding. Quality should be seen in terms of how well a product satisfies customer needs. Features are attributes that contribute to product functionality and deliver benefits. Design is especially important for differentiation. Packaging protects products and facilitates their use or storage. Labels provide information, attract attention, describe features and benefits, differentiate products and reinforce brand image. Branding identifies a product and differentiates it from competing products to stimulate customer response. Brand equity is the extra value customers perceive in a brand that builds long-term loyalty and boosts competitive advantage.

CASE STUDY: PANASONIC REFOCUSES ON THE COMPANY BRAND

The company formerly known as Matsushita Electric Industrial has rebranded itself after the best-known brand family in its portfolio: Panasonic. Matsushita, originally named after its founder, has a long history of growth and, until 2008, it marketed products under three brand families: Matsushita (used in its home country of Japan), National (for home appliances) and Panasonic (its global brand for televisions, DVD players, computers and other electronic products). Then Matsushita changed its name to Panasonic and put all of its products under that name to strengthen and unify its brand identity.

Today, Panasonic's global turnover exceeds £50 billion yearly and its marketers have plans for even more aggressive growth in the coming years. They aim to sharply increase Panasonic's home appliance business in Europe by marketing a new range of full-featured refrigerators, washing machines and air-conditioners under the Panasonic brand. This product strategy puts Panasonic into direct competition with upmarket European brands such as Miele and Electrolux, which have established brand images and enjoy considerable brand loyalty.

Panasonic is also using its company-brand strategy to support expansion in countries with fast-growing economies and sizeable middle-class populations (such as Brazil, India and China). To make this strategy work, it must overcome competition from local manufacturers as well as from South Korean powerhouses like Samsung Electronics that are increasingly focused on international markets. Rather than concentrate marketing and manufacturing efforts at the corporate headquarters in Japan, the chief financial officer says that in key markets, Panasonic is 'attempting to do everything locally – product planning, design, development, production, and parts procurement'.[29] The idea is to adjust product quality, performance, features and design to the needs and wants of customers in each market.

Meanwhile, Panasonic continues to promote its brand's global identification with advanced technology, efficiency and reliability. These associations are supported by the firm's long-time core competency of manufacturing proficiency and by the many product features that provide valued benefits such as low energy consumption and high performance. The company plans to introduce branded robots for home, hospital and industrial use in the coming years. More investments in marketing are ahead as Panasonic adds to its product line length and depth, all under the company brand.[30]

Case questions

1. From a marketing perspective, do you agree with the decision to change the company name to Panasonic and put that brand on all products? What are the implications for brand equity?

2. Where in the life cycle do most of Panasonic's products appear to be? How would you expect this to affect marketing decisions about expanding internationally?

 **APPLY YOUR KNOWLEDGE**

Select an organisation offering a branded good or service with which you are familiar and research its product and brand. Summarise your findings in a brief oral presentation or written report.

- From a customer's perspective, how would you describe the product's quality and performance? Do you think this perception of value matches what the marketer intended?

- How do the features deliver benefits to satisfy needs of the targeted customer segments?

- How do design, packaging and labelling contribute to your reaction, as a customer, to this product?

- Where does this product appear to be in its life cycle? How do you know?

- How would you describe this product's brand? What is the organisation doing to build brand equity?

- Would crowdsourcing be an appropriate approach to generating new ideas for products to be marketed under this brand? Why or why not?

BUILD YOUR OWN MARKETING PLAN

Going back to the marketing plan you've been preparing, is your product a tangible good or an intangible service? What level of quality is appropriate (and affordable) to meet the needs of the targeted customer segments? What needs do customers satisfy through products such as yours and what features must your product have in order to deliver the expected or desired benefits? What can you do with design, packaging and labelling to add value and differentiate your product? What brand image do you want to project? How do you want customers to feel about the brand and react towards it? What can you do to encourage brand loyalty? Think about your answers in the context of your earlier ideas and decisions, then draft the product and brand sections of your marketing plan.

ENDNOTES

1. Todd Wasserman, 'Adidas' Global Full-Court Press', *Adweek*, 15 October 2009, www.adweek.com; 'Adidas sees profits plunge by 95 per cent', *BBC News*, 5 August 2009, http://newsbbc.co.uk; 'Facebook starts localising content on brand fan pages', *Guardian*, 1 June 2009, www.guardian.co.uk/media; Uli Becker, 'India among fastest-growing markets now', *Economist Times*, 6 May 2009, http://economictimes.indiatimes.com; 'Adidas focuses on soccer market leadership in 2010', *The America's Intelligence Wire*, 10 June 2009, n.p.; Robert Lindsay, 'Adidas issues warning amid 97 per cent profit plunge', *Times Online*, 5 May 2009, http://business.timesonline.co.uk; Holger Elfes, 'Adidas leaps from hot sneakers to warm jackets', *BusinessWeek*, 9 December 2009, www.businessweek.com.

2. Michael Fitzgerald, 'Boomtown: The real money behind virtual goods', *Fast Company*, 1 July 2009, www.fastcompany.com.

3. Guido Jouret, 'Inside Cisco's search for the next big idea', *Harvard Business Review*, September 2009, http://hbr/harvardbusiness.org.

4. Gemma Charles, 'Builder's Breakfast crisps wins Walkers' flavour competition', *Marketing*, 6 May 2009, www.marketingmagazine.co.uk; David Teather, 'Calorie reducing, crisp making, porridge launching, lighter lunching', *The Observer*, 23 August 2009, www.guardian.co.uk/business/2009/aug/23/pepsi-uk-boss-salman-amin; 'Cajun squirrel among crisp flavours tested by Walkers', *Telegraph*, 9 January 2009, www.telegraph.co.uk/foodanddrink; Gemma Charles, 'Walkers plans relaunch to revive crisps brand Sensations', *Marketing*, 27 January 2009, www.marketingmagazine.co.uk; www.walkers.co.uk.

5. Quoted in Christina Passariello, 'L'Oreal's chief pursues price balm', *Wall Street Journal*, 28 August 2009, www.wsj.com.

6. Patrick Sawer, 'Sales of cosmetics buck economic gloom', *Telegraph*, 29 August 2009, http://www.telegraph.co.uk/fashion/fashionnews/6109610/Sales-of-cosmetics-buck-economic-gloom.html; Christina Passariello, 'L'Oreal's chief pursues price balm', *Wall Street Journal*, 28 August 2009, www.wsj.com; Zoe Wood, 'L'Oréal shares jump

10 per cent after firm beats profit forecast', *The Guardian*, 28 August 2009, www.guardian.co.uk; www.loreal.com; Rosie Baker, 'L'Oreal to launch Go 360 cleansers', *Marketing Week*, 21 December 2009, www.marketingweek.co.uk.

7. 'Analyst: 15–20 per cent of all iPhone sales in 2010 to be sold in China', *International Business Times*, 28 August 2009, n.p.; Arik Hesseldahl, 'The next iPod generation', *BusinessWeek*, 10 August 2009, p. 27; 'iPod Touch, iPhone sales total 37 million units', *Macworld*, July 2009, p. 18; www.apple.com.

8. Tom Dunmore, 'The internet TV revolution', *Mail Online*, 21 August 2009, www.dailymail.co.uk/sciencetech/; Dylan McGrath, 'High-def DVD war is high-stakes fight', *Electronic Engineering Times*, 15 January 2007, pp. 1ff; Adam Lashinksy, 'Shootout in gadget land', *Fortune*, 10 November 2003, pp. 74ff.

9. George MacDonald, 'Marks & Spencer launches personalised greetings cards business online', *Retail Week*, 10 September 2009, www.retail-week.com.

10. Emma Wells, 'Interiors: Design your own homeware online', *The Sunday Times*, 23 August 2009, www.timesonline.co.uk; Alice Rawsthorn, 'Nurturing the inner entrepreneur', *New York Times*, 17 August 2009, www.nytimes.com; Fabrizio Salvador, Pablo Martin de Holan and Frank Piller, 'Cracking the code of mass customization', *MIT Sloan Management Review*, 1 April 2009, http://sloanreview.mit.edu/the-magazine/articles.

11. Jill Park, 'Reckitt Benckiser calls for innovative ideas', *Packaging News*, 30 January 2009, www.packagingnews.co.uk/news; www.rb-idealink.com.

12. Amy Golding, 'The marketing profile: Phil Thomas of Reckitt Benckiser', *Marketing*, 11 August 2009, www.marketingmagazine.co.uk.

13. Quoted in 'O2 Inspiration Award news; case study: Belu Water', *The Evening Standard*, 25 January 2007, www.thisislondon.co.uk.

14. 'Green alternative to plastic, Belu Water, is idea worth bottling', *Telegraph*, 7 April 2009, www.telegraph.co.uk; Adam Smith, 'Bottled up', *Time International*, 24 August 2009, p. G-6; 'Belu brings first bio-bottle to UK', *Packaging News*, 1 August 2006, www.packagingnews.co.uk; www.belu.org.

15. Nadja Brandt, 'Luxury hotel chains dropping five-star ratings to conserve cash', *Bloomberg*, 25 August 2009, www.bloomberg.com.

16. Simon Arron, 'Tata Nano safety boost', *Telegraph*, 16 July 2009, www.telegraph.co.uk/motoring/news; 'The new people's car: the Tata Nano', *The Economist*, 28 March 2009, p. 64EU; Jyoti Thottam, 'Nano power', *Time*, 13 April 2009, p. GB1ff.

17. Kim Yoo-chul, 'Samsung's chip business to return to black', *The Korea Times*, 24 June 2009, www.koreatimes.co.kr.

18. Roland T. Rust, Debora Viana Thompson and Rebecca W. Hamilton, 'Feature bloat: The product manager's dilemma', *Harvard Business School Working Knowledge*, 8 May 2006, hbswk.hbs.edu.

19. Karl Greenberg, 'Q&A: CMO, Americas of Intercontinental Hotels Group', *Media Post Marketing Daily*, 21 September 2009, www.mediapost.com; Amy Wilson, 'InterContinental Hotels sees slow recovery', *Telegraph*, 11 August 2009, www.telegraph.co.uk; 'InterContinental Hotels deploy 'Hotel-in-a-Box' solution developed with IBM', *Europe Intelligence Wire*, 8 June 2009, n.p.; Gilmore Cheung, 'Hotel chain offers added value for customers on the mainland: Crowne Plaza', *South China Morning Post*, 27 March 2009, n.p.; Fred A. Bernstein, 'Holiday Inn reaches back to its Memphis Roots', *New York Times*, 26 August 2009, p. B6.

20. Jill Park, 'Beck's recruits pop stars to design limited edition labels', *Packaging News*, 1

September 2009, www.packagingnews.co.uk; Alex Brownsell, 'Beck's ties with Hard-Fi and Ladyhawke for music-themed labels', *Marketing*, 28 August 2009, www.marketingmagazine.co.uk.

21. See Department of Health website, http://www.dh.gov.uk/en/Publichealth/Healthimprovement/Tobacco/Tobaccogeneralinformation/DH_4083845.

22. David Kesmodel and Julie Jargon, 'Labels will say if your beef was born in the USA', *Wall Street Journal*, 23 September 2008, p. D1.

23. This section draws on concepts discussed in Kevin Lane Keller, *Strategic Brand Management*, 2nd edn (Upper Saddle River, NJ: Pearson Prentice Hall, 2003), Chapters 1 and 2.

24. See Donald R. Lehmann, Kevin Lane Keller and John U. Farley, 'The structure of survey-based brand metrics', *Journal of International Marketing*, vol. 16, no. 4, 2008, pp. 29–56.

25. Don E. Schultz, 'Branding geometry', *Marketing Management*, September–October 2003, pp. 8–9.

26. Steve McKee, 'The pros and cons of co-branding', *BusinessWeek Online*, 13 July 2009, www.businessweek.com.

27. Camille Alarcon, 'Kraft promotes Oreo Chocolate Creme launch', *Marketing Week*, 24 August 2009, www.marketingweek.co.uk; Elaine Wong, 'How Kraft's Double Stuf Oreo launch trumped expectations', *Brandweek*, 31 August 2009, www.brandweek.com; Tom Geogheagan, 'Can Oreo win over British biscuit lovers?', *BBC News Magazine*, 2 May 2008, http://news.bbc.co.uk/2/hi/uk_news/magazine/7376123.stm.

28. 'New customer research on customer referrals, commitment, loyalty', *Report on Customer Relationship Management*, August 2003, pp. 2ff.

29. Quoted in Kenji Hall, 'Panasonic posts losses but boosts sales overseas', *BusinessWeek Online*, 4 August 2009, www.businessweek.com.

30. Martyn Williams, 'Panasonic has big plans for robots', *PC World*, 16 October 2009, www.pcworld.com; Ronald Grover and Kenji Hall, 'Panasonic puts its chips on 3D TV', *BusinessWeek*, 28 September 2009, p. 58; Wailin Wong, 'Tech retailers turns off the "radio"', *Los Angeles Times*, 10 August 2009, p. B5; Yukari Iwatani Kane, 'For Matsushita, it's all about Panasonic', *Wall Street Journal*, 1 October 2008, www.wsj.com; Yuzo Yamaguchi and Kenneth Maxwell, 'Panasonic eyes Y1T/yr rev from white goods ops', *Wall Street Journal*, 1 September 2009, www.wsj.com.

7 Planning for pricing

Comprehension outcomes

After studying this chapter, you will be able to:

- Explain how customers' perceptions of value affect price decisions
- Identify internal and external influences on pricing
- Understand pricing for new products
- Discuss how to adapt prices

Application outcomes

After studying this chapter, you will be able to:

- Analyse the influences on your pricing decisions
- Set appropriate pricing objectives
- Make planning decisions about product pricing

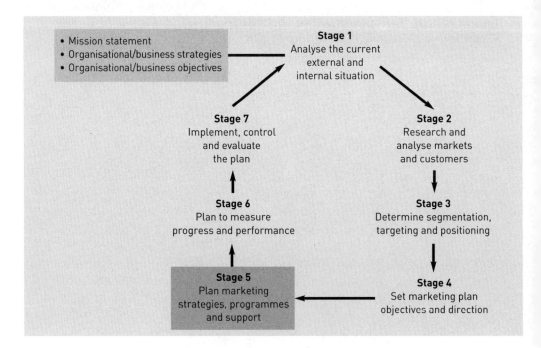

CHAPTER PREVIEW: LEGO BUILDS ON PRICING DECISIONS

Lego, nearly 80 years young, markets its iconic snap-together plastic blocks plus licensed character mini-figures and video games to children of all ages. The Danish company suffered losses in 2004 and almost went out of business as its product mix ballooned. Since then, Lego has followed a series of structured marketing plans to steadily increase turnover, even during recessionary periods, and improve profitability by refocusing on the value that Lego products offer customers.

Whereas some toymakers struggled financially during the recent economic downturn, consumers kept buying from Lego because they valued the high quality, durability and unique play experiences for which the brand stands. 'When families find money a bit tighter, they can't afford to get it wrong,' explained Lego's UK managing director. 'They look for brands they can trust and something that will last longer than a five-minute fix.'[1] Today, the company continues to increase profits by speeding up the introduction of new products such as board games, licensing popular characters from hit movies such as *Toy Story* and streamlining the supply chain for higher cost efficiency.[2]

Lego's marketers recognise that although they spend money on other marketing-mix elements (paying for product development and packaging, as two examples), pricing is the way they make money for the company. They also know that in the marketplace, it's what consumers perceive that counts – that customers actually determine whether the price of a set of Lego bricks or any other offer represents real value. Therefore, this chapter begins with a discussion of how customers perceive value and the difference between cost-based and value-based pricing. Next, you'll learn about the various external and internal influences on pricing that you must consider when preparing a marketing plan. Finally, you'll see how to handle specific pricing decisions, including setting pricing objectives, pricing new products, pricing multiple products and adapting prices.

Consult this chapter's checklist for questions to ask when pricing products during their life cycles. Also, to see how companies document their pricing strategies and activities, review the sample marketing plan in the Appendix.

UNDERSTANDING PRICE AND VALUE TODAY

Whether the price is one pound sterling, one euro or one bag of rice, customers will buy only when they perceive value – when a product's perceived benefits in meeting their needs outweigh the perceived price. Even when the price is collected in barter, customers will not complete a transaction if they perceive insufficient value. No matter how good or bad the economic circumstances, no matter what type of product you market, no matter what segments you're targeting, you can't make planning decisions about price without looking at value from your customers' perspective.

Perceptions of value

A product's value is perceived by customers according to the total benefits they receive. An individual customer may consider one benefit more important than the others, but the combination of all benefits is what provides value. Customers form value perceptions in the context of competing or substitute products that might meet their needs, on the basis of benefits such as:

- *Performance*. Does the product perform as it should in meeting the customer's needs? Does it perform better than competing products? Lego's brightly coloured bricks have a long history and many parents who are buying for their children still remember the fun of these toys from their own childhoods. Such long-lasting perceptions of performance shape how buyers think about, feel about and act towards Lego's products.

- *Features*. Does the product have all the features expected or desired to meet current needs and future or unspoken needs? How do the features compare with those of competing products? Lego continues to add new features to its products (such as accessories based on characters from *Indiana Jones*, *Toy Story* and other movies), supporting the value that buyers perceive in its products.

- *Quality*. Is the product defect-free, reliable and durable compared with competing products? Lego's bricks are designed for durability and manufactured to fit together properly yet snap apart easily. Today's bricks can be mixed with bricks made decades ago, a high level of quality that buyers appreciate and for which they're willing to pay a price premium.

- *Personal benefits*. Does the product deliver personal benefits such as status or self-expression? Lego bricks deliver the personal benefit of self-expression, enabling children and adults to build fanciful structures of their own design or to recreate favourite scenes from *Star Wars*.

- *Availability*. Is the product available whenever needed? Does the price change according to availability? How does this compare with that of competing products? Lego markets its toys through its own online store, through Lego stores and through retailers such as Argos, Tesco and Amazon.com, working with its channel partners to ensure sufficient supply even during holiday periods when demand peaks.

- *Service*. Does the service meet customers' expectations? Is it faster, more convenient or more personalised than that offered by competitors? Customers who buy directly from Lego expect speedy and accurate delivery of their orders.

Against the total perceived benefits, customers weigh the total perceived costs (time and money) associated with the product, including:

- *Initial purchase price*. What time and money must the customer spend to obtain the product initially? How does the purchase price compare with competing products?

- *Maintenance and repair costs*. What is the estimated cost of maintenance over the product's life? How often is maintenance or repair generally required and how much time or money might the customer lose while waiting for repairs or maintenance?

- *Ongoing fees*. Does the product require an annual usage charge or other fees after the initial purchase? Must the customer pay a tax to continue using or possessing the product?

- *Installation*. Does the product require installation? What is the cost in time and money for installing this product compared with competing products?

- *Training*. Do customers need training to use the product properly and if so, what is the cost in time and money compared with competing products?

- *Ancillary products*. Does the product require the purchase of ancillary products and at what cost? How does this compare with competing products?

- *Financing*. If applicable, what is the cost of financing the purchase of this product, what is the monthly payment (if any) and how do such costs compare with those of competing products?

Here's how marketers balance value and cost when using *freemium* pricing.

MARKETING IN PRACTICE: FREEMIUM PRICING

When consumers play *Sorority Life* on MySpace or Facebook, they pay nothing for the game – but do have to pay a small amount to buy virtual extras for their avatars. Marketers who use this kind of freemium pricing offer a basic good or service for free and put a price tag on premium levels of functionality and optional features. In the case of *Sorority Life*, marketed by Playdom, players suggested the virtual pink VW car as an avatar accessory. Playdom sold more than £60,000 worth of pink VWs in only two days as players made the purchase to express themselves and gain status through an extra not included with the free game.

Freemium pricing is a key feature of *app stores*, which offer downloadable applications for mobiles. Limited-functionality apps are often free, while versions with more functionality or options must be purchased. Apple's App Store offers tens of thousands of downloadable applications for the iPhone and iPod. Nokia also offers freemium apps in its Ovi store, and Microsoft offers freemium apps in its Windows Marketplace store. Now millions of apps have been sold, helping successful independent developers build profitable businesses using the freemium pricing model.[3]

Pricing based on value

Through research, you can determine how customers in your targeted segment(s) perceive the value of your product's total benefits and costs and the value of competing products. Then you can use this understanding of the customer's perspective to plan your pricing as well as your costs and your product design (see Figure 7.1(a)).

This is not the way marketers have traditionally planned for pricing. In the past, most started with the product and its cost, developed a pricing plan to cover costs and then looked for ways to communicate value to customer (see Figure 7.1(b)).[4] However, in today's networked world, when customers can so easily locate competitive products and compare prices online or via mobile, you can't afford to ignore the link between value and pricing when preparing your marketing plan.

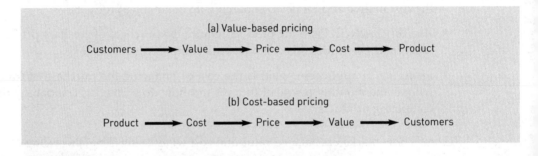

(a) Value-based pricing

Customers ⟶ Value ⟶ Price ⟶ Cost ⟶ Product

(b) Cost-based pricing

Product ⟶ Cost ⟶ Price ⟶ Value ⟶ Customers

FIGURE 7.1   Value-based pricing compared with cost-based pricing

Source: Adapted from *NAGLE, THOMAS T.; HOGAN, JOHN, THE STRATEGY AND TACTICS OF PRICING: A GUIDE TO GROWING MORE PROFITABLY, 4th,©2006.* Prentice Hall, p.4. Reproduced by permission of Pearson Education, Inc., Upper Saddle River, New Jersey.

Consider how Aldi, headquartered in Germany, uses value-based pricing.

MARKETING IN PRACTICE: ALDI

High quality and low costs are two main ingredients in Aldi's marketing plan for international growth. With 7,000 no-frills stores spread across Europe, the United States and Australia, and £2 billion in annual turnover, Aldi has the size and know-how to offer top-quality private-label products at deeply discounted prices. Although Aldi's stores carry up to 1,400 food, beverage, household and electronics products – far fewer than the average supermarket's 40,000 items – each line has been carefully developed to meet the tastes and price expectations of local shoppers.

Its private-label meats, yoghurts, flour, bottled water and other foods are made by the same suppliers used by Tesco, Superquinn and other supermarket chains, but produced and packaged to Aldi's specifications. The brands are Aldi's own, with names such as Harvest Moon for grain products and Alcafe for decaf coffee, which makes direct comparisons with national brands difficult. Yet consumers from all socio-demographic segments shop at Aldi stores because they recognise the special value that its products represent. Riding the wave of public interest in value-based pricing, Aldi is expanding rapidly, adding luxury items and advertising its private-label brands to attract savvy shoppers.[5]

ANALYSING INFLUENCES ON PRICING DECISIONS

Notice how Aldi looks closely at costs and product development as well as at customer needs and other external influences when it plans for pricing. Similarly, as you prepare your marketing plan, your pricing decisions must be made with a number of internal and external influences in mind.

Internal influences

Five major internal influences can affect the decisions you make about pricing: (1) organisational and marketing plan objectives; (2) costs; (3) targeting and positioning; (4) product decisions and life cycle; and (5) other marketing-mix decisions.

Organisational and marketing plan objectives

Price and every other marketing-mix element must tie back to the objectives of the organisation and the marketing plan. Because price generates revenue, it is a particularly important ingredient for achieving sales and profitability targets as well as for meeting societal objectives. If growth and market share are your key objectives, you might lower the product's price and reduce its perceived benefits or develop an entirely new product with fewer benefits that can be marketed at a lower price. Or you might develop a new product designed to sell for less as a way of meeting customer needs, as Nokia did by creating basic handsets for first-time mobile phone customers in Africa.[6]

Costs

Most companies price their products to cover costs, at least over the long run. In the short term, however, you may be willing to price for little or no profit when establishing a new product, competing with aggressive rivals or seeking to achieve another objective. If you compete primarily on the basis of price, you will be particularly concerned with managing variable costs and **fixed costs** (such as rent, insurance and other business expenses, which do not vary with production and sales). This keeps prices low and protects profit margins.

When you have limited control over the **variable costs** that vary with production and sales, such as the cost of raw materials and parts, you will find pricing for profit even more challenging. For example, Heineken, which owns Scottish & Newcastle, decided to raise beer prices after having to pay higher costs for materials used in product packaging.[7] Meanwhile, Airtel, India's largest telecommunications carrier, has increased profitability by bringing its variable costs under control as it expands. Instead of investing heavily to add on its own network, Airtel now leases network capacity from other carriers – which means it pays only for the network time its subscribers use.[8]

Although at times you may have difficulty determining a product's exact costs – especially if it has yet to be launched in the marketplace – you need cost information to calculate the **break-even point**. This is the point at which a product's revenues and costs are equal and beyond which the organisation earns more profit as more units are sold. Unless you make some change in price (which will affect demand) or variable cost, your product will not become profitable until unit volume reaches the break-even point. The equation for this calculation is:

$$\text{break-even point} = \frac{\text{total fixed costs}}{\text{unit price} - \text{variable costs per unit}}$$

If, for example, a product's total fixed costs are €100,000 and one unit's variable costs are €2, the break-even point at a unit price of €6 is:

$$\frac{€100,000}{€6 - €2} = 25,000 \text{ units}$$

Using this break-even point, the organisation will incur losses if it sells fewer than 25,000 units priced at €6 (which works out to total revenues of €150,000). Above 25,000 units, however, the company can cover both variable and fixed costs and increase its profits as it sells a higher quantity. Figure 7.2 is a graphical depiction of break-even analysis, which doesn't take into account changes in demand, how competitors might respond, how customers perceive the product's value and other external influences on pricing. Nor does break-even analysis reflect how the cost per unit is likely to drop as you produce higher quantities and gain economies of scale. Still, it provides a rough approximation of the unit sales volume that you must achieve to cover costs and begin producing profit, which is important for planning purposes.

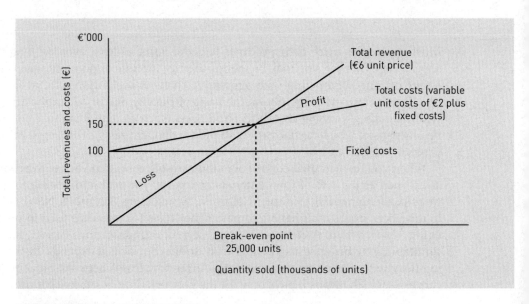

FIGURE 7.2   Break-even analysis

Targeting and positioning

Any pricing decisions should be consistent with your targeting and positioning decisions. Aldi uses low prices to target bargain-hunting shoppers across the economic spectrum, consistent with its positioning on the basis of value. If you're Tiffany and you target affluent customer segments with an upmarket positioning, you'll plan your pricing very differently from Aldi and others that target price-sensitive consumers.

MARKETING IN PRACTICE: TIFFANY

Tiffany, whose blue gift boxes have become a symbol of prestige, operates 206 jewellery stores around the world, including its famous flagship store in New York City. Of the company's £1.7 billion in annual turnover, 20 per cent comes from the sale of diamond engagement rings. However, after years of strong demand and rising revenue, Tiffany faced a major pricing challenge during the recent economic crisis. Consumers were postponing jewellery purchases or opting for less expensive items. In addition, the company was 'facing a headwind from continued heavy and unprecedented levels of discounting by many competitors', said one executive.[9]

Sales of Tiffany products priced at £30,000 or more fell sharply during the recession, although the sales decline in lower-priced items was less dramatic. The company realised that pricing decisions made to address the situation would have to be consistent with the company's traditional targeting and positioning. After studying the marketing environment, Tiffany decided to reduce the price of diamond engagement rings by about 10 per cent. Rather than advertise this pricing decision and risk damaging the brand image, Tiffany had its salespeople communicate the price change as they spoke with customers in the store. Why not change pricing on a broader scale and promote more discounts? 'It's about maintaining the long-term value of the enterprise,' the chief executive explained. 'If we were to abandon that, the consequences would be significant.'[10]

Marketing-mix decisions

Planning for pricing is influenced by (and influences) planning for a number of marketing-mix decisions, including communications. Obviously, many producers and channel members feature pricing in their promotions to attract customer attention and compete with direct rivals. Although marketers of luxury products may not make price a visible part of their communications activities, their pricing decisions will be affected by the benefits and value they emphasise in their marketing communications. In short, be sure your pricing fits with the other decisions you include in your marketing plan, including the way you manage products.

Product decisions and life cycle

If you look back at Figure 7.1(a), you can see that pricing decisions are closely inter-twined with product decisions. More companies are developing new products after they have determined customers' perceptions of value, set target costs and set a target price, rather than starting the pricing process after initiating production. Of course, your pricing decisions will change during the product life cycle. As discussed below, you may start with either market-skimming pricing or market-penetration pricing when launching a new product and then make changes in other stages.

By the time your product reaches the growth stage where competition is increasing, you should choose pricing strategies that support more differentiation in targeted seg-ments or pricing strategies geared to stimulating higher demand for more economies of scale and lower costs (or a combination of both).[11] Sales of a product in maturity will grow less rapidly even as more competitors are vying for the attention of customers, which necessitates another change in your pricing plan. Table 7.1 shows five options for pricing mature products, suggested by pricing experts Thomas Nagle and John Hogan.

Table 7.1 Pricing mature products	
Pricing alternatives	**Purpose**
Unbundle and price products individually	Compete by pricing goods and services individually rather than pricing an entire bundle
Re-examine customer price sensitivity and change price accordingly	Maintain or improve revenue and profits
Set prices based on better understanding of costs and capacity	Reflect realistic costs and earn more profit at times when demand outstrips capacity
Introduce related products	Leverage success of an existing product by adding related goods or services at a profit
Change channel pricing	Expand channel coverage while reducing channel margins

Source: Adapted from *NAGLE, THOMAS T.; HOGAN, JOHN, THE STRATEGY AND TACTICS OF PRICING: A GUIDE TO GROWING MORE PROFITABLY, 4th,©2006*. Prentice Hall, pp.275–77. Reproduced by permission of Pearson Education, Inc., Upper Saddle River, New Jersey.

Use the following checklist as you think about pricing products at different points in their life cycles.

ESSENTIAL MARKETING PLAN CHECKLIST NO. 11:
PRICING THROUGH THE PRODUCT LIFE CYCLE

Whether your marketing plan is for a new product or an existing product, you'll face pricing decisions as it moves through its life cycle. The following questions are a good starting point for considering key issues in pricing at each point in any product's life cycle. Place a tick alongside the questions that apply to your situation as you note your answers in the space provided.

☐ At introduction, how can pricing be used to encourage channel acceptance of a new product?

_____

☐ At introduction, what pricing approach will stimulate product trial and repeat purchasing among customers?

_____

☐ At introduction, how can pricing be used to manage initial supply and demand?

_____

☐ During growth, how can pricing be used for competitive purposes?

_____

☐ During growth, what pricing approach will lead to break-even and profitability?

_____

☐ In maturity, how can pricing encourage customer loyalty and defend market share?

_____

☐ In maturity, what pricing approach will achieve sustained profitability and other objectives?

_____

☐ In maturity, what pricing approach will support expanded channel coverage?

_____

☐ In decline, what pricing approach might slow the slide of unit sales and protect profits?

☐ In decline, how can pricing be used for profit as competitors withdraw from the market?

External influences

The five major external influences on pricing are: (1) customers; (2) market and demand; (3) competition; (4) channel members; and (5) legal, regulatory and ethical considerations.

Customers

Not all customers can or want to compare prices; not all customers are interested in buying the lowest-priced alternative. Research shows that consumers will accept a price if it is within what they consider an acceptable range for that good or service.[12] Customers may decide against buying a product that is priced unusually low because they suspect poor quality yet be willing to spend more if a product appears to offer value-added benefits, such as a prestige brand or special service. If your product is particularly innovative or meets unspoken customer needs, you may have to go against long-established traditions of pricing and service levels.

Business buyers in particular may feel pressure to acquire raw materials, components or services at the lowest possible prices, which in turn affects their suppliers' pricing strategies. Some business buyers and consumers constantly switch brands or suppliers in search of bargains, especially now that they can quickly and easily compare prices online. Your challenge as a marketer is to communicate your product's benefits so customers recognise the differentiation and perceive the value in relation to the price.

The UK movie industry is using a multimedia campaign to convince consumers to pay for the real thing rather than pirating or illegally downloading movies and programmes.

Market and demand

You also need to research the **demand** for your product in the target market – how many units are likely to be sold at different prices – and the effect of price sensitivity, or the **elasticity of demand**. When your research reveals **elastic demand**, a small percentage change in price will usually produce a large change in quantity demanded. If your research reveals **inelastic demand**, a small percentage change in price will usually produce a small percentage change in quantity demanded (see Table 7.2). Keep demand in mind as you prepare your marketing plan, because pricing decisions will significantly affect your ability to achieve sales and market share objectives.

MARKETING IN PRACTICE: PIRATE OR PAY?

Piracy is a major issue for the UK film studios and retailers, which lose millions of pounds every year to unauthorised DVD duplication and illegal movie downloads and sharing. In fact, DVD sales are falling as an estimated 7 million consumers illegally download entertainment content every year without paying. In one recent survey, three-quarters of the consumers who responded agreed with the idea of paying for cinema tickets and DVD rentals – yet fewer than half of the respondents thought they should pay for entertainment when downloaded or viewed online. The challenge for the industry has therefore been to discourage pirating and encourage paying.

In the past, hard-edged anti-piracy campaigns focused on the criminal aspect and warned of prosecution and imprisonment. Now the Industry Trust for IP [Intellectual Property] Awareness, supported by members such as the UK Film Council, Cineworld, HMV, Odeon and Granada Ventures, is adopting an attitude of gratitude, encouraging consumers to pay because the revenue supports their favourite actors, movies and programmes. With the theme 'You make the movies', the campaign emphasises the positive benefits. One advert thanked viewers for paying, saying: 'Your cinema ticket helps support the film industry in the UK. Thank you.' As the campaign began, Actor Matt Di Angelo, of the television programme *Hustle*, was quoted as saying that consumers 'need to realise that it's only by buying official DVDs, downloads and cinema tickets that we can enjoy the TV dramas and blockbuster films that we watch on a regular basis'.[13] Will this campaign reduce instances of piracy and illegal downloads?

Table 7.2	Pricing and elasticity of demand	
Pricing decision	**Inelastic demand**	**Elastic demand**
Small decrease	Small increase in demand	Larger increase in demand
Small increase	Small decrease in demand	Larger decrease in demand

Note that you can actually maintain or increase revenues by raising the price when demand is inelastic or by cutting the price when demand is elastic. Still, if you price a product excessively high, you risk reducing demand; price it too low and you may spark strong demand that you cannot profitably satisfy. Yet it can be difficult to research the exact elasticity of demand for a particular product, even though you can conduct pricing experiments and analyse sales history to get data for estimating the elasticity of demand. Remember that elasticity of demand can vary widely from one segment to another and one market to another.

Another consideration for marketers who target customers in other countries is the effect of currency fluctuations in foreign-exchange markets. Multinational corporations such as Unilever and Procter & Gamble must think about the effect of foreign-exchange rates when they import or export and buy from suppliers in other regions. Currency fluctuations – especially sudden or exchange changes – can push profit margins up or down, depending on the foreign-exchange situation and the prices set in each country.

Competition

Whether the product is confectionery or cars, competition exerts a strong influence on pricing decisions. Customers look at the costs and benefits of competing products when thinking about value, so be aware of what competitors are charging. However, it's risky to imitate another organisation's pricing simply for competitive reasons, because your organisation probably has very different costs, objectives and resources from those of your rival.

Should you become involved in a price war, your profit margins and prices will fall lower and lower. Another risk is that your product could face price competition from products that meet customers' needs in different ways, as when travellers can choose between air travel and train travel. In the planning process, therefore, you should consider any substitutes your customers might choose to meet their needs and how these choices could affect your pricing decisions. In addition, if customers become accustomed to waiting for price wars before they buy, you may have difficulty selling at what you previously considered to be normal pricing levels.

Price wars have broken out in many industries as competitors fight for customers and revenue.

MARKETING IN PRACTICE: PRICE WARS

For the past decade, Sony, Microsoft and Nintendo have become involved in periodic price wars as they cut prices on their video-game consoles to acquire new buyers and increase market share, particularly during the pre-Christmas buying season. Although steep price cuts mean lower per-unit revenue, these companies also gain from ongoing sales of games and accessories. As a result, the console marketers are willing to battle for customers during a short-term price war because they anticipate higher overall revenue in the long run.

Price wars often break out in the supermarket industry, where Tesco, Aldi and other competitors cut prices on selected items to bring shoppers into their stores or to defend market share when a rival store opens nearby. Mobile broadband marketers have used price wars to appeal to specific customer segments and increase revenue from non-voice services. During the recent financial crisis, many new car dealers survived by engaging in price wars. The objective was to attract buyers who otherwise might have purchased used cars or would not have bought any cars until the economic climate improved. Once economic conditions improved and new models were introduced, the dealers took less aggressive pricing measures.[14]

Channel members

When making channel arrangements, you must ensure that wholesalers and retailers can buy at a price that will allow profitable resale to business customers or consumers. Channel members have to be able to cover the costs they incur in processing customer orders, repackaging bulk shipment lots into customer-size lots, product storage and other operations. To make this work, think carefully about the costs and profit margins of all channel participants, along with the price perceptions of the targeted customer segment, when setting your product's price. (Note that when channel members discount selected items or participate in price wars, they typically have their own price objectives – such as defending market share.)

Even your choice of intermediaries depends on your product's price. If you market high-quality, high-priced products, you will have difficulty reaching your targeted segment through intermediaries known for stocking low-quality, low-priced products. If you market lower-quality, low-priced products, upmarket stores will not stock your products because of the mismatch with their target market. In short, carefully coordinate your channel decisions with your price decisions.

Legal, regulatory and ethical considerations

You have to abide by local, national and regional laws and regulations when planning to price your products. Among the kinds of issues your marketing plan should cover are:

- *Price controls and price fixing.* Some countries control the prices of products such as prescription drugs, which limits pricing choices. Some areas also forbid the use of price fixing and other actions considered anti-competitive.

- *Resale maintenance.* Companies in the United Kingdom and some other nations are generally not allowed to insist that channel members maintain a certain minimum price on their products. This paves the way for more competition and reinforces the need to consider pricing throughout the channel.

- *Industry regulation.* Government regulators can affect pricing in some industries by allowing or blocking the sale of certain products or bundles.

- *Government requirements.* Legal and regulatory actions can affect pricing by mandating product standards, tests or labelling; these requirements add to the costs that you will seek to recoup through product pricing.

- *Taxes and tariffs.* Prices for products sold in certain countries must include value-added tax (VAT) or sales taxes, which vary from nation to nation. In addition, import tariffs raise the price that customers pay for some products. Government taxes on services can also affect pricing decisions. Discount carrier Ryanair recently reduced its flights to and from certain British and Irish airports because 'increased travel taxes are affecting our ability to offer the lowest fares', according to an airline spokesperson.[15]

Going beyond legal and regulatory guidelines, look at the ethical implications. For example, is an airline or bank acting ethically when it promotes a special price without fully and prominently explaining any restrictions and extra fees? Is a pharmaceutical manufacturer acting ethically when it sets high prices for a life-saving drug that patients in some areas cannot afford? As challenging as such issues may be, building a reputation for ethical pricing ultimately enhances your brand's image and reinforces long-term customer loyalty.

MAKING PRICING DECISIONS

Once you understand the external and internal influences on pricing, you can set pricing objectives for the period covered by the marketing plan. If your product is new, you will decide between market-skimming and market-penetration pricing. As your product line expands, you will face decisions about pricing multiple products and you may need to plan to adapt your product's price.

Setting pricing objectives

Your objectives for pricing will be based on your organisation's objectives and those of the marketing plan. There are three categories of pricing objectives:

- *Financial objectives for pricing.* You may seek to maintain or improve profits, maintain or improve revenues, reach the break-even point by a certain date, support another product's revenues and profitability, or achieve a certain return.

- *Marketing objectives for pricing.* Here, you set relationship targets for pricing that will attract or retain customers, build or defend market share, build or change channel relations, or build brand image, awareness and loyalty.

- *Societal objectives for pricing.* You may set targets for covering the cost of using ecologically friendly materials and processes, providing reverse channels for recycling, generating cash for charitable contributions, or achieving other non-business objectives.

To illustrate, London is one of a growing number of cities that has set the societal objective of using pricing to reduce traffic jams and pollution. London charges drivers a fee of £8 to take their vehicles into central districts during weekdays. Local residents receive a discount, and certain vehicles (such as ambulances and taxis) pay nothing. The fee has cut daily traffic by 70,000 vehicles, increased the average speed during peak times and raised money to pay for public transportation improvements.[16]

Pricing new products

A new product presents a special pricing challenge because you must decide whether to use **market-penetration pricing** and price relatively low for rapid acquisition of market share or use **market-skimming pricing**, setting a relatively high price to skim maximum revenues from the market, layer by layer. With market-penetration pricing, the price may be so low that the product is unprofitable and/or priced lower than competing products in the short term. Yet such pricing may be effective in the long run if you are determined to boost volume and gain efficiencies that will lower costs as a foundation for future profitability.

Market-penetration pricing is not appropriate for every product, which is where internal and external influences come into play. Your customers may perceive less value in a luxury product that is launched with market-penetration pricing, for example. Also, market-penetration pricing may be inappropriate for the kinds of channel members you need to use to reach targeted customer segments. Finally, such pricing may not be consistent with your promotion decisions.

Apple, maker of iPhones, iPods and Mac computers, prefers market-skimming pricing for its new products. This pricing decision supports Apple's profitability as well as its cutting-edge image for new technology, design and features. When the company introduces a new model of an existing product – such as a new iPod Touch or Nano – it typically reduces the price of older models. This pricing decision clarifies the positioning of different products in the line and reinforces the distinction between newer and older models.[17]

You should consider market-skimming pricing for innovative or top-quality products, to make an upmarket impression on selected customer segments that are less price sensitive and place a premium on innovation. Market-skimming pricing is common with products employing new technology such as digital radio receivers. Not only do you take in more money to help cover costs with this approach, you have the flexibility to lower prices as you monitor competitive response, attain volumes that yield economies of scale and shift to targeting more price-sensitive segments. If your initial price is too high, however, you may set customer expectations too high, slow initial sales and lower repeat sales if the product does not fulfil those expectations.

Pricing multiple products

Your plan for pricing should take into account more than one product in the line or mix, any optional or complementary products and any product bundles. The way you price each product sets it apart from other products in your mix, reflecting or reinforcing customer perceptions of each product's value. You can then balance prices within the product line or mix to reach your total revenue or profit objectives. As an example, price competition among lower-priced models of car may produce slimmer profits for a carmaker even as prices on upmarket vehicles boost profit margins for those products.[18]

In services, a hotel company may market deluxe hotels, convention hotels and modestly priced tourist hotels, each with its own target market, pricing objectives and room rates in line with the perceived value. Many airlines market different classes of travel, charging higher prices for first class and business class than for economy class. Each class comes with specific features and benefits such as roomier seats for comfort, differentiations that are reflected in the price.

If you offer a bundle of goods or services you must determine how to price that bundle, given the competition and customers' perceptions of the bundle's value. One advantage of bundling is that competitors can't easily duplicate every aspect of a unique, specially priced bundle. If customers do not want everything in your bundle at the price set, however, they may buy fewer products individually or look at competitive bundles. And later in a product's life cycle, you may get more benefit by unbundling and pricing each part separately.

Adapting prices

Your plan should allow for adapting prices when appropriate, either by increasing perceived value or by reducing perceived cost. Depending on local laws and regulations – and the rest of your marketing plan – some ways in which you can adapt prices include:

- *Discounts.* You can plan special discounts for customers who buy in large quantities or during non-peak periods, pay in cash, or assume logistical functions such as picking up products that would otherwise be delivered.

- *Allowances.* You can invite customers to trade in older products and receive credit towards purchases of newer products. You may also offer customers refunds or rebates for buying during promotional periods.

- *Extra value.* To encourage intermediaries to carry your products, you may offer small quantities free when resellers place orders during a promotional period. For consumers, you may temporarily increase the amount of product without increasing the price.

- *Periodic mark-downs.* Retailers, in particular, plan to mark down merchandise periodically, at the end of a selling season, to attract or reward shoppers or to stimulate new product trial.

- *Segmented pricing.* Depending on your segmentation decisions, your pricing can be adapted for customers of different ages (such as lower prices for children and older customers), members and non-members (such as lower prices for professional association members), different purchase locations (such as lower prices for products bought and picked up at the main plant) and time of purchase (such as lower prices for mobile phone service during non-peak periods).

Internal or external influences may prompt you to raise or lower a product's price. For example, you can use a price cut to stimulate higher demand or defend against competitive price reductions. You may want to use a price increase to deal with rising costs or product improvements that raise perceived quality and value. Whether such price adaptations achieve their objectives will depend on customer and competitor reaction.

Planning for prices to vary

Some marketing plans call for pricing that isn't fixed but instead varies under certain circumstances. With **dynamic pricing**, marketers vary their prices from buyer to buyer or situation to situation. Most airlines plan for dynamic pricing, using software that aims to maximise the revenue for each flight. The software adjusts airfares depending on historical and actual demand for the flight, competition, the number of seats allocated to each class of service, the number of seats unfilled at a given time and other factors.[19]

If you're preparing a marketing plan for business goods or services or for certain expensive consumer products, you should be prepared for **negotiated pricing**, in which buyer and seller negotiate and then confirm the final price and details of the offer by contract. Some business and consumer marketers use **auction pricing**, inviting buyers to submit bids to buy goods or services through a traditional auction (such as those conducted by Sotheby's) or an online auction (such as those on eBay).

Auction pricing can be a good way to market excess or out-of-date stock to price-sensitive customers without affecting the fixed price set for other segments. It can also be used for special marketing situations. For example, Fox's Biscuits recently held a series of charity auctions on eBay for items that 'belonged' to Vinnie the Panda, the star of its adverts. Publicised on Twitter, Facebook and Fox's website, as well as through media contacts, the auctions raised money to benefit Crimestoppers.[20]

CHAPTER SUMMARY

Customers perceive a product's value according to the total benefits weighed against the total costs, in the context of competitive products and prices. During the planning process, marketers must research how customers perceive the value of their product and the value of competing products and, ideally, work backwards using the perceived value to make price, cost and product decisions. Internal influences on pricing decisions are organisational and marketing plan objectives, costs, targeting and positioning, product decisions and life cycle, and other marketing-mix decisions. External influences on pricing decisions are customers, market and demand, competition, channel members, and legal, regulatory and ethical considerations.

Two approaches to pricing new products are market-penetration pricing (to capture market share quickly) and market-skimming pricing (to skim maximum revenues from each market layer). Depending on local laws and regulations and the rest of the marketing plan, marketers can adapt prices using discounts, allowances, extra value, periodic mark-downs or segmented pricing. A marketing plan may not call for fixed prices but instead have prices that vary according to dynamic pricing, negotiated pricing or auction pricing.

CASE STUDY: IKEA PLANS FOR AFFORDABLE, PROFITABLE PRICING

The mission of Swedish furniture retailer Ikea is to improve everyday life by 'offering a wide range of well-designed, functional home-furnishings products at prices so low that as many people as possible will be able to afford them'.[21] With 300 stores in 36 countries and £17 billion in annual turnover, Ikea sells most of its stylish goods packed flat for customers to assemble at home – saving space and money at the same time. Although low prices are a high priority, the company's marketing plans also take into account sustainability and ecological issues.

Ikea's marketers carefully research customer needs, examine value perceptions and check competitive pricing to understand the current market situation. As they design a new product, they set a target price lower than rivals, estimate costs and plan features and specifications appropriate for the target price. They take into consideration sustainability as they consult with suppliers and come to agreement on costs and materials before they design the product, have it manufactured and ship it to stores.

As both manufacturer and distributor, Ikea can set its own retail prices with an eye towards profitability. However, its marketers must also follow legal and regulatory guidelines, which can affect costs and pricing from market to market. When Ikea opened its Dublin store, some of its prices were higher than in its UK stores, because of the Republic's higher VAT rate. Following local planning rules, the Dublin store also had to charge extra for using its car park during peak evening traffic periods, the only Ikea store in Europe to impose such fees.

Ikea's marketers are always looking for ways to improve internal efficiency, going so far as to switch fonts in the printed catalogue to save money. During the economic crisis, they scaled back expansion plans and lowered sales forecasts as consumers slowed their buying in most of the markets where Ikea has stores. What's ahead for Ikea's pricing plans as the global economy recovers?[22]

Case questions

1. Is Ikea using value-based pricing or cost-based pricing? How do you know? What are the implications for its marketing plans?

2. Which specific external and internal factors seem to be especially important influences on Ikea's pricing? Why must its marketers pay close attention to these particular influences when they plan for pricing?

 **APPLY YOUR KNOWLEDGE**

Choose a particular business product (such as a tractor or specialised software) and research the marketer's approach to pricing. Then write up your ideas or give an oral presentation to the class.

- What benefits does this product appear to offer to business customers?

- What initial and ongoing costs would business customers perceive in connection with buying and maintaining this product?

- If the product is new, what pricing approach is the company using to launch it? Why is this approach appropriate for the product?

- How does the price reflect the product's positioning and other marketing-mix decisions?

- How does the price of one competing or substitute product appear to reflect that product's value (from the customer's perspective)? If you were a customer, would you place a higher value on this competing product than on the product you have been researching? Why?

 **BUILD YOUR OWN MARKETING PLAN**

Continue developing your marketing plan by making pricing decisions about a new or existing product. What pricing objectives will you set for this product? If the product is new, will you use market-skimming pricing or market-penetration pricing – and why? Which external influences are most important to the pricing of this product? How do internal influences affect your pricing decision for this product? What price will you set for this one product and in what situations would you consider adapting the price? Would auction pricing or negotiated pricing be appropriate? Consider how these pricing decisions fit in with earlier marketing decisions and with the objectives you've set, then document them in your marketing plan.

STOP ENDNOTES

1. Quoted in Steve Hawkes, 'Block party', *The Sun*, 18 August 2009, www.thesun.co.uk.

2. 'Strong demand builds Lego sales', *BBC News*, 17 August 2009, http://news.bbc.co.uk/2/hi/business/8205974.stm; Steve Hawkes, 'Block party', *The Sun*, 18 August 2009, www.thesun.co.uk; Nelson D. Schwartz, 'Beyond the blocks', *New York Times*, 6 September 2009, pp. BU-1, BU-6; Adam Hartley, 'Official Lego iPhone photo app launches', *TechRadar.com*, 31 December 2009, www.techradar.com.

3. Chris Nuttall and David Gelles, 'Social game groups scrap over virtual spoils', *Financial Times*, 29 June 2009, www.ft.com; Chris Nuttall, 'Social gaming platforms closer to cashing in', *Financial Times Techblog*, 24 June 2009, www.blogs.ft.com/techblog; Alex Farber, 'Nokia Ovi app store reaches 10m downloads', *New Media Age*, 4 September 2009, www.nma.co.uk; Rupert Neate, 'Microsoft, Nokia, Orange and O2 challenge Apple's 'App Store'', *Telegraph*, 16 February 2009, www.telegraph.co.uk/finance.

4. This section draws on concepts in Thomas T. Nagle and John E. Hogan, *The Strategy and Tactics of Pricing*, 4th edn (Upper Saddle River, NJ: Pearson Prentice Hall, 2006).

5. Mary Portas, 'Shop! Mary Portas visits Aldi', *Telegraph*, 23 July 2009, www.telegraph.co.uk/foodanddrink; Gemma Soames, 'The rise of the Aldirati', *Sunday Times*, 26 April 2009, http://women.timesonline.co.uk; James Thompson, 'Credit crisis helps Aldi sales head for £2bn', *The Independent*, 7 November 2008, www.independent.co.uk; Suzanne Campbell, 'How Aldi changed the way we shop', *Independent Digital*, 27 August 2009, www.independent.ie/lifestyle/food-drink; Cecilie Rohwedder and David Kesmodel, 'Aldi looks to US for growth', *Wall Street Journal*, 13 January 2009, p. B1.

6. Michael Malakata, 'Nokia launches low-cost handsets in Africa', *ComputerWorld Kenya*, 10 April 2008, http://www.computerworld.co.ke/articles/2008/04/10/nokia-launches-low-cost-handsets-africa.

7. Catherine Boyle, 'S&N lifted profit but we wouldn't pay £7.6bn now, says Heineken', *Times Online*, 27 August 2009, http://business.timesonline.co.uk.

8. C.K. Prahalad, 'In volatile times, agility rules', *BusinessWeek*, 21 September 2009, p. 80.

9. Quoted in Alexandra Steigrad, 'Tiffany maintains outlook for year despite fall in net', *WWD*, 1 June 2009, p. 13.

10. Quoted in Brian Burnsed, 'Where discounting can be dangerous', *BusinessWeek*, 23 July 2009, p. 49. Other sources: Vanessa O'Connell and Amelie Baubeau, 'Corporate news: Tiffany struggles, sees signs of hope', *Wall Street Journal*, 29 August 2009, p. B5; Rachel Dodes, 'Corporate news: Tiffany unit shut down as jeweler struggles', *Wall Street Journal*, 11 March 2009, p. B3; Kumar Alagappan, 'Gem Diamonds signs supply deal with Tiffany unit', *Reuters*, 22 December 2009, www.reuters.com

11. This section draws on concepts in Thomas T. Nagle and John E. Hogan, *The Strategy and Tactics of Pricing*, 4th edn (Upper Saddle River, NJ: Pearson Prentice Hall, 2006).

12. Daniel J. Howard and Roger A. Kerin, 'Broadening the scope of reference price advertising research', *Journal of Marketing*, October 2006, pp. 185–204; Wayne D. Hoyer and Deborah J. MacInnis, *Consumer Behaviour*, 5th edn (Mason, OH: South-Western Cengage, 2010), p. 261.

13. Quoted in 'Film and TV stars back 'pay for downloads' campaign', *Telegraph*, 7 September 2009, www.telegraph.co.uk/culture/tvandra-

dio; also: Mark Sweney, 'Anti-piracy campaign aims to win over Generation Y-pay of internet users', *Guardian*, 7 September 2009, www.guardian.co.uk/technology; Mark Sweney, 'Campaign against film piracy tells moviegoers how precious they are', *Guardian*, 2 April 2009, www.guardian.co.uk/media; Harry Wallop, 'DVD sales fall for first time', *Telegraph*, 20 June 2009, www.telegraph.co.uk/technology.

14. 'Microsoft slash £100 off Xbox 360 in console price war', *Daily Mail*, 28 August 2009, www.dailymail.co.uk/sciencetech; Nic Fildes, 'Orange dongle deal kickstarts mobile broadband price war', *Times Online*, 5 August 2009, http://business.timesonline.co.uk; 'Aldi joins price wars with raft of 99p products', *Retail Week*, 24 April 2009, www.retail-week.com.

15. Quoted in Oliver Smith, 'Ryanair scraps services from Robin Hood Airport', *Telegraph*, 26 August 2009, www.telegraph.co.uk/travel; also: David Robertson and Robert Lindsay, 'Ryanair and easyJet spark airport price war', *The Times*, 18 August 2009, http://business.timesonline.co.uk.

16. 'In praise of ... London's congestion charge', *The Guardian*, 7 August 2008, www.guardian.co.uk; Daniel Gross, 'What's the toll? It depends on the time of day', *New York Times*, 11 February 2007, sec. 3, p. 7.

17. Shane Richmond, 'Apple event: everything we expected and less', *Telegraph*, 9 September 2009, http://blogs.telegraph.co.uk/technology; Yukari Iwatani Kane, 'Live-blogging Apple's iPod event', *Wall Street Journal*, 9 September 2009, http://blogs.wsj.com/digits.

18. Gail Edmondson, 'Classy cars', *BusinessWeek*, 24 March 2003, pp. 62–6.

19. Chris Rivers 'If airlines are in trouble, why are planes so full?', *McLeans*, 13 August 2009, http://www2.macleans.ca/2009/08/13/if-airlines-are-in-trouble-why-are-planes-so-full.

20. Chris Wilson, 'Fictional biscuit panda Vinnie raises cash for Crimestoppers', *The Mirror*, 3 August 2009, www.mirror.co.uk/news.

21. Ikea, *Our Business Idea*, www.ikea.com/ms/en_GB/about_ikea/the_ikea_way/our_business_idea/index.html.

22. Kate Watson-Smyth, 'Ikea: Flat pack and fabulous', *The Independent*, 14 October 2009, www.independent.co.uk; Simon Garfield, 'Verdana: Ikea's flat-pack font', *Guardian*, 2 September 2009, www.guardian.co.uk; 'Belfast Ikea has an edge on price over Dublin store', *Belfast Telegraph*, 23 July 2009, www.belfasttelegraph.co.uk; Peter Ranscombe, 'Ikea axes more jobs as slump in housing market takes toll', *Scotsman*, 8 July 2009, http://business.scotsman.com/consumerspending/Ikea; 'Ikea opens first store in Republic of Ireland', *Retail Week*, 28 July 2009, www.retail-week.com; 'Swedish home furnisher finds British market its weakest link', *Sunday Business*, 3 January 2007, www.thebusinessonline.com; Lisa Margonelli, 'How Ikea designs its sexy price tags', *Business 2.0*, October 2002, pp. 106–12; Tom Molloy, 'Shoppers here pay top dollar for IKEA icon', *Independent*, 10 September 2009, www.independent.ie; 'IKEA finally opens Dublin store', *RTE Business*, 27 July 2009, www.ret.ie/business/2009/0727/ikea.html.

Comprehension outcomes

After studying this chapter, you will be able to:

- Explain the roles of the value chain, marketing channels and logistics
- Describe the various channel levels and intermediaries
- Contrast exclusive, selective and intensive distribution
- Understand the balance between logistics costs and customer services

Application outcomes

After studying this chapter, you will be able to:

- Analyse the value chain for a good or service
- Decide on the number of channel levels and members
- Analyse and plan for logistics

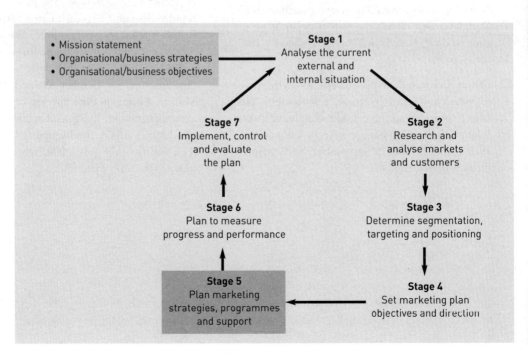

CHAPTER PREVIEW: TESCO, FOOD AND FINANCE SUPERMARKET

Building on its positive brand equity, strong customer relationships and extensive network of shops, Tesco has turned itself into a supermarket for food, finance and much more. Since 1997, the UK retailer's long-term growth strategy has been to expand into non-food offerings and enter new markets in Europe, Asia and North America. Customers can browse and buy when and where they like, whether they prefer to visit a nearby shop, click on one of Tesco's websites or place orders by phone. The food and household choices include goods from well-known manufacturers like Cadbury and Walkers plus Tesco's own-label value, discount and premium products.

Tesco Personal Finance (TPF), the company's financial services division, has 6 million customers and operates more than 3,000 cash points. TPF has more than two dozen offerings, from car and household insurance – in partnership with the insurer Fortis – to credit cards, savings accounts and personal loans; its marketing plan calls for offering current accounts and home mortgages in the near future. Tests of banking and insurance branches inside Tesco shops in Glasgow, Coventry, Blackpool and other cities will determine whether the division can increase both turnover and profits by opening additional branches.[1]

Tesco is a good example of the marketing-mix tool of 'place', how a company profits by enabling customers to take possession of a product in a convenient place and time, in a convenient form and quantity and at an acceptable price. Planning for this part of the marketing mix can be complex because these decisions must fit with your other marketing decisions while simultaneously meeting customers' needs and organisational objectives.

This chapter opens with an overview of the value chain and its effect on marketing planning. Next, you'll learn about planning for flows and responsibilities within the value chain, then consider decisions about channel levels and individual channel members. Finally, you'll gain insights into logistical issues that must be addressed as you plan. Use this chapter's checklists to think through decisions about channels and logistics during the planning process. The sample marketing plan, in the Appendix, illustrates how a marketer might summarise and explain ideas for channels and logistics for the coming year.

ANALYSING THE VALUE CHAIN

The **value chain**, also known as the *value delivery network* or *supply chain*, is the succession of interrelated, value-added functions undertaken by the marketer with suppliers, wholesalers, retailers and other participants (including customers) to source supplies and ultimately deliver a product that fulfils customers' needs. Figure 8.1 shows a simplified value chain and explains the key areas to be analysed during the marketing planning process. The point is to understand how each participant in the chain adds value to the good or service that your customers buy and use. Then your marketing plan can reflect a 'performance' view of the chain, including activities to enhance the combined efficiency and effectiveness of all partners, where possible.

Decisions about adding value inbound:

- How to manage suppliers and obtain materials plus other needed inputs (locating suppliers, buying parts, printing product manuals, etc.)
- How to manage logistics (arranging physical, informational and financial flows related to inbound orders, supply availability, deliveries, etc.)

Decisions about adding value through the marketer's functions:

- How to manage flows in marketing (interpreting market data to understand customer needs, developing suitable products and distribution, communicating product differentiation, etc.)
- How to manage flows to transform inputs into outputs (manufacturing tangible items, delivering intangible services)
- How to manage flows through customer service and internal operations (responding to customer enquiries, managing materials, etc.)

Decisions about adding value outbound:

- How to manage product availability for convenient customer interactions (arranging direct or indirect channels, selecting and supervising channel members to handle transactions, etc.)
- How to manage logistics (arranging physical, informational and financial flows related to allocating quantities and assortments to meet demand, expedite transportation, manage inventory, etc.)

Customers

| **FIGURE 8.1** | Areas of focus in a simplified value chain |

Imagine Heinz as the central link of the value chain. In its role as producer, it is responsible for coordinating the transformation of inputs (beans and spices, for instance) into outputs (baked beans) as well as inbound functions that occur upstream (bringing ingredients to food-production facilities) and outbound functions that occur downstream (getting canned goods to stores). The value added downstream occurs within a **marketing channel** (also known as a **distribution channel**), the set of functions performed by the producer or intermediaries, such as retailers, to make a particular product available to customers. Tesco, Morrisons, Ocado and other retailers are part of Heinz's marketing channel, buying its beans and ketchup to resell to consumers through shops and websites (all on the outbound side).

The profitable flow of products, information and payments inbound and outbound to meet customer requirements is accomplished through **logistics**. One or more parties must handle inbound transportation of ingredients and packaging materials so Heinz can produce its foods. Heinz or one of its suppliers must maintain inventory levels of food ingredients to ensure that sufficient quantities are on hand when needed. Heinz also has to track production quantities, accept and fill retailers' orders and despatch cartons of its foods to retailers on the outbound side of the value chain.

In planning for channel and logistics decisions, you should take into account the needs and behaviour of targeted customer segments, your SWOT analysis and competitive situation, your product's positioning and your marketing plan objectives. Then consider which functions in the value chain must be accomplished and which participants should be responsible for each. These decisions lay the groundwork for adding value and meeting customers' needs at an acceptable cost to the customer and an acceptable profit to the organisation.

Also think about how technology applies to your channel and logistics situation. For example, the BBC and other entertainment providers can take advantage of digital technology to deliver programmes on demand, when and where viewers want. The ability to deliver a good or service 'on demand' is another option to consider during your channel and logistics planning. Because of the number of alternatives available to you, you should analyse a variety of channel and logistics arrangements before you make a final decision and document it in your marketing plan.

Zara's careful management of its value chain has helped the retailer become a leader in 'fast fashion'.

MARKETING IN PRACTICE: ZARA

The Zara retail chain, based in Spain, has earned a reputation for moving quickly when a style takes off. Once its designers identify a new trend – with insights from store managers worldwide – they can have new fashions manufactured and on display in company stores within two to five weeks. Knowing that today's most in-demand style may be unwanted tomorrow, Zara makes much of its clothing in Spain, Portugal and Morocco, close to the company's design centre. Its plants use cutting-edge just-in-time systems to manage the flow of materials inbound, plan the timing of production and handle outbound details; its distribution experts use sophisticated software to track international shipments and customs documentation.

As a result, Zara has an extraordinary level of control over distribution and logistics and can restock its thousands of stores worldwide very quickly. It speeds merchandise by lorry from its centrally located warehouses to its European stores for next-day delivery and sends in-demand goods by air to stores outside Europe for two-day delivery. Customers know to stop by regularly because Zara stores receive small shipments of hot new merchandise all the time. By controlling supply and transportation costs, and offering customers the styles they want before fads fade, Zara has increased turnover and kept profit margins high.[2]

The value chain for services

If your marketing plan is for a service, be aware that your value chain should put particular focus on inbound activities, the service experience itself and outbound activities that involve the customer. Inbound functions cover supplies, information and payments related to providing the service; the service experience occurs in the central link (if delivered by your firm); and outbound functions cover service availability plus associated information and payments. Logistics for services are concerned with having the right supplies (and people) in the right place at the right time. Moreover, because services are perishable – they cannot be stored for future sale or consumption – your plan must carefully manage all flows to balance supply and demand.

Some services are using a variety of online channel connections to connect with customers. As an example, the Royal Society for the encouragement of Arts, Manufactures and Commerce (RSA) markets its London building as a venue that's elegant and 'green' for weddings, corporate meetings and other special events. In addition to maintaining its own website, the RSA markets through ethicalweddings.com, an online service that helps couples find venues, caterers, florists and other suppliers for the big day. RSA's marketing materials explain how it manages its outbound value chain to promote sustainability and reduce its carbon footprint – issues that are important to many customers seeking to rent a room or a building for a special occasion.[3]

Flows and responsibilities in the value chain

Each participant in the value chain is responsible for certain functions and activities that help make goods and services available to customers in the next link of the chain. Having a wide variety of supplies, materials or products immediately available at all times in all locations (or ready to be despatched quickly on demand) is the most desirable situation but often too costly for an organisation and its customers. Yet customers are likely to be unsatisfied – and may turn to competitors – if a marketer has too few supplies or products available, the wrong quantities or models available, and/or slow or expensive transactions. When you plan your value chain, therefore, you will face difficult trade-offs between value added and cost.

Ensuring the quality and integrity of ingredients, production and packaging is a particularly vital responsibility in the value chain for food. When tainted milk sickened more than 250,000 children in China, government testing revealed melamine contamination in dairy products made by a number of large local producers. Many consumers concerned about quality switched to buying dairy products made by the Swiss food marketer Nestlé, which operates its own plants in China and was not implicated in the scandal. Nestlé soon expanded its Chinese research and development centres, implemented even stricter testing procedures and wound up winning higher brand recognition and market share.[4]

Reverse channels

Your marketing plan should consider the need for a **reverse channel**, a flow that moves backwards through the value chain to return goods for service or when worn out and to reclaim products, parts or packaging for recycling. This is particularly important if you're marketing online and want to reassure customers that they can return or exchange what they buy. Amazon.com, for example, has arranged with a specialised company to handle any customer returns, which frees the retailer to concentrate on its retailing business.[5] In establishing reverse channels for recycling broken or outdated appliances and consumer electronics products, UK and European manufacturers and retailers must comply with Waste Electrical and Electronic Equipment (WEEE) regulations.

Properly planned and implemented, reverse channels can offer opportunities for enhancing sustainability and may help differentiate products or brands as eco-leaders. However, some companies have been accused of **greenwashing**, meaning that consumers perceive these companies as marketing products or brands on the basis of 'green' activities that have little or no actual ecological impact. Therefore, when you plan for reverse channels to handle recycling or other green activities, be sure your arrangements will lead to the desired outcome and help you reach your objectives.

Here's a brief look at reverse channels for recycling electronics products.

MAKETING IN PRACTICE: REVERSE CHANNELS FOR ELECTRONICS RECYCLING

Manufacturers and retailers follow a variety of marketing plans for ensuring that reverse channels are available for recycling electronics and appliances such as PCs, mobiles and televisions. Dell is a good example of a manufacturer that plans for its own reverse channels to ensure ecologically safe disposal of old or unwanted products in every country where it markets its computer equipment. Some UK appliance retailers, such as Comet and Selfridges, have banded together in a Distributor Take Back Scheme that provides a common reverse channel for recycling the electronics products they sell.

Electronics recycling has grown into a marketing opportunity for some businesses and a fundraising opportunity for some charities. Manchester-based Eazyfone is a fast-growing small business that is profiting from increased public interest in recycling used mobiles. Air Miles offers points for members who recycle their old mobiles through the travel reward programme's partner, ShP Limited. ShP runs other mobile recycling schemes as well, including one in which consumers who sell their old mobiles to ShP can request that some of the proceeds be donated to the charity of their choice.[6]

PLANNING FOR CHANNELS TODAY

Depending on your organisation's situation and objectives, you can plan for a value chain that includes direct or indirect channels. With **direct channels**, you make products available directly to customers. For example, Ikea uses direct channels, marketing its furniture and home wares through its own stores, its own retail website and its own catalogues. With **indirect channels**, you work through **intermediaries**, outside businesses or individuals that help producers make goods or services available to customers. To illustrate, the entertainment company Walt Disney works with major retail chains in India to distribute its video products and uses a wholesaler channel to get its videos into smaller shops around India.[7]

Figure 8.2 shows how goods or services would reach customers through direct and indirect channels. It also shows the three major types of intermediaries, each of which adds value in a particular way:

- **Wholesalers** buy from producers, sort and store products, create smaller lots for buyer convenience and resell to other intermediaries or to business customers. Some take on duties normally handled elsewhere in the value chain, such as monitoring a customer's inventory.

- **Retailers** are companies such as Selfridges, Mothercare, Amazon.com and Carrefour that buy from producers and resell products, giving consumers easy and convenient access to an array of products. Many retailers also sell their own range of private-label products in their stores, on their websites and in their catalogues. Amazon also serves as a channel for other retailers that want to reach customers online.

- **Representatives, brokers and agents** (such as insurance agents) bring producers together with customers but generally do not take ownership of the products they market. These intermediaries add value through their knowledge of the market, customers and products.

Channel arrangements take time to plan and implement because you'll be working through a variety of intermediaries and each will have its own objectives and plans. Therefore, although today's business environment is highly dynamic, it usually takes time to add, eliminate or modify channels if you identify changes in your marketing situation.

In your marketing plan, you will have to specify the number of intermediary levels you want to use for each product – in other words, the length of the channel.

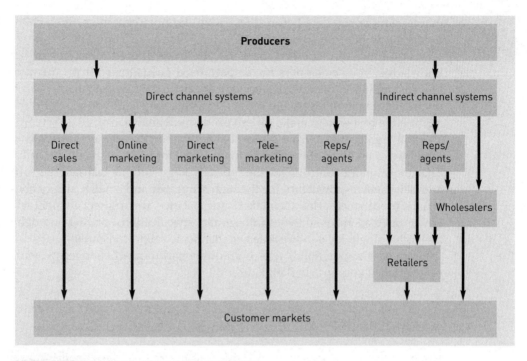

FIGURE 8.2	Marketing channel arrangements

Source: Adapted from *BEST, ROGER J., MARKET-BASED MANAGEMENT: STRATEGIES FOR GROWING CUSTOMER VALUE AND PROFITABILITY, 2nd,©2000.* Prentice Hall, p.199. Reproduced by permission of Pearson Education, Inc., Upper Saddle River, New Jersey.

Channel length decisions

Longer channels have more intermediary levels separating the producer and its customers; shorter channels have fewer intermediaries. A direct channel is the shortest because there are no intermediaries and the producer deals directly with its customers through any or all of the methods shown on the left in Figure 8.2. This is appropriate when you want as much control as possible over dealings with customers and your organisation can handle all outbound functions. If your markets and segments are not well defined or you lack the resources and knowledge to work directly with customers, however, using a direct channel can be inefficient at best and ineffective at worst.

The zero-level channel can work well for both business and consumer marketers, despite differences in products, customers, prices and markets. Nippon Steel, one of the world's largest steel producers, uses direct channels to sell to construction companies, carmakers, shipbuilders and other businesses in its home country of Japan and in other markets.

Longer channels, such as the two- and three-level indirect channels illustrated on the right in Figure 8.2, send products through a series of representatives or agents, wholesalers or retailers before they reach the final customer. Such channel arrangements allow intermediaries to add value when your company is targeting multiple or geographically dispersed markets, you have limited resources or little customer knowledge, your customers have specialised needs, or your products require training, customisation or service. Although the price paid by customers reflects a profit for intermediaries at all levels and covers the value they add, you may find that long channels are the best way to make certain products available.

Some organisations use a direct channel for certain segments (usually business customers) and an indirect channel with one level for other segments (usually consumers). This allows more control over the typically large-volume transactions with businesses and delegates responsibility for the higher number and smaller size of consumer transactions to intermediaries. Carmakers, for instance, use a direct channel when selling to government agencies so they can negotiate specifications, pricing and delivery, but use a separate single-level indirect dealer channel to sell to consumers.

Grameen Danone Foods uses both direct and indirect channels to market its nutrition-enriched yoghurts in Bangladesh.

MARKETING IN PRACTICE: GRAMEEN DANONE FOODS

Grameen Danone Foods, a joint venture of the French dairy food firm Danone and Grameen Bank, is a social business dedicated to fighting malnutrition and poverty in and around Bogra, Bangladesh. Grameen Danone buys milk from hundreds of local farmers and produces up to 500,000 pots of enriched yoghurt under the Shokti Doi brand every week. Some of the output is sold through 'Grameen ladies', local entrepreneurs who carry insulated bags to keep the yoghurt chilled as they walk door to door and who earn a small profit on each pot they sell.

More than three-quarters of Grameen Danone's output is transported in refrigerated lorries for distribution through small village stores and larger shops in Bogra and the city of Dhaka, where Shokti Doi is positioned as a snack. These shops receive refrigerators or insulated boxes to keep the yoghurt at the proper temperature. Grameen Danone supports its distributors with an advertising campaign to increase brand awareness and promote the product's benefits. It has also introduced new products and flavours as it gets ready to build additional product facilities and expand distribution into neighbouring regions of Bangladesh.[8]

Channel member decisions

If you decide to work with at least one level of intermediary, your marketing plan should indicate how many and what type of channel members you'll need for each level in each market. These decisions depend on the market, the product and its life cycle, customer needs and behaviour, product pricing and product positioning. Table 8.1 summarises the three broad choices in number of channel members, along with the value for customers, producers and channel members.

Table 8.1 Exclusive, selective and intensive distribution

	Exclusive distribution	Selective distribution	Intensive distribution
Value added for customer	• Individual attention • Knowledgeable sales help • Availability of training, other services	• Choice of outlets in each area • Some services available	• Convenient availability in many areas • Competition among outlets may lower price
Value added for producer	• Reinforces positioning of expensive or technical product • Closer cooperation and exchange of information • More control over service quality	• Ability to cover more of the market • Less dependent on a small number of channel members	• Higher unit sales • Ability to cover an area completely • Lower cost per unit
Value added for channel member	• Association with exclusive brands enhances image • Can become expert in certain product categories and lines • Can tailor services to targeted customers	• Benefit from producer's marketing support in the area • Potential to build sales volume and qualify for higher discounts	• Attract customers seeking high-volume, high-demand offerings • Enhance overall merchandise mix
Concerns for producer	• Higher cost per unit • Potentially reach fewer customers	• Medium costs, medium control	• Less control over service quality • More difficult to supervise • Possible conflict among channel members

If you use **exclusive distribution**, one intermediary will handle your product in a particular area. If you use **selective distribution**, a fairly small number of intermediaries will sell your product in the area. If you use **intensive distribution**, many intermediaries will handle your product in the area. As a producer, how do you choose? As the table indicates, you can enhance the luxury image of upmarket or specialised goods and services by using exclusive distribution. New products that require extensive customer education may be sold in exclusive or selective distribution. Also, products that require expert sales support or for which customers shop around are often marketed through selective distribution. Finally, consider intensive distribution for inexpensive, everyday products – especially impulse items – because of the opportunity to achieve higher sales volumes.

In addition, you have to select specific intermediaries for each channel. In a marketing plan for an existing product or a new entry in an existing line, you may want to reassess the value each member is providing, add more channel members to expand market coverage if needed, and replace ineffective or inefficient members as necessary. As coverage increases, however, so does the possibility for conflict among channel members over customers, market coverage, pricing and other issues.

When preparing a marketing plan for a new or existing product, allow for educating channel members about the product's benefits; they should be induced to promote it actively. Also look ahead to think about whether a particular intermediary will be a strong partner in marketing the product (and possibly later products) now and in the future. Debenhams and Asda are among the growing number of retailers with websites where buyers can rate and review the products they purchase. Ratings and comments help the intermediaries and the producers understand what customers like, dislike and want.[9] Bear in mind that some retailers may stock your product online only, due to limited space in branch shops. And some retailers may give your product special consideration because they want variety in their merchandising assortment.[10]

The following checklist will help you think about channel issues for your marketing plan.

ESSENTIAL MARKETING PLAN CHECKLIST NO. 12:
PLANNING FOR MARKETING CHANNELS

A good channel strategy starts with customer research and a thorough understanding of the current marketing situation. Also consider how channel choices and changes might affect your competitive position and your organisation's ability to achieve its objectives. Place a tick alongside each question below as you note your answer in the space provided.

☐ How do customers prefer or expect to gain access to the product?

_____

☐ What channels and channel members are best suited to the product, positioning and brand image?

_____

☐ What are the organisation's channel costs and will customers pay for access through these channels?

_____

☐ Are the right assortments of products available at the right time and in the right quantities, with appropriate support?

_____

☐ How much control does the organisation want over channel functions?

☐ How can channel decisions be used to manage the product life cycle?

☐ What geographical, ecological, legal and regulatory considerations affect channel decisions?

☐ How many channel levels and members are appropriate, given the organisation's situation, objectives and targeting decisions?

☐ Do channel members have capable sales and support staff, are they equipped to store and display the product and are they financially sound?

PLANNING FOR LOGISTICS TODAY

A good logistics plan can help you compete by serving customers more effectively or by saving money. This is especially important for small businesses and in fast-growing industries, where customer relationships are just being formed. Whatever your plan, you will need clear-cut, non-conflicting objectives. If your objective is to make more products available or get them to customers more quickly, expect your costs to be higher. If your objective is to cut the total cost of logistics, you might maintain lower inventory levels, raising the possibility that you might run out of some products. Your logistics strategy must be realistic for your situation now and in the future, striking a balance between your customers' needs and your organisation's financial, marketing and societal objectives.

Wal-Mart has built a highly profitable retail empire, including its Asda stores, based on its core competency of logistics management. See the box on the next page.

Inventory decisions

Your decisions about inventory must be made even before the first product moves into the channel. Pre-production, you should identify the inventory level of parts and supplies required for the planned output. Post-production, think about how much inventory of a particular product is needed outbound to meet customer demand, balanced with organisational constraints of budgets, production and storage capacity. Zara, for example, produces limited quantities of each fashion, knowing it can get additional inventory to stores in just a few weeks, if needed.

MARKETING IN PRACTICE: WAL-MART AND ASDA

One reason that Wal-Mart has increased annual turnover to £240 billion worldwide and become the largest retailer on the planet is its mastery of logistics. Think of the complexities of getting the right assortment of merchandise from 100,000 suppliers to one of 8,100 Wal-Mart and Asda stores, ready for purchase by the retailer's 200 million weekly shoppers. Thousands more customers click to buy on Walmart.com or Asda.com or other Wal-Mart-owned websites, which only complicates the process of determining what and how much to stock in each store, how to get merchandise from suppliers to distribution centres, and how to fulfil customer orders received online. The company has also asked its suppliers to begin providing detailed data about the ecological impact of each product's production and packaging so it can label merchandise with a 'green rating' and help shoppers make more informed buying decisions.

In many areas, Wal-Mart gives online shoppers the option of picking up their purchases in a local store rather than paying to have items shipped to a home or business address. To keep sufficient quantities of the most popular items in stock at all times, Wal-Mart has reduced the number of product lines it sells and is devoting more shelf space to top-selling merchandise. At the same time, Wal-Mart and Asda cater to local needs and buying patterns by stocking some locally produced merchandise in each store. 'Our job is to provide the right range for customers,' explains Asda's chief merchandising officer.[11]

As Figure 8.3 indicates, logistics decisions about pre- and post-production inventory, storage, transportation, order processing and fulfilment depend on whether your objectives are linked to less service (lower cost) or more service (higher cost).

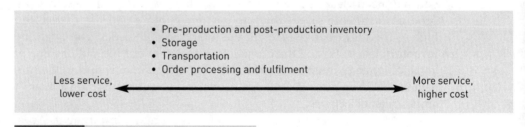

FIGURE 8.3 Implementing logistics objectives

If your inventories are too low, customers will not find products when and where they want and your channel members will lose sales; if your inventories are too high, the organisation's investment is tied up and you risk having some products going out of style, spoiling or becoming obsolete. If you're a retailer, you have to consider what shoppers will buy (and when), what your suppliers can provide (at short notice, if needed) and when you must pay your suppliers. The online retailer Amazon.com has enough experience across its product range that it can accurately predict buying habits and adjust inventory levels accordingly. This helps the company maintain a strong financial position because it's often able to resell the goods it's purchased before it's time to pay its suppliers.[12]

Increasingly, producers, suppliers and channel members are collaborating to forecast demand and have the right amount of inventory when and where needed. Mistakes can be costly – resulting in empty shelves and disappointed customers or, just as bad, warehouses full of obsolete or overpriced products. You must be able to respond quickly when your retail partners reorder items that sell unusually well; also remember that retailers may delist products that fail to live up to their sales expectations.

Storage decisions

Where will you store materials before production and where will you store finished products until needed to fill intermediary or customer orders? How long will you store materials and finished products? Such storage decisions are based, in part, on your inventory decisions and your customers' requirements. If you promise a business customer just-in-time stock replenishment, you might store products in a nearby warehouse or distribution centre for speedy delivery on schedule. Also examine how much space is needed for storing inventory at the site where customers actually gain access to the product.

Look at the product itself and typical variations in demand when planning for product storage. Is your product perishable? Is it especially large (or small) or fragile? Does it have other physical characteristics that affect storage? Are large quantities needed quickly during periods of peak demand? Is demand erratic or steady? What are the implications for your marketing plan? Evaluate your alternatives to determine whether your organisation should maintain its own storage facilities or outsource warehousing to a specialist.

Transportation decisions

In the course of planning inbound and outbound logistics, choose the transportation modes that are appropriate for your product, your budget and your customers' needs and value perceptions. Choices include road transport by lorry (convenient for door-to-door shipments), rail transport (for bulky or heavy items), air transport (when time is a factor and budgets allow), water transport (when time is not a factor but cost is) and pipeline transport (for liquids and natural gases). Often products are despatched by more than one mode of transportation, such as lorry to water, rail or air and back to lorry.

Table 8.2 shows some of the key questions to ask when making transportation decisions for your marketing plan.

Table 8.2 Questions to ask when planning for transportation

Question	Transportation choices
How quickly must products be at their destination?	Air is speediest; water is slowest
Is steady, predictable receipt of products desirable?	Pipeline allows for fairly steady transport of liquids and gases; water is least predictable
What level of transportation cost is acceptable to the organisation and its customers?	Pipeline and water are least expensive; air is most expensive
Is transportation available from the point of despatch directly to the point of delivery?	Road transport offers the most convenient door-to-door delivery
How do product characteristics affect transportation options?	Water and rail easily and cost effectively accommodate large, bulky products; lorries are often used to transport products that require a temperature-controlled environment

If you're a producer, your flexibility in transportation choices depends, in part, on legal and regulatory rules governing competition in pricing and schedules, as well as your balance of cost and customer service. If you are marketing transportation services, use your marketing plan to differentiate yourself from competitors through convenience, speed, special product handling or another benefit that your customers value. For example, the logistics company Blue Dart holds an estimated 45 per cent of the air express market in India. It differentiates itself by owning its own cargo planes and maintaining specially equipped airport facilities so it can deliver supplies and products when and where business customers direct.[13]

Some marketers outsource the process of transporting orders to specialist firms that take care of all the details. In South Africa, Woolworths contracts with Niche Logistics to deliver orders to customers who order online or by mobile. Woolworths has 12 stores that pack orders for nearby customers and prepare them for pickup by drivers from Niche Logistics. To avoid traffic congestion, each driver is assigned a time to arrive at a particular store and, once orders are loaded, follows carefully planned routes to make that day's deliveries on schedule.[14]

In some situations, the reliability of transportation throughout the value chain can mean the difference between life and death. Riders for Health, a UK NGO, is dedicated to ensuring the proper functioning of motorcycles and other vehicles used to transport medicines, vaccines and blood samples in seven African nations. This attention to transportation reliability has had immediate and measurable effects on health in the region. Since Riders for Health started improving medical supply transportation in Gambia, vaccines are being delivered where and when needed. As a result, the full immunisation rate among Gambian infants has risen from 62 per cent to 73 per cent.[15]

Order processing and fulfilment decisions

Whether you're targeting business or consumer markets, you'll have to include order processing and fulfilment in your marketing plan, with decisions about the method and timing of:

- accepting orders and billing for purchases

- confirmation of order and available inventory

- picking and packing products for despatch

- documenting and tracking the contents of shipments

- handling returns, errors and damaged goods.

Many organisations aim for better customer service through reduced order cycle time as part of their marketing plan activities. This means your customers (whether consumers or businesses) will have as short a wait as possible between placing an order and receiving delivery. Also consider whether you and your customers would benefit from paying to outsource order processing and fulfilment. For a fee, the pioneering online retailer Amazon.com will provide fulfilment functions for producers and other retailers; it stores merchandise until purchased, then packs and ships to fulfil orders placed through Amazon or through other channel members.

You can use the following checklist as a guide to some of the key questions you need to ask when you plan for logistics.

ESSENTIAL MARKETING PLAN CHECKLIST NO. 13:
PLANNING FOR LOGISTICS

Keep your channel strategy in mind as you think about the logistics decisions that are right for your customers, your organisation and your competitive situation. Tick each question as you answer by writing notes in the space provided.

☐ What logistics arrangements would enable customers to obtain products quickly, conveniently and at an acceptable price?

_____

☐ How can logistics add more value for the customer and the organisation by boosting benefits or decreasing costs or both?

_____

☐ What influence are the organisation's SWOT and resources likely to have on logistics decisions? Can any aspect of logistics be outsourced if necessary without compromising objectives or service?

☐ How can logistics be used for competitive advantage and to support positioning?

☐ What is the optimal balance of logistics costs and customer service, given the marketing plan objectives?

 **CHAPTER SUMMARY**

The value chain (also called the value delivery network or supply chain) is the succession of interrelated, value-added functions that enables a producer to create and deliver a product that fulfils customers' needs through connections with suppliers, wholesalers, retailers and other participants. The marketing (or distribution) channel refers to the set of functions performed by the producer or by intermediaries in making a product available to customers at a profit. Marketing channels are outbound functions downstream in the value chain, closer to the customer. Logistics refers to the flow of products, information and payments inbound and outbound to meet customer requirements.

Marketers can use direct channels, in which the organisation deals directly with customers, and/or indirect channels, in which the organisation works through other businesses or individuals (intermediaries). The three major types of intermediaries are wholesalers, retailers, and representatives, brokers and agents. In a channel with one or more levels, marketers can choose exclusive, selective or intensive distribution. The main functions involved in logistics are pre- and post-production inventory, storage, transportation, order processing and fulfilment. Increasing customer service levels generally increases logistics costs, reducing logistics costs generally reduces the level of customer service, a point to keep in mind while planning.

CASE STUDY: HOW LUXOTTICA SEES CHANNEL AND LOGISTICS PLANNING

Luxottica Group, based in Milan, Italy, has a definite vision of how spectacles should be designed, manufactured and marketed around the world. Of the company's €5.2 billion in annual turnover, 60 per cent comes from retailing and 40 per cent from wholesaling.

Among Luxottica's brands in the retailing sector are Sunglass Hut, LensCrafters, Ilori, BrightEyes and Oakley; among the eyewear brands it markets to wholesale customers are Arnette, Luxottica, Persol, Ray-Ban and Oakley. In addition, Luxottica licenses a number of designer brands for the eyewear collections it manufactures, including Stella McCartney, Burberry, Polo Ralph Lauren, Chanel, Versace and Prada.

To achieve its long-term goal of global growth, Luxottica continues to acquire eyewear brands and retail chains, add new stores, strengthen its connection with independent opticians and enhance its logistical operations for flexibility and efficiency. For example, it has taken a stake in one of Latin America's largest eyewear retail chains, MultiOpticas Internacional, to enter promising new urban markets. In Australia, where it already operates 835 retail stores under the Sunglass Hut and other names, Luxottica is opening smaller branches inside Australia's Myers department stores to reach shoppers in new ways.

On the wholesale side, the company distributes its brands to independent eyewear stores in 130 nations through 9 logistics centres and 30 commercial branches. The Elite Client programme provides particular rewards to independent stores that are long-time, high-volume buyers. In exchange for their loyalty and their buying commitments, Elite Clients receive special treatment such as early stocking opportunities for new products. Rewarding intermediary loyalty has helped Luxottica increase revenues from this segment.

During challenging economic times, Luxottica has adapted by closing underperforming stores, eliminating low-performing brands and reallocating some of its marketing budget to support in-store displays. It has also expanded and revamped some of its logistics centres for more efficiency in order processing and fulfilment; this will also allow for additional inventory storage as the company grows in the coming years.[16]

Case questions

1. What are the advantages and disadvantages of rewarding independent stores for loyalty and high-volume purchasing through a programme such as Elite Client? Do you think Luxottica should expand this programme?

2. If you were planning logistics for Luxottica's sales to independent stores, what specific issues would you pay the most attention to, and why?

 **APPLY YOUR KNOWLEDGE**

Select a common consumer product, then research and analyse its value chain and its channel arrangements. Prepare a written report or an oral presentation summarising your analysis.

- Draw a diagram to show a simplified value chain for this product. Is a reverse channel necessary or desirable? Why?

- Is this product available through direct channels such as by mail or from the producer's website? How does this channel arrangement benefit customers and the organisation?

- Is the product available through indirect channels such as retailers? Why is this appropriate for the product, the market and the targeted customers?

- Is the product available through exclusive distribution? Through intensive distribution? Do you agree with this decision?

BUILD YOUR OWN MARKETING PLAN

Continue developing your marketing plan by making decisions about channel arrangements and logistics. Should you market this product directly to customers or through indirect channels or a combination? How long should your channel be, and what value will each level add? Will you use intensive, selective or exclusive distribution, and why? What kinds of channel members would be most appropriate? Does your product require any special transportation, storage or post-purchase support? What specific customer needs should you take into account when planning logistics and how will you balance cost with customer service? Record your decisions and explain their implications in your marketing plan.

ENDNOTES

1. 'Exclusive interview with Tesco Personal Finance', *International Supermarket News*, 2 September 2009, www.internationalsuper-marketnews.com; 'Row parts ways with Tesco Personal Finance', *Marketing*, 15 July 2009, p. 3; 'Retail giants head into markets', *Post Magazine*, 25 June 2009, n.p.; Melanie Stern, 'Bags of experience', *Accountancy Age*, 27 November 2008, n.p.; 'Tesco plans mortgages for next year', *Daily Mail*, 21 August 2009, n.p.; Vladimir Guevarra, 'Tesco, Fortis UK form insurance partnership', *Wall Street Journal*, 11 September 2009, www.wsj.com; Margot Patrick and Lilly Vitorovich, 'Tesco moves ahead on banking', *Wall Street Journal*, 21 August 2009, p. B4; www.tescoplc.com; 'Tesco sees "solid" sales growth', *BBC News*, 8 December 2009, http://news.bbc.co.uk/2/hi/business/8400828.stm.

2. Lisa Berwin, 'Inditex store expansion assault pushes UK operation into loss', *Retail Week*, 2 October 2009, www.retail-week.com/city/annual-results/inditex-store-expansion-assault-pushes-uk-operation-into-loss/5006833.article; 'Zara owner automates', *Logistics Manager*, 4 June 2009, p. 8; Joseph Weber, Kerry Capell and David Welch, 'The overseas adventurers', *BusinessWeek*, 22 June 2009, p. 39; Kerry Capell, 'Zara thrives by breaking all the rules', *BusinessWeek*, 20 October 2008, p. 66; Sarah Morris, 'Inditex profit tops forecast, sales picking up', *Reuters*, 10 December 2009, www.reuters.com.

3. Laura Fitzpatrick, 'A bride helps plan ethical weddings', *Time*, 21 September 2009, p. 59; Giles Broadbent and Andrew Williams, 'Green living: Ethical weddings', *Wharf*, 13 May 2009, http://www.wharf.co.uk/2009/05/green-living-ethical-weddings.html.

4. Wing-Gar Cheng, 'Nestlé China growth may double after evading scandal', *Bloomberg*, 7 September 2009, www.bloomberg.com.

5. Brian Hindo, 'Outsourcing: What happens to that scarf you really hated', *BusinessWeek*, 15 January 2007, p. 36.

6. James Ferguson, 'Eazyfone's first profits at £3.3m', *Manchester Evening News*, 2 September 2009, www.manchestereveningnews.co.uk; Fred Pearce, 'Greenwash: E-waste trade is the unacceptable face of recycling', *Guardian*, 28 May 2009, www.guardian.co.uk/environment; Gareth Jones, 'More commercial retailers split profits with charities', *Professional Fundraising*, September 2009, www.professionalfundraising.co.uk; 'Travel reward scheme Airmiles has launched a mobile phone recycling programme', *Marketing Week*, 10 August 2009, www.marketingweek.co.uk.

7. Udita Jhunjhunwala, 'Disney India moves into video distribution', *Screen Daily*, 7 May 2009, www.screendaily.com.

8. Liam Black, 'Pots of gold', *Guardian*, 18 February 2009, www.guardian.co.uk; James Melik, 'Danone's yogurt strategy for Bangladesh', *BBC*, 8 July 2009, http://news.bbc.co.uk; Karl Weber, 'Social business goes from the drawing board to the real world', *Harvard Business Publishing Good Business Blog*, 5 December 2008, http://blogs.harvardbusiness.org; 'Grameen Danone Food Ltd – Overview 210609', www.slideshare.net/danonecommunities/grameen-danone-food-ltd-overview-210609.

9. Dan Leahul, 'Debenhams and Asda launch online customer review sections', *Revolution*, 2 July 2009, www.revolutionmagazine.com/news.

10. Joanna Perry, 'A matter of choice: Is bigger product range good for shoppers?', *Retail Week*, 25 September 2009, www.retail-week.com.

11. Quoted in Zoe Wood, 'Brands fighting for shelf space now that Wal-Mart believes less is more', *Guardian*, 16 August 2009, www.guardian.co.uk. Other sources: Sean Gregory, 'Walmart's latest move to crush the competition', *Time*, 9 September 2009, www.time.com; Tom Leonard, 'Wal-Mart announces "green" labelling plans', *Telegraph*, 16 July 2009, www.telegraph.co.uk; http://walmartstores.com.

12. Brad Stone, 'Can Amazon be Wal-Mart of the web?', *New York Times*, 20 September 2009, pp. BU 1, BU7.

13. 'Can India's logistics industry deliver a better model for transporting goods?', *Knowledge@Wharton*, 10 September 2009, http://knowledge.wharton.upenn.edu/india.

14. 'A businessman's driving ambition to deliver the goods', *Business Day (South Africa)*, 10 September 2009, www.businessday.co.za.

15. Marguerite Rigoglioso, 'In Africa and at home, supply chains are getting kinder and greener', *Stanford Graduate School of Business*, May 2009, www.gsb.stanford.edu/news; www.riders.org.

16. Vincent Boland, 'Luxottica expands in Latin America', *Financial Times*, 28 May 2009, p. 17; 'Stella sees bright future with Luxottica', *WWD*, 31 August 2009, p. 8; Allison Manning, 'Conveying a new vision', *Modern Materials Handling*, 1 January 2009, p. 44; 'Elite opportunity', *Optician*, 17 October 2008, n.p.; 'Luxottica Group adapts to economic environment', *Ophthalmology Times*, 15 April 2009, p. 49; 'Sunglass Hut to open in 65 Myer Australia stores', *Reuters India*, 17 August 2009, http://in.reuters.com; www.luxottica.com.

9 Planning for communications and influence

Comprehension outcomes

After studying this chapter, you will be able to:

- Understand the role of marketing in communicating with and influencing customers and other target audiences
- Outline the planning process for marketing communications and influence
- Discuss how communications tools are used to reach target audiences in support of marketing plan objectives

Application outcomes

After studying this chapter, you will be able to:

- Set communications and influence objectives consistent with marketing plan objectives
- Select appropriate communications tools
- Plan a campaign to engage with and influence target audience(s)

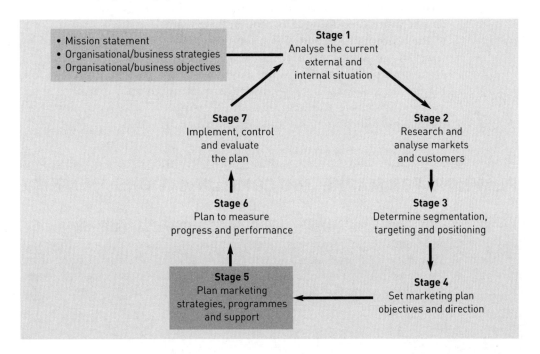

CHAPTER PREVIEW: HOW DELL CONNECTS WITH CUSTOMERS

How can a global corporation with more than £37 billion in annual turnover afford to maintain an ongoing dialogue with consumers and business customers? The US-based computer manufacturer Dell is doing just that, and the results are rewarding for all. Dell's idea is to communicate with customers, potential buyers, members of the media, technology columnists, influential bloggers and everyone else interested in its computer equipment, accessories and services. In addition to advertising in traditional media such as newspapers, magazines and television, Dell communicates and influences opinions and actions through catalogues, direct mail, e-mail and newsletters plus an ever-expanding online presence that includes websites and postings on blogs, YouTube, Facebook, LinkedIn, Flickr, Twitter and other social networking sites. It also invites customers to rate and review its products online for everyone to see.

In the first two years after Dell began announcing special promotional deals and new products on Twitter, it sold more than £2 million worth of products through such postings. Customers appreciate hearing about the latest promotions and getting voucher codes for additional savings. Now 200 Dell staff members tweet not just to promote specific deals but also to provide support, answer questions, monitor public sentiment, discuss technology and otherwise engage with external and internal audiences on a more personal level. Twitter is 'a great way to fix customer problems and hear what customers have to say, it's a great feedback forum and it leads to sales – how can you miss?', says a Dell employee who tweets.[1]

Strategies for marketing communications and influence – in other words, for promotion – help you engage the people and organisations that are important to your brand, the way Dell is doing. In this chapter, you'll learn the basics of how to plan for communications, including the need for post-implementation analysis and evaluation. You'll also be introduced to word of mouth, buzz marketing and social media marketing and to the concept of integrated marketing communications. This chapter includes a brief overview of planning for advertising, sales promotion, personal selling, direct marketing and public relations – the most visible and creative aspects of many marketing plans. Use this chapter's checklist to think through your decisions about media. And look at the sample marketing plan, in the Appendix, for examples of how companies document their communications and influence decisions.

PLANNING FOR MARKETING COMMUNICATIONS AND INFLUENCE

You might have the best product on the planet, the best price or the most convenient distribution, but your marketing plan will accomplish nothing unless you have a strategy for communicating with customers and other important audiences. Until a few years ago, it was traditional for marketers to rely on one-way techniques such as advertising to get messages to broad groups of customers. These days, if you're a smart marketer like Dell, you'll strive for two-way communications to foster ongoing conversations with targeted audiences as a way to build relationships over time.

As you plan your communications, you'll develop a *customer-influence strategy* to engage your customers and key publics through marketing communications and to influence how these people think, feel and act towards your brand or offering. Increasingly, Dell and other marketers are including word of mouth, buzz marketing and social media marketing as part of their influence strategies.

Word of mouth, buzz marketing and social media marketing

Word of mouth means people telling other people about a marketing message, a particular product or another aspect of the offering or the marketing. Word of mouth has considerable credibility because it's not marketer-controlled and it reflects what people in the market think, feel and do. As a marketer, you can try to initiate positive word of mouth, and you may even reward word of mouth. However, you can't control whether your audience picks up on the message and passes it along when or as you intended. And, because word of mouth spreads in an unpredictable way, your message will probably not reach everyone in your target audience.

A more intense form of word of mouth is **buzz marketing**, in which you target opinion leaders with communications that influence them to be active in spreading brand or product information to other people. Buzz marketing can spread product or brand information especially quickly on the Internet. Yet because this is word of mouth, marketers can't control exactly what's being said, where and when the message spreads or how long it will circulate. Often buzz about a brand will fade as quickly as it builds.

In **social media** – online media such as blogs, social networking sites such as Bebo and video- and photo-sharing sites such as YouTube and Flickr, all of which facilitate user interaction – consumers create much of the content (in the form of text, videos, podcasts or photos) and respond to content posted by other users. The immense popularity of such sites has led to the rise of **social media marketing**, the intentional use of social media to achieve marketing plan objectives such as increasing brand awareness, attracting website visitors and maintaining dialogues with various publics.[2]

For many firms, social media marketing has become a priority because research suggests that brand and product mentions in a social-media context can affect customers' attitudes and feelings and may also affect purchasing decisions of friends within social networks.[3] Some companies also plan for branded *e-communities*, web pages where consumers can share information and images, ask questions and post product comments. Kraft Foods, which markets Oreo and other food brands, hosts one e-community for recipe exchange and another for cooking tips, to stimulate online discussion and enhance the image of its brands.

Unilever's chief marketing officer observes that 'brands are now becoming conversation factors where academics, celebrities, experts and key opinion formers discuss functional, emotional and, more interestingly, social concerns', adding: 'Of course, the conversation is no longer one way or 30 seconds.'[4] Remember, as a marketer, you aren't in control of all messages that appear in all social media, and you can't expect all word of mouth to be positive. See Table 9.1 for examples of how social media marketing is being used today.

Table 9.1 Social media marketing

Social medium	Example of marketing use
Blog	Managing directors at John Lewis use corporate blogs to announce store openings, improvements to the retail website and other news
E-community	Asda encourages internal communication with 'The Green Room', a company video blog by and for the retailer's employees
Social networking site	Facebook fan page for Apple's iTunes store features free music samples, free tutorials, behind-the-scenes videos and more to encourage brand engagement
Flickr	Dell posts photos of new technology products and industry events on its official Flickr page, inviting comments from viewers
Twitter	Complementing its advertising, Fox's Biscuits uses a 'Vinnie Says' Twitter account to communicate with brand fans
YouTube	Comic Relief maintains a Red Nose Day channel featuring both professional and consumer-generated videos to raise awareness and raise money for charity

For reasons of transparency and trust, you must be willing to accept some online criticism and complaints along with praise and questions. Snacks and beverage marketer PepsiCo understood this when it set up branded social media pages: 'We are allowing open conversation in branded areas, and we are encouraging dialogue good, bad or ugly,' says the director of global social media.[5] The head of social media for the other giant of global beverage marketing, Coca-Cola, emphasises the need to listen and respond to negative comments: 'We're getting to a point if you're not responding, you're not being seen as an authentic type of brand.'[6] And, to comply with fair trading regulations, be completely transparent about your company's identity when trying to spark word of mouth in any media.[7]

Marketers of all sizes are using social media marketing to communicate with and influence their customers. Albion, a bakery and cafe in London, has more than 1,300 people subscribed to its Twitter messages. The bakery tweets to alert customers when cupcakes, muffins and breads are just out of the oven. 'We tested it by telling people we had fresh scones, and five minutes later we had sold out,' says one of the owners.[8] EMC, which markets technology equipment, software and consulting services to businesses worldwide, maintains several Twitter accounts, including one for news releases, one for job recruitment and one for its annual customer event. Individual EMC managers and employees tweet as well. The company's social media specialist says Twitter is a good way to communicate because 'people are people, and people connect with people'.[9]

Understanding marketing communications tools

As you plan to engage your audience(s), consider how one or more of the five major marketing communications tools shown in Figure 9.1 might help you achieve your objectives. The following is a brief description; each tool is examined again later in the chapter.

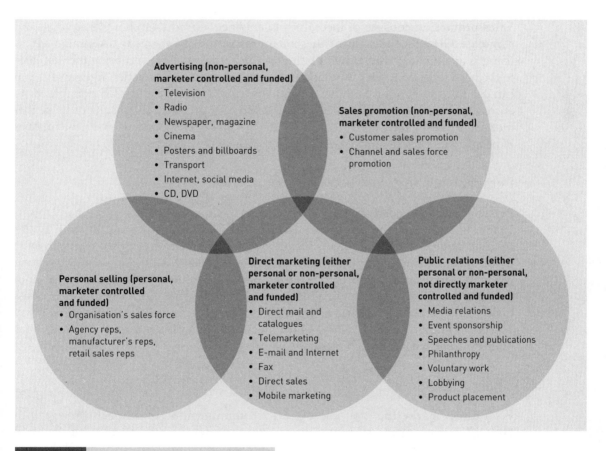

Advertising (non-personal, marketer controlled and funded)
- Television
- Radio
- Newspaper, magazine
- Cinema
- Posters and billboards
- Transport
- Internet, social media
- CD, DVD

Sales promotion (non-personal, marketer controlled and funded)
- Customer sales promotion
- Channel and sales force promotion

Personal selling (personal, marketer controlled and funded)
- Organisation's sales force
- Agency reps, manufacturer's reps, retail sales reps

Direct marketing (either personal or non-personal, marketer controlled and funded)
- Direct mail and catalogues
- Telemarketing
- E-mail and Internet
- Fax
- Direct sales
- Mobile marketing

Public relations (either personal or non-personal, not directly marketer controlled and funded)
- Media relations
- Event sponsorship
- Speeches and publications
- Philanthropy
- Voluntary work
- Lobbying
- Product placement

| FIGURE 9.1 | Tools for marketing communications |

Advertising

Advertising is non-personal promotion paid for by an identified sponsor. This is a cost-effective way to inform large numbers of customers or channel members about a brand or product, persuade customers or channel members about a brand's or product's merits, encourage buying, and remind customers or channel members about the brand to encourage repurchase. Although television advertising remains popular, many companies see online advertising and social networking sites as less costly methods of communicating with more targeted audiences. One of the fast-growing types of advertising is *paid search*, in which companies pay for clickable website links to appear alongside the results of online searches when people enter certain keywords into Google and other search engines.

Sales promotion

Sales promotion consists of incentives to enhance a product's short-term value and stimulate the target audience to buy soon (or respond in another way). Although advertising is an excellent way to build brand image and awareness and bring the audience to the brink of action, sales promotion provides impetus to take action right away. You can use sales promotion to induce customers to try a new product, for example, or to encourage channel members to stock and sell a new product. The results of most promotions are easily measured by counting the number of coupons redeemed, the number of people who click on links in e-mail newsletters or on websites, and so on.

Personal selling

Personal selling – especially useful for two-way communication – can take many forms, including traditional in-person sales, Internet sales and telemarketing. Sending a sales representative to call on customers is extremely costly, whereas personal selling in most retail, telemarketing and Internet settings is less expensive. Still, companies marketing costly or complicated products to business markets may need sales reps to learn about customers' needs, recommend solutions, explain features and benefits, answer questions, demonstrate product use and complete sales transactions. Sales reps are also key players in learning about customers for marketing planning purposes, as well as for building trust and strengthening relationships.

Direct marketing

With **direct marketing**, you use two-way communication to interact directly with targeted customers and stimulate direct responses, particularly purchasing, that will ultimately lead to an ongoing relationship. This communication may occur through letters and catalogues, television, radio, e-mail, Internet ads, newspaper ads, telemarketing, faxes, mobile phones or personal selling. The objective for an initial direct marketing contact might be to get a customer to buy or ask for product information or simply agree to receive further messages. One of direct marketing's most important advantages is the ability to measure actual results in terms of purchases or requests for information, for example.

Public relations

Public relations (PR) activities promote dialogue to build understanding and foster positive attitudes between the organisation and its publics. A marketing plan might call for a news conference to launch a new product, for example, or a special event to polish brand image. Because the firm doesn't directly control or pay for media mentions, and because the communication is not sales directed, PR is very believable. However, there's no guarantee that the information will reach the intended audience in the preferred form or at the preferred time, if at all. Also remember that media coverage may be positive or negative, no matter what message a marketer tries to convey.

Here's a look at how Barclaycard reaches and influences multiple audiences using a variety of communications tools.

MARKETING IN PRACTICE: BARCLAYCARD

London-based Barclaycard introduced the first UK credit card in 1966; today it serves 24 million cardholders as well as 88,000 retailers and merchants worldwide. Among the UK audiences targeted with specific communications are college students and graduates, charity donors, football fans, frequent travellers, businesses that provide employees with credit cards for official use, businesses that accept credit cards as payment, and government agencies that give credit cards to employees for official use. Barclaycard coordinates messages in radio, on television, in cinemas, in print and in online media to attract new cardholders, convey the brand's benefits and reinforce brand choices by current cardholders. It also uses internal communications to inform employees about its mission and strategy and motivate this audience to actively support the organisation's goals and objectives.

When Barclaycard's marketers planned the multimedia Waterslide campaign to highlight the benefit of convenience, they supported the brand theme with social-media activity on Facebook and YouTube plus a special website and a downloadable iPhone app featuring a waterslide game. In addition, they have arranged for the company to sponsor events that appeal to the interests of specific cardholder segments, such as the Mercury Music Prize and the Freerunning Championships. Also, they publicise Barclaycard's activities using news releases and media briefings and call attention to corporate achievements by posting financial and sustainability reports online for customers and non-customers to read.[10]

Defining the target audience

As you can see in Figure 9.2, your first planning decision is to define the audience that you'll target. This may be customers in a certain segment, people who influence buyers or users, people who are currently competitors' customers, current or potential channel members, members of the general public, members of the media, government officials or regulators, or other publics. As you've seen, Barclaycard defines a number of target audiences for its communications because influencing these people will help it achieve its marketing plan objectives.

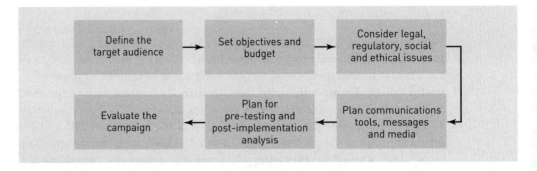

FIGURE 9.2 Planning a communications and influence campaign

If you target intermediaries in an effort to move or push your product through the channel to customers, you're using a **push strategy** to stir channel interest using sales promotion, advertising or other communications techniques. Manufacturers with established channel relationships often use a push strategy to induce their wholesale and retail partners to carry new products. An alternative approach is a **pull strategy**, which targets customers so they will request and buy the product from channel members. This pulls the product through the channel from producer to customer. When Nissan used a pull strategy to encourage European car buyers to check out the low-priced Pixo at local dealerships, it ran a consumer-influence campaign that included advertising and mobile marketing.[11]

In your marketing plan, define who each campaign should reach and, through research, indicate what audience members think or feel about the brand, product, organisation or idea, their attitudes and behaviour toward competitors, what kind of message, appeal, delivery and timing would be most effective, what the message should contain and how it should be conveyed. Look beyond generalities and develop a profile of a typical audience member in as much detail as possible, including age, gender, family situation, lifestyle, media preferences, product attitudes and loyalty, payment preferences, timing of buying decisions and other factors.

The purpose of careful audience definition and research is to identify nuances that will help shape the content of your messages. This will also help you determine when and where your messages are likely to have the most influence on audience members. For example, the marketing director of the UK charity National Childbirth Trust observes that 'new mums and mums-to-be are most heavily influenced by information distributed by the NHS [National Health Service] and other key sources, and by the views and experiences of friends and family, rather than broad media channels'.[12] Knowing this, the charity supplements its media activities with messages aimed at getting parents involved to volunteer in its local centres, share information with new parents in their communities, raise money and help shape political and legal actions affecting parents and children.

A growing number of firms are using **mobile marketing** to send information, directions, coupons and other messages to target audiences through text and e-mail received on mobiles as well as through websites optimised for handset screens. Here are a few examples of mobile marketing around the world.

MARKETING IN PRACTICE: USING MOBILE MARKETING

In the UK, Kellogg launched a year-long multimedia 'Big Bake' campaign to get customers involved with its cereals by getting them to try recipes at home and compete for an opportunity to star in an ad. The company printed recipes on its cereal boxes and included a mobile-phone code and a special website address on the box and in ads. Customers were invited to use their mobiles or digital cameras to snap and submit photos showing their families making one of the featured recipes. The contest attracted thousands of entries and considerable attention in conventional and online media, plus additional coverage about the family selected for the television advert (which was posted online after it aired).[13]

In Germany, BMW is using mobile marketing to build sales of snow tyres, which are required by law during winter months. In a pilot programme, customers whose mobile numbers are in BMW's database received photos of the car model they purchased, along with recommendations for appropriate winter tyres, including prices. Customers could click through the message to call a dealer or send a text message to ask the dealer to call them. The programme has been successful in driving sales: during the first two years of this programme, 30 per cent of the message recipients bought snow tyres from BMW.[14] In Canada, Volkswagen uses mobile marketing to give customers detailed driving directions to nearby petrol stations that offer diesel fuel. Because several VW models require diesel fuel but not every station offers it, this builds goodwill by helping customers find a convenient place to refuel wherever they happen to be driving.[15]

Setting the objectives and the budget

Your campaign will aim to achieve marketing objectives that move the target audience through a hierarchy of cognitive, affective and behavioural responses. A **cognitive response** refers to a customer's mental reaction, including brand awareness and knowledge of product features and benefits. An **affective response** is a customer's emotional reaction, such as being interested in or liking a product. A **behavioural response** is how the customer acts, such as buying a product or applying for credit. Customers move through these responses in different order, depending on how involved they are in making that type of purchase, product differentiation in that category and the influence of consumption experience (see Figure 9.3).

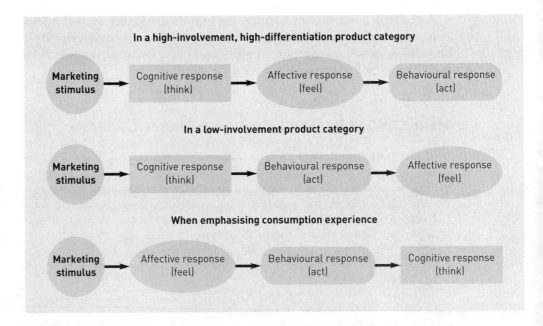

In a high-involvement, high-differentiation product category

Marketing stimulus → Cognitive response (think) → Affective response (feel) → Behavioural response (act)

In a low-involvement product category

Marketing stimulus → Cognitive response (think) → Behavioural response (act) → Affective response (feel)

When emphasising consumption experience

Marketing stimulus → Affective response (feel) → Behavioural response (act) → Cognitive response (think)

FIGURE 9.3   Using communications to provoke audience response

Source: After *SOLOMON, MICHAEL R., CONSUMER BEHAVIOR: BUYING, HAVING, AND BEING, 5th,©2002.* Prentice Hall, pp.200–202. Reproduced by permission of Pearson Education, Inc., Upper Saddle River, New Jersey.

Usually your communications and influence objectives will relate to building long-term relationships by attracting customers' attention, communicating about the product or brand, persuading customers to seek out and buy the product once, supporting a positive attitude leading to repeat purchases and ultimately loyalty. Specific advertising objectives may be set to complement or support objectives for personal selling, direct marketing or other tools in your plan. You may also set sales or profit objectives, particularly when you can measure and attribute the results to a particular campaign or message. Further, you may use communications to enhance your firm's image or build brand awareness. (Review Chapter 5 for more about setting objectives.)

The marketing communications budget is developed and allocated in the context of your organisation's overall marketing budgeting process and budget-approval process, which may be driven from the floor up or the top down (or a combination). One floor-up option is to allocate funding according to the objectives and the cost of the tasks needed to achieve those objectives. This directly ties tasks and objectives for better accountability in terms of whether the tasks actually achieve the objectives. However, this method may lead to unrealistic budget requests and may complicate planning if particular tasks can't easily be linked to specific objectives.

Other budgeting methods include the affordability method (a top-down method based on how much the organisation can afford to spend), percentage-of-sales method (spending a certain percentage of annual sales revenue or an average industry percentage of sales) and competitive parity (budgeting according to what rivals spend). In practice, you may use several methods to construct a preliminary budget, look closely at costs and the market situation, consider both long- and short-term objectives, and then arrive at a reasonable budget. (See Chapter 11 for more on budgeting.)

Considering legal, regulatory, social and ethical issues

When planning, be aware of a wide range of legal, regulatory, social and ethical issues as you think creatively. On the most basic legal and ethical level, your communications should not be deceptive, distort facts or falsify product benefits. Find out whether certain types of messages are illegal and whether the rules are changing. For instance, some nations outlaw comparative advertising while others forbid television commercials promoting tobacco products. Until recently, independent UK broadcasters were not allowed to accept payment for featuring branded products during television programmes. This ban has now been lifted and marketers are looking at new ways to use *product placement* in their plans for communicating with and influencing audiences.[16]

Be aware that some industries impose self-regulation on product communications. In the UK, the alcohol industry has established strict voluntary rules against advertising alcoholic products to under-age consumers, and studies by the Advertising Standards Authority indicate that marketers are adhering to these guidelines. Despite industry self-regulation, however, the British Medical Association has called for a comprehensive ban on alcohol advertising to combat binge drinking.[17]

Also take privacy into consideration. The European Union has strict rules about what personal data companies may collect and under what circumstances they are allowed to exchange such information. Retailers must first obtain permission before gathering customer data, sharing or selling it and using it for store marketing purposes. Companies must delete personal data after a set period, and they are forbidden to send personal data collected in the European Union to countries without equally strong privacy laws. Such concerns about collection, storage, use and disclosure of personal data continue to make privacy a hot issue for marketers.

Planning for tools, messages and media

Most marketing plans employ more than one communications tool to achieve their objectives. Your exact choices depend on your target audience, objectives and budget, other marketing-mix decisions, and legal, regulatory, social and ethical considerations. They also depend on message and media strategy (discussed more fully later in this chapter). For instance, television advertising is generally more expensive than print advertising, so if you have a small budget or want to reach highly targeted audiences you may avoid television or use it sparingly. If your message involves an actual product demonstration, you will probably find radio inappropriate.

Planning for pre- and post-implementation analysis and evaluation

To get the information you need for making better decisions about communications and influence, you should plan time and money for research to pre-test messages, creative approaches and use of media. The purpose is to gauge the target audience's response and have the opportunity to make changes, possibly pre-test additional elements and then launch the complete campaign. For example, you can conduct pre-tests to measure recognition (does a sample of the audience recognise what is being promoted?), recall (does the sample remember the message and what it communicated?), affective reaction (do the message, product and brand provoke positive reactions?) and behavioural intentions (are people likely to buy the product or take another action on the basis of the promotion?).

You should also plan for measuring and evaluating the results after full implementation. Specifically, determine whether the message or media failed to reach the target audience at times, and why, how well the audience understood the message, what the audience thought and felt about the product or brand, message and media, which messages and media were especially effective in provoking the desired audience response, and how well the tools, messages and media are supporting the overall positioning and working with other marketing-mix strategies.

Cadbury's communications agency commissions research to understand how adverts are being perceived and to measure their effectiveness.

MARKETING IN PRACTICE: CADBURY

When the Fallon ad agency first proposed an advert featuring a 'gorilla' drumming along to the Phil Collins hit *In the Air Tonight*, Cadbury's chief executive wasn't sure it would do much to build Dairy Milk sales. Yet 'Gorilla' became one of the most popular and parodied adverts of recent years, accomplishing a number of marketing and financial objectives for Cadbury. After just a few months on the air, 'Gorilla' scored a 91 per cent awareness level among British consumers and helped increase Dairy Milk sales by 9 per cent. It won the grand prize at the Cannes Lions International Advertising Festival and has been viewed on YouTube more than 3 million times.

Long before the advert appeared on television, Fallon analysed audience reaction in multiple pre-tests. '"Gorilla" was researched again and again,' says the agency's director of strategy. 'In this case, research didn't only help build the confidence to do something incredibly courageous for the brand, it told us some things we didn't expect, like older audiences loved it as much as younger ones.'[18] Inspired by fan remixes posted on YouTube, Fallon changed the advert a year after its debut; this time, the gorilla was seen drumming along to Bonnie Tyler's *Total Eclipse of the Heart*.[19]

Integrated marketing communications

Your marketing plan should strive for **integrated marketing communications (IMC)**, coordinating content and delivery of all marketing messages in all media for an organisation, product or brand. This approach to communications ensures consistency and will help you achieve your objectives. For proper integration, carefully select communications tools and media that are appropriate for your audience, product and positioning. Consider how factors in the external marketing environment – especially social–cultural trends and technological developments – might affect your ability to get messages across to the audience and the audience's ability to understand and respond to your messages.[20]

When planning a communications campaign, think about how the overall effect of the messages and media will influence customer receptivity, attention, interest and response. Also check that the content of each message is consistent with that of all other messages and with your brand's competitive points of differentiation. Be aware that customers may respond to any or all messages, regardless of media, and be prepared to react to both positive and negative customer responses. Finally, plan to measure results so you can determine whether your campaigns are having the desired effect on the target audience.

PLANNING ADVERTISING

Planning for advertising follows the general planning pattern shown in Figure 9.2. Note that you'll generally wait to make detailed decisions until after your marketing plan is being implemented. Still, you have to plan the general direction of both message and media in order to allocate the overall budget among advertising and other communications and influence activities.

Planning messages

What will the message actually say? What will it look (and/or sound) like? These are the two main decisions in planning messages. Some messages follow a 'hard-sell' approach to induce the target audience to respond now; others take a more 'soft-sell' approach, persuading without seeming to do so.

Message planning is inseparable from media planning because the copy in the advertisement, the design and the creativity of its execution depend on media choice. A creative decision to show the product in action, for instance, can be executed through a visual medium such as television or the web. Creativity is, in fact, crucial for attracting attention, building awareness and shaping positive attitudes, as Cadbury found with its 'Gorilla' advert. Although all decision details need not be finalised until the marketing plan is actually implemented, you should have some idea of message and media strategy so you can plan budgets, timing and marketing-mix coordination.

Planning media

Media planning has become more complex due to the multiplicity of media choices and vehicles and the resulting smaller audience sizes for each – **audience fragmentation**.

You'll always have budget constraints as you seek to balance reach and frequency. **Reach** refers to the number or percentage of people in the target audience exposed to an advertisement in a particular media vehicle during a certain period. Higher reach means the message gets to more people, but this usually comes at a cost. **Frequency** is the number of times the target audience is exposed to a message in a particular media vehicle during a certain period. Higher frequency means you expose more people to your message on more occasions, again at a cost.

Should you plan to spend more on reach or more on frequency? Which media and vehicles will get your message to the right people at the right time and in the desired frequency? For example, Hindustan Unilever recently decided to aim for high short-term reach and frequency across India using a one-day television network 'roadblock' plan. It arranged for all Star India channels to air only adverts for Lifebuoy and other Hindustan Unilever consumer products during that day, an unusual media plan that sparked word of mouth as well.[21]

An alternative to paying for high reach that may include people outside the target audience (which sometimes happens with television adverts, for example) is to use more precisely targeted media. When Tommy Hilfiger introduced a new range of wristwatches, one of the brand's UK boutiques advertised the watches using a special vinyl wrap inside the shopping-centre's lift. This decision to target by proximity made sense because the shoppers were already in the vicinity of the boutique; in fact, three wristwatches were sold even before the range was arranged in the shop's display case.[22]

The following checklist summarises planning considerations for media.

ESSENTIAL MARKETING PLAN CHECKLIST NO. 14:
PLANNING FOR MEDIA

Your marketing plan should explain the basic reasoning behind your choices of media and message, although it need not cover every detail of every communications and influence campaign. Based on the tools you will use, your budget and objectives, the marketing environment and the profile of your target audience, think about each of the following aspects of media planning. Put a tick next to each question after you've entered your answers in the space provided.

☐ What media do audience members use and prefer? Are these media available in the geographic region being targeted?

☐ Can the media reach the right people in appropriate numbers to deliver messages during the customers' buying cycle?

☐ Will the audience consider some media excessively intrusive or annoying?

☐ Will the use of certain media require special attention to privacy concerns?

☐ What media are used by competitors and how might competing messages affect audience receptivity, understanding and response?

☐ Should media be used to deliver the message continuously, intermittently or seasonally?

☐ Will the budget cover the projected media cost for the desired reach and frequency?

☐ What is the expected payback based on anticipated audience reaction?

PLANNING SALES PROMOTION

Include sales promotion in your marketing plan when you want to stimulate faster response from consumers and business customers, channel members (sometimes called *the trade*) and the sales force. Although such promotions add value for only a limited time, some marketers use them as part of a longer-term strategy to strengthen relationships with the target audience. Sales promotion spending now exceeds advertising spending in a number of industries, reflecting increased competitive pressure and the need to produce immediate results.

However, because sales promotion often adds value by reducing perceived cost – lowering the product's price, in effect – over-use may heighten price sensitivity among customers, diminish brand strength and hurt profitability. Moreover, says promotion specialist Stephen Callender, 'Promotions that go wrong make a brand's strategies appear ill-thought out. That leads to insidious damage to the brand's credibility.'[23] Thus, you should set clear objectives, understand applicable laws and regulations, choose your techniques carefully, monitor implementation and evaluate results to make your sales promotion programmes successful.

Planning for customer sales promotion

Table 9.2 shows a variety of common sales promotion techniques you can use, depending on your communications objectives and strategy. Consider sales promotion to target consumers or business customers when you want to:

- *Encourage product trial.* Potential customers have to try a product at least once before they can form a definite opinion and decide to buy it again (and again). Sales promotion is therefore commonly used to introduce a product and to stimulate higher sales during the maturity stage.

- *Reinforce advertising for a product or brand.* An exciting sales promotion can help customers notice and remember your advertising messages.

- *Attract interest.* Simply getting customers to visit a store or contact a manufacturer about a product can be a challenge. Some marketers use coupons, samples or other techniques in an attempt to get customers to take the first step.

- *Encourage purchase of multiple products.* Depending on your product mix, you can use sales promotion to stimulate customer purchases of two, three or even more products.

- *Encourage continued product purchase and usage.* You want to build customer loyalty, increase sales and reduce customer acquisition costs. Airlines do this with their frequent-flyer programmes; supermarkets do this with their frequent-shopper programmes. When planning for vouchers and other promotions, Unilever thinks about the long-term effect on customer purchasing and relationships rather than trying to 'drive volume in one month'.[24]

Table 9.2 Sales promotion techniques targeting customers

Technique	Description
Sample	Free trial of a good or service
Voucher or coupon	Certificate or special code redeemable for money off a product's price
Premium	Free or low-priced items offered to induce purchase
Sweepstake or draw, contest, game	Chance to win cash or prize through luck, knowledge or skill
Refund, rebate	Returning part or all of a product's price to the customer
Price pack	Special price marked by producer on package or for multiple products bought together
Loyalty reward	Opportunity to earn gifts or cash for continuing to buy a certain offering or from a certain marketer
Point-of-purchase display or demonstration	In-shop materials promoting a product or in-shop demonstration of a good or service
Branded speciality	Everyday item such as a 1-shirt or calendar bearing a brand or logo, for reminder purposes

Field marketing is used to engage the target audience by bringing sales promotion to (and sometimes taking orders from) customers 'in the field' – in stores, shopping districts and city centres, using an outside agency. Nintendo is one of many companies that rely on field marketing to sample and demonstrate their products where consumers live, work or play.

MARKETING IN PRACTICE: NINTENDO

The video-game console market is intensely competitive, with Nintendo, Sony and Microsoft fighting for market share and profits. One way Nintendo builds brand preference and boosts sales for its consoles is by using field marketing in major global markets. To introduce the Wii in the UK, Nintendo planned a full schedule of advertising supported by a field marketing tour of dozens of shopping centres, family destinations and special attractions. It used similar field marketing tours in the US and other countries to allow consumers of all ages to try the controller and sample the games for themselves. To stimulate word of mouth, Nintendo also provided Wii consoles to cruise ships, senior centres and gaming events.

Nintendo's marketing worked: in the Wii's first two years, demand far outstripped supply, especially during the year-end holiday shopping period. More recently, Sony and Microsoft have lowered prices on some PlayStation and Xbox consoles to capture additional market share. With the economic crisis slowing consumer spending on non-essentials and focusing buyers on value, Nintendo did the same. The company returned to field marketing with sampling tours and announced loyalty rewards for European customers who get friends and family to connect their Wii consoles. Other communications and influence activities, including a high-profile advertising campaign, are helping to maintain the Wii's sales momentum.[25]

Planning for channel and sales force sales promotion

Particularly when using a push strategy, you may find sales promotion effective in enlisting the support of channel members and motivating sales representatives. Specifically, you can use channel and sales force promotions to:

- *Build channel commitment to a new product*. So many new products are introduced every year that channel members rarely have the space (or the money) to carry them all. Channel promotions can focus attention on a new product, encourage intermediaries to buy it, motivate the sales force to sell it and provide appropriate rewards.

- *Encourage more immediate results*. Sales promotion aimed at channel members and sales representatives offer inducements to take action during a specific time period.

- *Build relationships with channel members.* Keeping the ongoing support of major retail or wholesale businesses takes time and effort. Channel promotion offers opportunities for interactions that benefit the producer and its channel members.

- *Improve product knowledge.* Support the marketing effort by offering training and information through channel and sales force promotion.

Sales force promotions include contests (with cash or prizes as rewards), sales meetings (for training and motivation) and special promotional material (to supplement personal sales efforts). In planning a channel promotion, you may use monetary allowances (either discounts or payments for stocking or displaying a product), limited-time discounts (for buying early in the selling season or during other specified periods), free merchandise (extra quantities provided for buying a minimum quantity or a certain product), cooperative advertising (sharing costs when a channel member advertises a particular brand or product) or trade shows (setting up a booth or room at a convention centre to demonstrate products and interact with channel members or business buyers). Some companies are experimenting with virtual trade shows held on special websites or in virtual worlds like Second Life. The purpose is to provide information to channel members or prospective customers in an innovative and entertaining yet cost-efficient way.[26]

PLANNING PERSONAL SELLING

One of the most compelling reasons to include personal selling in a marketing plan is to establish solid relationships with new customers and maintain good relationships with the current customer base. Personal attention can make all the difference when your customers have unique problems, require customised solutions or place very large orders. It's especially important in marketing plans targeting business buyers who require considerable assistance assessing the specifications, benefits and usage requirements of expensive or complex goods and services. When the InterContinental Hotel Group planned to refresh its Holiday Inn hotel brand with a new logo, new room decor and new amenities, it expanded its sales force by 25 per cent to communicate the changes to businesses that rent hotel space for meetings and send many employees on business trips.[27]

Be sure to coordinate personal selling with all other marketing plan decisions to achieve the desired results. In addition, remind sales people to look beyond individual transactions and build long-term relationships with customers. Avon Products has many decades of experience with personal selling.

MARKETING IN PRACTICE: AVON PRODUCTS

Avon Products, the US-based beauty company, has 6 million independent reps selling its personal care products face to face in residential neighbourhoods and office buildings around the world. Its largest markets, after the US, are in Latin America and Asia. When Avon's reps meet customers, they demonstrate products, provide samples, take orders and deliver ordered products as quickly as possible. 'We bring the store to them, there's better service, it's easier to shop,' explains the president of Avon Philippines. 'We have redesigned our marketing to focus on "smart" value; I don't mean cheap, I mean great products at a great price.'[28]

Worldwide, the company sells four lipsticks every second and launches hundreds of new products every year. Demand in developing nations has been growing so quickly, even during tough economic times, that Avon is continually recruiting new reps and expanding its distribution centres to have products available for immediate despatch. More sales reps are the key to meeting goals for long-term sales gains in targeted regions. Over the past three years, Avon has recruited 1 million reps to sell its products throughout China. This has helped push the company's annual turnover in the region beyond £210 million.[29]

When planning for personal selling, consider:

- *Need*. Should your company have its own sales force or sell through retailers, agents, manufacturers' representatives or independent reps such as Avon's sales force? Some online businesses offer 'live chats' with reps who can answer questions and check on product specifications or inventory levels right away.

- *Organisation*. Will you organise reps according to geographic market, product, type of customer, size of customer or some other structure?

- *Size*. How many sales reps should you have, based on your objectives and current sales levels?

- *Compensation*. How will you determine sales force compensation?

- *Management*. How will you recruit, train, supervise, motivate and evaluate sales reps? How will sales reps be educated about legal, regulatory and ethical guidelines?

- *Process*. How will you generate sales leads? How will sales personnel access information about prospects and customers? What logistical activities must be coordinated with sales transactions, and who will be responsible?

PLANNING DIRECT MARKETING

Although mail order and telemarketing are hardly new, a growing number of organisations now include these and other direct marketing techniques in their plans for communications and influence. Why? With better technology, marketers can target audiences more precisely, adjust messages and timing according to audience need and form a dialogue to build relationships cost effectively. Direct marketing costs more than advertising in mass media, yet its interactive quality, selectivity and customisation potential may add enough flexibility to make the difference worthwhile. Just as important, you can easily measure customer response and modify the offer or the communication again and again to move customers in the desired direction and achieve your objectives.

In planning direct marketing, first decide what response you want to elicit from the target audience(s), in accordance with your objectives. Many marketers use direct marketing to generate leads for sales representatives; the desired response is to get a potential customer to indicate interest in the product by calling, e-mailing or sending a reply by post. Banks and mobile phone companies frequently use direct marketing – especially mailings – to attract new customers, bring former customers back and encourage current customers to buy more.

Now you're ready to select appropriate media and formulate an appropriate offer, based on research into the target audience's media and buying patterns. Different audiences and markets require different media and offers. Be sure your direct marketing campaign fits with the product's positioning and allow time in the marketing plan schedule for testing the message and the mechanisms for response (such as a freephone number, URL, e-mail address or postage-paid envelope). One of the advantages of direct marketing is that you can quickly see what actually works and use the results to refine your campaign or the overall marketing plan.

British Telecom, for instance, relies on a range of direct marketing media to reach customers and prospects and encourage a direct response from these audiences. 'We use a lot of channels for direct response: the traditional channels of direct mail, door drops and inserts,' says the retail marketing director, 'We also use television for direct response and quite a lot of online, pay per click.'[30]

PLANNING PUBLIC RELATIONS

At one time or another, nearly every organisation has prepared news releases, arranged news conferences and answered questions from reporters. Yet media contact is only one aspect of this flexible and powerful tool. You can use public relations not just to convey the organisation's messages but also to build mutual understanding and maintain an ongoing dialogue between your organisation and key members of the 'public'. Moreover, your message has more credibility when conveyed by media representatives than when communicated directly by your organisation, as noted earlier.

Defining the 'public'

The 'public' in public relations may refer to people in any number of target audiences, such as customers and prospective customers, employees, channel members, suppliers, news reporters, investors and financial analysts, special interest groups, legislators and regulators, and community leaders. Each of these audiences can affect your plan's success and performance, but not all will be addressed in the same way; in fact, not all may be addressed in a single marketing plan.

In general, you can use PR to achieve one or more of the following objectives:

- *Identify and understand stakeholder concerns.* Through PR contacts such as community meetings, surveys and other methods, you can learn what your stakeholders think and feel about important issues such as your products, image, ecological record and so on. Some companies host or monitor online communities where members of the public exchange ideas and concerns about sustainability and other issues.

- *Convey the organisation's viewpoint or important information.* Knowing your target audience's views, you can adapt your organisation's position if appropriate. At the very least, you can use PR to explain your management's viewpoint or educate the public, especially vital in the midst of a crisis. Often the company website is the first place your publics will check for news and views, so be sure to post information and label links accordingly.

- *Correct misperceptions.* If one or more target audiences have misperceptions about some aspect of your organisation – such as the quality of its products – you can plan to use PR to counteract the inaccuracies by providing more information, answering questions and allowing for periodic updates.

- *Enhance the organisation's image.* Many organisations apply PR techniques to enhance their image. If an organisation has been embroiled in controversy, PR can show what management is doing to improve and how it has gone beyond minimum requirements to satisfy its publics.

- *Promote products and brands.* You can use PR to communicate the features, benefits and value of your products and promote your brands.

Planning and evaluating PR activities

Your marketing plan may include a variety of PR techniques. One of the most commonly used is the news release, written and distributed to media representatives via printed document, e-mail, Web link or *podcasting* (distributing an audio or video file via the Internet). For more significant news, you may want to call a news conference, let media reps hear management speak and hold a question-and-answer session. Also consider whether you should seek publicity through special events or special appearances.

When the mayor of London visited New York City to promote tourism, his highly publicised visit resulted in considerable coverage in multiple media on both sides of the Atlantic.[31]

Although it's nearly impossible to make a direct link between purchasing and PR, you can plan to evaluate how PR activities have engaged your target audience and how you've moved them in the direction of certain cognitive, affective and behavioural responses. For example, before and after a PR event, you can count how many blogs mention your product or brand, determine whether online comments are positive or negative and what commenters are talking about, count how many visitors your website attracts, note how many people buy and what/when they buy, count how many new followers you acquire on Twitter, and count how many viewers your YouTube video attracts.

Also dig deeper to examine what people say about your brand online. Are their comments positive or negative? What other issues are customers discussing online that are important to your product or brand? What can you learn from these discussions that will help you do a better job of engaging customers in dialogue, applying transparency, meeting their needs and influencing how they think, feel and act towards your product?

 **CHAPTER SUMMARY**

Strategies for marketing communications and influence – for promotion – help you engage and influence the thoughts, feelings and behaviour of audiences that are important to your brand. Word of mouth, buzz marketing and social media marketing are part of the influence strategies developed by many organisations. The purpose of integrated marketing communication (IMC) is to ensure that content and delivery of all the marketing messages in all media are coordinated and consistent, and that they support the positioning and objectives of the product, brand or organisation. Communications tools include advertising, sales promotion, public relations, direct marketing and personal selling.

The steps in communications planning are: (1) define the target audience; (2) set objectives and budget; (3) consider relevant legal, regulatory, social and ethical issues; (4) select and plan for the use of specific tools, messages and media; (5) plan pre- and post-implementation analysis; and (6) evaluate the campaign. When planning advertising, consider message appeal, creativity and appropriateness for media, and balance reach and frequency in the context of the budget. Use sales promotion to stimulate faster response from customers or channel members by adding limited-time value (or reducing perceived cost). If personal selling is appropriate, consider in-person sales, Internet sales or telemarketing. Use direct marketing to build relationships with targeted audiences cost effectively and be able to measure response. Plan for public relations to foster positive attitudes and an ongoing dialogue with key publics.

CASE STUDY: SERIOUS MARKETING FOR COMIC RELIEF

Founded in 1985, Comic Relief has a serious purpose: to end poverty and social injustice. The London-based charity uses marketing communications to raise awareness of the issues and raise money so it can make grants to groups that work toward these goals in the UK and in Africa. With the support of corporate partners such as BT, BBC, Sainsbury's and TK Maxx, Comic Relief has raised hundreds of millions of pounds over the years by getting consumers and businesses involved in a fun way and encouraging them to make a serious difference through donations. Comic Relief's two main fundraising events are Red Nose Day and Sport Relief, held in alternating years (Red Nose Day in 2011 and 2013, Sport Relief in 2010 and 2012).

Leading up to Red Nose Day in 2009, Comic Relief planned fun messages in traditional media such as television and radio plus e-mail messages, social media interaction and other online activities. The charity worked with the BBC to publicise the event and the charity by featuring Red Nose-theme content on both BBC online and BBC iPlayer. Media coverage in advance of the fundraising 'BT Red Nose Climb' to the top of Kilimanjaro added to the excitement; day by day, thousands of people followed along on Twitter as the climbers tweeted during their trek up and down the mountain.

Adverts and special videos on YouTube drew millions of viewers and sparked word of mouth about Red Nose Day; they also prompted consumers to create their own Red Nose videos for YouTube viewing. The dedicated website Rednoseday.com drew more than 2 million visitors who clicked to learn how to organise their own fundraisers, find out more about the causes, view adverts, play games, learn about the sponsors, download ad banners and donate money. To raise money, the iTunes UK store sold special Red Nose Day singles and videos; it also donated part of the purchase price of the Top 40 songs to Comic Relief during that week.

On Red Nose Day, celebrities hosted special pages on social networking sites such as Bebo and MySpace, trading comments with visitors and encouraging online donations and support. The charity's Facebook fan page drew 225,000 fans, who discussed that evening's special television programming and bought thousands of virtual red noses to benefit Comic Relief. Television viewers were reminded to donate by calling a special number, sending a text message or clicking online. Companies supported Red Nose Day with their own fundraising events. Kia Motors, for instance, donated £100 from the sale of each limited-edition Picanto Red car and Kia dealerships held local fundraisers to achieve the company's goal of donating £100,000 to Comic Relief. Future Sport Relief and Red Nose Day events will move deeper into social media marketing to build more buzz and raise more money for Comic Relief's causes.[32]

Case questions

1. When Comic Relief communicates with its target audiences, what cognitive, affective and behavioural responses is it trying to influence?

2. If you were the director of marketing for a Red Nose Day corporate sponsor, what types of objectives would you set for communications about your company's involvement, and how would you define your target audience?

 **APPLY YOUR KNOWLEDGE**

Choose a particular product, find two or more advertisements, promotions, websites or other communications in which it is featured, and analyse the company's communication and influence activities. Then prepare a brief oral presentation or written report explaining your analysis.

- What target audience(s) do you think these communications are designed to reach?

- What cognitive, affective or behavioural response(s) might these communications provoke?

- What objectives do you think the company has set for these communications?

- How would you recommend that this firm measure results for the communications you're analysing?

- What legal, regulatory, social or ethical considerations are likely to affect this firm's planning for communications and influence?

- What specific suggestions can you offer to help this marketer do a better job of communicating with or influencing its audience(s)?

 **BUILD YOUR OWN MARKETING PLAN**

Outline your communications and influence activities as you continue developing your marketing plan. What target audience(s) do you want to reach? What are your specific objectives for each audience? What is an appropriate budget, given the available resources, reach and frequency preferences and the chosen tools? Identify any legal, regulatory, social or ethical issues that would affect your communications and influence decisions. Will you use advertising, sales promotion, personal selling, direct marketing and/or public relations – and why? Should you try to stimulate word of mouth (possibly using social media) to achieve your objectives? Outline one campaign, indicating objectives, target audience, general message and media decisions, approximate budget and how results will be measured. Finally, document your ideas in a written marketing plan.

(STOP) ENDNOTES

1. Quoted in Claire Cain Miller, 'Dell says it has earned $3 million from Twitter', *New York Times*, 12 June 2009, http://bits.blogs. nytimes/2009/06/12. Also: Tim Parry, 'Dell does $4 million on Twitter', *Multichannel Merchant*, 1 September 2009, www.multichannelmerchant. com; Chris Daniels, 'Dell's new campaign highlights entrepreneurial "heroes"', *PR Week*, 11 September 2009, www.prweekus.com; www.dell. com; Daniel Ionescu, 'Dell proves that Twitter can be profitable', *PC World*, 9 December 2009, www. pcworld.com.

2. David Heitman, 'Social media marketing for non-profits', *Fast Company blog*, 17 September 2009, www.fastcompany.com/blog/david-heitman/ marketing-and-pr-challenging-economy-edition/ social-media-marketing-non-profits.

3. Raghuram Iyengar, Sangman Han and Sunil Gupta, 'Do friends influence purchases in a social network?', *Harvard Business School Working Paper 09-123*, 21 May 2009, http://hbswk.hbs.edu.

4. Quoted in Jack Neff, 'Lever's CMO throws down the social-media gauntlet', *Advertising Age*, 13 April 2009, p. 1.

5. Quoted in Theresa Howard, 'Signing on to social media', *USA Today*, 1 June 2009, www. usatoday.com.

6. Quoted in Sarah E. Needleman, 'For companies, a tweet in time can avert PR mess', *Wall Street Journal*, 3 August 2009, www.wsj.com.

7. 'Close-up: live issue – cutting a path through new trading regulations', *Campaign*, 6 June 2008, p. 11.

8. Quoted in Mark Prigg, 'Bakery tries to attract customers using Twitter', *London Evening Standard*, 8 April 2009, www.thisislond.co.uk.

9. Rich Karpinksi, 'B-to-B followers flock to Twitter', *BtoB*, 6 April 2009, p. 1.

10. 'Barclaycard takes Waterslide campaign onto mobile in push for iPhone', *New Media Age*, 23 July 2009, p. 4; David Woods, 'Exclusive: Staff engagement levels rise at Barclaycard despite the downturn', *Human Resources*, 10 September 2009, www.hrmagazine.co.uk; 'Barclaycard opens up to online branding', *New Media Age*, 30 April 2009, p. 19; 'Barclaycard highlights "convenience" message', *Marketing*, 22 October 2008, p. 3; barclaycard.co.uk.

11. 'Nissan launches umbrella strategy to push city cars', *Marketing Week*, 2 July 2009, p. 8; Ben Bold, 'Yahoo! and Nissan team up to highlight "simplicity" campaign', *Brand Republic*, 2 September 2009, www.brandrepublic.com;

12. Quoted in Louise Jack, 'Making your messages strike home', *Marketing Week*, 17 September 2009, www.marketingweek.co.uk.

13. Dan Butcher, 'Kellogg runs MMS campaign for cereal recipes', *Mobile Marketer*, 9 April 2009, www.mobilemarketer.com; 'TV date for snap, crackle and pop', *The Sentinel (Staffordshire)*, 19 March 2009, http://www.thisisstaffordshire. co.uk/news/TV-date-snap-crackle-pop/article-781544-detail/article.html.

14. Mike Hibberd, 'Driving force', *Telecoms.com*, 28 September 2009, www.telecoms.com/14830/

driving-force; Rita Chang, 'Getting personal with mobile marketing can boost sales, loyalty', *Advertising Age*, 10 August 2009, p. 14.

15. Andrew Wahl, 'Mobile marketing: always on the move', *Canadian Business*, 28 September 2009, www.canadianbusiness.com.

16. 'Product placement for TV approved', *BBC News*, 13 September 2009, http://news.bbc.co.uk/2/hi/entertainment/8252901.stm; Jackie Schneider, 'No product placement on UK TV shows', *Guardian*, 9 December 2009, www.guardian.co.uk.

17. Rebecca Smith, 'Ban all alcohol advertising and sponsorship, says BMA', *The Telegraph*, 9 September 2009, www.telegraph.co.uk; Mark Sweney, 'BMA demands total ban on alcohol ads', *The Guardian*, 8 September 2009, www.guardian.co.uk/media; 'ASA news: ASA survey shows advertisers comply with alcohol rules', *Advertising Standards Authority*, 8 September 2009, www.asa.org.

18. Quoted in 'Close-up: Is the researcher killing the creative?', *Campaign*, 24 July 2009, p. 11.

19. 'Cadbury feeling sweet', *Times Online*, 6 March 2009, http://business.timesonline.co.uk; Marcus Leroux, 'How Cadbury hope to beat their iconic drumming gorilla ad', *Times Online*, 2 February 2009, http://business.timesonline.co.uk; Agi Zabo, 'Cadbury Gorilla still so sweet', *Media Week*, 23 September 2008, www.mediaweek.co.uk.

20. See Ilchul Kim, Dongsub Han, and Don E. Schultz, 'Understanding the diffusion of integrated marketing communications', *Journal of Advertising Research*, March 2004, pp. 31–45.

21. 'Marketing: Unilever blocks whole day on Star India's entire network', *Business Line*, 17 September 2009, n.p.

22. Dan Matthews, 'How to ... take it outside', *The Marketer*, n.d., www.themarketer.co.uk.

23. Quoted in Belinda Gannaway, 'Hidden danger of sales promotions', *Marketing*, 20 February 2003, pp. 31ff.

24. 'Vouchers: Case study – Unilever', *Marketing Week*, 14 May 2009, p. 27.

25. Mark Sweney, 'Ant and Dec star in Nintendo ads', *The Guardian*, 16 October 2009, www.guardian.co.uk/media; Don Clark, 'Nintendo cuts price of Wii console', *Wall Street Journal*, 24 September 2009, www.wsj.com; Amy Johannes, 'The graying of Nintendo', *Promo*, 1 September 2007, www.promo.com; Ellie Gibson, 'Wii will sell out this Xmas – Nintendo', *Games Industry Biz*, 11 March 2006, www.gamesindustry.biz.

26. April Joyner, 'Nice meeting your avatar: industry trade shows go virtual', *Inc.*, May 2009, p. 98.

27. Deirdre van Dyk, 'Global business: Dreaming of a rebound', *Time*, 12 October 2009, pp. Global 1–4.

28. Quoted in Johanan D. Poblete, 'Direct selling going strong', *BusinessWorld (Philippines)*, 24 August 2009, n.p.

29. 'Avon boss on the offensive', *Telegraph*, 10 October 2009, www.telegraph.co.uk; Stuart Grudgings, 'Beauty booms as Brazil consumers shrug off crisis', *Reuters*, 16 September 2009, www.reuters.com; Gene Marcial, 'Avon: Calling more sales reps', *BusinessWeek*, 6 July 2009, p. 60; 'Ding dong! Empowerment calling', *The Economist*, 30 May 2009, p. 70.

30. Noelle McElhatton, 'Real world – Clients tell us how Royal Mail postal strikes are affecting their businesses', *Marketing Direct*, 22 September 2009, www.marketingdirectmag.co.uk.

31. 'Boris Johnson visits New York to declare London "open for business"', *Daily Mail*, 11 September 2009, www.dailymail.co.uk.

32. 'Britain goes red nose mad', *The Times*, 7 March 2009, www.timesonline.co.uk; 'Kia nose how to support Comic Relief', *Europe Intelligence Wire*, 5 March 2009, n.p.; 'The Lesson: Sport Relief'; *The Guardian*, 4 March 2008, p. 7; www.sportrelief.com; www.rednoseday.com; www.comicrelief.com.

10 Supporting the marketing mix

Comprehension outcomes

After studying this chapter, you will be able to:

- Explain why a marketing plan should include customer service and internal marketing strategies
- Understand planning for customer service and internal marketing

Application outcomes

After studying this chapter, you will be able to:

- Plan for customer service to support the marketing plan
- Plan for internal marketing to support the marketing plan

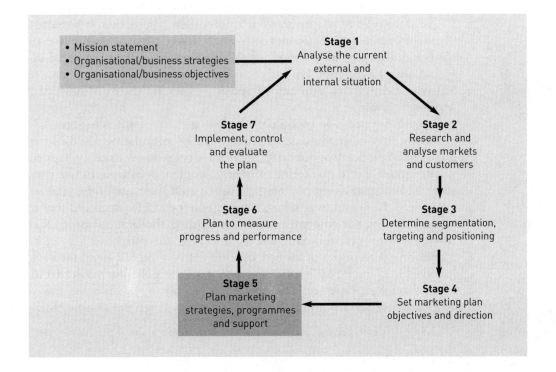

- Mission statement
- Organisational/business strategies
- Organisational/business objectives

Stage 1
Analyse the current external and internal situation

Stage 2
Research and analyse markets and customers

Stage 3
Determine segmentation, targeting and positioning

Stage 4
Set marketing plan objectives and direction

Stage 5
Plan marketing strategies, programmes and support

Stage 6
Plan to measure progress and performance

Stage 7
Implement, control and evaluate the plan

CHAPTER PREVIEW: NET-A-PORTER FASHIONS SERVICE STRATEGY

Natalie Massenet, who founded the London-based luxury fashion retail website Net-a-Porter.com in 2000, aims to provide affluent customers worldwide with the personal service, special style tips and exclusive merchandise selection they would receive in a high-street fashion boutique. Her retail website looks like an upmarket fashion magazine, with multiple photos of each item, detailed descriptions and size information, videos of the latest runway trends, and interviews with top designers. It also offers an exclusive e-mail newsletter with weekly updates about new fashion arrivals, seasonal style trends and designers' thoughts on upcoming collections.

Net-a-Porter's special competitive edge is superior service. Shoppers are pampered with such extras as expedited express despatch to 170 countries, elegant packaging, free style advice, personal shoppers and free returns. Those who live or work in London and New York City can pay an additional fee to receive their designer purchases the same day, delivered directly to their door in the company's signature black-and-white vans. Careful attention to customer service has helped Net-a-Porter grow year after year. Even during the recent economic downturn, Net-a-Porter booked 10,000 orders per week, with an average order of £513, and achieved annual turnover topping £84 million. The retailer delights shoppers in more than 100 nations and signs up 1,200 new customers every week.

The challenge for Net-a-Porter is to continue its growth momentum. The company now offers an iPhone app so users can browse its fashion magazine and shop for the newest styles at any hour, from any location, via mobile. It has also introduced a discount outlet site, theOutnet.com, with marked-down fashions at hefty savings. 'Although the core Net-a-Porter business isn't price sensitive, we found our sale section would attract a different kind of customer – someone just as passionate about fashion, but who didn't place as much emphasis on owning the must-have of the moment,' Massenet explains.[1]

Superior service is an especially compelling point of differentiation for Net-a-Porter, attracting new customers, encouraging loyalty, stimulating word-of-mouth referrals and generating positive publicity. Superior service doesn't simply happen – it requires planning and skilful marketing to internal audiences as well. In this chapter covering stage 5 of the marketing planning process, you'll learn about the vital support role of customer service and internal marketing. You'll consider decisions that must be made when planning for customer service, including those about process and outcome; service levels, service before, during and after the purchase; service recovery; and monitoring perceptions of service. In addition, you'll think about the various decisions involved in planning for internal marketing. Use this chapter's checklist to plan for customer service support. For ideas about how a company incorporates internal marketing and customer service into its marketing activities, see the sample marketing plan in the Appendix.

THE ROLE OF CUSTOMER SERVICE AND INTERNAL PLANNING TODAY

Net-a-Porter's marketing plan must delineate its decisions about product (the assortment of fashion merchandise carried), price (how much to charge for each item), channels and logistics (how customers can obtain its merchandise) and communications and influence (how to connect with and influence customers). All of these marketing-mix decisions are vital, yet they must also be supported by excellent customer service for the retailer to provide the extra value its brand represents. From the customer's perspective, service is an integral part of the experience of dealing with a product or brand. Thus, if a retailer doesn't deliver ordered merchandise on time, for instance, or a manufacturer fails to respond to questions about product specifications, these lapses are perceived as poor customer service.

Unsatisfactory and inconsistent customer service quality can hinder your ability to achieve marketing plan objectives, even if you've meticulously researched targeting and positioning and planned highly creative marketing activities. As you know from your own experience, people often tell others about incidents of good or bad customer service, generating positive or negative word of mouth that can help or hurt a product or brand image. This is an important consideration for marketers of tangible goods as well as marketers of intangible services, especially in today's global marketplace with choices galore.

Bad publicity about customer service can hurt an entire industry's reputation. For example, in one well-publicised survey, only 52 percent of UK customers said they were satisfied with the service they were receiving from their energy suppliers.[2] When the Financial Ombudsman Service releases its annual ranking of UK banks and credit-card companies according to the number of service complaints, widespread media coverage brings the listing to the attention of the entire country.[3] Negative publicity may influence the way current customers think and feel about a company, even if they've been satisfied with its service in the past.

As a result, it's best to view complaints not as annoyances but as opportunities to identify areas for improvement. Plan to give any customers who complain tangible reasons to continue the relationship and also reinforce the loyalty of customers who haven't complained. This is a particular concern for retailers because of the intensely competitive nature of the industry.

As Figure 10.1 indicates, planning for customer service supports the marketing effort outside the organisation and is, in turn, implemented with the support of the internal marketing strategy, which focuses on people and processes inside the organisation.

MARKETING IN PRACTICE: CUSTOMER SERVICE SUPPORT IN RETAILING

Product assortment, location and pricing are key decisions in retail marketing, but customer service support is at least as vital, from the customers' perspective. HMV, the entertainment retailer, employs an outside firm to conduct 'mystery shopping' research and talk with customers as they leave its stores. According to an HMV executive: 'Understanding our customers' experiences and what we can do to improve them has never been more important.'[4]

The Carphone Warehouse retail chain believes good service is so important that employee bonuses depend, in part, on customer feedback. To obtain monthly shopper feedback, a research company sends text messages to 30 customers per shop, asking them to rate various aspects of the service they received. Each month that the shop achieves preset service targets, staff members are eligible for special pay. 'It therefore pays – quite literally – for us to listen to our customers,' says a Carphone Warehouse manager.[5]

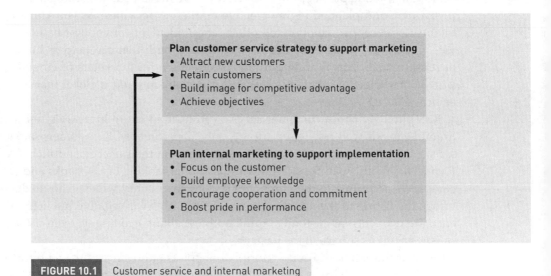

Plan customer service strategy to support marketing
- Attract new customers
- Retain customers
- Build image for competitive advantage
- Achieve objectives

Plan internal marketing to support implementation
- Focus on the customer
- Build employee knowledge
- Encourage cooperation and commitment
- Boost pride in performance

FIGURE 10.1   Customer service and internal marketing

Marketing applications of customer service

Depending on your marketing plan, good customer service may be part of your positioning or inherent in your marketing strategy for building customer relationships and achieving the objectives you've set.

Customer relationships

Consider how customer service can add value, helping to attract and retain customers, especially if your service level is competitively superior. Good customer service is as important in the online world as it is in any other marketing situation. These days, most manufactured goods can't be marketed without attention to quality service support (such as ensuring that orders are delivered when and where promised), as marketers for divisions of Yamaha are well aware.

MARKETING IN PRACTICE: YAMAHA

With aggressive market-share goals in mind, the Japanese manufacturer Yamaha is emphasising customer service, especially in fast-growing target markets. In India, where Yamaha Motors markets motorcycles, one objective is to achieve 100 percent customer satisfaction. Knowing that customers expect speedy maintenance and repairs, the company more than doubled the number of service centres it operates and expanded the number of shops carrying spare parts for repairs. This customer-service initiative helps Yamaha reinforce brand loyalty, support its dealers and differentiate itself within a highly competitive environment.[6]

Yamaha also makes and markets pianos and keyboards, guitars, drums and other musical instruments worldwide. To communicate with channel partners and help them achieve superior customer service, Yamaha Music maintains a comprehensive Yamaha University website with product training tools, videos and quizzes. For consumers, the company makes product manuals available online, along with podcasts of master classes and performances on Yamaha instruments. In-shop demonstrations allow Yamaha's experts to meet salespeople and buyers to gain first-hand knowledge of their needs, interests and questions.[7]

Remember, customers have many choices, so a reputation for good customer service can tip the balance when a consumer or business is deciding whether to buy from *you*. If your current customers remain loyal, you'll need fewer or less expensive customer acquisition programmes to meet your marketing objectives. Moreover, not having to fix a service problem saves money, which can help move you towards your financial objectives.

Marketing plan objectives

To achieve objectives such as increasing market share and enhancing brand image, look for ways to leverage good customer service as a competitive strength. Also consider how to use special customer services to increase sales in specific target segments or markets. Quality customer service can help you defend market share and establish or maintain strong ties with channel members. It will also be a particular priority if your objective is to retain or attain the role of market leader.

Here's how entrepreneur Mike Welch, managing director of Blackcircles.com, uses customer service to support his marketing plans for long-term growth.

MARKETING IN PRACTICE: BLACKCIRCLES.COM

Mike Welch founded Blackcircles.com in Edinburgh as an online tyre retailer in 2001. In less than a decade, by offering top-quality service, he had increased annual turnover to £10 million. Aware that customers are interested in convenience as well as value, Welch has signed up 1,000 garages around the UK so buyers can have tyres fitted locally. During the buying process, a customer chooses a participating garage near home or office, enters the most convenient date and time for tyre fitting and provides payment information. Blackcircles promptly confirms the order with an e-mail containing directions to the local garage and arranges to have the tyres delivered in time for the customer's fitting appointment.

Blackcircles researches service satisfaction by surveying buyers within two weeks after a purchase and posts the results on the website, along with customer testimonials. Often the reported satisfaction level approaches 100 percent. Of the company's new customers, 40 percent choose Blackcircles because of referrals from current customers. The founder has always recognised that great customer service is vital to generating positive word of mouth. From the start, his plan was 'to treat every customer as a new potential communicator of our message to their friends and family', Welch says. 'The same stands today, we are obsessive about customer service.'[8]

Marketing applications of internal marketing

Good customer service – and, in fact, effective implementation of the entire marketing plan – depends on **internal marketing**, a carefully coordinated set of policies and activities designed to build internal employee relationships and reinforce and reward internal commitment to the marketing effort and to good customer service. At the very least, internal audiences need advance notice of new promotions, new products and other marketing activities so that they are prepared when customers respond.

On a larger scale, planning for internal marketing covers decisions about hiring and training managers and employees, motivating and rewarding them for working to satisfy customers and communicating with them about marketing plans and performance. In short, robust internal marketing lays the foundation for implementing your marketing plan and delivering good, consistent customer service.

You can use internal marketing in the following areas:

- *Focus on the customer*. Some employees in functions with little customer contact – such as finance or human resources – may get caught up in the daily pressures of work and lose their customer focus. Internal marketing is a good way to refocus on the customer and remind employees that their performance is essential for implementing plans that serve and satisfy customers. The US discount retail chain Target uses internal marketing to keep store managers informed about upcoming promotions so they'll be ready when shoppers ask for featured products. In turn, managers use internal marketing to communicate with staff members about external marketing objectives and initiatives.[9]

- *Build employee knowledge.* Be sure employees at every level know at least the general outline of the marketing effort, are informed about the needs and expectations of targeted customers and understand what the organisation wants to achieve. This knowledge gives them the background they need to serve customers and solve any service problems.

- *Encourage organisation-wide cooperation with and commitment to the plan.* Success really is in the details. If your organisation's employees do not understand the plan or resent it, they may not give details the proper attention, let alone implement every tactic to full effect. Remember that marketing is not the only function affected by the marketing plan; manufacturing, finance and all the other departments must cooperate to achieve the objectives and you need senior management's support. Use internal marketing to build relations inside the organisation and encourage commitment among those responsible for approving the plan and making it succeed through implementation.

- *Boost pride in performance.* Internal marketing can increase employees' sense of involvement and boost their pride in performing over and above expectations. For example, the Marco Polo Hongkong Hotel gives widespread internal recognition to employees who deliver outstanding service, based on guest comments. Such feedback shows employees that the organisation and its customers appreciate good customer service. 'Guests judge us immediately. They will not come again if we deliver mediocre service,' the general manager observes.[10]

The next two sections highlight how you can plan for customer service and for internal marketing as you prepare your marketing plan. Many of the examples in the following pages are from service businesses but the customer service ideas can be adapted for many situations.

PLANNING FOR CUSTOMER SERVICE

Knowing what your customers want and value, you face process decisions about how to make the customer service experience as pleasant as possible. You also face outcome decisions related to whether the customer service is delivered on time, as promised and in a satisfactory manner. Your customers will be dissatisfied if they receive the promised quality of service but find the experience of arranging for it tedious or inconvenient. Meanwhile, customers who are satisfied with both the process and the outcomes are likely to become loyal.

The specific process and outcome decisions that you will make depend on your objectives, marketing strategies, resources and capabilities. You must also consider what levels of customer service you will promise and be able to deliver, including whether self-service is appropriate, decide on the type of customer service you will offer before, during and after a purchase, formulate a process for recovering from any customer service lapses, and plan to monitor service comments (see Table 10.1).

Table 10.1 Key customer service strategy decisions

Decision	Purpose
Process	To create a satisfactory experience for customers who expect or require service delivery
Outcomes	To deliver service on time, as promised and with the expected result for customer satisfaction
Timing	To provide needed service before, during or after a purchase
Service recovery	To handle complaints, fix lapses in service delivery, anticipate potential problems and identify areas for improvement
Perception monitoring	To understand how customers perceive the organisation's customer service

Determining service levels

Few companies can afford the highest level of customer service, with completely personalised attention immediately available on request, but then again, not every customer in every segment can afford (or will expect) such service. As you saw in the chapter-opening example, Net-a-Porter targets high-income shoppers who expect and receive superior service that sets the online retailer apart from its rivals. However, low price doesn't necessarily mean low service levels. For instance, Amazon.com's customers appreciate the low prices, on-time delivery and 30-day returns guarantee.

In many industries where price competition is commonplace, there is a trend towards eliminating extras and cutting costs, often by automating service procedures. Ryanair and easyJet are two no-frills, low-fare airlines that minimise customer service costs by getting customers to buy tickets online and pay extra for inflight food and drinks and for seat reservations. Self-service can supplement other service choices, especially during periods of peak demand. Some supermarkets have self-service checkout, for example; vending machines, a form of self-service, dispense everything from deli sandwiches to DVDs.[11] Yet companies may choose to maintain customer service levels even when they reduce prices for competitive reasons. When Sony, Microsoft and Nintendo cut the prices of their video-game consoles, they didn't change their service-support strategies.

The level of customer service you plan should be consistent with the following elements:

- *Customer needs and expectations.* What do targeted customers want, need and expect in terms of customer service? Use marketing research to identify the service levels that would satisfy customers in each targeted segment, uncover trends in customer turnover and determine whether customers are defecting because of poor customer service. If you segment your market according to service usage and expectations, you may find promising opportunities and steer the organisation away from unprofitable segments. For instance, depending on customer requirements, price sensitivity and other factors, you may plan a high level of service to support your most expensive products and a lower level of service to support your least expensive products.

- *Positioning and competitive strategies.* What level of service is consistent with your product's or brand's positioning? What level of service would help the product or brand compete more effectively? Because Commonwealth Bank in Australia understands the value of a positioning based on good customer service, its managers redesigned service processes to produce better service outcomes. As one example, they eliminated redundant bank procedures, rearranged branch layouts and changed staffing (process), aiming to reduce queue times to five minutes or less (outcome). Good service will be even more important in the future because, the bank's head of retail banking services says, 'in terms of what will shape the industry, I can sum it up in a single word – convenience'.[12]

- *Other marketing-mix decisions.* Is the product new or complicated? To provide service for customers who buy its high-end televisions, for example, Philips India has opened a series of Star Service Centres that stock parts and diagnose product problems. To showcase its advanced lighting products, it set up shop-in-shop areas with special displays and service.[13] How is pricing likely to influence customers' expectations of customer service? Do the product's promotions promise or imply a high level of customer service? What level of customer service can your channel members deliver? How will a certain level of customer service fit in with the strategies and objectives in your marketing plan?

- *Organisational resources and strengths.* What level of customer service fits in with your organisation's financial and human resources? Is technology available to support or substitute for customer service delivery? Is good customer service delivery a particular strength? Can or should customer service be outsourced? In deciding about customer service levels, you should carefully analyse the cost–benefit trade-offs for each targeted segment.

Brands that include superior service in their positioning, making it an integral element in the brand promise, must be ready to deliver on that high level every day. Mercedes-Benz does this as part of its marketing plan implementation.

MARKETING IN PRACTICE: MERCEDES-BENZ

The German car manufacturer Mercedes-Benz brings buyers into dealerships around the world by communicating its vehicles' top-notch engineering, design and performance. Positive experiences with the product and with support services such as routine maintenance generate revenue and encourage brand loyalty. However, if customers have complaints, they expect local dealers to come up with solutions.

In Europe, Mercedes is driving for higher customer service satisfaction by benchmarking against top dealerships and providing its employees and dealers with additional service training. Dealers that improve their customer-satisfaction scores will be rewarded with higher margins. In Canada, where Mercedes-Benz owns 17 dealerships, the company's marketing plan emphasises delivery of a consistently high level of service. 'We do not want to have heroes,' says the president of Mercedes Canada. 'We do not want to have Mr Superman or Mrs Superman. We just want to have people who do a great job every day, independent of who is on shift and in charge today, and [know] that our customers can rely on that.'[14]

Planning for service before, during and after purchases

Depending on your product and market, customers may have questions and require service assistance before they buy. Business buyers in particular may need help with product specifications or configuration, installation options and warranty or repair information. During the negotiation of a very large or complex business purchase, buyer and seller may agree on a certain level of post-purchase service to be delivered under contract. In negotiating such contracts, be sure you understand what your customers require and how you can meet those requirements at a profit once the purchase has been completed.[15]

If you market directly to customers, you must be prepared to provide at least some service before a purchase transaction. If you market through intermediaries, you will be relying on channel members to answer customers' questions and demonstrate features. Your marketing plan may therefore include tactics for channel training and sales promotion activities targeting wholesale or retail sales representatives. Before Apple and Microsoft release new operating system software, for instance, they provide training and support materials to resellers who will, in turn, deal with customer purchases, questions and concerns.

At the time or place of the purchase, your customers may want help in testing a product, completing the paperwork for a transaction, arranging for delivery or pick-up, arranging payment method or terms, taking advantage of promotions connected with purchasing, or other purchase-related service tasks. If your customer service falls short here, customers may not complete the purchase; conversely, if you deliver good customer service during the purchase transaction, you will build customer satisfaction and encourage repeat purchasing.

If you market through intermediaries, you'll plan for point-of-purchase service through activities such as product and sales training. For upmarket or technical products, however, your marketing plan may call for delivering point-of-purchase service on your own. When Apple established its own chain of retail stores, the company was aiming to control the environment in which its products are displayed and demonstrated and to control the quality of customer service delivered at the point of purchase. Some manufacturers establish special showrooms where potential customers can browse and try products. Nokia, for instance, recently set up an 'experience centre' in Nigeria to showcase its mobile phones and applications; it refers customers to nearby authorised dealers for the actual purchase.[16]

To encourage repeat business and strengthen customer relations, you'll probably have to deliver some sort of customer service after the purchase. This may include training buyers in product use, explaining maintenance or repair procedures, exchanging defective products, returning products for refunds, installing replacement parts, or other post-purchase services. Some companies use technology to detect the need for post-purchase service even before customers notice any problems. Many provide targeted customer segments with special services. Every weekday morning, for example, the Fujitsu Premium Care Centre in Singapore designates priority queues for students who bring in a notebook computer for repair.[17]

When customers seek service months or years after they buy your product, you have an opportunity to reinforce their image of and loyalty to your brand. By providing the level of maintenance or repair service that customers expect, you remind them of why they selected your brand in the first place and give them yet another reason to choose your brand next time. IWC Schaffhausen, which makes upmarket wristwatches, trains staff members in its branded boutiques to provide special attention to customers whose watches need servicing, as one of the ways it shows appreciation for their loyalty.[18]

Monitoring service perceptions

Your marketing plan should provide for monitoring what customers think of the service you're delivering. Monitoring and protecting your reputation ultimately enables you to maintain strong relationships with customers and other stakeholders. In fact, inviting online reviews of customer service, product quality and other aspects of your business can build trust and enhance your reputation for transparency and customer responsiveness.[19] On average, such reviews tend to be quite positive – even higher in the UK than in the US. 'If you inspire passion in somebody in a good way or a bad way, that is when they want to write a review', says an executive at Amazon.com.[20]

You should analyse comments made in letters, phone calls, e-mail and on your company website. Also monitor what customers (and others) say about your service and your brand elsewhere on the web by searching for comments on:

- *Review websites.* Yelp and other websites invite customers to post reviews and ratings of restaurants, shops and other establishments in London, Glasgow, Los Angeles and other cities.

- *Retail websites.* Amazon.com pioneered the idea of getting customers to rate and critique products and sellers. Now many other online retailers are doing the same.

- *YouTube.* Customers sometimes post videos online to let the world know about good or bad service experiences. When Canadian singer Dave Carroll was dissatisfied with the response after he complained to United Airlines that his guitar had been damaged by baggage handlers, he posted a series of YouTube music videos about his experience. *United Breaks Guitars* and its sequels have been seen by more than 6 million people. In response, United Airlines donated cash to charity, at Carroll's request, and began using the incident in its training for baggage handlers and customer-service employees.[21]

- *Blogs and miniblogs.* Many consumers, journalists and industry observers blog or tweet their complaints and compliments.

Inevitably, your monitoring will turn up a negative comment, so be ready to respond by communicating with the customer, taking action to correct the problem and adding to the customer's public comment with a note about what you've done to make things right. Some companies invite people to tweet their opinions and expectations and have service experts ready to resolve any complaints that are registered. British Telecom maintains a Twitter account for customer service assistance; BT's representatives on duty show their names in the 'profile' section to add a personal touch. However, resist the temptation to anonymously post online comments about your goods or services, which is illegal in the UK and ethically questionable in any case.

Planning for service recovery

Because customer service may not be delivered perfectly every time, you should plan for **service recovery**: how your organisation will recover from a service lapse and satisfy customers. Service recovery offers an excellent opportunity to demonstrate understanding of customers' expectations and needs and – equally important – rebuild ties with customers by implementing a speedy and satisfactory resolution. According to one study, at least 70 per cent of dissatisfied customers will keep buying from a company if their complaints are resolved satisfactorily. If you please these customers you can turn them from potential defectors into advocates for your organisation, a good way to stimulate positive word of mouth.[22]

Internal marketing is vital for service recovery, because employees must have the commitment, skills and authority to clarify the extent and nature of a service lapse, offer a suitable response and see that it is implemented as promised. As you plan for service recovery, focus on both process and outcome (see Figure 10.2). Customers will be more dissatisfied if you provide no convenient method for receiving complaints or fail to resolve their complaints satisfactorily. At times, customers may only want a way to express their dissatisfaction, know that their voices are heard and receive a sincere apology. In one recent study of online comments about a wholesaler, nearly half of the consumers who had posted negative or neutral reviews were willing to withdraw their comments after the company apologised.[23]

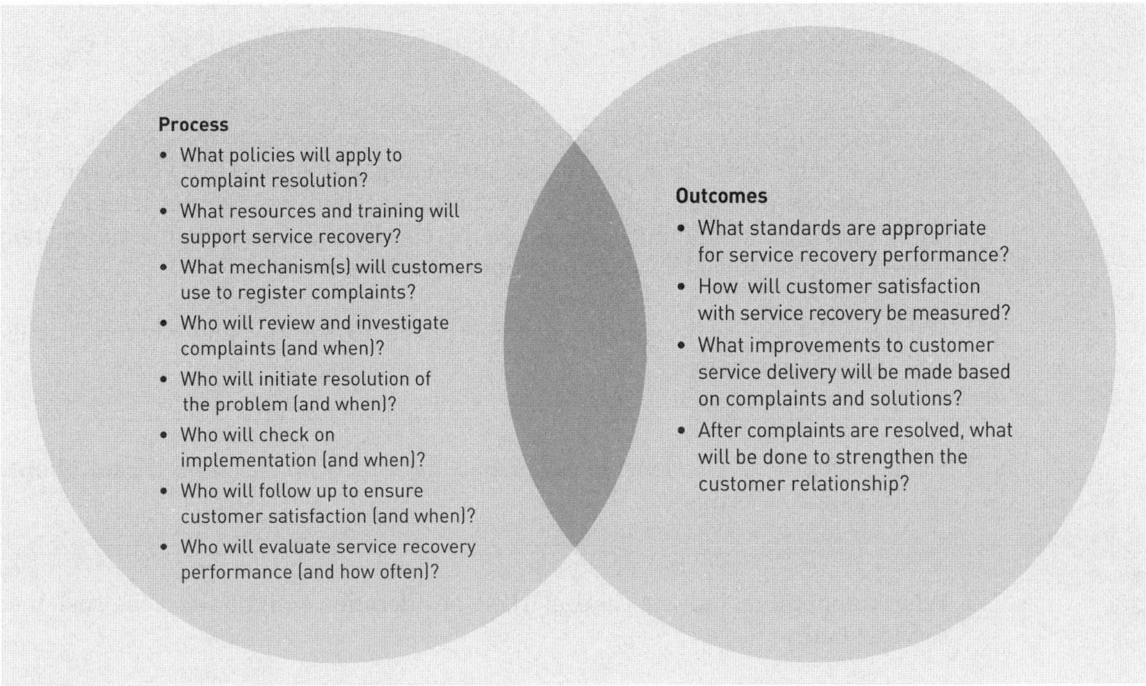

Process

- What policies will apply to complaint resolution?
- What resources and training will support service recovery?
- What mechanism(s) will customers use to register complaints?
- Who will review and investigate complaints (and when)?
- Who will initiate resolution of the problem (and when)?
- Who will check on implementation (and when)?
- Who will follow up to ensure customer satisfaction (and when)?
- Who will evaluate service recovery performance (and how often)?

Outcomes

- What standards are appropriate for service recovery performance?
- How will customer satisfaction with service recovery be measured?
- What improvements to customer service delivery will be made based on complaints and solutions?
- After complaints are resolved, what will be done to strengthen the customer relationship?

FIGURE 10.2   Planning service recovery process and outcomes

Be aware, however, that the number of complaints usually understates the actual number of service failures experienced by your customers, because not every dissatisfied customer will take the time to complain. Your organisation could be losing customers due to an ineffective service recovery plan, and you might never know the reason. By encouraging two-way communication with your customers and paying close attention to negative and positive comments, you'll build trust and gain valuable insights into service problems and achievement.[24]

Be sure to seek the input of staff members who deal directly with customers when determining what tools and support you need to correct service mistakes. Also solicit suggestions from these employees for practical ways to improve delivery and prevent service lapses. And try to involve top management in service recovery, as doing so will go a long way towards proving your organisation's commitment to satisfaction and to keeping the customer relationship alive.

As you consider how to incorporate customer service support into your marketing plan, use the following checklist.

ESSENTIAL MARKETING PLAN CHECKLIST NO. 15:
PLANNING FOR CUSTOMER SERVICE SUPPORT

This checklist will guide you through the main issues to research and analyse as you plan for customer service to support your marketing activities. After you write your ideas in the spaces provided, put a tick next to the questions you've answered. If your marketing plan is for a hypothetical firm, use this checklist as a guide to the information you'd need to gather to make decisions about customer service.

☐ What level of service do targeted customers need, expect and prefer before, during and after the purchase?

_____

☐ What customer service level is reasonable and practical, based on organisational resources and objectives?

_____

☐ What competitive, industry and market considerations might affect the customer service plan?

_____

☐ What legal, regulatory, ecological, technological, social or ethical issues might affect the customer service plan?

_____

☐ How will you monitor customer perceptions of your service activities?

_____

☐ How will you train and reward employees and channel members for providing good customer service?

_____

☐ What service recovery plans and policies do you need?

_____

PLANNING FOR INTERNAL MARKETING

Ideally, you want your internal marketing activities to engage the hearts and minds of managers and employees at every organisational level – the internal equivalent of what good external marketing seeks to achieve. First, of course, you will 'market' the marketing plan to gain senior management approval and support. Then, for the approved plan to succeed, you need internal marketing to build enthusiastic commitment among the organisation's middle managers, front-line managers and employees. This means going beyond a catchy slogan or one-time special event to develop an ongoing internal marketing strategy that you can adapt as the situation changes.

Although the specifics of internal marketing strategy will differ from organisation to organisation, most touch on the following:

- *Hiring and training*. Even when you are not directly involved in personnel decisions, you can influence hiring procedures to ensure that new employees have a positive attitude towards customer service. You should also influence or participate in training to build the staff's knowledge of the customer and of the marketing effort.

- *Standards*. What, exactly, constitutes performance in implementing marketing programmes? Your performance standards should be consistent with the marketing plan's (and the organisation's) objectives, with other job-related standards, with what customers want and with what you are promising and promoting.

- *Communication*. This is essential for reinforcing objectives and standards, coordinating programmes and implementing responsibilities, keeping employees informed and keeping them interested and connected. You can use any number of communication techniques, from printed newsletters and voice-mail messages to internal websites and teleconferences. For instance, the Marco Polo Hongkong Hotel has condensed its service basics into five succinct messages introduced at a company party, repeated at staff meetings and printed on pocket calendars for employees to check daily. The hotel also circulates the results of customer service studies and compliments submitted by guests.

- *Participation*. Inviting participation in the marketing planning process can encourage stronger support and commitment among those who are charged with implementation. Customer contact personnel, in particular, may be able to suggest how your proposed programmes can be improved. In other words, view internal marketing communication as a two-way, relationship-building dialogue, with information flowing to you and from you.

- *Monitoring and rewards*. Are employees performing up to the standards that have been set and cooperating for smooth implementation of marketing programmes? If not, what needs improvement? If so, how should you reinforce and reward good performance? Your internal marketing reward system must be consistent with the organisation's overall system of motivation, performance evaluation and rewards.

See Chapter 12 for more about controlling marketing plan implementation.

CHAPTER SUMMARY

Customer service supports the external marketing effort and, in turn, must be supported by internal marketing focusing on people and processes inside the organisation. Customer service can help the organisation attract new customers, retain current customers, build image for competitive advantage and achieve its objectives. Internal marketing can help the organisation focus on customers, increase employee knowledge, encourage internal cooperation and commitment to marketing and boost pride in performance.

Marketers face decisions about process (the experience customers will have in arranging for customer service) and outcomes (delivering service on time, as promised and to the customer's satisfaction). They also face decisions about the appropriate level of customer service to be promised and delivered, the delivery of customer service before, during and after a purchase, how to monitor customer comments about service, and the process of recovering from any customer service lapses.

CASE STUDY: INTERNAL MARKETING AND SERVICE SUPPORT AT INTEL

Computers were massive room-size machines used by corporations and colleges when Intel was founded in California in 1968. Today, Intel brings in £22.5 billion in annual turnover by marketing sophisticated computer chips and wireless networking components to manufacturers of laptops, mobiles, medical devices, next-generation windmills and other products. Planning for future growth while it navigates challenging economic circumstances and addresses questions about antitrust allegations, Intel's goal is 'to be the preeminent provider of semiconductor chips and platforms for the worldwide digital economy'.[25]

To achieve this long-term corporate goal, Intel's marketers must plan carefully for internal marketing and service support. Nearly two decades of 'Intel Inside' campaigns, implemented through the company's marketing plans, have built the brand into a household name, contributed to pull strategies and provided a solid foundation for reaching market-share and revenue objectives. Recent campaigns have featured the accomplishments of Intel employees responsible for breakthroughs such as the invention of the USB connection, with employees singing the five-note Intel theme that ends each advert. The company uses social media such as Twitter and Facebook to communicate with and influence business and consumer buyers, following transparency guidelines that require employees to identify themselves as working for Intel.

Although Intel's products do not stand alone – they are incorporated into other manufacturers' products – the company invests millions to understand how its customers' customers think about, feel about and act towards technology. Its marketers encourage employees at all levels to share their insights and suggest ideas for tomorrow's goods and services, a valuable dialogue that brings different views into the process. To ensure that all those inside Intel know about company strategy, plans, campaigns and cutting-edge technological advances, the management and marketing teams keep up a steady stream of internal communications. In addition, Intel's sales personnel can log onto the company's internal sites and the Second Life virtual world for training, support and product information.

As part of its marketing plan targeting resellers that customise computer and networking systems using Intel chips and components, Intel provides three levels of service through its channel partners programme. Participating partners receive priority technical support and expedited shipment of replacement parts, marketing materials and information for personal selling, opportunities to learn about the latest Intel offerings at conferences and in-person or online training sessions, and loyalty rewards to encourage ongoing purchasing. They can also listen to Intel podcasts, live-chat with a support specialist about particular issues, ask or answer questions in Intel-sponsored online communities and 'ask an expert' for special assistance. Finally, Intel's marketers have detailed plans for service recovery to keep both resellers and manufacturers satisfied.[26]

Case questions

1. Why would Intel offer service support for resellers at three different levels? What criteria would you suggest that Intel use to determine how much service support to provide at each level?

2. What are the internal marketing benefits of having employees participating in social media and recording the Intel theme for company adverts?

 **APPLY YOUR KNOWLEDGE**

To see how customer service supports a firm's marketing mix, select a retailer with a nearby store location and an online presence. Visit one store, browse the website and then analyse this retailer's approach to customer service. Prepare a brief oral or written report summarising your analysis.

- Where on the website does the retailer place its customer service policies? Where in the store are such policies displayed? Are the policies practical and easy to understand?

- How would you describe the level of service in the store? Is it consistent with the retailer's positioning and competitive situation, its pricing and its other marketing activities?

- What customer service is offered online? Does the website invite shoppers to interact with service representatives via e-mail, online chat, telephone or some other method?

- Are pre-purchase, point-of-purchase and/or post-purchase services offered in the store? What self-service options, if any, are available? How do these differ (if at all) from the services offered to online customers?

- What changes in customer service would you suggest for this retailer? Why?

- Briefly search for online comments about this retailer. Summarise what you find and what the store's responses were, if any. What would you recommend this retailer to do to enhance and protect its service reputation online?

 ## BUILD YOUR OWN MARKETING PLAN

Continue your marketing plan by making decisions about customer service and internal marketing. First, what is an appropriate level of customer service to support your positioning and other marketing-mix decisions? Do you know how this level of service fits with customers' needs and expectations? Does your customer service add more value than that offered by competitors? What pre-purchase, point-of-purchase and post-purchase customer service will you plan to offer and what resources will you need? Should you offer any self-service options? How will you use internal marketing to communicate the marketing plan and build commitment inside the company? How will you monitor customer perceptions of your service support? Outline a customer service or internal marketing programme, as applicable, indicating the specific audience or market being targeted and what you expect to achieve. Explain how this programme will contribute to meeting your plan's objectives.

 ## ENDNOTES

1. Quoted in Rhiannon Harries, 'Discount dreamland: Net-a-Porter's sister site offers high-end glamour at an 80 percent markdown', *Independent*, 3 May 2009, www.independent.co.uk/life-style/. Other sources: 'Net-a-Porter launches iPhone application', *Retail Week*, 17 July 2009, www.retail-week.com; John Brodie, 'A winning formula for fashion retail', *Fortune*, 2 September 2009, http://money.cnn.com/2009/09/02/technology/net_a_porter.fortune; www.theoutnet.com; www.net-a-porter.com; Lucie Greene, 'Why gift concierges are thriving', *Financial Times*, 12 December 2009, www.ft.com.

2. Ali Hussain, 'Consumers unhappy with energy suppliers', *Times Online*, 22 September 2009, www.timesonline.co.uk.

3. Josephine Cumbo, 'High street banks top complaint list', *Financial Times*, 16 September 2009, www.ft.com.

4. Quoted in James Verrinder, 'HMV appoints Retail Eyes for customer service task', *Research*, 22 September 2009, www.research-live.com.

5. Quoted in Joe Fernandez, 'Even negative views improve brand image', *Marketing Week*, 10 September 2009, www.marketingweek.co.uk; also: Michael Garwood, 'Mystery shop affects bonuses', *Mobile News*, 21 September 2009, www.mobilenewscwp.co.uk.

6. 'Yamaha drafts aggressive script for India', *India Business Insight*, 1 November 2009, n.p.; 'Yamaha India targets 1.4 lakh unit bike exports by 2010-end', *Wheels Unplugged*, 17 September 2009, www.wheelsunplugged.com; 'Yamaha sales jump 60 pc in 2009', *Economic Times*, 1 January 2010, http://economictimes.indiatimes.com.

7. 'Creating a single Yamaha', *Music Trades*, January 2009, pp. 99ff; http://uk.yamaha.com.

8. Quoted in Graham Charlton, 'Q&A: Mike Welch of online tyre seller Blackcircles.com', *Econsultancy*, 20 March 2009, http://econsultancy.com; also: Linda Jones, 'If you only do one thing this week ...' *Guardian*, 7 September 2009, www.guardian.co.uk; www.blackcircles.com.

9. 'Target masters art of internal communications', *MMR*, 17 November 2008, p. 31.

10. Quoted in Wendy Ng, 'Guests help hotel to raise levels of service excellence', *Asia Africa Intelligence Wire*, 29 March 2003, n.p.

11. Maria Halkias, 'Self-service kiosks bloom, saving time for shoppers and costs for stores', *Dallas Morning News*, 28 September 2009, www.dallasnews.com.

12. 'Impudent newcomers take on incumbents in retail banking', *Australian Banking & Finance*, 30 September 2006, pp. 6ff; 'Harley focuses on the service experience', *Australian Banking & Finance*, 15 July 2003, p. 11.

13. 'Philips to up investment in India, China by 27 per cent', *Press Trust of India*, 22 September 2009, www.business-standard.com/india; 'Philips now for Star Service at premium end', *Asia Africa Intelligence Wire*, 28 July 2003, n.p.

14. Quoted in Nicolas Van Praet, 'How Mercedes got its groove back', *Financial Post (Montreal)*, 8 June 2009, www.montrealgazette.com. Also: Jason Stein and Diana T. Kurylko, 'Mercedes begins push to bolster CSI scores', *Automotive News*, 16 October 2006, p. 8; Harold Hamprecht, 'Mercedes wants friendly, profitable dealers', *Automotive News Europe*, 6 February 2006, p. 22.

15. Ritu Jain, 'Why customer service needs to be more than mere lip service', *Industry Week*, 18 September 2009, www.industryweek.com.

16. 'Nigeria: Nokia debuts first experience centre in Otigba Market', *All Africa*, 28 September 2009, http://allafrica.com.

17. N. Ravindran, 'Meeting customer needs despite challenges', *Today's Manager*, June–July 2009, pp. 35ff.

18. Christina Binkley, 'How to sell a $35,000 watch in a recession', *Wall Street Journal*, 4 August 2009, www.wsj.com.

19. Jennifer Alsever, 'Even bad reviews boost sales', *Fortune Small Business*, 28 September 2009, http://money.cnn.com/2009/09/28/smallbusiness/retail_democracy.fsb.

20. Quoted in Geoffrey A. Fowler and Joseph de Avila, 'On the Internet, everyone's a critic but they're not very critical', *Wall Street Journal*, 5 October 2009, www.wsj.com.

21. 'Singer gets his revenge on United Airlines and soars to fame', *Guardian*, 23 July 2009, www.guardian.co.uk; Dan Reed, 'United Airlines' makeover aims to refresh and renew', *USA Today*, 17 September 2009, www.usatoday.com.

22. Jena McGregor, 'Customer service champs', *BusinessWeek*, 5 March 2007, pp. 52ff.

23. Douglas MacMillan, 'Why it pays to apologise', *BusinessWeek*, 12 October 2009, p. 22.

24. Stefan Michel, 'Turning customer frustration into customer loyalty', *Jakarta Post*, 25 February 2009, p. 17.

25. Goal quoted on Intel website, www.intc.com/strategy.cfm.

26. James Ashton, 'Computing? We've only just begun, says Intel chief', *Sunday Times*, 11 October 2009, p. 9; Ellen McGirt, 'Intel risks it all (again)', *Fast Company*, November 2009, pp. 88ff; Barbara Lippert, 'I love you, tomorrow', *MediaWeek*, 5 October 2009, p. 18; 'Intel antitrust allegations detailed', *InformationWeek*, 21 September 2009, www.informationweek.com; Lauren McKay, 'Social shepherds: if you expect employees to stay within the lines, you need to draw the lines first', *CRM Magazine*, June 2009, p. 15; Scott Morrison, 'A second chance for Second Life – Northrop, IBM use virtual world as setting for training, employee meetings', *Wall Street Journal*, 19 August 2009, p. B5; www.intel.com.

Planning metrics and performance measurement

Comprehension outcomes

After studying this chapter, you will be able to:

- Explain the role of metrics in planning to track progress towards marketing performance
- Understand how to use forecasts, budgets and schedules in marketing planning

Application outcomes

After studying this chapter, you will be able to:

- Select metrics to measure progress towards financial, marketing and societal objectives
- Prepare for forecasting, budgeting and scheduling to support your plan

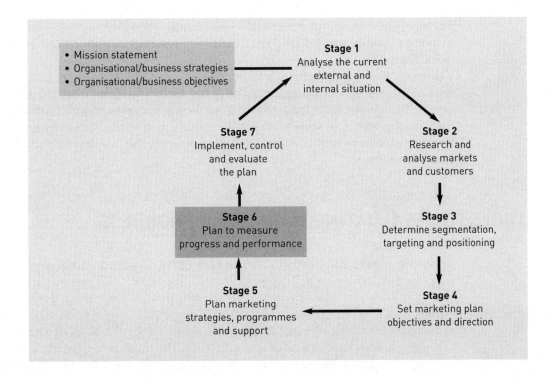

CHAPTER PREVIEW: MALAYSIA AIRLINES

A few years ago, Malaysia Airlines was struggling to recover from heavy losses as costs skyrocketed, cash ran low and competition increased. Managers needed a turnaround marketing plan that would show results quickly. As part of the situation analysis, they measured the profitability of each route and flight. Then they dropped the most unprofitable routes and created a marketing plan to improve the profitability of the routes targeted as the most financially promising. The plan also aimed to boost the customer base by increasing passenger loads, especially on routes with capacity, through a combination of careful pricing and upgraded services.

After implementing the marketing plan, managers arranged to measure results through a daily summary of profitability by region and, within each region, by route and individual flight. Now Malaysia Airlines' executives use the daily profitability report to assess the financial results of marketing programmes such as the Global Low Fares campaign, designed to introduce the airline to new customers worldwide and to fill more seats on each flight. The airline is also using mobile marketing to sell tickets, allow passengers to check in and communicate flight details. This 'enhances the product and in the long run, reduces our cost and helps us increase revenue while customers get more satisfaction', says the chief executive.[1]

Malaysia Airlines must measure marketing performance to determine whether its plans are having the intended effect. The time to plan for measuring progress is before implementation, so measurement standards and checkpoints can be established in advance. Then, after implementation, you can see when and where performance is not meeting expectations and prepare to improve results by applying marketing control (see Chapter 12).

In Stage 6 of the marketing planning process, you will decide how to track performance towards your marketing, financial and societal objectives. This chapter will teach you about the four tools for measuring marketing progress and performance: metrics, forecasts, budgets and schedules. See the sample plan in the Appendix for ideas about how these tools are applied in the marketing plan; review this chapter's checklist as you plan your metrics.

TOOLS FOR EVALUATING MARKETING PROGRESS

Every programme and tactic in your marketing plan should contribute, if only in a small way, towards achieving your objectives and, ultimately, your organisation's goals. As shown in Table 11.1, you can measure marketing plan progress using these four tools:

- **Metrics** are specific numerical standards used on a regular basis to measure selected performance-related activities and outcomes. The point is to examine interim results by applying metrics measurements at set intervals and analyse progress towards meeting marketing plan objectives. Marketing expert Tim Ambler stresses that the metrics used by top management should be vital to the business, precise, consistent and comprehensive.[2]

- **Forecasts** project the estimated level of sales (for example, by product or market) and costs (for example, by product or channel) for the specific period covered by the marketing plan. By comparing actual sales and costs with forecast levels, you can spot deviations and prepare to adjust your assumptions or your activities as trends develop.

- **Budgets** are time-defined allotments of financial resources for specific programmes, activities and products. You might, for example, prepare one overall advertising budget and allocate it across specific campaigns, programmes, products or geographic areas. After implementing the marketing plan, you check whether actual spending is above, below or at the budgeted level.

- **Schedules** are time-defined plans for coordinating and accomplishing tasks related to a specific programme or activity, such as new product development. You will prepare individual schedules showing starting and ending dates as well as responsibilities for the major tasks within a programme, plus an overall schedule reflecting the key tasks and target dates for implementing marketing plan programmes.

Table 11.1 Measuring marketing plan performance

Tool	Description	Use
Metric	Specific numerical standard measuring an outcome that contributes to performance	Target for interim achievement against which to measure actual outcome
Forecast	Forward-looking estimate expressed in unit or monetary terms	Projected level of sales or costs against which to measure actual results
Budget	Funding allotment for specific programme or activity	Guideline for spending, against which actual expenditures are measured
Schedule	Series of target dates for tasks related to a particular programme or activity	Guideline for anticipated timing against which to measure actual timing

If you achieve the expected results day after day, you will move ever closer to accomplishing both short-term objectives and long-term goals. However, avoid overemphasising short-term measurements because of the risk that you might lose sight of what customers really want and what your organisation is striving to achieve. At the same time, don't wait too long to act if you identify significant shifts in competition or other elements that begin to affect the progress you expected to make towards your objectives. In short, try for a balanced perspective as you apply the metrics, forecasting, budgeting and scheduling tools discussed in the remainder of this chapter.

MEASURING PROGRESS WITH METRICS

After implementation, how will you (and your management) know whether progress is being made towards achieving the marketing plan's objectives? Metrics allow you to measure the outcomes and activities that really contribute to performance. Organisations are concerned about holding marketing accountable for achieving the expected results, which is why the use of metrics is an important part of marketing planning. Like Cisco Systems, you'll need clear objectives and baseline measures against which to compare interim results and ultimate performance.

MARKETING IN PRACTICE: CISCO

With £5.3 billion in annual turnover, Cisco Systems is a global powerhouse in computer networking systems and uses marketing to communicate with and influence business customers, channel partners, consumers and the community. Its marketing plan includes objectives for increasing brand awareness, enhancing brand image, increasing traffic on product websites, generating sales leads and converting leads to sales, and productivity of communications. One marketing team focuses specifically on social media such as Twitter, which Cisco uses to share corporate and product information, understand brand perceptions and provide speedy customer support. Among the many metrics used to measure social-media results are how many followers Cisco's Twitter accounts and blogs attract, how many times the brand is mentioned in other blogs, and the number and type of brand comments made on Twitter.

Cisco's marketers also track the results of specific keyword search initiatives to increase company website and product website rankings among the results of online searches and to improve the volume of traffic to specific sites. Not long ago, one objective was to have more of Cisco's 'priority pages' appearing on the first page of Google search results; according to the company's search marketing manager, metrics show that at least half of Cisco's priority pages now appear on the first page of Google results. Achieving that objective supports brand reputation and recognition as well.[3]

Yet just because you can measure something doesn't mean you should measure it – nor should you measure everything. The key is to identify the specific metrics that apply to the most significant activities and results affecting marketing performance. Consider four categories of metrics to measure progress towards objectives: internal in-process, external in-process, internal performance (end-result) and external performance (end-result) metrics (see Table 11.2).

Table 11.2	Categories of process and performance metrics	
	Time of measurement	
Measurement perspective	**In-process metrics**	**End-result metrics**
Internal (in-company)	Product defects Late deliveries Billing errors Accounts receivable Inventory turnover	Net profit/earnings Return on sales Profit margin per unit Return on assets Asset turnover
External (in-market)	Customer satisfaction Relative product quality Relative service quality Intentions to purchase Product awareness	Market share Customer retention Relative new product sales Revenue per customer Market growth rate

Source: Adapted from *BEST, ROGER J., MARKET-BASED MANAGEMENT: STRATEGIES FOR GROWING CUSTOMER VALUE AND PROFITABILITY, 2nd,©2000.* Prentice Hall, p.32. Reproduced by permission of Pearson Education, Inc., Upper Saddle River, New Jersey.

Achieving in-process market metrics paves the way for achieving marketing and financial objectives. For example, the metric of product awareness measures progress towards the marketing objective of strengthening and expanding customer relationships: the higher the awareness, the higher the probability that prospects will become customers. In contrast, internal and external performance metrics measure results that more directly contribute to specific financial and marketing objectives. Procter & Gamble, which spends millions on marketing communications every year, calculates the return on investment for programmes, brand by brand, using an external measurement perspective. This is how the company learned that public relations is an unusually effective tool for three of its brands, yielding a 275 percent return on investment.[4] Apply your measurements before, during and after programme implementation so you can make changes if necessary to improve performance.

Hilton Worldwide is one of many companies using a marketing dashboard to track actual performance. A **marketing dashboard** is a computerised, easy-to-read depiction of marketing outcomes, as measured by key metrics, used to monitor progress and identify deviations from expected results. Hilton's dashboard monitors customer loyalty, revenues and other metrics chosen by management. Being able to track performance and determine where improvement is needed has helped the company increase profit margins at its 3,300 hotels and resorts and prepare to expand beyond 4,000 properties in the next few years.[5] Kodak, which makes imaging equipment, uses a marketing dashboard to monitor key metrics such as return on marketing investment, changes in market share and changes in sales revenue.[6]

Selecting metrics

Hilton's metrics cover not only short-term results (measuring current revenues) but also longer-term objectives (measuring customer loyalty). When you select metrics, look for measures that will help you evaluate progress throughout the course of each programme and into a new marketing plan period, so you can follow progress and assess results. See Table 11.3 for sample metrics.

Table 11.3 Sample metrics for marketing plan objectives	
Type of metric	**Examples**
Metrics to measure progress towards financial objectives	• Metrics to measure sales and profitability by unit, product line, market, channel, customer segment • Metrics to measure return on investment by product, programme, activity
Metrics to measure progress towards marketing objectives	• Metrics to measure change in customer relationships by number or percentage of new customers acquired, number or percentage of existing customers retained • Metrics to measure efficiency of support activities by product, process, personnel or facility
Metrics to measure progress towards societal objectives	• Metrics to measure change in public image by periodically assessing attitudes and perceptions of various publics • Metrics to decrease ecological impact by measuring reduction in carbon footprint, reduction in waste, increase in recycling

When selecting metrics:

- *Match metrics to programme and marketing plan objectives.* Be sure your metrics are relevant to your objectives. A company seeking 10 per cent higher sales in the coming year would check performance by regularly measuring unit or monetary sales and market share. However, if its marketers measure the number of sales leads generated but have no metric for conversion rates, they won't know the ultimate outcome of lead generation, which directly influences sales objectives.

- *Measure activities or outcomes that show progress towards fulfilling the organisation's mission and moving in the desired direction.* Your metrics should track results that are consistent with your mission, direction and goals. The mission of Virgin Atlantic is 'to grow a profitable airline where people love to fly and people love to work'.[7] The airline's marketers might use metrics such as increase in profitability, increase in number of passengers flown and percentage of employees retained to understand whether they are making progress towards that mission every month and every year. If your direction is growth, be sure to establish metrics that will help you determine whether (and how quickly) your marketing is taking you in that direction.

- *Measure the non-financial and financial outcomes that can be quantified and that matter to customers.* Supported by marketing research, you can select and measure metrics for changes in customers' perceptions of company image, product quality and value, all of which affect customers' attitudes and behaviour. You might use metrics to track the number of defectors, percentage change and reason for defections. To follow the development of customer relationships, track your progress in acquiring customers, selling additional products to current customers, retaining customers, reactivating dormant relationships and re-establishing relations with defectors. Consider metrics to track profit per customer and acquisition costs in line with your objectives so you have data for future marketing decisions.[8]

- *Measure appropriate internal metrics.* By tracking internal performance using metrics such as measuring order fulfilment accuracy and on-time shipping, you can quickly identify areas for improvement in processes and procedures that affect customer satisfaction and loyalty. Also consider metrics that will help you identify which of your supply-chain and channel partners are most responsive. All your internal metrics should reflect processes or outcomes that make a difference to the customer or to your competitive performance in the marketplace.[9]

- *Use metrics to reinforce ongoing priorities.* You can use metrics to track the proportion of sales made to more profitable customers compared with those made to less profitable customers as a way to reinforce marketing priorities for long-term success. Also, using metrics to track the ratio of new product sales to existing product sales can show the extent to which new product innovation is fuelling growth. Emerson Electric, a US-based industrial equipment manufacturer, uses metrics to gauge its new-product success by determining how much of its sales are attributable to breakthrough innovations compared with how much of its sales are attributable to incrementally improved products.[10]

The specific metrics selected depend on your organisation, its mission and objectives, your marketing plan objectives and the programmes you will implement. Most companies select metrics to measure profitability and profit margins, sales, product awareness and number of new products, among others – with profitability and sales metrics seen as the most valuable in assessing progress.[11] Other vital areas to monitor through metrics are channel and sales force performance; product portfolio performance; new product pricing, price changes and effect on profitability; and the value of individual customers and relationships.[12]

Google's managers select metrics that relate to the tech company's mission, long-term goals, short-term objectives and customer needs.

MARKETING IN PRACTICE: GOOGLE

Google's mission is to 'organise the world's information and make it universally accessible and useful'. The tech company uses metrics to measure its progress in speeding online search innovations to market, including how many of its 6,000 experiments are eventually launched and how quickly users adopt these changes. Some of the more innovative experiments appear on the Google Labs section of Google.com, where engineers can monitor how many users try each innovation and what users do with the innovations. In some cases, Google can test an improvement in a matter of hours to gauge viability and user response. By super-charging its rate of innovation, Google plans to maintain its market-share lead over newcomers such as Microsoft's Bing search engine.

Google also evaluates improvements using metrics that might seem unusually exacting but that make a difference in the user's experience. After one recent search engine improvement was implemented, Google engineers found that the time between search results being viewed and the user clicking on one of the links was narrowed by a tiny fraction of a second – meaning the user found a relevant result more quickly than before the improvement. 'This was a small idea,' says a Google engineer, 'but we have a real responsibility as a company to respect people's time' – in line with the company's mission.[13]

Rather than simply replicate the metrics common to your industry, select or modify metrics for your organisation's particular situation. Many retailers, for instance, set goals for opening a certain number of shops. The high-street bakery and sandwich chain Greggs has a long-term goal of operating 2,000 UK shops. Although number of stores is an important metric to measure growth, the chief executive also recognises that 'location, location, location is key', adding, 'It's not a race to see who's got the most shops.'[14]

You can select narrowly defined metrics to track progress towards particularly crucial outcomes or activities, such as the number of new products in development. Also fit your metrics to your long-term goals. One financial goal of Pizza Hut, an international chain of pizza restaurants, is to increase turnover by deriving more than £600 million worth of sales from online sources by 2012. To do this, its marketers are testing communications and vouchers using Facebook and other social media. The company can evaluate the outcome of each promotion individually and in the aggregate using metrics such as source, size and timing of orders, all of which indicate interim progress towards the 2012 goal.[15]

Applying metrics

You will need pre-implementation numbers for every metric so you can track progress from that point forward. If possible, obtain benchmark metrics (from your industry or best-in-class organisations) against which to compare your progress. UK companies that market via direct mail, for example, are benchmarking against PAS 2020 standards for processes and outcomes that are ecologically sound, reduce waste, increase recycling and improve productivity.[16]

Depending on your organisation, objectives and technology, you may apply selected metrics daily, weekly, monthly, quarterly or yearly. In especially volatile markets, you may check metrics more than once a day or even on an hourly basis. Be sure to analyse the direction and rate of change in measurements taken at different intervals as well as the total progress from pre-implementation levels. This will show how quickly you are moving towards your objectives (and reveal problem areas for attention). Check your previous results to see the progress measured in comparable pre-implementation periods as a way of identifying unusual trends. By documenting your measurements, you will have historical data for comparison with future results. Also analyse your metrics in the context of competitive results whenever possible – an especially important point with measures such as market share, profitability and quality perceptions.

Remember that the metrics you apply today may not be as useful tomorrow because of environmental shifts, new competition, changes in organisational strategy, or evolving customer attitudes and behaviour. For example, the number of people who click to view display ads online has dropped year by year, yet research shows that people who see such ads are more likely to visit the brand or product site than people who don't see the ads. As a result, Internet advertisers are testing different metrics for measuring cognitive, affective and behavioural responses to communications and influence programmes.[17]

Finally, keep the use of metrics in perspective. Marketing judgement is vital for interpreting what metrics measure. Quantifiable measures are necessary but so are innovation and insight.[18] In fact, metrics are only one input in decisions about adjusting marketing programmes if interim results fail to meet expected results, as discussed in Chapter 12. Use this chapter's checklist as you consider suitable metrics for your marketing plan.

ESSENTIAL MARKETING PLAN CHECKLIST NO. 16:
PLANNING METRICS

Your choice of metrics will determine exactly what you're able to track as you implement your marketing plan and move closer to your objectives. Be sure the metrics you choose are relevant to your organisation and the targets you've set. Also consider how often to apply your metrics so you can identify any problems quickly and make changes as needed.

☐ What metrics will help you and your management track the marketing results that contribute to achieving long-term objectives and fulfilling the mission?

☐ What metrics will help you track marketing results that relate to managing the life cycle of a customer relationship, including satisfaction, loyalty and retention?

☐ What metrics will help you measure progress towards achieving the plan's financial, marketing and societal objectives?

☐ What metrics will help you determine whether specific marketing programmes have achieved their objectives?

☐ What metrics will help you track how each marketing-mix element contributes to interim performance?

☐ What metrics will help you assess performance of your customer support services and internal marketing initiatives?

☐ How often should you measure interim progress using each metric?

FORECASTING AND THE PLANNING PROCESS

The purpose of forecasting is to project future demand, sales and costs so you can make marketing decisions and coordinate internal decisions about manufacturing, finance, human resources and other functions. (Depending on the coming year's forecasts, your organisation may need to expand or reduce manufacturing capacity, change inventory levels, reallocate budgets and increase or reduce the workforce.) Forecasting is challenging because of the dynamic business environment, unpredictable competitive moves, changeable demand and other uncertainties that can affect marketing performance.

Moreover, your product forecasts must take into account the interrelationships between products in the marketplace. For business markets, apply the principle of **derived demand**: the demand you forecast for a business product will be based, in part, on (derived from) the demand forecast for a related consumer product. When industry analysts forecast higher consumer sales of digital cameras, for example, manufacturers of electronic storage devices and removable chips raise their forecasts for selling to camera manufacturers, and so on through the supply chain.

Forecasts are, at best, only informed estimates, even when based on statistical data and carefully adjusted for the effect of external influences such as market growth, economic conditions, technological developments and industry trends. Tesco uses detailed regional weather forecasts to fine-tune its forecasts of consumer demand for seasonal items such as barbecue foods.[19] Still, aim to make your forecasts as accurate as possible to improve the quality of information supporting the decision-making process. You may want to develop forecasts for the most optimistic situation, the most pessimistic situation and the most likely situation you will face, then, if possible, statistically estimate the probability of each. This helps you think about the diverse ways in which your product, industry, competition and market may develop.

More companies are reforecasting future sales and costs using actual results throughout the planning and implementation period. This is especially important during periods of unusual volatility or uncertainty, such as the financial crisis that hurt the global economy not long ago. Canon, the Japanese company that markets office equipment and cameras around the world, forecasts sales by product and market. It also forecasts foreign exchange rates for the yen, because these affect its costs and its export strength. After implementing its marketing plans, Canon adjusts its forecasts every quarter based on current and projected economic circumstances and currency fluctuations.[20]

Types of forecasts

What forecasts do you need for your marketing plan? Most organisations start at the macro level by forecasting industry sales by market and segment, then move to the micro level by forecasting sales for their company, sales by product, sales costs by product, and sales and costs by channel. With these forecasts in hand, you can estimate future changes in sales and costs to examine trends by product and by channel. Such analyses will show the magnitude of projected sales increases or decreases for your market, segment and individual products as well as the expected rate of change over time for sales and costs.

Market and segment sales forecasts

The first step is to project the level of overall industry sales in each market and segment for the coming months and years, using the external audit and the market analysis completed earlier in the planning process. Here you will forecast sales in the qualified available market and in your targeted segment of this market, adjusted for external influences such as expected legal restrictions and the economic outlook. Once you've forecast the size of the market, you can forecast the share you aim to achieve with your marketing plan, as well as estimating the future share for each competitor. Then bring industry sales forecasts down to the segment level to support your targeting and strategy decisions. The next step is to project sales for your company and for each product.

Company and product sales forecasts

Use your market and segment forecasts, your market and customer analyses and your knowledge of the current situation to develop sales forecasts at the company and product levels. Also factor in earlier decisions about direction, strategy and objectives when thinking about future company sales. Car manufacturers typically project industry, company and product sales three to five years in advance because of the lead time needed to design new vehicles, build or retrofit assembly facilities and plan for other operational activities. They consult forecasts from industry groups, such as the UK's Society of Motor Manufacturers and Traders, and adjust their forecasts in accordance with the latest economic indicators and other external influences. During the recent economic downturn, many car manufacturers lowered their sales forecasts, then raised the forecasts after a number of nations began offering incentives for consumers to buy new cars and scrap older models.[21]

Most marketers prepare month-by-month sales forecasts for the coming year, although some firms prefer week-by-week forecasting and some project sales 15–18 months ahead. Manufacturers of industrial equipment and cars typically prepare monthly sales forecasts for at least two years ahead, on the basis of top-down and floor-up input, so they can plan supply acquisition and production capacity. Involving value-chain partners can improve accuracy and give suppliers the data they need for better forecasting to meet your organisation's needs. If your marketing plan covers at least one new product introduction, forecast those sales separately so you can measure results and track progress towards product-specific objectives. Also consider the effect that other value-chain participants could have on your product forecasts.

Costs of sales forecasts

Now you're ready to forecast the total costs you can expect to incur for the forecast sales levels and project when these costs will occur. This gives you an opportunity to consider the financial impact of your forecasts and revise them if necessary. Your forecasts will be more realistic if you discuss cost figures with line managers or others who are knowledgeable about the products and markets. You may need to adjust your overall cost forecasts after the marketing plan is implemented. Nonetheless, estimating these costs during the planning process helps you allocate funding to individual programmes and products.

Channel forecasts

Companies that work with multiple channels and channel members often forecast sales and costs for each, including the cost of logistics. In addition to providing benchmarks against which to measure actual channel results and costs, these forecasts give you an opportunity to reconsider your channel and logistics decisions if the costs seem too high (or surprisingly low). Even companies that own their own stores can use channel forecasts to project sales on a store-by-store basis. Ideally, you should forecast unit sales and revenue results by product and by channel (perhaps down to the store or wholesale level) so you can track progress after implementation and make changes if actual performance varies significantly from forecasts.

Forecasting approaches and data sources

There are a number of approaches to forecasting sales and costs, as shown in Table 11.4. Some rely on statistical analysis or modelling, whereas others rely on expert judgement.

Note that for a forecast developed with a time series or causal analysis to be at all accurate, you must have sufficient historical sales data. Also, be aware that judgemental forecasting approaches such as the jury of executive opinion can be very valuable if applied in a systematic way. Incorporate external information and expertise to avoid too narrow an internal focus.

Table 11.4 Selected approaches to forecasting

Forecasting technique	Description	Benefits/limitations
Sales force composite estimate	Judgemental approach in which sales personnel are asked to estimate future sales	Can provide valuable insights from customer-contact personnel but may introduce bias
Jury of executive opinion	Judgemental approach in which managers and sometimes channel members or suppliers are asked to estimate future sales	Combines informed judgement of many but may give too much weight to some individuals' estimates
Delphi method	Judgemental approach, in which outside experts participate in successive rounds of input, leading to a consensus forecast	Minimises possibility of bias or overweighting one individual's estimates but is time consuming and accuracy depends on choice of experts
Online prediction market	Judgemental approach in which employees or invited stakeholders indicate their confidence in certain predictions through online trading in a mock stock market	Combines judgement of many people and can be an efficient forecasting method, but may involve bias towards longer-term predictions
Survey of buyer intentions	Research-based approach in which buyers in a given market are asked about their purchasing intentions	Solicits market input but may not be indicative of customers' actual behaviour
New product test marketing	Research-based approach in which a new product's sales performance in limited markets is tested and the results used to forecast future sales	Reflects actual customer input but may be affected by competition or other factors
Time series analyses	Statistical approaches in which the patterns of historical data are analysed to predict future sales; examples: moving averages, exponential smoothing	Uses actual purchase data to produce forecast estimates quickly but assumes that similar buying trends will continue
Causal analyses	Methods that statistically determine the relationship between demand and the factors that affect it; examples: regression analysis, neural networks	Provides insights into relationships between factors that affect demand but requires sufficient data for analysis

Some companies are supplementing executive opinion and other forecasting methods with online prediction markets.

MARKETING IN PRACTICE: ONLINE PREDICTION MARKETS

Online prediction markets operate like mock stock markets to 'crowdsource' forecasts by seeing how thousands of people (usually employees, but sometimes people outside the organisation) rate the possibilities of each predicted outcome. Each participant is given a certain amount of 'money' to invest in one or more of the predictions being considered. Like the market value of a share of stock, the market value of each prediction goes up or down depending on how much money is invested in it at any given time. Using an online prediction market as input for a forecast allows management to tap the collective knowledge and experience of all the participants by seeing which predictions attract the most investment.

For example, the US conglomerate General Electric has 10,000 employees 'investing' in up to 50 predictions about future goods and services. Its managers examine the movement of these predictions and consult specialists and business leaders for their expert advice when formulating specific forecasts. Another example: when Hewlett-Packard used online prediction markets to forecast the future price of memory chips that are incorporated into its computers, the results were 70 per cent more accurate than the computer company's usual forecasting methods.[22]

In preparing forecasts, review the background information you've gathered about your markets, customers, channels and costs. Also consult industry associations, government information and financial analysts' reports when estimating future sales and costs, especially at the macro level. Before you rely on any secondary data for forecasting purposes, carefully check the source, collection method, credibility, completeness and timeliness. For a final 'reality check', compare your forecasts with the actual outcome of recent periods to identify major anomalies.

PREPARING BUDGETS AND SCHEDULES

With sales and cost forecasts complete, you can develop an overall marketing budget and, within that budget, estimate spending for specific programmes and activities in line with your marketing plan objectives. Every marketer must make hard choices because marketing budgets (and other resources) are never unlimited. As with forecasts, some marketers budget for the most optimistic, most pessimistic and most likely scenarios so they are prepared to tackle threats and opportunities.

Your organisation may set budget requirements for return on investment, limit the amount or percentage of funding that can be allocated to certain activities or products, set specific assumptions, cap cost increases, or prefer a particular budget method or format. Your marketing budget should be linked to corporate-level goals and initiatives. Enhancing brand image and preference to fuel future growth is an ongoing priority for many companies as they approve marketing budgets. This is why Kimberly-Clark, which markets paper products such as Kleenex tissues and Huggies disposable nappies, maintains its marketing budget even during trying economic periods. 'The worst thing you can do is pull in your brand-building spending and become more of a commodity,' says its chief executive.[23]

Budgeting methods

Budgets may originate in the marketing department and move upwards for review (floor up), at the top management level and move downwards for specific allocations (top down), or be constructed through a combination of floor-up and top-down methods (see Figure 11.1). The **objective and task budget method**, a floor-up option common in large organisations, allocates marketing funding according to the cost of the tasks to be accomplished in achieving marketing plan objectives. If you can relate specific tasks to specific objectives, this method offers good accountability; however, the combined cost may result in too high a budget, given your organisation's resources. For this reason, some corporations use the **econometric modelling method** to calculate programme or activity budgets using formulas that take into account anticipated customer response, budget constraints, product profitability, competitive spending and other relevant variables.[24]

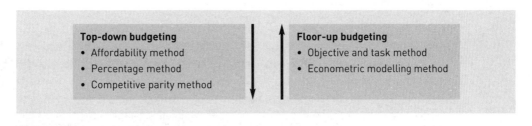

Top-down budgeting
- Affordability method
- Percentage method
- Competitive parity method

Floor-up budgeting
- Objective and task method
- Econometric modelling method

FIGURE 11.1 Top-down and floor-up budgeting methods

Your organisation may use one of the top-down budgeting methods. With the **affordability budget method**, senior managers set the amount of the marketing budget on the basis of how much the organisation can afford (or will be able to afford during the period covered by the plan). Although simple, this method has no connection with market conditions, opportunities, potential profits or other factors. With the **percentage budget method**, the overall marketing budget is based on a percentage of the previous year's annual turnover, next year's expected turnover, the product's price, or an average industry percentage. Note that this method has no connection to market conditions. With the **competitive parity budget method**, managers set a total marketing budget at least equal to that of competitors. But because no two organisations are exactly alike, mimicking another organisation's budget may be disastrous for yours.

The top-down budgeting methods are relatively easy to apply, but they fail to relate costs to objectives. Compared with the affordability method, the objective and task budgeting is more sophisticated, results in larger marketing budgets and is related to better profitability.[25] In practice, most marketing budgets combine top-down and floor-up methods, guided by higher-level strategic planning and product or brand-level input relative to objectives and costs.

Budgets within budgets

At this point, you can create separate budgets for specific marketing activities and programmes, schedule planned expenditures and fix responsibilities for spending. This allows you to compare the actual outlays with the budgeted outlays after the marketing plan has been implemented. You will want to prepare budgets (for annual, monthly and perhaps weekly costs) covering individual marketing-mix programmes matched with appropriate objectives (such as projected profit or return on investment).

In addition, you can establish budgets within your overall budget reflecting planned expenditures by market, segment, region, business unit, product or line/category, brand, activity or responsibility. This allows examination of performance market by market, product by product and activity by activity so you and your managers can change budget priorities as appropriate. Set your budgeting priorities and make your allocation decisions based on a careful analysis of the external and internal marketing environment. Today, a growing number of marketers are shifting spending to boost their budgets for online marketing.

MARKETING IN PRACTICE: SPENDING MORE ON ONLINE MARKETING

Mercedes-Benz's marketers continually research the media habits of the car manufacturer's customers, market by market. When they found that UK consumers had increased their involvement with digital media, they decided to reallocate spending, with half of the overall budget now going towards online marketing programmes. Burberry, the upmarket UK clothing marketer, has also reallocated money to invest more heavily in online marketing. Its marketers know that customers are using the Internet to follow fashion trends and brands. The company also sees opportunities to extend its reach and stretch its budget by reallocating spending. 'We have to be conscious of the economic environment, and digital is an increasingly viable and economic way to reach consumers,' says the director of strategic marketing.[26]

Reckitt Benckiser, which offers household brands like Finish dishwashing detergent, has also shifted some of its marketing budget in recent years. Seeking more efficiency and lower cost compared with traditional television campaigns, RB boosted its budget for advertising on websites that feature news and entertainment videos. RB is closely monitoring response and will decide whether to increase its online marketing budget beyond the £12.5 million it's currently spending for adverts on video sites.[27]

Planning schedules for implementation

When planning schedules for implementation, you will estimate the timing and deadlines for each programme or task to coordinate concurrent activities, prevent conflicts, obtain needed resources and track progress towards completion. Although you may not have to include detailed programme schedules when documenting your marketing plan for management review, you need a schedule to summarise the timing and responsibilities for major programmes. Then, if tasks do not start or finish on schedule, you can determine the effect on other tasks, work to regain the expected timing and get back on track towards results. Also review the new timing (and cost changes, if any) with management and communicate with the major customers and suppliers who would be affected.

As with budgeting and forecasting, you may want to develop schedules for the most optimistic, most pessimistic and most likely situations – and be ready to make changes in response to emerging opportunities, threats or other factors. Organisations planning marketing activities related to the 2012 Summer Olympic Games in London have had to follow strict schedules to be ready on time.

MARKETING IN PRACTICE: 2012 OLYMPICS

Royal Mail began planning to market a series of Olympics-themed stamps almost as soon as London was chosen as the host city for 2012. The goal was to celebrate the sports, highlight London's role as host and build anticipation for this special event. It commissioned artists to design the Olympic-themed stamps and carefully planned printing, distribution and publicity schedules for issuing the stamps in sets during 2008, 2009, 2010 and 2012. The first set of four stamps was released at the conclusion of the 2008 Summer Olympics in Beijing; through precise scheduling, the stamps were put on sale with widespread publicity simultaneously in China and in the UK.

Olympic sponsors of the London Games have their own schedules, budgets and forecasts to prepare. Three years before the Games began, Hornby was awarded a licence to produce and market official Games toys and souvenirs under its four brands. The toy company moved quickly to forecast sales by product, range and brand, design the merchandise, create packaging and communications in compliance with licensing specifications, prepare for production, work with channel partners to develop point-of-purchase displays, and schedule shipments to retailers so merchandise would be available when and where needed. Following a tight schedule, Hornby introduced miniatures of the London Olympic stadium and other models only a few months after announcing the licensing deal, stocking stores for the holiday selling season in 2009.[28]

CHAPTER SUMMARY

Metrics are used to measure selected performance-related activities and outcomes numerically and on a regular basis. The purpose is to analyse interim results at set intervals and track progress towards meeting marketing-plan objectives, long-term objectives and the organisation's mission. Types of metrics include internal in-process metrics, external in-process metrics, internal performance (end-result) metrics and external performance (end-result) metrics. A marketing dashboard is a computerised, easy-to-read depiction of marketing outcomes, as measured by key metrics, used to confirm progress and identify deviations from expected marketing results. Plan to apply selected metrics daily, weekly, monthly, quarterly or yearly, and review metrics regularly in light of internal and external environmental changes.

Marketers use forecasts to project the estimated level of sales and costs for the marketing plan period so they can compare actual results and identify deviations. Some prepare forecasts for the most optimistic, most pessimistic and most likely situation. Budgets are used to allot financial resources to specific programmes, activities and products and then compare actual spending to budgeted spending to pinpoint deviations. Budgets may be developed using floor-up methods (objective and task, econometric modelling), top-down methods (affordability, percentage budget, competitive parity) or a combination of methods. Marketers use schedules to define the timing of tasks to plan and implement specific programmes and activities.

CASE STUDY: ACTION FOR CHILDREN PLANS MARKETING TO MAKE A DIFFERENCE

In 1998, at the height of the dot-com era, 30 people from the information technology industry decided to sleep rough to raise awareness about homeless children and raise money to fight the problem. These Byte Night 'sleepers' raised £35,000 to be donated to the registered charity Action for Children (known as the National Children's Home until being rebranded in 2008). Ten years later, more than 500 IT professionals were participating in Byte Night activities in Edinburgh, Manchester, Birmingham, Thames Valley and London, publicising the issue of homeless children and collecting £470,000 in donations for the charity.

The mission of Action for Children, founded more than 140 years ago, is 'to help the most vulnerable children and young people break through injustice, deprivation and inequality, so they can achieve their full potential'. In partnership with local groups, churches and families, Action for Children fulfils this mission through hundreds of UK projects that address child neglect, help children with disabilities, offer community services and more. To support these projects, Action for Children's marketers set financial, marketing and societal objectives and plan metrics, forecasts, budgets and schedules for implementation and performance measurement.

Planning for the 2009 Byte Night, Action for Children set specific targets for number of participating sleepers and amount of money raised per sleeper in London, Thames Valley, Newcastle, Gateshead, Manchester and Scotland. For example, sleepers in London aimed to raise £5,000 per team or £2,000 per individual; sleepers in Manchester aimed for £2,500 per team or £500 per individual. The overall objective was to top the 2008 results by having 700 people sleeping rough on Byte Night and raising £500,000 in donations. Sleepers were asked to register online in advance and, with permission, the charity publicised their names and company affiliations in news releases and other communications. Participants were also encouraged to enlist friends and generate word of mouth before, during and after the event using blog posts, Twitter tweets, Facebook posts, Flickr photos, YouTube videos and e-mail messages.

Action for Children's marketers planned to gauge progress towards their objectives by counting the number of mentions online and in traditional media, counting the number of individuals and companies that got involved and counting the amount of money raised. Results showed that Byte Night 2009 was highly successful, despite the difficult economic climate. It attracted more than 700 sleepers from Dell, Intel, Accenture, Barclays, Experian, BT, Ernst & Young and many other organisations and it achieved the objective of raising £500,000 in donations. Before Byte Night publicity faded, Action for Children launched its largest-ever multimedia campaign, with Big Brother's Davina McCall starring in adverts and YouTube videos about preventing child neglect.[29]

Case questions

1. What are the marketing implications of Action for Children publicising specific fundraising targets for each sleeper?

2. What additional metrics would you recommend that Action for Children use to measure the performance of its marketing plan for the next Byte Night fundraiser? Explain your answer.

 **APPLY YOUR KNOWLEDGE**

Review your work researching a company's marketing, financial and societal objectives in the 'Apply your knowledge' exercise in Chapter 5. In a brief oral or written report, answer the following questions about measuring progress towards those objectives.

- Does the company explain any metrics used to measure interim progress? What metrics would you recommend, given your knowledge of this company and its objectives?

- Has the company revealed any of its forecasts or budgets? If so, what are they based on and how do they relate to its objectives?

- What secondary data sources would you consult if you were preparing a forecast for one of this company's products? Be specific.

- Has the company discussed any schedules for marketing activities, such as launching a new product or starting a new advertising campaign? If so, what connection do you see between the schedules and forecasts or budgets?

BUILD YOUR OWN MARKETING PLAN

Move ahead with your marketing plan by researching and estimating sales and costs, plus forecasts for industry, company and product sales, cost of sales, and sales and costs by channel. What sources will you use? Do your forecasts represent the most optimistic, most pessimistic or most likely situation? Are they appropriate for the current marketing situation? Next, develop a month-by-month marketing budget using the objective and task method and a budget for a specific programme or activity such as advertising. List any factors that would affect your budgets for the most optimistic, most pessimistic and most likely situations. Now identify appropriate metrics for your financial, marketing and societal objectives. Explain how, when and why you will use them to measure progress towards objectives. Document your decisions in a written marketing plan.

ENDNOTES

1. Quoted in B.K. Sidhu, 'Continuity under new stewardship', *Malaysia Star*, 12 September 2009, http://biz.thestar.com; also: Jeeva Arulampalam, 'MAS: No plans to lay off staff', *New Straits Times Press*, 23 June 2009, www.btimes.com; 'Turning around a struggling airline', *The McKinsey Quarterly*, November 2008, www.mckinseyquarterly.com; Julie Goh, 'Malaysia Airlines plans $778 mln rights offering', *Reuters UK*, 22 December 2009, http://uk.reuters.com/article/idUKSGE5BL06420091222.

2. Tim Ambler, *Marketing and the Bottom Line* (London: Financial Times Prentice Hall, 2000), p. 5.

3. Christopher Hosford, 'Cisco Systems optimises organic search from the inside out', *B to B*, 14 September 2009, p. 16; 'Metrics gather momentum', *B to B*, 8 June 2009, p. 3; www.cisco.com.

4. Sean Callahan, 'Marketers stay in the conversation', *B to B*, 9 February 2009, p. 1.

5. Christopher Hosford, 'Hilton's dashboards graphically depict five 'value drivers' at hotel properties', *B to B*, 11 December 2006, p. 18; William Kay, 'Hilton launches worldwide hotel expansion drive', *Sunday Times*, 9 July 2006, p. 3; Barbara De Lollis, 'Hilton Hotels changes name to Hilton Worldwide', *USA Today*, 23 September 2009, www.usatoday.com.

6. Elisabeth A. Sullivan, 'Measure up', *Marketing News*, 30 May 2009, pp. 8–11.

7. See www.virgin-atlantic.com/en/gb/allaboutus/missionstatement/index.jsp.

8. See Werner Reinartz, Manfred Krafft and Wayne D. Hoyer, 'Measuring the customer relationship management construct and linking it to performance outcomes', *Insead,* January 2003, www.insead.edu.

9. See Roger More, 'Market-focused products generate sustainable businesses', *Canada.com,* 21 September 2009, www.canada.com.

10. Brian Hindo, 'Emerson Electric's innovation metrics', *BusinessWeek,* 5 June 2008, www.businessweek.com.

11. Tim Ambler, *Marketing and the Bottom Line* (London: Financial Times Prentice Hall, 2000), p. 163.

12. See Paul W. Farris, Neil T. Bendle, Phillip E. Pfeifer and David J. Reibstein, *Marketing Metrics: 50+ Metrics Every Executive Should Master* (Upper Saddle River, NJ: Wharton School Publishing, 2006), pp. 2–5.

13. Quoted in Robert D. Hof, 'Can Google stay on top of the web?', *BusinessWeek,* 12 October 2009, pp. 44–9; also: Rob Hof, 'Live: New stuff from Google Labs', *BusinessWeek,* 20 April 2009, www.businessweek.com; Rob Hof, 'Google search guru Singhal: we will try outlandish ideas', 2 October 2009, www.businessweek.com; Gregg Keizer, 'Google's Chrome grabs No. 3 browser spot from Safari', *Computerworld,* 2 January 2010, www.computerworld.com.

14. Marcus Leroux, 'Greggs still has faith in the high street', *Times Online,* 21 September 2009, http://business.timesonline.co.uk.

15. Emily Bryson York, 'Facing more competition from freezer aisle, Pizza Hut calls for agency review', *Advertising Age,* 29 September 2009, www.adage.com.

16. 'Direct marketing: Environmental awareness is now standard', *Marketing Week,* 23 July 2009, p. 25.

17. Kunur Patel, 'What to measure? Only 16 per cent of the web is clicking display ads', *Advertising Age,* 30 September 2009, www.adage.com.

18. John Nardone and Ed See, 'Free yourself from the tyranny of metrics', *Advertising Age,* 20 November 2006, p. 12.

19. Julia Werdigier, 'Tesco, British grocer, uses weather to predict sales', *New York Times,* 2 September 2009, www.nytimes.com.

20. Robin Harding, 'Canon turns small profit, cuts sales forecast', *Financial Times,* 28 July 2009, www.ft.com.

21. Louise Barnett, 'Car deals surge thanks to scrappage scheme', *Daily Express,* 7 October 2009, www.dailyexpress.co.uk; 'Scrappage scheme boosts car sales', *BBC News,* 6 August 2009, http://news.bbc.co.uk/2/hi/business/8186992.stm.

22. Jonathan Richards, 'Prediction markets: the future of decision-making', *Times Online,* 4 September 2008, http://technology.timesonline.co.uk/tol/news/tech_and_web/article4539072.ece; Teck-Hua Ho and Kay-Yut Chen, 'New product blockbusters: The magic and science of prediction markets', *California Management Review,* Fall 2007, pp. 144–58.

23. Quoted in Burt Helm, 'Best global brands: gutsy marketers spend into the teeth of a recession', *BusinessWeek,* 29 September 2008, www.businessweek.com.

24. Gary L. Lilien and Arvind Rangaswamy, *Marketing Engineering,* 2nd edn (Upper Saddle River, NJ: Prentice Hall, 2003), pp. 312–15.

25. Nigel Piercy, 'The marketing budgeting process: marketing management implications', *Journal of Marketing,* October 1987, pp. 45–59.

26. Quoted in 'Burberry joins push online by luxury brands', *New Media Age,* 7 May 2009, p. 1. Also: Justin Pearse, 'Mercedes allocates half its UK marketing budget to digital', *New Media Age,* 23 September 2009, www.nma.co.uk.

27. Michael Learmonth, 'Kill or cure: How Reckitt's big buy rocked online ads', *Advertising Age*, 7 September 2009, p. 1.

28. Amy Golding, 'Royal Mail reveals London 2012 Olympics stamps', *Marketing*, 25 August 2009, www.marketingmagazine.co.uk; 'Ahead of the Games', *Marketing*, 29 July 2009, p. 14; 'Hornby set to unveil 2012 Olympics toys and souvenirs', *Marketing Week*, 23 July 2009, p. 7; 'Stamps mark Olympic flag handover', *BBC News*, 22 August 2008, http://news.bbc.co.uk.

29. Mark Sweney, 'Davina McCall to star in Action for Children campaign', *Guardian*, 12 October 2009, www,guardian.co.uk; 'Byte Night plans IT industry charity tactics for 2009 campaign', *Public Technology.net*, 8 June 2009, www.publict-echnology.net; www.bytenight.org.uk; www.actionforchildren.org.uk.

Comprehension outcomes

After studying this chapter, you will be able to:

- Explain the role of marketing control
- Understand how marketing control works at various levels
- Discuss planning for annual, financial, productivity and strategic control

Application outcomes

After studying this chapter, you will be able to:

- Diagnose interim marketing results and plan corrective action
- Use marketing control to evaluate plan performance
- Prepare for contingency and scenario planning

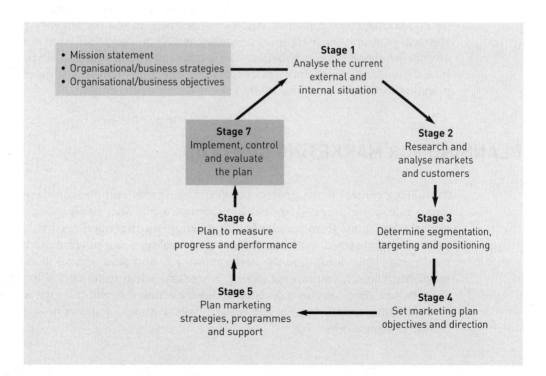

- Mission statement
- Organisational/business strategies
- Organisational/business objectives

Stage 1
Analyse the current external and internal situation

Stage 2
Research and analyse markets and customers

Stage 3
Determine segmentation, targeting and positioning

Stage 4
Set marketing plan objectives and direction

Stage 5
Plan marketing strategies, programmes and support

Stage 6
Plan to measure progress and performance

Stage 7
Implement, control and evaluate the plan

CHAPTER PREVIEW: JDSU PLANS FOR DIFFERENT FUTURES

Paying close attention to customers and preparing responses to possible future trends during planning can help a company do a better job of marketing implementation. JDSU, an £800 million company that manufactures fibre optic components and optical products for telecommunications firms and other business customers, looks ahead to a variety of possible situations when formulating marketing plans. Its managers start the planning process months in advance, examining broad external influences and monitoring customers' views and intentions as they plan for both favourable and unfavourable situations.

Although JDSU's turnover was increasing before the worst of the recent economic turmoil, its sales people said their customers were becoming more cautious about future spending. As the rate of new orders slowed and the financial crisis became more severe, marketing managers considered the implications and decided to begin adjusting the current year's activities. They implemented the plan they had created for operating in an unfavourable environment, eliminating several of their less profitable products and reducing costs by changing suppliers and consolidating research and development sites. At the same time, JDSU's marketers began looking ahead to when the world economy was likely to improve, planning for various levels of future demand and financial circumstances so the company would be prepared for whatever the future might bring.[1]

JDSU's preparations illustrate the importance of stage 7 in the marketing planning process, the point at which the plan is implemented, controlled and evaluated. Even the best plan will be ineffective without proper implementation and the ability to respond quickly to changing circumstances; a poor plan will not be improved by superb implementation. In this chapter, you'll learn about the importance of marketing control, including the levels of marketing control and the use of annual, financial, productivity and strategic control. Also, you'll consider how to use contingency planning and scenario planning for marketing purposes, which helped JDSU cope with an unusually challenging economic situation. The sample marketing plan in the Appendix shows how a company might apply principles of marketing control. For more ideas about planning for implementation, see the checklist later in this chapter.

PLANNING FOR MARKETING CONTROL

Marketing control is the process of setting standards and measurement intervals to gauge marketing progress, measuring interim results after implementation, diagnosing any deviations from standards and making adjustments if needed to achieve the planned performance. Without marketing control, you can't determine whether your marketing plan is leading to the performance you and your organisation expect. With marketing control, you can see exactly where and when results fall short of or exceed expectations, then come to a decision about the action you will take, the way JDSU did by eliminating some products and cutting costs. Figure 12.1 shows how the marketing control process works.

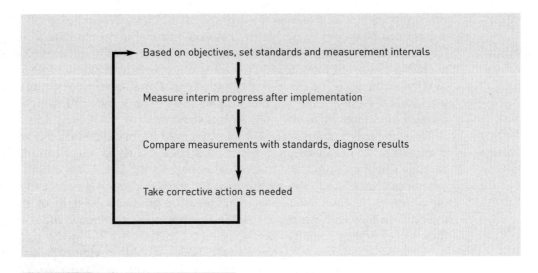

Based on objectives, set standards and measurement intervals

Measure interim progress after implementation

Compare measurements with standards, diagnose results

Take corrective action as needed

FIGURE 12.1 Applying marketing control

The use of marketing control assumes that the organisation is willing and able to make changes after implementing the marketing plan. Marketing control is intended to help you identify the warning signs of an emerging problem early enough to take corrective action. This may entail a small change or a major decision such as discontinuing a product or increasing marketing spending.

At times, the use of marketing control can raise ethical questions. Will marketers set less stringent standards or lower short-term sales forecasts in order to qualify for bonuses or promotions? Will they honestly and adequately explain deviations from expectations and amend or reverse their earlier decisions if necessary? Will marketers apply marketing control laxly or inconsistently if they feel pressured by senior managers to produce ever-higher quarterly results? This can lead to concentration on short-term progress to the detriment of long-term objectives and, as in several highly publicised instances, decisions to make current sales or profits look better than they actually are.

Control of marketing strategy must be coordinated with control of corporate strategy to ensure that your organisation achieves its long-term goals and short-term objectives. Tesco, for example, uses a 'steering wheel' divided into five sections (financial focus, customer focus, operational focus, employee performance focus and community focus) to communicate its progress in each area. The purpose is to make all employees aware of the company's progress and provide guidance for their actions in supporting Tesco's movements toward its targets. 'Tesco doesn't want one leader,' the chief executive explains. 'We want thousands of leaders who take initiative to execute the strategy.'[2]

The marketing control process

The marketing control process starts with the objectives you have already set and the detailed forecasts, budgets, schedules and metrics you have developed to track post-implementation progress toward objectives. Next, determine exactly which standards must be met to show progress at each interval of measurement. Suppose your forecast calls for selling 500 units of a product in June, your financial metrics specify an average gross profit margin of 30 per cent, and your advertising budget for June totals £3,000. During June you can get early indicators of progress by measuring actual results weekly; at the end of June you can measure full-month results and see whether you are meeting your forecast, metrics and budget standards.

The standards and measurement intervals used for marketing control will vary from organisation to organisation. Supermarket chains such as Tesco can measure store, product category, brand and individual item sales by day, week, month, quarter and year; some track store sales by the hour for staffing purposes as much as for marketing purposes. Fashion retailers like Zara measure product sales daily or at even shorter intervals so they can identify fast-selling merchandise for immediate reorder and see the effect of pricing and other decisions.

Whatever standards and intervals you choose should provide sufficient information and time to recognise an emerging problem and be able to diagnose it. You do this by comparing actual interim results with pre-set standards, examining the magnitude and direction of variations and calculating the rate of change from the previous period's results. Assume that your non-profit organisation actually receives £2,000 in contributions during November, although your monthly forecast standard is £2,500. Your results are 20 per cent lower than the standard, which is a sizeable variation. However, sharply lower November results would signal an even more problematic trend if your October contributions were 10 per cent lower than the standard and your September contributions were 5 per cent lower.

How can you diagnose the cause and significance of any deviations from standards? Examine your actual results and recent trends in the context of your marketing activities, previous results and overall industry results. For example, when marketers for Thailand's Central Restaurants Group found that turnover in the company's Auntie Anne's pretzel shops was lower than expected, they compared the size of the average order and the number of customers to the same period in the previous year. Although the analysis showed no change in the size of the average order, it revealed that the chain was serving fewer customers, an outcome consistent with the overall decline in consumer visits to local shopping centres. Based on this deviation from the sales forecast, Central Restaurants increased its marketing budget and planned new products to improve results.[3]

Use internal and external audits to identify and analyse changes that may have affected your progress. Internally, you might find staffing shortages, budget cuts or operational difficulties contributed to worse-than-expected results. Externally, you might find that better-than-expected results were due, in part, to a competitor's troubles or reduced unemployment in targeted markets. Look upstream and downstream in the value chain: on the supply side, production may depend on just-in-time deliveries; on the demand side, sales may depend on demand for certain consumer products. Also look for answers by researching customer behaviour, perceptions, attitudes and relationships.

If measurements show no deviations, you can continue implementation as planned. You may do this even if you find deviations, to allow more time for a definite trend to develop and avoid acting prematurely. If you decide to respond to a deviation, you can take one of three corrective actions: (1) adjust marketing programmes, schedules or budgets; (2) adjust the standards or measurement intervals for your metrics; or (3) change the assumptions factored into your marketing plan, such as the prevailing economic climate or increased price competition. In turn, changing a key assumption may cause you to change your objectives or other aspects of the marketing plan. Finally, if interim results are much better than expected, you can use your diagnosis to maintain these outstanding results and enhance the implementation of other programmes (see Table 12.1).

Table 12.1 Responding to the diagnosis of interim results

Action	Description
Continue with implementation	Leave programmes, timing, budgets, responsibilities, metrics and measurement intervals as planned
Adjust implementation to solve a problem	Change marketing programmes, timing, budgets, responsibilities as suggested by diagnosis of deviation
Adjust standards or measurement intervals	Switch metrics or make other changes that will allow more accurate or timely identification of potential problems
Adjust marketing plan assumptions	Change relevant assumptions on which strategies and programmes are based to fine-tune planning and implementation
Maintain outstanding results and enhance implementation	Use the diagnosis to find ways of sustaining superior results and enhancing the implementation of other programmes

Levels of marketing control

During plan implementation, you can apply marketing control at a number of different levels, as your organisation chooses. These levels include:

- *Business unit.* Is the marketing plan of a particular business unit achieving interim results as expected? How do these results compare with the results of the company's other units and with the industry in general?

- *Marketing-mix activities.* Are the planned product, channel, pricing and communications activities achieving the desired results? Is each product meeting sales targets and other interim standards? Are sales through each channel (and channel member) up to expectations? Are advertising campaigns achieving their awareness and response objectives? Are price changes stimulating sales to the desired degree?

- *Programme.* How is each programme performing relative to the standards for interim results? Which programmes are yielding better results and which are yielding disappointing results?

- *Product or line.* Are individual products (or the entire line) meeting standards for interim progress toward objectives? Are the products or line moving toward market share targets?

- *Segment.* What are the interim results for each customer segment being targeted?

- *Geography.* What do interim results look like for each branch or region? What area-specific elements could cause deviations in certain branches or regions?

- *Manager.* For accountability, what is the status of each manager's results compared with agreed-upon standards?

- *Brand.* Is each brand performing up to the pre-set standards, in financial and marketing terms? How do interim results compare with those of other brands in the portfolio and with those of competing brands?

Organisations usually apply marketing control at multiple levels, both macro and micro. H&M and other fashion retailers give special emphasis to marketing control at the product and store level; consumer packaged-goods marketers such as Unilever look closely at the business unit, region, product line and brand levels. Panera Bread, a US restaurant chain, applies marketing control on an hourly basis, store by store, posting specific details on an internal website so store managers can adjust their activities accordingly.[4]

Don't depend on only one or two levels of control; if you do, you'll get an incomplete or distorted picture of interim results and might therefore take action inappropriately. Remember, forecasts and schedules are targets; your actual results may be slightly higher or lower at each measurement interval as you move toward achieving full-year performance. When applying marketing control, you want to act soon enough to make a difference in the final outcome of your marketing plan without overreacting.

Types of marketing control

To determine the overall effectiveness of your marketing plan at its conclusion and to gauge progress while it is being implemented, you will use annual, financial, productivity and strategic control, applied at the various levels you have chosen. Table 12.2 summarises these four types of marketing control, which are discussed in more detail in the following sections.

Table 12.2 Annual, financial, productivity and strategic control

Annual control	Financial control
● Evaluate full-year and interim marketing plan performance ● Identify ineffective or unsuitable programmes and activities ● Identify ineffective or mishandled implementation	● Use financial measures to assess performance ● Compare actual financial results with metrics, budgets, forecasts ● Analyse profit and cost results at multiple control levels
Productivity control	**Strategic control**
● Evaluate the efficiency of marketing planning, processes, activities ● Assess productivity due to higher output or lower costs ● Gauge ability to transfer marketing learning and tactics	● Evaluate performance in managing the marketing function ● Evaluate performance in managing key relationships ● Evaluate marketing performance with regards to social responsibility and ethics

Annual control

Annual control allows you to evaluate the current marketing plan's performance in preparation for developing next year's marketing plan. This annual control process provides an important check of what your plan has achieved and where improvements can be made, feeding back to the environmental scanning and analysis for next year. Start with a broad overview of the plan's performance. How do the full-year results match up with the primary marketing, financial and societal objectives such as increasing sales and profits, strengthening customer loyalty or improving corporate image?

Looking at performance measured by a few vital objectives can suggest strengths and weaknesses to be further investigated through internal analysis. Now look at whether other marketing plan objectives were achieved, and by what margin. Using these targets, was full-year performance below expectations, at the expected level or above expectations? At the micro level, how did each programme and marketing activity perform relative to its objectives? What can you learn from the pattern of interim progress measurements throughout the year that will help in next year's forecasting and implementation? Can line managers and others responsible for implementation and customer contact offer constructive feedback about the programmes, objectives, activities or anything else connected with the marketing plan?

A particular challenge is distinguishing ineffective or unsuitable programmes and activities from ineffective or mishandled implementation so you can make changes during the next planning cycle. Did a programme fail to meet objectives because its planning was flawed or because its implementation was flawed? How do the current conditions differ from those previous situations, and what conclusions can you draw? At worst, annual control will reveal poor marketing performance and the need to address bad planning or bad implementation. At best, it will indicate superior marketing performance and confirm the soundness of the plan or the implementation – or identify an unintended result brought about by the organisation's marketing.

Financial control

Businesses and non-profit organisations alike apply **financial control** to evaluate the marketing plan's interim and overall performance according to key financial measures such as sales (or contributions), profits, gross and net margin, costs and return on investment. Interim measurements show progress toward full-year objectives; full-year financial results clarify the big picture of marketing performance. You can compare actual expenditures with planned budgets, actual sales and costs with forecasts, and profit objectives with profit results at multiple levels (by product, market, segment, channel and so forth).

Productivity control

The purpose of **productivity control** is to evaluate the marketing plan's performance relative to the efficiency of key marketing processes and activities. Whereas financial control is concerned with financial measures of performance, productivity control focuses on improvements to processes and activities that either decrease costs or increase output. Different organisations apply productivity control in different ways (and at different intervals). Some common business examples include:

- *Overall plan productivity*. Has the current plan yielded better results with smaller-than-usual marketing budgets? Has the current plan maintained expected results without budget increases? Have implementation costs increased without corresponding increases in marketing results?

- *Communications productivity*. Without higher budgets, are advertising reach and brand/product awareness increasing over time? With lower budgets, are reach and brand/product awareness levels sustained? Which sales promotions yield the best response for the investment? If your current plan has a different combination of communications and influence programmes than in previous years, are you achieving more efficiency and effectiveness?

- *Sales force productivity*. Is the sales force contacting more prospects and making more sales without higher budgets? With lower budgets, is the sales force maintaining productivity on the same measures? Which sales people and territories are the most productive?

- *Product and development productivity*. Are more new products being generated on a stable development budget? Are more new products moving from the concept stage to commercialisation, resulting in higher sales and profit potential? Are some products more productive (yielding higher profitability relative to their costs) than others? Should some products be dropped because they are less productive?

- *Channel productivity*. Are some channels more important for long-term sales and profit productivity? Do some channels require disproportionately high investment for the level of return? Can results be maintained with lower channel costs?

- *Price productivity*. Did a price promotion stimulate revenues to offset the lower profit margin? Did a reduced price stimulate sufficient sales to bring a product to the break-even point earlier than planned? Did a price increase yield higher total profit despite lower unit sales?

- *Segment and customer productivity*. Are the marketing costs for some segments or customers too high relative to the payback? Which yield the best returns on investment? Should some be dropped because they are relatively unproductive in generating returns? Are you able to reach your targeted segments as planned? What marketing changes would allow you to target more efficiently and effectively?

Strategic control

Strategic control is used to evaluate marketing's performance in managing strategic areas such as the marketing function itself, key relationships, social responsibility and ethics. Applied annually or semi-annually, generally by marketing management and top executives, strategic control shows whether marketing is doing its job, whether the organisation is forging relationships with publics that are important, and whether social responsibility and ethics objectives are being achieved. The purpose is to assess strengths and weaknesses in these areas, identify where improvement is needed and build on success when developing marketing plans.

To assess the marketing function's performance, your organisation can conduct a **marketing audit**, a formal, detailed study of the planning process, plan implementation, personnel skills, use of resources and responsiveness. As part of the marketing audit, management should look at the skills and motivation of marketing personnel. Also consider a *brand audit* for each brand in your portfolio to determine whether your planning and implementation are having the desired effect on awareness, image, preference and loyalty.

Customer relationships are at the heart of any company's success, which is why strategic control should evaluate marketing performance in acquiring and retaining new customers, building loyalty, increasing satisfaction and supporting positive perceptions. Examine your firm's performance in managing relationships with shareholders, suppliers, channel partners and other groups that can significantly affect your ability to achieve objectives and goals.

Finally, use strategic control to assess marketing's performance with regard to social responsibility and ethics. Is marketing effectively conveying the organisation's involvement in socially responsible causes or green initiatives? Are societal objectives being set and achieved? Are marketing decisions being made and implemented in an ethical manner? What else can marketing do to demonstrate that the firm is socially responsible and committed to strict ethical standards? Many marketers, including the US retail chain Gap Inc., make public the results of their social responsibility audits.

MARKETING IN PRACTICE: THE GAP

The Gap, founded in 1969 as a retailer of denim jeans, rings up £9 billion in annual turn-over from more than 3,100 stores under the Gap, Banana Republic, Old Navy, Piperlime and Athleta brands. The comprehensive social responsibility programmes now under way at The Gap can be traced back to the mid-1990s, when some of its overseas suppliers were accused of using child labour. In response, the company set ambitious goals for improving living and working conditions around the factories where its clothing is made; management has been monitoring performance ever since. The company demonstrates its transparency by issuing a yearly social responsibility report showing progress toward targets such as supplier compliance with its requirements for improving employee conditions.

Over time, The Gap has expanded its societal objectives to push for such improvements as recycling shipping materials, preventing water pollution, providing safe drinking water, conserving energy and donating to local causes. It also works with experts and activist groups to identify additional social issues where its involvement can make a dif-ference to stakeholders while supporting the company's business goals and marketing objectives. A 'digital dashboard' on the company's website shows at a glance how the company is doing on the most significant social responsibility metrics.[5]

Use the following checklist as a guide to assessing the implementation of your marketing plan.

ESSENTIAL MARKETING PLAN CHECKLIST NO. 17:
EVALUATING IMPLEMENTATION

When you plan for implementation, you must be ready to identify potential problems and make changes quickly if actual results vary from expected results. Also you must be prepared to gather data so you can evaluate how well the organisation did in imple-menting the marketing plan. These questions will start you off in the right direction when you look back on your planning and implementation activities.

☐ Were the appropriate personnel (internal and external) involved in planning and implementation?

☐ Were suitable metrics and measurement intervals selected for measuring progress toward achieving the plan's financial, marketing and societal objectives?

☐ Were marketing plan decisions made after investigating multiple options to address each opportunity, threat and competitive situation?

☐ Were marketing metrics, forecasts, schedules, budgets and implementation responsibilities clearly delineated, realistic, coordinated properly and communicated effectively?

☐ Were marketing resources, internal activities and value chain activities properly coordinated and managed during implementation?

☐ How did marketing personnel deal with interim results that deviated from standards?

☐ How can marketing planning and implementation be improved in the future?

CONTINGENCY PLANS AND SCENARIO PLANNING

To supplement your implementation plan, you may need a **contingency plan** to be implemented in response to or anticipation of significant changes in the marketing situation that could disrupt important marketing activities. Look at your forecasts, schedules and budgets representing the most pessimistic and the most optimistic scenarios that could occur during the planning period, identify the worst-case scenarios that could be most damaging to your ability to achieve marketing plan objectives, then create plans for coping with those scenarios. Table 12.3 presents the main components of contingency planning for marketing. Note that top management may incorporate marketing contingency plans into a comprehensive organisation-wide contingency plan.

Contingency plans may also be the outcome of a sophisticated scenario-planning process in which managers develop detailed descriptions of future situations to anticipate and plan for major shifts in external forces, industry trends, technological developments and organisational resources.[6] With **scenario planning**, marketers look beyond historical trends and short-term projections to envision broad, long-term changes in the marketing environment that could affect future performance, then prepare contingency plans for these possible situations. The purpose is to have plans ready for implementation so your organisation can adjust its activities if and when these scenarios become realities.[7] Here are a few examples of how companies are applying scenario planning in marketing.

Table 12.3 Contingency planning for marketing

Planning action	Purpose
Identify emergency situations and analyse their potential consequences for marketing	To understand the marketing activities, people and operations most likely to be disrupted by each possible emergency
Consider how emergencies might affect the organisation's suppliers, wholesalers and retailers	To prepare for the possibility of disruptions due to emergency situations elsewhere in the value chain
List advance preparations that can be made to minimise disruptions and restore normalcy	To have materials and procedures ready in the event of an emergency
Establish warning signs of impending crises	To help recognise when an emergency is developing and provide triggers for contingency plan implementation
Assign specific actions, responsibilities and priorities for containment and customer service	To prevent the crisis from becoming more severe by organising and coordinating an effective initial response to contain the problem and continue serving customers
Create a contingency communication plan	To keep internal and external publics informed about the situation, the response and future steps
Resolve the crisis and analyse outcomes of contingency plan	To improve the contingency planning process by eliminating ineffective actions and learning from experience for better advance preparation

MARKETING IN PRACTICE: SCENARIO PLANNING

The Danish toy manufacturer Lego formulates a number of contingency plans for marketing so no matter what direction the economy moves in, the company is ready to take action. Its senior managers meet monthly to re-evaluate external conditions and discuss the situations they are most likely to face in the coming months. As a result, Lego has been able to increase sales despite global recession and mounting competition.[8]

MasterCard has an international team travelling the world to research different scenarios for growth by seeking input from the credit-card company's workforce. Using internal communications such as webcasts, the team then presents a range of scenarios to inform and inspire all employees in preparation for the different paths that the firm's future marketing initiatives might follow. Estée Lauder, which markets cosmetics, uses scenario planning to plan for rapid changes in global economic conditions and consumer demand. When considering worst-case scenarios, the chief executive asks brand managers: 'What must you have? What would you like to keep going? And what can you give up?'[9]

Contingency plans are valuable for coping with major challenges and large-scale emergencies brought on by uncontrollable external factors such as natural disasters, an outbreak of a disease, terrorism, sabotage, computer system failures or transport cuts, extreme economic conditions, unusual competitive pressures or the sudden withdrawal of a key supplier or customer. A severe, prolonged crisis may physically threaten employees, customers or suppliers, damage facilities or equipment, destroy products and supplies, and shut down channels. Less severe emergencies may disrupt (but not cripple) internal or external marketing activities.

Be sure to examine multiple links in your organisation's value chain to pinpoint and plan for potential problems.[10] If possible, conduct a simple SWOT analysis of the key partners in your value chain to understand where they stand. Ideally, you and your suppliers and distributors should work together to develop contingency plans for situations such as:

- supply challenges, such as insufficient or unpredictable availability of raw materials and parts

- transportation challenges, such as a strike or severe weather disrupting deliveries

- financial challenges, such as a reduction in credit availability

- personnel challenges, such as difficulty recruiting or retaining skilled staff

- communications challenges, such as interruption of postal or telecommunications services, and

- market-by-market challenges, such as logistical difficulties or opportunities in particular locations.

For example, during the H1N1 swine flu virus outbreak, many companies established contingency plans to ensure that their marketing activities would continue without interruption. Reckitt Benckiser, Lloyds and other firms also asked ad agencies and key suppliers to prepare contingency plans for operating in the event of many employees being taken ill.[11]

 ## CHAPTER SUMMARY

The process of marketing control consists of: (1) setting standards and measurement intervals to gauge progress toward marketing objectives; (2) measuring interim results after implementation; (3) comparing measured results with standards and diagnosing any deviations; and (4) taking action as needed. The purpose is to pinpoint where results are below or above expectations, understand why and decide to leave the programmes and implementation unchanged, make changes to solve problems, or apply lessons learned to improve progress toward standards and, ultimately, objectives. The decisions made at the end of the process feed back to the beginning, providing feedback for changing standards, measurement intervals or even objectives.

Annual plan control is used to evaluate the current marketing plan's performance in preparation for developing next year's marketing plan. Financial control is used to evaluate the marketing plan's performance according to key financial measures such as sales and profits. Productivity control is used to evaluate the marketing plan's performance relative to the efficiency of key marketing processes and activities. Strategic control evaluates effectiveness in managing strategic areas such as the marketing function and social responsibility/ethics. Formulate contingency plans in advance to be ready to respond to potentially disruptive changes in the organisation's situation. Use scenario planning to look beyond historical trends and short-term projections and envision broad, long-term changes in the marketing environment that could significantly alter future performance.

CASE STUDY: HONDA STEERS MARKETING TOWARDS PROFITABLE FUTURE

With some smart adjustments, Honda's marketing plans for profitable growth have kept the automotive giant from severe losses, despite gyrating petrol prices and a global economic crisis. The company produces 3.5 million cars and 14.5 million motorcycles every year. Just a few years ago, many automakers were launching larger, more powerful vehicles, which often deliver higher per-unit profits. In contrast, Honda's marketing plans have avoided introductions of big pickup trucks and cars with massive engines. Instead, its plans focus on deriving more than 75 per cent of turnover from selling four key models worldwide: the Civic, the Accord, the Fit/Jazz and the CR-V, a small sport-utility vehicle. Its plans also call for manufacturing the most popular models in the markets where they are sold, to stay close to customers and be able to respond to local conditions.

The recession initially had little effect on Honda. As sales slowed, however, the company recognised the need to modify existing marketing plans in light of new economic realities. Honda's marketers quickly dropped plans to introduce a new sports car and postponed plans to launch the Acura brand in Japan. They also made the difficult decision to cut costs by eliminating Honda's expensive sponsorship of Formula One racing, which had been one of the company's most visible marketing programmes externally and internally.

In the UK, where economic stimulus incentives boosted purchasing of fuel-efficient vehicles, Honda's five-door Jazz import became particularly popular. As a result, the company retooled its Swindon factory to produce the Jazz locally for UK and European buyers, reopening the plant just as overall demand was improving. Honda also blunted the effect of the yen's ups and downs in the foreign exchange market by shifting some of its production outside Japan.

Although Toyota's Prius is the world's best-selling hybrid, high demand in Japan – fuelled, in part, by government incentives – has caused some delays in delivery to customers. Honda, meanwhile, has been able to deliver its Insight hybrid to Japanese buyers within a month of orders being placed. Looking ahead, Honda's marketers are readying hybrid-engine versions of many car models. To ensure sufficient supply of lithium-ion batteries in Japan, they have forged a joint venture to supplement their purchases from Sanyo, which has been providing batteries for the Insight. Sales of small, fuel-efficient models have been so strong that Honda recently increased its forecast for sales in Japan.[12]

Case questions

1. Automakers have to plan years in advance for new model introductions. What questions might Honda's marketers have considered when weighing the decision to retain or drop plans for introducing a new sports car during the economic downturn?

2. What worst-case scenario(s) and contingency plan(s) would you recommend Honda consider for its hybrid vehicles and why?

 **APPLY YOUR KNOWLEDGE**

Review your research and responses for the 'Apply your knowledge' exercises in Chapters 5 and 11. Now answer the following questions about your chosen company's marketing control. Prepare a brief written or oral report summarising your ideas.

- What revenue and profit results has this company announced in recent months? How does this performance compare with the company's forecasts and/or budgets?

- If the company's actual financial performance is different from the planned results, what corrective actions have been taken?

- Did this company recently report changes related to marketing relationships, such as market share? How do these compare with the expected performance? What marketing control steps, if any, do you think this company should take right now – and why?

- Based on what you know of this company, identify one issue that could interfere with achieving marketing plan objectives and explain how you would address this in a contingency plan.

BUILD YOUR OWN MARKETING PLAN

Finalise your marketing plan by selecting the levels at which you will apply marketing control and the types of marketing control you will need to prepare for. How often will you measure results and what standards are most important for monitoring interim progress? How would you diagnose a situation in which actual expenditures exceeded budgeted costs? What corrective action might you take if actual unit sales for an important channel fell below your forecast? Should you reconsider your measurement intervals or standards if actual performance deviates significantly from your plan? Is it important to apply marketing control by segment, geography, manager and/or brand? What areas will require strategic and productivity control? What worst-case scenario might require contingency planning? Document your thoughts in a written marketing plan.

ENDNOTES

1. Cari Tuna, 'Theory & practice: Pendulum is swinging back on "scenario planning"', *Wall Street Journal*, 6 July 2009, p. B6; Lindsay Riddell, 'Q & A: Look at company's culture, what motivates the people', *San Jose Business Journal*, 1 February 2008, n.p.; www.jdsu.com.

2. 'Earning customers' lifetime loyalty', *Balanced Scorecard Report*, March–April 2009, n.p.

3. 'Central Group's Auntie Anne's pretzelshop sets budget for marketing', *The Nation*, 22 July 2009, www.nationmultimedia.com.

4. Gregg Cebrzynski, 'Panera Bread managers 'harvest' key sales data via intranet to support internal marketing', *Nation's Restaurant News*, 3 November 2008, p. 12.

5. Masha Zager, 'Doing well by doing good', *Apparel*, August 2009, pp. 10ff; 'A stress test for good intentions', *The Economist*, 16 May 2009, p. 67; Dan McDougall, 'Child sweatshop shame threatens Gap's ethical image', *The Observer*, 28 October 2007, www.guardian.co.uk.

6. See Babette E. Bensoussan and Craig Fleisher, *Analysis Without Paralysis: 10 Tools to Make Better Strategic Decisions* (Upper Saddle River, NJ: FT Press, 2008), Chapter 9.

7. 'An interview with Peter Schwartz', *Economic Times*, 16 May 2009, n.p.; Larry Lapide, 'Scenario planning for a successful future', *Supply Chain Management Review*, October 2008, p. 8.

8. 'Managing in the fog', *The Economist*, 28 February 2009, p. 67.

9. Quoted in Matthew Boyle, 'The budget knives come out', *BusinessWeek*, 13 October 2008, p. 30; also: Reena Jana and Damian Joseph, 'Keeping employees creative in a downturn', *BusinessWeek Online*, 23 July 2009, www.businessweek.com.

10. Robert Handfield, 'United they'll stand', *Wall Street Journal*, 23 March 2009, p. R6.

11. Alex Brownsell, 'Marketing departments require ad agencies to put contingency plans in place for swine flu', *Marketing*, 22 September 2009, www.marketingmagazine.co.uk.

12. 'Honda extols the three joys rather than doom and gloom', *Sunday Times*, 10 October 2009, www.timeslive.co.za/sundaytimes; Kae Inoue and Yuki Hagiwara, 'Toyota may avoid future Prius delays with Panasonic–Sanyo deal', *Bloomberg*, 8 October 2009, www.bloomberg.com; Ian Rowley, 'What put Honda in the passing lane', *BusinessWeek*, 19 October 2009, pp. 57–8; 'Honda brings Jazz to UK', *The Engineer Online*, 8 October 2009, www.theengineer.co.uk; 'Honda repeats goal to raise Japan sales', *Reuters*, 8 October 2009, www.reuters.com; Yoshio Takahashi, 'Honda's return to profit is made uncertain by yen', *Wall Street Journal*, 2 October 2009, www.wsj.com.

The fictitious company Lost Legends Luxury Chocolatier is planning to market premium gourmet chocolates to adults in the United Kingdom and, later, in Western Europe. As this sample plan indicates, many confectionery companies target the children's chocolate sweets market, but fewer are active in the adult segment and fewer still in upmarket chocolates. The UK has the highest per capita consumption of and spending on chocolates, compared with other European nations, making it a very attractive market for our gourmet products. Also, our gourmet range will tap rising demand for dark chocolate products, which is forecast to grow more quickly than overall chocolate demand.

This sample plan illustrates the marketing steps that Lost Legends Luxury Chocolatier will take to launch its first products and compete with established confectionery companies. Notice how the contents, order of topics and section headings are tailored to fit the company's situation. Also notice that details (such as product-by-product pricing, detailed programme schedules and detailed budgets) are not in the main body of this plan but would be available in the appendix of an actual plan for readers who want more specifics.

EXECUTIVE SUMMARY

Lost Legends Luxury Chocolatier is a new company planning to market premium gourmet chocolates to UK adults and, later, to adults in Western Europe. In monetary terms, this market is smaller than the children's chocolate sweets market. However, confectioners offering gourmet, premium-priced chocolates under well-regarded brands can potentially earn higher profit margins by targeting specific market segments. We will target three consumer segments and three business segments at the high end of the gift, holiday and affordable personal luxury market, enhancing our positioning with Fairtrade Marked cocoa supplied by a plantation known for superior quality. Our Belgian Legends product line will be introduced in September to allow time for building brand awareness and product trial prior to the Christmas period, when our seasonal Limited Edition Legends line will be featured.

Our financial objectives relate to first-year turnover in the UK market, a minimum level of sales for each retail outlet, achieving break-even within 16 months and aiming for 10 per cent gross profit margin by the end of our second year. Our marketing objectives relate to first-year brand awareness among consumers and businesses, arranging for retail distribution, launching the e-commerce website and planning for new products to be introduced in the second year. Our societal objectives relate to supporting sustainability and using recycled materials in product packaging.

Key strengths are our family recipes, patented roasting process, cost-effective hand production and glamorous history. Weaknesses include lack of brand awareness and image, limited resources and lack of channel relationships. Our marketing plan will address three major opportunities: higher demand for premium chocolates, especially dark chocolates, growing interest in treats with mystique and growing interest in socially responsible products. The main threats we must counter are intense competition, market fragmentation and uncertain supply prices.

CURRENT MARKETING SITUATION

The company was founded by the British descendants of a nineteenth-century Bruges chocolate maker who was famous for his unusually dark and intensely flavoured chocolates. In this pre-automation era, he mixed small batches using the finest ingredients, kneaded and tempered the chocolate to achieve a smooth, refined texture, and poured his confections into hand-made moulds one at a time. Dozens of his recipes were handed down from generation to generation as the family moved from Bruges to the London area, but the chocolates were never produced commercially until now. After experimenting with roasting cocoa beans and updating the recipes as they prepared for a St Valentine's Day party, two entrepreneurial family members were inspired to patent the roasting process and launch a new business. The name 'Lost Legends Luxury Chocolatier' was chosen because it captured the romance of dark, rich Belgian chocolates made in the old-fashioned way from treasured recipes.

Europe has a long tradition of chocolate making, from leading brands such as Barry Callebaut, Lindt, Nestlé, Cadbury, Perugina and Lenôtre to locally owned and operated gourmet chocolatiers. The top brands enjoy high awareness and high customer loyalty. Upmarket stores such as Harrods and Fortnum and Mason also sell private-label branded chocolates as well as domestic and imported upmarket brands, which adds to the competitive pressure. Nonetheless, a number of smaller companies are successfully targeting specific niches within the adult chocolate market by offering hand-made chocolates, exotically flavoured chocolates, Fairtrade chocolates, all-natural chocolates, lower-fat chocolates, holiday chocolates and gift chocolates. In fact, Fairtrade chocolates have gone mainstream now that Cadbury Dairy Milk, the UK's best-selling chocolate bar, is made with certified Fairtrade cocoa.

In this environment, Lost Legends Luxury Chocolatier will compete at the higher end of the gift, holiday and affordable personal luxury market. Our positioning is based on the hand-made, top-quality nature of our premium chocolates made from the finest, freshest, all-natural ingredients, our distinctive product and package differentiation, our exclusive brand image, carefully controlled production output, and highly selective distribution. Much of our marketing focus will be on our use of Fairtrade Marked cocoa, a programme ensuring that growers receive a fair price for their cocoa. By actively promoting socially responsible sourcing of top-quality cocoa (and other ingredients), we can encourage positive associations with our brand and products. We can also support the mystique aspect of our positioning by using only cocoa grown on a specific plantation renowned for the distinctive quality of the beans it produces.

MARKET SUMMARY

Although North and South America are the largest global markets in terms of chocolate sales, sales in Europe have been slowly increasing. UK sales of chocolate exceed £4.3 billion annually and annual per capita UK consumption is estimated at 10 kg. By comparison, estimated annual per capita consumption of chocolate in Germany is 8 kg per year; in France, 6 kg per year; in Spain, 3 kg per year; and in Italy, 2 kg per year.

As the recent economic recovery progresses, UK sales of all chocolates are forecast to grow by about 2 per cent per year up to 2015, while sales of dark chocolates are forecast to grow by up to 10 per cent per year. Eastern Europe is expected to experience rapid growth in chocolate consumption, so we will explore opportunities there after establishing our brand and building sales in our UK home market and then in Western Europe. Fairtrade chocolate has become increasingly popular over the past decade, and now accounts for more than £26 million in UK sales annually, another key trend in our favour.

Looking at customer buying patterns, chocolate sales are subject to seasonality. Sales increase markedly before holiday periods such as Easter, Christmas and St Valentine's Day. Chocolate is not only a seasonal treat: one survey shows that more than half of UK consumers buy chocolate year-round without a special occasion in mind. However, sales can drop in extremely hot weather because (1) stores must keep chocolate products chilled, which reduces the opportunity for impulse purchases, and (2) customers tend to buy sweets that are less perishable and retain their quality. We plan to introduce our first products in September, building awareness and word of mouth so we can attract buyers during the critical year-end holiday period.

Consumer market

The three consumer market segments targeted by Lost Legends Luxury Chocolatier are middle- to high-income adults who: (1) like (or want) to reward themselves or their families with the affordable luxury of gourmet chocolates; (2) view upmarket chocolates as a suitable gift; (3) buy fine chocolates as a tradition for St Valentine's Day, Christmas, Easter or another holiday.

According to research, women account for the majority of purchases in this segment, and they are increasingly interested in product and packaging as expressions of pampering and personality. Although they are aware of prices, they are also loyal to their upmarket chocolate favourites. Not surprisingly, the affluent adults in our targeted segments have sophisticated tastes, high expectations and demanding standards.

We will give buyers of premium chocolate another reason to feel good about Lost Legends Luxury Chocolatier: they will be buying a brand that is socially responsible as well as top quality, an uncommon benefit combination among upmarket brands. Even before Cadbury's Dairy Milk was made of Fairtrade cocoa, more than 40 per cent of UK consumers had tried Fairtrade chocolates. This indicates an interest in the social responsibility aspect of chocolate products, which we will satisfy through our product.

As shown in Table A1.1, we plan to provide features that deliver valued benefits for the different needs of these targeted consumer segments.

Table A1.1 Targeted consumer segments

Targeted segment	Characteristics and needs	Feature/benefit
Adults with middle to high income levels who buy fine chocolates for themselves or their families	• Prefer the cachet of luxury brands • Like small indulgences • Willing to splurge for themselves or loved ones • Appreciate the taste and quality of premium chocolates	• Customers can select type and quantity of chocolates to accommodate tastes and budget • Premium brand image enhances perception of chocolates as special treat • Fairtrade Marked cocoa balances self-indulgence with social responsibility
Adults, primarily women, with middle to high income levels who buy fine chocolates for gifts	• Seek a gift that reflects personality of giver or recipient • Seek a gift with high perceived value • Seek a gift to delight the senses • Seek a gift that is unique yet not excessively extravagant • Seek a gift with emotional associations • Seek a gift that is socially responsible	• Distinctive yet sustainable gift packaging adds to visual appeal, personality, perceived value • Top-quality, limited-edition chocolates make our products unique and uncommon • Fairtrade Marked cocoa balances gift status with sense of social responsibility
Adults with middle to high income levels who buy fine chocolates for holidays	• View holidays as occasions to enjoy special treats • Have or want to create a tradition of enjoying special chocolates on certain holidays	• Seasonal/holiday packaging adds to our product's appeal for special occasions • Limited-edition range reinforces exclusivity • Fairtrade Marked cocoa combines holiday tradition with social responsibility

Business market

The business market segments targeted by Lost Legends Luxury Chocolatier consist of professionals and business people who select or give gifts: (1) to clients and other business contacts; (2) to colleagues or managers on holiday occasions; (3) customised by product, packaging or business logo. These segments represent a significant opportunity to build repeat purchasing and loyalty among businesses that require unique corporate gifts with wide appeal for various occasions. Many small chocolate shops accept or invite customised orders but Lost Legends Luxury Chocolatier will aggressively target this segment and seek to build longer-term customer relationships spanning gift-giving occasions.

Table A1.2 summarises the features and benefits we can deliver to satisfy the needs of these targeted segments of the business market.

Table A1.2   Targeted business segments

Targeted segment	Characteristics and needs	Feature/benefit
Professionals and executives who give gifts to clients and other business contacts, or who are responsible for selecting such gifts on the firm's behalf	• Want a gift with high perceived status and value • May influence selection but not actually purchase gifts • May give gifts but not actually make the purchase • May make the purchase but not actually give the gift	• Purchasers can select type and quantity of chocolates to accommodate budget and occasion • Premium brand image enhances perception of chocolates as gift • Fairtrade Marked cocoa balances luxury with social responsibility
Professionals and business people who give gifts to colleagues or managers at holiday times	• Seek a gift with high perceived value • Seek a gift that is recognised as unique and exclusive • Seek a gift that is socially responsible	• Distinctive yet sustainable gift packaging adds to visual appeal and perceived value • Top-quality, limited-edition chocolates make our products unique and uncommon • Fairtrade Marked cocoa balances gift status with sense of social responsibility
Professionals and business people who give customised gifts	• Want to reinforce corporate name in a tangible, memorable way • Want to give a gift not available to the general public • Want recipients to anticipate high-quality customised gifts • Want recipients to feel good about the social responsibility aspect of the gift	• Chocolates and packaging can carry business logo as visual reinforcement of corporate name • Special packaging customised for business clients reinforces the uniqueness and exclusivity of the gift • Fairtrade Marked cocoa combines holiday tradition with social responsibility

Market trends and growth

The overall European chocolate confectionery market is projected to grow modestly for the remainder of this decade, a positive trend for our product. Moreover, UK chocolate sales represent 25 per cent of the total European market for chocolates, which supports our decision to launch first in the United Kingdom. Gourmet chocolate brands clearly have higher wholesale and retail value than mass-market chocolates, although per capita consumption does not match that of mass-market chocolates.

A growing number of Fairtrade chocolates have gained distribution in national chains such as Waitrose as well as in independent shops. National advertising and sales promotions support sales of Cadbury, Nestlé, Mars and other mainstream chocolate marketers, especially prior to Easter and other holidays. Chocolate made from cocoa beans native to specific regions or plantations, such as the organic chocolates made by Montezuma in West Sussex from cocoa grown in the Dominican Republic and Peru, carry a special mystique.

Further, product proliferation in the European chocolate market is adding to competitive pressure. In fact, chocolate products represent a significant fraction of all new food products introduced during any given year. Both for-profit and not-for-profit companies are introducing chocolate bars, truffles and novelties made from Fairtrade ingredients. Smaller companies are making speciality chocolate products for niche markets, such as chocolates for people who want to avoid dairy products, chocolates for people who are diabetic and chocolates for people who prefer natural or organic flavourings and ingredients. Established companies constantly introduce variations of truffles, bars, bonbons, pralines and other favourites to satisfy customers' variety-seeking behaviour and encourage loyalty. In many cases, companies are offering their products directly to customers through online and printed catalogues.

Marketing research

To stay in touch with our targeted segments and track emerging market trends, we are commissioning qualitative research that will investigate perceptions, attitudes and behaviour related to premium chocolate products in general and Lost Legends Luxury Chocolatier in particular. We will use both secondary and primary research to support new product development, plan public relations activities, understand our competitive situation and monitor progress towards awareness objectives. In addition, we will commission marketing research to examine customer and channel satisfaction and identify opportunities and threats to which we must respond. Finally, we will solicit feedback through our website, social media and manufacturer's representatives as part of our ongoing research.

CURRENT PRODUCT OFFERINGS

Initially we will offer two main product lines, both based on modern adaptations of family recipes and a proprietary cocoa bean-roasting process we recently developed. The first, Belgian Legends, features 12 dark chocolates named for Belgian cities, such as Antwerp (dark, fruity flavour) and Bruges (extra dark, sprinkled with *fleur de sel*). This product line will be available all year and both the chocolates and packaging can be customised for corporate gift giving. In subsequent years, we will add between two and four new varieties in this line and retain the best-selling eight to ten chocolates from the previous year, as measured by volume. We will also offer special packaging for three important holiday seasons: Easter, Christmas and St Valentine's Day.

Our product plan has the following advantages: (1) the product line and packaging are freshened and updated on a regular basis; (2) customers can find their favourites year after year, holiday after holiday; (3) the product line and the names of individual chocolate varieties reflect our family's background and tradition. The plan supports steady year-round purchasing and encourages impulse and gift purchases during peak selling periods.

The second product line, Limited Edition Legends, features chocolates in one of two seasonal shapes and matching packaging: seashells for summer and snowflakes for winter. Each season we will bring back the seashell or snowflake favourites in new packaging. By restricting production and distribution of these limited-edition chocolates, and planning each seasonal announcement as a media event, similar to those for new wine vintages, we will build customer anticipation and demand. Premium chocolates have been offered in limited editions for some time, but mainstream manufacturers such as Cadbury, Nestlé and Mars have brought the practice to a wider audience by offering limited editions of well-known chocolate treats.

The use of limited editions has the following advantages: (1) the temporary introduction of seasonal varieties will give sales a strong, relatively predictable boost during specific periods; (2) loyal customers will be able to buy some favourite chocolates in every season; (3) the perceived value as a gift will be higher because these varieties are not available throughout the year. As a result, we can capture customer interest in between the peak holiday periods and fulfil consumer and corporate needs for unique, value-added gifts.

BUSINESS ENVIRONMENT

Lost Legends Luxury Chocolatier will begin operations in an environment shaped by national and regional political forces, economic uncertainty, powerful social–cultural forces, including concerns about social responsibility, new production and communications technologies, specific legal considerations, increased emphasis on sustainability, and strong competition. This section discusses how the business environment is likely to affect our marketing and performance and this is followed by a SWOT analysis of our strengths, weaknesses, opportunities and threats.

- *Political forces.* As chocolate makers, we must be knowledgeable about political conditions in the nations where we obtain our cocoa and other supplies. We must also monitor the political situation domestically and throughout Europe as we plan to expand through exporting.

- *Economic uncertainty.* Economic conditions are not uniform throughout the European market, which will affect our ability to forecast sales and profits during the first year. Industry records show that demand falls slightly during economic downturns, because buying premium chocolate allows consumers to indulge themselves in a small way. Yet because buyers of upmarket chocolates routinely seek out new specialities, our initial sales should be strong despite the economic uncertainty. We must also monitor the economic climate in Ghana, where we source our Fairtrade Marked cocoa beans.

- *Social–cultural trends.* The Fairtrade Marked system, designed to ensure that growers are equitably compensated for their cocoa beans, is emblematic of a larger movement towards socially responsible business operations, with which we will be associated. As consumers and business customers become more knowledgeable about the social issues connected with chocolate production, our offerings are likely to be perceived favourably. Our products take advantage of the trend towards supporting small, local brands in a world dominated by giant multinational corporations. We also recognise that attitudes towards sweets are influenced by concern about nutrition and unhealthy foods. Yet some research suggests that the flavanol in chocolate can have health benefits. Our communications will therefore suggest that fine chocolate products be enjoyed as special treats, not as a steady diet.

- *Technological trends.* Although our chocolates will be hand-produced, the special roasting process for our cocoa beans relies on new technology that we have protected through patent. Technology will enable us to communicate more efficiently and effectively with our customers, suppliers and channel partners. In addition, our automated inventory-management system will help us forecast future demand, plan for supplies, plan for production and plan for distribution to ensure that we and our intermediaries have the right products in stock when needed.

- *Ecological trends.* With a focus on sustainability, we are buying Fairtrade Marked cocoa that is grown in an ecologically-sound manner. We are also planning earth-friendly packaging using recycled materials and inks that do not pollute.

- *Legal factors.* Our company must comply with all regional and national laws and regulations governing product quality, labelling, ingredients and many other aspects of the business. For example, any 'organic' chocolate product must comply with EU rules for organic certification. Similarly, our communications must comply with applicable laws.

- *Competition*. We face competition from Callebaut, Lindt, Neuhaus, Perugina, Nestlé, Cadbury and Godiva, among other major rivals. These companies have established brands and sizeable advertising budgets, yet they are not immune to industry competition and the effect of economic conditions on product sales. Montezuma and other speciality chocolate makers are promoting their products online and in selected upmarket shops. Lost Legends Luxury Chocolatier will preserve our exclusivity by restricting distribution to selected shops, using our heritage and sense of social responsibility to differentiate our products, promoting our patented roasting method and our commitment to hand-made quality.

SWOT analysis

Lost Legends Luxury Chocolatier can leverage several core competencies and key strengths in addressing potentially lucrative opportunities in both consumer and business market segments. As a new and unknown company, however, we must counter a few critical weaknesses that could threaten our ability to build profitability by serving the targeted segments. Table A1.3 summarises our SWOT analysis.

Table A1.3 SWOT analysis

Strengths	Weaknesses
• Unique, time-tested recipes • Patented roasting process • Cost-effective hand production • Glamorous history and heritage	• Lack of brand awareness, image • Limited resources • Lack of channel relationships
Opportunities	**Threats**
• Higher demand for premium chocolates, particularly dark chocolates • Growing interest in treats with mystique • Growing interest in socially responsible products	• Intense competition • Market fragmentation • Uncertain supply prices

Strengths

Among the internal capabilities that support our ability to achieve long-term and short-term objectives are:

- *Unique, time-tested recipes*. No other chocolatier sells the unusually rich, flavourful chocolates we can offer, updated from dozens of original recipes developed in the Steenstraat section of Bruges – a city renowned for delicious hand-made chocolates.

- *Patented roasting process.* Our legally protected, proprietary process for roasting cocoa beans results in a distinctively rich flavour and complex aroma that add sensory appeal to the finished product.

- *Cost-effective production.* Drawing on family records and supplier connections, we have perfected a cost-effective method for producing consistently high-quality chocolates by hand.

- *Glamorous history.* Publicising the legend of our family's original recipes and generations of chocolate making will evoke vivid images of old-fashioned quality and enhance the brand's glamour.

Weaknesses

Some of the internal factors that might prevent Lost Legends Luxury Chocolatier from achieving our objectives include:

- *Lack of brand awareness and image.* Lost Legends Luxury Chocolatier is a new company and therefore has no brand awareness in its targeted segments. We must effectively position our brand, create a premium image and communicate product benefits in order to build positive perceptions and attract customers.

- *Limited resources.* Much of our first-year budget is committed to funding production and internal operations, leaving limited funds for paid marketing messages. We will therefore put more emphasis on social media, online marketing, special packaging, sampling, public relations and special events to generate buzz, gain brand awareness and attract buyers.

- *Lack of channel relationships.* Most of our competitors own their own shops or have long-established relationships with leading retailers serving affluent customers. We are in the process of convincing exclusive speciality shops, leading department stores and other select retailers that our products are compatible with their merchandise assortments and will be profitable to carry.

Opportunities

We plan to exploit the following key opportunities:

- *Higher demand for premium chocolates.* More people see premium gourmet chocolates as an affordable luxury and therefore buy such products for themselves and for gifts. UK customers are familiar with premium chocolates and accustomed to paying more for ultra-high-quality products, especially those made from Fairtrade ingredients. Also, corporate demand for premium chocolates is rising due to interest in status products that can be given as gifts to almost any business contact (unless restricted by religious or cultural traditions).

- *Growing interest in treats with mystique.* Research suggests that customers (both consumers and business buyers) want more than a chocolate treat – they want to know the story behind the product and share in the product's mystique. Our company's connection with the family's legendary Bruges chocolates is an intriguing story to be publicised; the unique recipes, limited-edition products and special packaging add to the mystique.

- *Growing interest in socially responsible products.* The use of Fairtrade Marked cocoa (and coffee) will appeal to consumers who like the idea of supporting socially responsible products. It will also differentiate our products from those of companies using cocoa beans not grown by Fairtrade farmers. More than two dozen companies already produce Fairtrade chocolate products for the UK market, which shows how interest has grown and suggests that competition is likely to become more intense as this niche expands.

Threats

We recognise the need to counter the following threats as we begin marketing our chocolates:

- *Intense competition and market fragmentation.* In addition to the major luxury chocolate makers with established brands, national advertising campaigns and sizeable market share, many smaller, local chocolate makers are attracting loyal customers. Among the more than two dozen companies that feature Fairtrade chocolates in the UK market are Divine Chocolate, Green & Black's, Chocaid and Traidcraft. The resulting market fragmentation threatens our ability to build a solid customer base effectively and efficiently.

- *Uncertain supply prices.* Initially, we will be buying supplies in limited quantities and will not qualify for the most favourable volume discounts. Also, the price of ingredients can vary widely according to crop conditions, weather and other factors. Thus, we must allow for an extra margin when we set retail prices and recalculate break-even and profit levels as we come to know our supply prices.

Key issues

Because weather is an uncontrollable environmental factor, it has a major effect on chocolate sales and cocoa bean production. Heat waves generally hurt sales and can affect chocolate production; cool weather allows both channel members and consumers more flexibility in storing chocolates. Lost Legends Luxury Chocolatier will forecast modest sales for the hottest summer months and be ready to increase production output if the weather is not extremely warm. Extreme weather conditions or crop diseases in Ghana will hurt cocoa bean production, making this key ingredient scarce and expensive. We must be prepared to buy from alternative Fairtrade sources if our primary growers cannot fulfil their contracts, in order to meet our first-year sales objectives. In this event, we will plan to absorb higher costs and assume smaller profit margins for a limited period to avoid raising prices.

Product and package design are becoming increasingly important drivers of gift chocolate purchasing. Some companies are targeting niche markets such as golf-ball-shaped chocolates for men who play golf. Others are packaging premium gift chocolates in keepsake boxes that communicate status and elegance. Companies that emphasise Fairtrade connections generally explain their positioning on labels and packaging. We will monitor these trends and research additional opportunities during the coming year.

MISSION, DIRECTION AND OBJECTIVES

The mission of Lost Legends Luxury Chocolatier is to bring the family's expertise and tradition of making top-quality, premium chocolates to adult consumers and business buyers who buy luxury sweets for themselves or as gifts. All of our chocolate products will be updates or variations of cherished family recipes and produced by hand from the finest, freshest ingredients. We are committed to contracting for Fairtrade Marked cocoa, coffee and other ingredients from socially responsible sources. Our priority is to build our brand first in the UK market and then gradually expand our focus to other European markets.

Our initial year's direction is controlled growth through the establishment of the brand, development of two main product lines and targeting adults in consumer and business segments. In the second year, we will pursue growth through both market penetration and market development. Because of ongoing plans for limited-edition chocolate products, our growth will depend on product development as well. Based on this mission and direction, we have formulated the following primary objectives for our marketing plan:

- *Financial objectives.* The main financial objectives for Lost Legends Luxury Chocolatier are to (1) achieve first-year turnover of £500,000 in the UK market; (2) achieve full-year retail sales of at least £10,000 per outlet in the retail channel; (3) reach the breakeven point for UK operations within 16 months; and (4) achieve 10 per cent gross profit margin in our second year of operation.

- *Marketing objectives.* The main marketing objectives are to (1) generate first-year brand awareness of 35 per cent within consumer segments and 40 per cent within business segments; (2) place our products in 50 exclusive shops and high-end department stores located in affluent UK areas; (3) have our UK direct-sales website fully operational when the first products launch; and (4) research and develop between two and four new Belgian Legends variations, based on family recipes and traditions, for introduction in the second year.

- *Societal objectives.* The main societal objectives are to (1) support socially responsible trade by buying all cocoa and coffee from Fairtrade Marked sources; and (2) increase the proportion of recycled materials used in product packaging from 50 per cent at start-up to 65 per cent by the end of the first full year.

TARGETING AND POSITIONING DECISIONS

As shown in Tables A1.1 and A1.2, we are targeting specific segments of the consumer and business markets. In demographic terms, these are adults with middle to high income levels, professionals and business people. In behavioural terms, the targeted consumer segments consist of adults who buy fine chocolates for themselves, for the holidays or as gifts. The targeted business segments consist of business people who buy fine chocolates as gifts, customised or not. Because the corporate gift market is growing faster than the consumer chocolate market, and because of the potential for higher customer lifetime value and better return on investment, we will put more emphasis on the targeted business segments.

We will use differentiated marketing to reinforce the positioning of Lost Legends Luxury Chocolatier as a marketer of gourmet chocolates hand-made from 'legendary' family recipes using strictly fresh, high-quality ingredients drawn from socially responsible sources. This positioning sets us apart competitively and helps establish a positive, upscale image in the minds of the consumers and business customers we are targeting.

PRODUCT AND BRAND DECISIONS

Both of our initial product lines are based on updates of traditional family recipes and use our proprietary, patented cocoa bean-roasting process. The 12 chocolates in the Belgian Legends line are named for Belgian cities: Antwerp, Bruges . . . The chocolates in the Limited Edition Legends line will be shaped like seashells (for the summer season) and snowflakes (for the winter season).

Packaging for both product lines will carry through the Belgian theme with stylised nineteenth-century artwork of the major cities on the boxes, velvet and satin ribbons, and choice of holiday or seasonal ornament to top each box. Our Lost Legends Luxury Chocolatier packaging will be instantly recognisable because of the distinctive colours and graphics. Customised orders will allow for corporate logos on each chocolate and on the ribbon and box. Limited-edition chocolates will also be individually wrapped in foil that is changed from season to season, adding to the feeling of luxury and exclusivity. Although some packaging will be retained year to year, we will build customer anticipation by introducing elaborate new packaging for each holiday (Christmas, St Valentine's Day and Easter) and each new limited-edition range. Table A1.4 summarises our main product marketing decisions.

Table A1.4	Summary of product marketing decisions
Product mix	(1) Offer Belgian Legends range year round (2) Offer Limited Editions range seasonally, one for summer and one for winter
Product life cycle	(1) Retain the top-selling 8–10 chocolates in Belgian Legends range each year (2) Replace the slowest-selling chocolates yearly with new flavours/variations (3) Bring back Limited Edition Legends in summer and winter to extend growth part of life cycle
New product development	(1) Develop at least two new Belgian Legends flavours or variations each year by updating family recipes (2) Track customer preferences, channel feedback, supplier ideas and market trends as input for new product decisions
Quality and performance	(1) Use only the finest, freshest, all-natural ingredients (2) Obtain Fairtrade Marked cocoa from a single plantation renowned for its quality (3) Hand-produce chocolates that meet highest customer standards for competitively superior taste and texture
Features and benefits	(1) Offer a range of flavours and variations to satisfy different customers' tastes, preferences and need for novelty (2) Offer year-round, holiday and customised packaging to satisfy needs for gift status (3) Use packaging materials from sustainable sources to demonstrate commitment to environmental protection
Brand	(1) Emphasise the 'legends' concept to communicate the long family heritage of gourmet, hand-made chocolate (2) Link the brand to attributes such as exclusivity, superior taste and quality, fresh, natural ingredients, socially responsible sourcing
Design and packaging	(1) Offer chocolate in distinctive shapes and combinations that convey a sense of luxury and tradition (2) Create sustainable, attractive packaging that communicates the Bruges background and tradition of our chocolates (3) Offer special seasonal packaging for Limited Edition range (4) Offer special holiday packaging for Belgian Legends range (5) For corporate orders, design custom chocolates and packaging with company logos

The coming year's product development efforts will focus on researching and creating new chocolates to replace the slowest sellers in the Belgian Legends line. All new products must fit the high-quality tradition of our family recipes yet incorporate new flavours or other product elements that will trigger repeat purchasing from current customers and attract new customers. Also, every new product should take advantage of our proprietary bean-roasting process and our commitment to socially responsible sourcing of ingredients.

The competitively distinctive 'legends' concept is central to our brand image. For identity purposes, the Lost Legends Luxury Chocolatier name will appear on every package, along with the name of the product line (Belgian Legends or Limited Edition Legends). Packaging, public relations and other aspects of our marketing will emphasise the 'legends' concept. We want customers to associate our brand with a decades-old family history of making top-quality chocolates by hand in the Bruges tradition, using the finest, freshest ingredients. And we want them to respond to our brand's association with social responsibility, as demonstrated through purchases of Fairtrade Marked cocoa and coffee.

(In an actual marketing plan, more information about individual products, design, packaging and new product development would be shown here, with additional detail being shown in an appendix.)

PRICING DECISIONS

We will price our two product lines differently. On the basis of our research, we will make Belgian Legends available in 200 g, 300 g and 500 g packages with introductory retail prices of £14, £18 and £29. Our wholesale prices will be 50 per cent lower than the retail prices, not including quantity pricing for retailers who sell a higher volume of our products. The Limited Edition Legends range will be priced at £1 higher per package, reflecting the limited period of availability and allowing Lost Legends Luxury Chocolatier to recoup higher costs related to these seasonal products. Holiday packaging will add between £1 and £2 to retail prices, depending on the package and ornaments selected. These prices support our premium positioning and the high value that our products represent.

For comparison, the following is a sample of competitive prices:

- Large UK chocolate maker offers a satin gift box with 1,800 g of assorted fine chocolates for £65 and a smaller, star-shaped satin gift box with 280 g of chocolates for £14. The company provides a special Web page for corporate orders.

- Family-owned chocolate marketer sells a package of 26 mini-bars of dark chocolate for £25 and a collection of 25 truffles, total weight 325 g, for £16. Corporate gifts are priced based on quantity and customisation, available in hampers or branded packaging.

- Speciality gift company sells a 150 g box of gourmet chocolates for £7 and a 400 g box for £14. Chocolates in more deluxe packaging are priced at £19 for 300 g and £33 for 550 g.

- Mid-sized UK chocolate maker that uses organic Fairtrade ingredients sells three 150 g gourmet bars for £10 and a 500 g gift box of gourmet chocolates for £24.

Our pricing for corporate orders will be higher than the pricing for our consumer products, depending on quantity, level of customisation and delivery instructions. For customers' convenience, we will pack and address all corporate orders, include a business card or a seasonal greeting, and despatch all gifts for a nominal delivery fee. Once a corporate customer has provided names and addresses of gift recipients, we will keep the information on file and automatically provide it for updating when the customer places another order.

By aggressively pursuing these more profitable corporate orders, we expect to attain our objective of breaking even on UK operations within 16 months. However, the timing is subject to change if the cost of cocoa (or other ingredients) rises dramatically. As shown in the financial details section, our pricing is planned to support the objective of attaining 10 per cent gross profit margin on our second-year turnover.

(In an actual marketing plan, more information about pricing, costs and breakeven would be shown here, with additional detail included in the appendix.)

CHANNEL AND LOGISTICS DECISIONS

One of our major first-year objectives is to establish strong relationships with 50 upmarket shops that cater to affluent UK customers and have temperature-controlled storage for our chocolates. By restricting distribution to only one retail outlet in a given area of the country, we can strengthen our luxury image and more effectively reach higher-income customers. We will also use exclusive distribution to our advantage by educating store personnel about our patented roasting process, our Fairtrade Marked ingredients, our recipes and our family 'legends'. During the initial product introduction period, we will provide channel members with sample chocolates and display packaging, posters publicising the 'legends' concept, product nutrition information and literature about Fairtrade Marked sourcing.

To reinforce exclusivity, we will phase in Limited Edition Legends during each season. In the first week, only the top 20 per cent of our retail outlets (measured by volume) will receive the snowflake or seashell chocolates. During the second week, the next 20 per cent of the outlets will receive these seasonal chocolates. By the third week, all of our outlets will carry the product line. This approach rewards retailers that do the best job of selling our chocolates and gives their customers access to seasonal chocolates before anyone else. We will be using a push strategy to educate retail sales staff about our company and products.

We will also have our own UK direct-to-consumer website operational by the time we launch the Belgian Legends line. The site will follow the 'legends' theme in describing our company background, recipes and hand-production methods. We will allow visitors to view each product and package in a larger format and check ingredients, nutrition information and other details before buying. The site will have separate ordering pages for consumer and business buyers and allow pre-orders for seasonal and holiday offerings (to be fulfilled through retail partners). Although non-UK buyers will be able to order online for direct delivery, we will open a separate European website during our second-year expansion.

Our logistics plan includes obtaining quality ingredients (including cocoa and coffee from Fairtrade Marked sources) and packaging components on schedule and in sufficient quantities, maintaining constant, optimal product temperature and protective packaging when delivering to retail outlets, checking that retailers store and display chocolates under proper conditions, and using shipping containers that preserve product quality when fulfilling orders placed online or by corporate customers.

(In an actual marketing plan, more information about channel relationships and logistics would be shown here with additional detail included in the plan's appendix.)

MARKETING COMMUNICATIONS DECISIONS

Given the company's start-up costs, our marketing communications and influence strategy will rely less on paid advertising than on public relations and special events, sales promotion, personal selling and direct marketing (see Table A1.5). Our marketing messages will use the emotional appeal of status, incorporate the 'legends' concept and be consistent with our product's upscale, superior-quality positioning. Initially, we are choosing media that will bring our messages to the attention of prospective channel members and executives who buy or influence the purchase of corporate gifts.

Consumer advertising in upmarket magazines will be considered in our second year of operation. Throughout, we will use social media to engage our channel members, business customers and consumers, to stimulate positive word of mouth and to monitor response from our target audiences. We will also investigate the use of paid search for particular keywords during our second year.

We are designing public relations programmes to support our financial and societal objectives and to achieve our marketing objectives of (1) generating first-year brand awareness of 35 per cent within consumer segments (and 40 per cent within business segments) and (2) placing our products in 50 exclusive shops and department stores. Our sales promotion programmes will encourage channel participation and reward the outside manufacturer's representatives handling our products for arranging distribution through appropriate upmarket shops and department stores. The major consumer sales promotion planned for the first year is to have UK luxury hotels and restaurants giving away product samples to their customers as an introductory 'taste' of our legendary chocolates.

Our direct marketing effort will centre on the website, with separate sections devoted to product and company information, the 'legends' behind our family recipes, corporate ordering, store locations and social responsibility activities. Visitors will be invited to e-mail feedback, comment on our blog and subscribe to our free monthly newsletter. We will also keep a dialogue going with audiences through messages and videos posted on social media such as Twitter, Facebook and YouTube.

(In an actual marketing plan, more information about programmes, messages and schedules would be shown here, with additional detail included in the plan's appendix.)

Table A1.5   Summary of decisions about marketing communications and influence

Technique	Activities
Advertising	• Targeted magazine ads to build brand awareness and acceptance among channel members, corporate customers • Channel-only advertising campaign to announce seasonal products as part of push strategy • Use social media to engage and influence consumers, businesses and channel members through online ads that link to our website, Facebook fan page and Twitter posts
Public relations	• Media interviews, special events, news releases, social media interaction to build brand awareness and positive word of mouth among consumers, businesses, channel members • Create buzz by arranging tasting events with several celebrity opinion leaders • Communicate 'legends' concept and associate it with the brand image • Communicate use of Fairtrade Marked cocoa to influence public perception of our social responsibility • Through social media interaction and other methods, gather information about each public's attitudes and perceptions to shape messages and policies
Sales promotion	• Channel sales promotion to pave the way for personal selling by manufacturer's reps, as part of push strategy • Selective consumer sales promotion in the form of product samples distributed through luxury hotels, restaurants, shops • Create brand-building point-of-purchase displays for shops • Participate in industry trade shows • Sales force promotion to reward reps for placing our chocolate in upscale shops, part of push strategy
Personal selling	• Contract with manufacturers' sales reps to visit targeted retail shops and place our products, part of push strategy • Arrange for periodic personal, telephone and e-mail follow-up to gather feedback from channel and from customers • Provide ongoing training support to retail sales staff and manufacturers' reps
Direct marketing	• Encourage corporate customers, in particular, to visit our website and order customised products • Invite consumers to visit our website to learn more about the 'legends' concept, see our products, locate nearby shops and submit queries or comments to management • Invite consumers to continue the dialogue by subscribing to our e-mail newsletter, becoming Facebook fans or following us on Twitter

CUSTOMER SERVICE AND INTERNAL MARKETING

To support our marketing plan, we need good customer service to build positive relationships with channel members, corporate customers and consumers. We recognise that customers who buy premium chocolates expect perfection, as do our retailers. Therefore the manufacturer's reps who call on our retailers will be allowed to replace chocolates and settle channel complaints as necessary. We are holding monthly briefing sessions to keep our reps and our employees fully informed about our products, marketing programmes, product-line performance and future plans. Further, we will keep reps and employees updated about the latest products and promotions by holding virtual training sessions every month, posting podcast messages from our owners and sending reps the monthly e-mail newsletter one week before customers receive it.

We have a separate plan for delivering pre-purchase service, post-purchase service and service recovery to our business buyers. Two employees will be responsible for answering business customers' questions before orders are placed, monitoring order fulfilment, communicating with customers about delivery schedules, tracking deliveries, contacting customers after the sale to check on satisfaction, and handling any questions or complaints as quickly as possible. On the basis of our interaction with business customers, we will adjust offerings, policies and procedures to improve our service over time and build our share of this potentially profitable market. Should any complaints or concerns be posted on Twitter or other social media, we have designated an employee to respond immediately and resolve issues quickly.

(In an actual marketing plan, additional information about service support and implementation would be included here and in the plan's appendix.)

MARKETING PROGRAMMES

Given below are summaries of our main integrated marketing programmes leading up to our product introductions in September and mid-November and continuing during the year-end holiday period. Associated schedules, budgets and responsibilities are included in the appendix.

- *August.* Our push strategy will be strongest one month before the Belgian Legends product range is introduced, to prepare channel members. Employees and manufacturer's reps will visit each participating retailer to provide product training, samples and display materials. Full-page colour advertisements in major confectionery and chocolate industry magazines and online ads on selected industry websites will introduce the brand and the 'legends' concept. Simultaneously we will start our public relations efforts with media interviews and news releases focusing on the 'legends' concept and the family's Bruges-style chocolate recipes. One special media event planned for August is the arrival of a shipment of Fairtrade Marked cocoa. Family members will blog about the cocoa and the importance of Fairtrade; the company will also post podcasts and YouTube videos for downloading or forwarding. In addition, we will seek to influence targeted segments and resellers through communications on Twitter and Facebook.

- *September*. To launch the new product range, Lost Legends Luxury Chocolatier's founders and family members will travel to each retail outlet in an elegant horse-drawn coach and present the manager or owner with an ornate package containing all Belgian Legends varieties. This public relations event, to be covered by media outlets and taped for posting on YouTube, will focus attention on the legendary family heritage of chocolate making and the old-fashioned gourmet quality of our products. During this month participating upmarket hotels and restaurants will receive their first deliveries of Belgian Legends samples, also delivered by family members arriving by coach. Manufacturer's reps will follow up to ensure that every channel member has sufficient inventory and marketing material for the launch.

- *October*. We will place colour advertisements in business magazines and in the business section of London newspapers to generate response from professionals and executives who buy premium chocolate as gifts for clients, colleagues and other business contacts. All advertisements will include the Fairtrade Marked logo and a brief description of this trade programme. Our website will also be prominently featured, along with the store-location function. Our public relations programme for the month will focus on Fairtrade Marked sourcing. Our manufacturer's reps will participate in a sales contest to pre-sell the Limited Edition Legends line, which is launched in mid-November. Our first e-mail newsletter will be sent this month. Customers and channel partners will be invited to watch a three-minute YouTube video about our unique manufacturing process, our seasonal chocolates and our use of Fairtrade cocoa.

- *November*. Our website home page will promote Christmas gifts, especially the seasonal Limited Edition Legends chocolates and special holiday packaging. Our channel promotions will highlight the Limited Edition Legends range for gift giving and encourage retailers to order early. Public relations and social-media activities will draw attention to the original family recipes on which our products are based and to the limited-edition concept. We will also send holiday samples to opinion leaders to generate buzz and influence brand perceptions and preference.

- *December*. Our website will offer suggestions for last-minute chocolate gifts for consumers and business contacts. Manufacturer's reps will visit every participating retailer to check on inventory, provide sales assistance, deliver additional display materials and provide other support as needed. Publicity and special events will showcase the 'legends' concept and our family's tradition of gourmet chocolate making. Marketing research will gauge interim awareness levels and attitudes among the targeted consumer and business segments. Our monthly e-mail newsletter, blog posts, Facebook messages, tweets and YouTube videos will focus on the history of chocolate and chocolate gift ideas. Internally, we will be preparing for the summer line of Limited Edition Legends and for other new products.

(In an actual marketing plan, additional programme details would be shown in the appendix.)

FORECASTS AND FINANCIAL DETAILS

We are forecasting £500,000 in annual company turnover during our first full year of operation, with a minimum of £10,000 in sales per participating retail outlet. Our forecasts call for annual turnover increases of 20 per cent during the next three years. We expect to reach the breakeven point on UK operations within 16 months and achieve 10 per cent gross profit margin by the end of our second year.

Due to constant variations in the price of ingredients such as cocoa, coffee and sugar, we can only estimate our cost of goods and then for only two or three months in advance. As our volume increases and we buy supplies in larger quantities, we will be able to stabilise variable costs for up to six months. Therefore, our financial projections are subject to revision during the year.

(In an actual marketing plan, additional details would be shown in the appendix.)

IMPLEMENTATION AND CONTROL

To ensure that our two product ranges are launched on time, we will adhere to weekly schedules and assign management responsibilities for supervising manufacturer's reps, coordinating sales promotion activities, and briefing the public relations, advertising, research and website experts.

Among the metrics we have selected to monitor progress towards our objectives are:

- unit and monetary sales (analysed daily, weekly, monthly and quarterly by product, range, channel, outlet, type of customer)

- profitability (analysed monthly by product range, type of channel, overall sales)

- customer perceptions of and attitudes towards brand (twice-yearly research supplemented by monitoring of social media and direct customer feedback)

- business customer retention and profitability (monthly analysis)

- competitive standing (annual research)

- channel member participation and satisfaction (quarterly analysis)

- image as socially responsible company (twice-yearly research)

- use of recycled materials in packaging (quarterly analysis)

- order fulfilment speed, accuracy (monthly analysis).

We will review interim progress weekly during the first year of operation, comparing actual results with forecasts, schedules and budgets and adjusting activities if needed. We have also developed a comprehensive contingency plan to ensure a continuous supply of Fairtrade ingredients if unfavourable weather conditions or crop diseases threaten cocoa production in Ghana.

(In an actual marketing plan, additional details about implementation and control would be included in the appendix, along with summaries of any contingency plans.)

Sources

Market background and environmental trends based on information from: Leonie Nimmo and Dan Welch, 'Chocolate revolution transforms the world's favourite treat', *Guardian Environment Blog,* 14 October 2009, www.guardian.co.uk; Zoe Wood, 'Socially aware chocoholics rejoice as Cadburys Dairy Milk goes Fairtrade', *Guardian,* 22 July 2009, www.guardian.co.uk; Alice Calupny, 'Miracle Chocolate from Swiss maker?', *BusinessWeek,* 17 July 2009, www.businessweek.com; Stephen Baker, 'Following the luxury chocolate lover', *BusinessWeek,* 25 March 2009, www.businessweek.com; Carolyn Cui, 'Cocoa prices create chocolate dilemma', *Wall Street Journal,* 13 February 2009, www.wsj.com; 'Ferrero launches new Rondnoir pralines', *Talking Retail,* 27 September 2008, www.talkingretail.com; Martin Hickman, 'Britain's chocolate connoisseurs driving market in estate-produced 'vintage' bars', *Independent,* 22 March 2008, www.independent.co.uk.

Glossary

advertising Non-personal promotion paid for by an identified sponsor (Chapter 9)

affective response Customer's emotional reaction, such as being interested in or liking a product (Chapter 9)

affordability budget method Method in which senior managers set the total marketing budget on the basis of how much the organisation can afford or will be able to afford during the period covered by the plan (Chapter 11)

annual control Type of marketing control used to evaluate the current marketing plan's full-year performance as a foundation for creating next year's marketing plan (Chapter 12)

attitudes Consumer's assessment of and emotions about a product, brand or something else (Chapter 3)

auction pricing Approach to pricing in which buyers are invited to submit bids to buy goods or services through a traditional auction or an online auction (Chapter 7)

audience fragmentation Trend towards smaller audience sizes due to the multiplicity of media choices and vehicles (Chapter 9)

available market All the customers within the potential market who are interested, have adequate income to buy and have adequate access to the product (Chapter 3)

Balanced Scorecard Broad performance measures that help organisations align strategy and objectives to manage customer relationships, achieve financial targets, improve internal capabilities and attain sustainability (Chapter 5)

behavioural response Customer's action in response to a marketing communication, such as buying a product (Chapter 9)

behavioural tracking Monitoring what consumers and business people do online as they visit websites, click on ads and fill virtual shopping trolleys (Chapter 3)

benefits Need-satisfaction outcomes that a customer expects or wants from a product (Chapter 6)

blog Short for *web log*, an informal online journal where people can exchange ideas and opinions (Chapter 3)

brand equity Extra value that customers perceive in a brand, which builds long-term loyalty (Chapter 6)

brand extension Widening the product mix by introducing new products under an existing brand (Chapter 6)

brand promise Marketer's vision of what the brand must be and do for consumers (Chapter 1)

branding Giving a product a distinct identity and supporting its competitive differentiation to stimulate customer response (Chapter 6)

break-even point Point at which a product's revenues and costs are equal and beyond which the product earns more profit as more units are sold (Chapter 7)

budget Time-defined allotment of financial resources for a specific programme, activity or product (Chapter 11)

business (organisational) market Companies, institutions, non-profit organisations and government agencies that buy goods and services for organisational use (Chapter 3)

business strategy Strategy determining the scope of each unit and how it will compete, what market(s) it will serve and how unit resources will be allocated and coordinated to create customer value (Chapter 1)

buying centre Group of managers or employees that is responsible for an organisation's purchases (Chapter 3)

buzz marketing More intense form of word of mouth in which the organisation targets opinion leaders, with the aim of influencing them to spread information to other people (Chapter 9)

cannibalisation Situation in which one product takes sales from another marketed by the same organisation (Chapter 6)

category extension Widening the mix by introducing product lines in new categories (Chapter 6)

cause-related marketing Marketing a brand or product through a connection to benefit a social cause or non-profit organisation (Chapter 5)

cognitive response Customer's mental reaction, such as awareness of a brand or knowledge of a product's features and benefits (Chapter 9)

competitive parity budget method Method in which senior managers establish a total marketing budget at least equal to that of competitors (Chapter 11)

concentrated marketing Targeting one segment with one market mix (Chapter 4)

consumer market People and families who buy goods and services for personal use (Chapter 3)

contingency plan A plan to be implemented in response to or anticipation of a significant change in the marketing situation that could disrupt important marketing activities (Chapter 12)

core competencies Organisational capabilities that are not easily duplicated and that serve to differentiate the organisation from competitors (Chapter 1)

crowdsourcing Generating new product ideas or marketing materials from concepts, designs, content or advice submitted by customers and others outside the organisation (Chapter 6)

customer lifetime value Total net long-term revenue (or profit) an organisation estimates it will reap from a particular customer relationship (Chapter 4)

data mining Sophisticated analyses of database information used to uncover customer buying and behaviour patterns (Chapter 2)

demand How many units of a particular product will be sold at certain prices (Chapter 7)

derived demand Principle that the demand forecast for a business product ultimately derives from the demand forecast for a consumer product (Chapter 11)

differentiated marketing Targeting different segments with different marketing mixes (Chapter 4)

direct channel Marketing channel used by an organisation to make its products available directly to customers (Chapter 8)

direct marketing The use of two-way communication to engage targeted customers and stimulate a direct response that leads to a sale and an ongoing relationship (Chapter 9)

distribution channel Set of functions performed by the producer or participating intermediaries in making a particular product available to customers; also known as the *marketing channel* (Chapter 8)

diversification strategy Growth strategy in which new products are offered in new markets or segments (Chapter 5)

dynamic pricing Approach to pricing in which marketers vary prices from buyer to buyer or situation to situation (Chapter 7)

econometric modelling method Use of sophisticated econometric models incorporating anticipated customer response and other variables to determine marketing budgets (Chapter 11)

elastic demand Relationship between change in quantity demanded and change in price, in which a small percentage change in price produces a large percentage change in demand (Chapter 7)

elasticity of demand How demand changes when a product's price changes (Chapter 7)

environmental scanning and analysis The systematic and ongoing collection and interpretation of data about internal and external factors that may affect marketing and performance (Chapter 2)

ethnographic research Observing customer behaviour in real-world situations (Chapter 3)

exclusive distribution Channel arrangement where one intermediary distributes the product in an area (Chapter 8)

external audit Examination of the situation outside the organisation, including political–legal factors, economic factors, social–cultural factors, technological factors, ecological factors and competitive factors (Chapter 2)

features Specific attributes that contribute to a product's functionality (Chapter 6)

field marketing Working with outside agencies on sales promotions that take place in stores, shopping districts and office locations (Chapter 9)

financial control Type of marketing control used to evaluate the current marketing plan's performance according to specific financial measures such as sales and profits (Chapter 12)

financial objectives Targets for achieving financial results such as revenues and profits (Chapter 5)

fixed costs Business costs such as rent and insurance that do not vary with production and sales (Chapter 7)

forecast Projection of the estimated level of sales and costs during the months or years covered by a marketing plan (Chapter 11)

frequency The number of times people in the target audience are exposed to an advertisement in a particular media vehicle during a certain period (Chapter 9)

goals Longer-term targets that help a business unit (or the organisation as a whole) achieve performance (Chapter 1)

greenwashing Perception that a company is marketing its products or brands on the basis of 'green' activities that have little or no actual ecological impact (Chapter 8)

indirect channel Marketing channel in which intermediaries help producers make their products available to customers (Chapter 8)

individualised (customised) marketing Tailoring marketing mixes to individual customers within targeted segments (Chapter 4)

inelastic demand Relationship between change in quantity demanded and change in price, in which a small percentage change in price produces a small percentage change in demand (Chapter 7)

integrated marketing communications (IMC) Coordinating content and delivery of all marketing messages in all media to ensure consistency and to support the chosen positioning and objectives (Chapter 9)

intensive distribution Channel arrangement in which as many intermediaries as possible distribute the product in an area (Chapter 8)

intermediaries Businesses or individuals that specialise in distribution functions (Chapter 8)

internal audit Examination of the situation inside the organisation, including resources, offerings, previous performance, important business relationships and key issues (Chapter 2)

internal marketing Coordinated set of activities and policies designed to build employee relationships within the organisation and reinforce internal commitment to the marketing plan and to good customer service (Chapter 10)

lifestyle The pattern of living reflecting how consumers spend their time or want to spend their time (Chapter 3)

line extension Lengthening a product line (or range) by introducing new products (Chapter 6)

logistics Flow of products, associated information and payments through the value chain to meet customer requirements at a profit (Chapter 8)

market The group of potential buyers for a specific offering (Chapter 3)

market development strategy Growth strategy in which existing products are offered in new markets and segments (Chapter 5)

market leader Firm that holds the largest market share and leads others in new product introductions and other activities (Chapter 1)

market-penetration pricing New product pricing that aims for rapid acquisition of market share (Chapter 7)

market penetration strategy Growth strategy in which existing products are offered to customers in existing markets (Chapter 5)

market segmentation Process of grouping consumers or businesses within a market into segments based on similarities in needs, attitudes or behaviour that marketing can address (Chapter 4)

market share The percentage of unit or monetary sales in a particular market accounted for by one company, brand or product (Chapter 3)

market-skimming pricing New product pricing in which a high price is set to skim maximum revenues from the market, layer by layer (Chapter 7)

marketing audit Formal, detailed study of the marketing planning process and the marketing function to assess strengths, weaknesses and areas needing improvement (Chapter 12)

marketing channel Set of functions performed by the producer or participating intermediaries in making a particular product available to customers; also known as the *distribution channel* (Chapter 8)

marketing control Process of setting standards and measurement intervals to track progress towards objectives, measure post-implementation interim results, diagnose any deviations and make adjustments if needed (Chapter 12)

marketing dashboard A computerised, easy-to-read depiction of marketing outcomes, as measured by key metrics, used to confirm progress and identify deviations from expected results (Chapter 11)

marketing objectives Targets for achieving results in marketing relationships and activities (Chapter 5)

marketing plan Internal document outlining the marketplace situation, marketing strategies and programmes that will help the organisation achieve its goals and objectives during a set period, usually a year (Chapter 1)

marketing planning Structured process that leads to a coordinated set of marketing decisions and actions, for a specific period, through analysis of the current marketing situation, clear marketing direction, objectives, strategies and programmes, customer service and internal marketing support, and management of marketing activities (Chapter 1)

marketing strategy Strategy developed to determine how the marketing-mix tools of product, place, price and promotion, supported by service and internal marketing strategies, will be used to meet objectives (Chapter 1)

marketing transparency Open and honest disclosure of marketing activities and decisions that affect stakeholders in some way (Chapter 1)

mass customisation Developing products tailored to individual customers' needs on a large scale (Chapter 4)

metrics Numerical standards used to measure a performance-related marketing activity or outcome (Chapter 11)

mission statement Statement of the organisation's fundamental purpose, pointing the way towards a vision of what it aspires to become (Chapter 1)

mobile marketing Getting information, directions, vouchers or other messages to target audiences via mobile through text, e-mail and websites optimised for handset screens (Chapter 9)

motivation Internal force driving a consumer's behaviour and purchases to satisfy needs and wants (Chapter 3)

multibrand strategy Using two or more brand names in an existing product line or category (Chapter 6)

negotiated pricing Approach to pricing in which buyer and seller negotiate and then confirm the final price and details of the offer by contract (Chapter 7)

neuromarketing Using brain science and body responses to investigate and understand consumer reactions to marketing activities (Chapter 3)

niches Small subsegments of customers with distinct needs or requirements (Chapter 4)

objective and task budget method Method in which money is allocated according to the total cost of the tasks to be accomplished in achieving marketing plan objectives (Chapter 11)

objectives Shorter-term performance targets that lead to the achievement of organisational goals (Chapter 1)

opinion leader Person who is especially admired or possesses special skills and therefore exerts more influence over certain purchases made by others (Chapter 3)

opportunity External circumstance or factor that the organisation aims to exploit for higher performance (Chapter 2)

organisational (corporate) strategy Strategy governing the organisation's overall purpose, long-range direction and goals, the range of businesses in which it will compete and how it will create value for customers and other publics (Chapter 1)

penetrated market All the customers in the target market who currently buy or previously bought a specific type of product (Chapter 3)

percentage budget method Method in which senior managers set the overall marketing budget on the basis of a percentage of the previous year's annual turnover, next year's expected turnover, the product's price or an average industry percentage (Chapter 11)

personas Fictitious yet realistic profiles representing how specific customers in targeted segments would typically buy, behave and react in a marketing situation (Chapter 4)

PESTLE Acronym for political, economic, social–cultural, technological, legal and ecological factors in the environment, analysed during the external audit (Chapter 2)

positioning Use of marketing to create a competitively distinctive place (position) for the product or brand in the mind of the target market (Chapter 1)

potential market All the customers who may be interested in a particular good or service (Chapter 3)

primary data Data from research studies undertaken to address a particular situation or question (Chapter 3)

product development strategy Growth strategy in which new products or product variations are offered to customers in existing markets (Chapter 5)

product life cycle Product's movement through the market as it passes from introduction to growth, maturity and decline (Chapter 6)

product line depth Number of variations of each product within one product line (Chapter 6)

product line length Number of individual products in each product line (Chapter 6)

product mix Assortment of product lines offered by an organisation (Chapter 6)

productivity control Type of marketing control used to evaluate the marketing plan's performance in managing the efficiency of key marketing activities and processes (Chapter 12)

psychographic characteristics Complex set of lifestyle variables related to activities, interests and opinions that marketers study to understand the roots and drivers of consumer behaviour (Chapter 3)

public relations (PR) Promoting a dialogue to build understanding and foster positive attitudes between the organisation and its publics (Chapter 9)

publics Groups such as stockholders, reporters, citizen action groups and neighbourhood residents that are interested in or can influence the organisation's performance; also known as *stakeholders* (Chapter 1)

pull strategy Targeting customers with communications to stimulate demand and pull products through the channel (Chapter 9)

push strategy Targeting intermediaries with communications to push products through the channel (Chapter 9)

qualified available market All the customers within the available market who are qualified to buy based on product-specific criteria (Chapter 3)

quality Extent to which a good or service satisfies the needs of customers (Chapter 6)

reach The number or percentage of people in the target audience exposed to an advertisement in a particular media vehicle during a certain period (Chapter 9)

relationship marketing Marketing geared towards building ongoing relationships with customers rather than stimulating isolated purchase transactions (Chapter 1)

repositioning Changing the competitively distinctive positioning of a brand in the minds of targeted customers (Chapter 4)

retailers Intermediaries that buy from producers or wholesalers and resell to consumers (Chapter 8)

reverse channel Channel flow that moves backwards through the value chain to return goods for service or to reclaim products, parts or packaging for recycling (Chapter 8)

sales promotion Incentives to enhance a product's short-term value and stimulate the target audience to buy soon or to respond in another way (Chapter 9)

scenario planning Type of planning in which managers look beyond historical trends and short-term projections to envision broad, long-term changes in the marketing environment that could affect future performance, then prepare contingency plans to cope with these possible situations (Chapter 12)

schedule Time-defined plan for coordinating and accomplishing tasks connected to a specific programme or activity (Chapter 11)

secondary data Information collected in the past for another purpose (Chapter 3)

segments Customer groupings within a market, based on distinct needs, wants, behaviours or other characteristics that affect product demand or usage and can be effectively addressed through marketing (Chapter 1)

selective distribution Channel arrangement in which a relatively small number of intermediaries distribute a product within an area (Chapter 8)

service recovery How the organisation plans to recover from a service lapse and satisfy the customer (Chapter 10)

social media Online media such as blogs, Bebo and YouTube that facilitate user interaction (Chapter 9)

social media marketing The intentional use of social media to achieve specific marketing plan objectives (Chapter 9)

societal objectives Targets for achieving results in social responsibility areas (Chapter 5)

strategic control Type of marketing control used to evaluate the marketing plan's effectiveness in managing strategic areas such as the marketing function, key relationships and social responsibility/ethical performance (Chapter 12)

strength Internal capability or factor that can help the organisation achieve its objectives, capitalise on opportunities or defend against threats (Chapter 2)

subculture Discrete group within an overall culture that shares a common ethnicity, religion or lifestyle (Chapter 3)

sustainable marketing Establishing, maintaining and enhancing customer relationships to meet the objectives of the parties without compromising the ability of future generations to achieve their own objectives (Chapter 1)

SWOT analysis Evaluation of an organisation's primary strengths, weaknesses, opportunities and threats (Chapter 2)

target market All the customers within the qualified available market that an organisation intends to serve (Chapter 3)

targeting Determination of the specific market segments to be served, order of entry into the segment and coverage within segments (Chapter 1)

threat External circumstance or factor that may hinder organisational performance if not addressed (Chapter 2)

undifferentiated marketing Targeting the entire market with one marketing mix, ignoring any segment differences (Chapter 4)

value From the customers' perspective, the difference between a product's perceived total benefits and its perceived total price (Chapter 3)

value chain Sequence of interrelated, value-added actions undertaken by marketers with suppliers, channel members and other participants to create and deliver products that fulfil customer needs; also known as *supply chain* or *value delivery network* (Chapter 8)

variable costs Costs for supplies and other materials, which vary with production and sales (Chapter 7)

virtual product Product that exists in electronic form as a digital representation of something, such as a virtual gift purchased for a Facebook friend (Chapter 6)

weakness Internal capability or factor that may prevent the organisation from achieving its objectives or effectively addressing opportunities and threats (Chapter 2)

wholesalers Intermediaries that buy from producers and resell to other channel members or business customers (Chapter 8)

word of mouth People telling other people about a product, advert or some other aspect of an organisation's marketing (Chapter 9)

Index

Note: Pages entries in **bold** denote Glossary entries.